EMBATTLED
FREEDOM

CIVIL WAR AMERICA

Peter S. Carmichael, Caroline E. Janney,
and Aaron Sheehan-Dean, editors

This landmark series interprets broadly the history and culture
of the Civil War era through the long nineteenth century and
beyond. Drawing on diverse approaches and methods, the
series publishes historical works that explore all aspects of
the war, biographies of leading commanders, and tactical and
campaign studies, along with select editions of primary sources.
Together, these books shed new light on an era that remains
central to our understanding of American and world history.

Embattled Freedom

Journeys through the Civil War's Slave Refugee Camps

AMY MURRELL TAYLOR

THE UNIVERSITY OF NORTH CAROLINA PRESS

Chapel Hill

This book was published with financial support from the University of Kentucky College of Arts and Sciences and Department of History and with the assistance of the John Hope Franklin Fund of the University of North Carolina Press.

Manufactured in the United States of America

Designed by Jamison Cockerham
Set in Arno, Trattatello, Scala Sans, Archive Antiqua
by Tseng Information Systems, Inc.

Front cover: Camp Nelson Refugee Home, courtesy of the Camp Nelson Photographic Collection, Special Collections Research Center, University of Kentucky. Back cover: the Mill Creek settlement in 1864, courtesy of the Library of Congress.

The University of North Carolina Press has been a member of the Green Press Initiative since 2003.

LIBRARY OF CONGRESS CATALOGING-IN-PUBLICATION DATA
Names: Taylor, Amy Murrell, author.
Title: Embattled freedom : journeys through the Civil War's slave refugee camps / Amy Murrell Taylor.
Other titles: Civil War America (Series)
Description: Chapel Hill : University of North Carolina Press, [2018] | Series: Civil War America | Includes bibliographical references and index.
Identifiers: LCCN 2018020213 | ISBN 9781469643625 (cloth : alk. paper) | ISBN 9781469643632 (ebook)
Subjects: LCSH: United States—History—Civil War, 1861–1865—African Americans. | Slaves—Emancipation—United States. | United States—History—Civil War, 1861–1865—Refugees. | Refugee camps—Southern States—History—19th century. | United States. Army—History—Civil War, 1861–1865.
Classification: LCC E453 .T18 2018 | DDC 973.7/115—dc23
LC record available at https://lccn.loc.gov/2018020213

for Scott

contents

figures

maps

acknowledgments

The years I spent learning about the lives and the struggles of those seeking freedom in the 1860s have made me ever more grateful for the vast network of support that surrounds me today. To begin, my research would not have been possible without fellowships from the National Endowment for the Humanities and the American Council of Learned Societies. These funding programs allowed me to bury myself in the National Archives for two years and to let my curiosity take me in time-consuming, but ultimately rewarding directions. I am also grateful for the financial support provided by a Faculty Research Award Program Grant from the University at Albany, an Individual Development Awards Program Grant from United University Professions and the State University of New York, and an associate professor course release from the College of Arts and Sciences, University of Kentucky.

A crucial part of my research involved visiting the places described in these pages, and I want to thank a number of people who helped me envision where refugee camps once stood. In Hampton, Virginia, members of the Contraband Historical Society welcomed me to one of their meetings, and Phillip Adderley generously gave me a tour that made everything clearer. I am also thankful for my conversations with the late Gerri Hollins and with Thulani Davis, both descendants of refugees who lived in and around Fort Monroe, and for the research shared with me by Joan Charles. In Kentucky, an email to Stephen McBride, director of interpretation and archaeology at Camp Nelson, resulted in an in-depth tour, many suggestions, and after I moved to Kentucky, an ongoing conversation about the site that continues to this day. I was also fortunate to get to know Joseph Brent of Mudpuppy and Waterdog, Inc., whose work to preserve and interpret Helena's Civil War history was crucial—and helped me to plot my fieldwork in Arkansas.

Many people along the way shared their knowledge of archival sources and turned what I thought was a deeply buried subject into one that nearly overwhelmed me with its abundance. I am not sure how to begin thanking Leslie Rowland, who invited me to the offices of the Freedmen and Southern Society Project and shared the project's extensive indexes; she also gave me my first introduction to the complex organizational scheme of the notorious Record Group 393. At the National Archives and Records Administration in Washington, D.C., I benefited from the assistance of Trevor Plante, and at the NARA's now-closed regional branch in Pittsfield, Massachusetts, from that of Tyrone Keels. My research in Virginia was aided by the assistance of Donzella Maupin and Andreese Scott of the Hampton University Archives; David Johnson of the Casemate Museum; and Graynell Drummond and Bethany Austin of the Hampton History Museum. I also owe a big thanks to Chris Densmore of the Friends Historical Library at Swarthmore College; Anne Thomason and Tom Hamm at the Friends Collection at Earlham College; Jacob Lee and James Holmberg at the Filson Historical Society; Jaime Burton at Berea College; and Shane Williams at the Helena Museum. Thanks also to the staff of Congressman Paul Tonko for tracking down two pension records that had not yet been deposited in the National Archives.

Early on in my research I received a series of envelopes in the mail from the extraordinarily generous Michael Parrish, each filled with photocopies of sources he thought (correctly) would assist me. I am grateful for his thoughtfulness and collegiality. Other colleagues who kindly shared photocopies and leads on sources are Bill Andrews, Peter Carmichael, John Coski, David Hochfelder, Terry Johnston, Patrick Lewis, Aaron Sheehan-Dean, Daniel Sutherland, and Monica Tetzlaff. Several research assistants came to my aid at critical points too. I am thankful for the hard work of Jennifer Thompson Burns and Jasmine Bumpers at the University at Albany and Ruth White at the University of Kentucky. Rose Buchanan of North Carolina State University also lent a hand when I could not travel to Raleigh. Later on in the project I got a big boost from Jeff Levy and Dick Gilbreath at the Pauer Center for Cartography & GIS at the University of Kentucky, who took my unfinished maps and made them useful and publishable. For earlier iterations of the maps, I want to thank Kati Engel and Marilyn Nickels, both formerly of the National Park Service.

As I tried to make sense of the tangled history I was uncovering, I had many conversations with many smart people, all of whom asked just the right questions or had just the right answers to push my thinking along. I am most grateful for the opportunity to have received feedback during presentations at the Nineteenth Century Workshop at Georgetown University, the University of Georgia's "Weirding the Civil War" Conference, the University of Tennessee Humanities Center, the Civil War Study Group at the University of Cincinnati, the Civil War Weekend at Virginia Tech, Maryville College's Community Conversations Series, the Kentucky Association of Teachers of History annual conference, the Civil War Institute at Gettysburg College, Baylor University's Symposium on Religion and the Civil War, and the University of Kentucky's Southern History Workshop. For making these opportunities possible—and so enjoyable   I want to thank Chandra Manning, Adam Rothman, Stephen Berry, Luke Harlow, Chris Phillips, Paul Quigley, Aaron Astor, Randolph Hollingsworth, Peter Carmichael, and Michael Parrish. Public interest in the Civil War's refugees from slavery also grew rapidly as I worked on this book, and I was fortunate to have opportunities to learn from local historians and preservationists while giving talks at the Mitchelville Preservation Project Inaugural Forum, the Tennessee Civil War Sesquicentennial Signature Event, the National Trust for Historic Preservation's Summit on "Contraband Heritage," the New York State Library, and the Clark County, Kentucky, Public Library.

I owe a debt to other colleagues who took the time to read my work, ranging from conference papers to the whole book manuscript. Thanks especially to David Blight, John Boles, Joan Cashin, Chandra Manning, Steven Mintz, Leslie Rowland, Leslie Schwalm, and Heather Williams. Stephen Berry deserves huge thanks for his constant encouragement—and for his signature blend of incisive and imaginative feedback on both short pieces and the entire manuscript. Our profession needs more Steve Berrys. Edward Ayers left an indelible imprint on my thinking as a historian years ago and continued to make key observations about this work that improved it for the better. His example also never ceases to inspire. Conversations with many other colleagues advanced my thinking along the way too. For that I want to thank Jane Beck, Carl Bon Tempo, Emory Campbell, Catherine Clinton, Abigail Cooper, Jim Downs, Carole Emberton, Matt Gallman, Judy Giesberg, David Gleeson, Thavolia Glymph, Lesley Gordon, Charles Irons, Watson Jennison, Susanna Lee, John Lovett, Anne Marshall, Jim Marten, Louis Masur, Andy Morris, Megan Kate Nelson, Scott Nesbit, Kenneth Noe, Michael Perman, Christopher Phillips, George Rable, Joshua Rothman, Anne Sarah Rubin, Bethany Sharpe, Diane Sommerville, Margaret Storey, William G. Thomas, and Susannah Ural.

The editorial staff at the University of North Carolina Press made this whole process easier—and the end product better. Mark Simpson-Vos and Aaron Sheehan-Dean grasped what I was trying to do from the very beginning and offered important advice at several key points. I am grateful for the time they put into this book—and for their enthusiasm all along the way. The two anonymous readers for UNC Press also offered enormously valuable insights. And I want to thank Dino Battista, Mary Carley Caviness, Cate Hodorowicz, Jessica Newman, and Iza Wojciechowska for handling all my pesky inquiries with patience and skill and for everything else they did to turn the manuscript into a book.

While working on this book I moved from New York to Kentucky, which really meant that I doubled the support network that I rely upon so heavily. My friends and colleagues at the University at Albany—Allen Ballard, Iris Berger, Susan Gauss, Richard Hamm, Susan McCormick, and Kendra Smith-Howard—offered invaluable encouragement and feedback as I got this project under way. And my new colleagues at the University of Kentucky helped me bring it to a close, especially Tracy Campbell, Francie Chassen-Lopez, Anastasia Curwood, Abigail Firey, Dan Gargola, Tina Hagee, Vanessa Holden, Kathi Kern, Kathy Newfont, Karen Petrone, Gerald Smith, and Akiko Takenaka. My larger village of friends who listened but made sure I maintained perspective include Margaret Brackett, Allison Cowett, Jessica Dasher, Jeena and Sean Madden, Keaghan and Dan Turner, and the incomparable Bordeaux Bookworms. My parents, Joyce and Darwin Murrell, always think whatever I'm doing is cool and worthwhile, and for that unwavering support I continue to be hugely grateful. I also have to thank Susan Matthews-Duvall for sage advice on balancing my time between personal and professional obligations.

Researching and writing this book while raising young kids tested me in ways that I never predicted. I never could have done it without all the caregivers who loved my children as their own and allowed me the time to devote to my work. Thanks especially to our friends at Cloverpatch Early Childhood Services and the Sidney Albert Albany Jewish Community Center. Still, even with all that help, there were moments when finding writing time meant carrying my laptop from room to room of our busy house, chasing a zone of quiet for writing a few paragraphs. But in all the noise was the good humor of Katie, who lives for a big laugh and kept me laughing in turn, and the welcome distraction of watching Food Network shows with Alex and dreaming of her future as a baker. They could not have been more patient with my absences and my distracted state of mind, so I will take under consideration their idea to be rewarded with a second dog. No one, though, sacrificed more than Scott, who temporarily set aside his own ambitions so I could pursue mine and made sure our little family hummed along happily. He kept me supplied with bourbon and chocolate, amused with political commentary, and energized with his firm belief in what I was trying to do. I dedicate this book to him because he does not often seek credit — but deserves every bit of it that he can get.

EMBATTLED FREEDOM

Prologue

Hampton, Virginia, September 1861. It was just five months into the U.S. Civil War and this once-thriving coastal town seemed on the verge of collapse. Charred stumps occupied the places where mature trees once stood; lone chimneys rose above the burned-out ruins of houses and stores and churches; and once-grand homes looked nothing like they did weeks before, having collapsed into piles of bricks. And yet, amid all the rubble and ashes, Edward and Emma Whitehurst saw more than a town destroyed. They began rolling barrels of flour into one of the abandoned buildings and dragged in bushels of potatoes. They placed pigs in the side yard to be fattened up and readied for slaughter and, as the late summer heat bore down on them, got to work baking ginger cakes. In these moments, this husband and wife, enslaved from the days they were born but now miles away from the white man who claimed to be their owner, became storekeepers. And if they could make a go of it in this war-ravaged town, if the Union soldiers and other people like them seeking freedom from slavery were willing to come inside and buy their goods, then they could sell their way into a new life as free people.[1]

Helena, Arkansas, July 1863. Nearly two years later and over 1,000 miles away, this low-lying town on the western bank of the Mississippi River had been continually deluged. If it wasn't the flooding river waters, which left knee-deep mud along the town's streets, then it was the arrival of thousands of Union troops to occupy this cotton-trading town, as well as the intermittent appearance of Confederate forces firing on the area from passing riverboats. Eliza Bogan, a woman who had spent her life harvesting cotton under the threat of the lash on a plantation just northwest of town, was now left to figure out if she could safely remain and call this place her new home. She spent her nights in a crudely built cabin that had a roof and a door but no floor to protect her from the river muck; her husband had been sent hundreds of miles away as a new soldier in the Union army; and her seven children remained back on her old plantation under the surveillance of their enslaver. Illness raged and death claimed the lives of one in four people in the tents and cabins around her. And now rumor had it that the Confederates were making inroads again, closing in on Helena and the nearly 4,000 freedom-seeking people who had taken refuge there that year.[2]

Camp Nelson, Kentucky, August 1864. A year later, on a high bluff over-looking the Kentucky River, the Union supply depot known as Camp Nelson hummed with the sounds of an army preparing to extend its reach across the wartime South. A sawmill produced lumber for erecting soldier barracks, a blacksmith shop made and repaired government wagons, and steam-driven machines pumped in water from the river. Elsewhere across this stretch of roll-ing farmland were the sounds of newly recruited soldiers drilling in prepara-tion for distant campaigns. But amid all of this was the voice of Gabriel Bur-dett, a minister trying to worship openly and freely in a way he never could while enslaved in a neighboring county. Some days he claimed space for reli-gious worship outside in the open air, other days inside a barracks. He exhorted those in attendance to do God's work and to live according to his laws, so that one day they would all be delivered to freedom. Because in this place, in this war zone, Burdett knew well, they were not yet there.[3]

Slavery collapsed in the United States in a massive dislocation of hundreds of thousands of people like Edward and Emma Whitehurst, Eliza Bogan, and Gabriel Burdett. All had been enslaved in early 1861 — and all of them knew that if freedom was to come during the Civil War, it was not going to come directly to them. Freedom had to be searched for and found. It required leaving the plantations of their enslavement, by foot or by boat or by wagon, and taking to the region's roads and waterways. And it required moving into encampments filled with soldiers like Camp Nelson, or into the rubble and ruin of burned-out cities like Hampton, or inside the mud-soaked tents and cabins lining the Mississippi River in towns like Helena. Their pursuit of freedom pushed them deeper and deeper into a war zone, into the most contested spaces of the na-tion's bloodiest war, where they remained for as long as the war lasted, or for as long as they could survive it.

The Whitehursts, Bogan, and Burdett were not the first to make this jour-ney. It was just days after the war broke out in April 1861 that a group of seven enslaved people from the Florida panhandle town of Milton traveled by foot across thirty miles of bogs and swamps to arrive at Fort Pickens, an island installation off the coast of Pensacola that remained under Union control. Three more enslaved people began following the First Rhode Island Regiment in Maryland as it arrived in that state ready to help defend Washington, D.C., in early May. And around the same time, the same scenario occurred along the Virginia coast, where groups of enslaved people repeatedly appealed to officials at the Union-held Fort Monroe to open their lines. Yet, "in all cases they are returned," according to reports, and the fort's commander, Col. Justin Dimmick, assured Confederate Virginians that "no molestation of their slave system would be suffered."[4] The same thing happened in Florida and Maryland. Union officials initially responded to freedom-seeking people by enforcing federal law—the Constitution and the 1850 Fugitive Slave Act, which together empowered federal agents to return fugitive slaves to their owners. And President Abraham Lincoln had recently promised in his inaugural address that he would not interfere with slavery in the South.[5]

Yet the enslaved continued to press Union authorities to interfere. They knew that the Union army was in a nearly untenable position during these early encounters: determined to uphold federal law—its duty in the war anyway—yet required to uphold a particular law that served the interests of their enemies, the slaveholding Confederates. Neither Dimmick nor the commanders of Fort Pickens and the Rhode Island regiment appeared to be particularly troubled by this conflict, but other officials soon were.

On May 24, 1861, in response to another group of men, women, and children who arrived at Fort Monroe, and just days after replacing Dimmick in command there, Gen. Benjamin F. Butler vowed to abandon the fugitive slave policy for the first time. He wrote in a letter to General-in-Chief Winfield Scott that "the Fugitive Slave Act did not affect a foreign country, which Virginia claimed to be ... [and] she was taken at her word."[6] Butler was no abolitionist: he had already turned back runaway slaves in Maryland earlier that month, and before that he had supported the proslavery Southern Democratic candidate, John C. Breckinridge, over the Republican Abraham Lincoln in the 1860 presidential election. But his encounter that morning with this group of enslaved people from nearby Hampton had convinced Butler that there was no sense in returning "this species of property" to assist the enemies when his own military operation, especially his quartermaster's department, was in need of their labor. "As a military question," Butler argued, "it would seem to be a measure of necessity to deprive their masters of their services."[7]

Butler would famously call these men, women, and children around him "contraband" of war; his order to his subordinates requiring their admission and protection inside Union lines would go down in history as his "contraband order." His action, rightfully, has been held up as a pivotal moment that set a precedent for the federal government's evolving policy on slavery and emancipation. His order did not grant those individuals their legal freedom exactly; to be "contraband" was to be considered little more than enemy "property" to be seized by the Union. But it did open space for enslaved people inside the Union army's lines, physical spaces in which to live beyond their owners' reach and to begin imagining the future. And as these spaces opened along rivers, across former plantations, and in cities—anywhere occupied by the Union—those seeking freedom worked to make these places their own, to make them begin to conform to their visions of freedom. Which is what Edward Whitehurst was doing in his store, what Eliza Bogan was doing in her cabin, and what Gabriel Burdett was doing from his new pulpit. This book is the story of what happened next—to these individuals, and to the many thousands more who fled slavery alongside them. It is the story of life inside the Civil War's slave refugee camps.

Introduction

The United States had never seen anything like it before. Nearly 500,000 men, women, and children would continue to flee the farms and plantations of their enslavement in search of refuge behind the lines of the Union army throughout the Civil War. It was unprecedented in scale. Enslaved people had always run away from slavery in the decades before the war, aiming for places in Northern states or in Canada where they could start a new life as free people. And previous wars had accelerated their flight. The British Army opened its lines to freedom-seeking slaves during the Revolution, offering to liberate those who were willing to shoulder arms and fight on its behalf; the same thing happened again during the War of 1812. Those conflicts threatened slavery but only to a degree, freeing "tens of thousands," according to some estimates, before peace returned and slavery continued to expand unabated across the American South.[1] By the 1860s, however, the nation's descent into civil war set in motion hundreds of thousands of men, women, and children — entire families, neighborhoods, and communities — in a mass exodus from slavery that would strain and then destroy the institution once and for all.

Their movement went in a vastly different direction from that of those who had previously run to Northern states or to foreign powers. The Civil War's refugees from slavery remained in the South, turning away from the region's edges to find freedom in its heart, in the very same plantation districts and amid the very same urban slave markets that had long confined them in slavery. They went wherever the Union army went and wherever they could find a military commander willing to let them stay. They set up tents in cotton fields and inside military installations both large and small. They erected cabins on the edges of encampments and took over abandoned buildings in

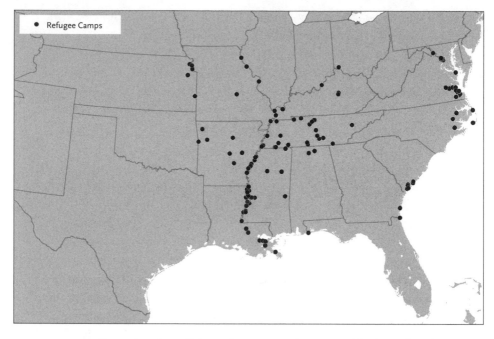

MAP 1. Known locations of slave refugee camps that emerged by the war's end in April 1865 (Pauer Center for Cartography & GIS, University of Kentucky)

cities under military occupation. Together their settlements multiplied quickly across the wartime landscape, creating a series of refugee camps (or "contraband camps," in the words of some federal authorities), in which some of them lived for months, others for years. They worked, worshipped, ate, slept, and endured disease, hunger, and assault inside the camps. They met soldiers from far Northern states, some of them helpful, some of them not; they encountered missionaries eager to teach them what they had not already taught themselves about reading and writing and worshipping. They searched for and found family long separated, or sometimes created new kinship ties. They started to build new lives that they believed would leave slavery behind — and would turn the promise of freedom from an abstraction into a lived reality. And this occurred many, many times over, in nearly 300 settlements that stretched from the coast of Virginia to Kansas, from Missouri down to New Orleans (map 1).[2]

As the camps multiplied, so too did an entirely new federal bureaucracy established to oversee and protect the residents within them. The U.S. War Department added a layer to the army's vast organizational structure in order to manage refugee affairs, appointing officers to positions such as superintendent of contrabands or superintendent of freedmen within particular geographic departments of the army, or in some places creating a whole new Department of Negro Affairs with a superintendent at its command. The secretary of war, Edwin Stanton, likewise kept a close eye on what was going on, dispatching commissioners to visit camps and publish reports that recommended what could, and what should, be done to provide federal protection to freedom-seeking people.[3] Never before had federal government agents intervened so directly to protect the interests of those in bondage—it marked, in fact, a reversal of the approach taken by other federal officials who had enforced the 1850 Fugitive Slave Act. Around the wartime camps we can instead see federal power expanding on behalf of former slaves in ways that anticipated, and laid the groundwork for, the more well-known Freedmen's Bureau that emerged by the war's end.[4]

And yet, even as this bureaucracy survived into the postwar period, the camps themselves did not last long. Never intended by military authorities to be permanent, many of the settlements were closed down very quickly at the end of the war or during its immediate aftermath, as Union troops withdrew and returned north, and much of the land reverted to its antebellum owners. Tents were collapsed, buildings were destroyed, and the refugee camps were effectively erased from the Southern landscape. Little to no traces remain today, even as antebellum mansions, military fortifications, breastworks, and sunken roads still remain to remind visitors of the history that surrounded those structures. Without such physical representations, and with a delayed acknowledgment in both popular and academic historical writing of slavery's role in bringing on the Civil War, it is no wonder that the story of how half a million men, women, and children risked their lives for freedom has left little imprint on Americans' historical memory. The refugees have not ranked—at least not yet—among the war's great heroes, nor have they received thick biographies or had their names affixed to buildings or road signs or military installations. The story of this monumental exodus from slavery still remains relatively unknown among Civil War enthusiasts and historians alike.[5]

Embattled Freedom thus began as an act of recovery. Its goal was to reconstruct, from the crumbling pages of military records, newspapers, and missionary reports, the way that the refugee camps looked and were experienced by those who lived there—to reimagine a physical landscape that can no longer be seen. As the research got under way, other recovery efforts emerged in some of the places where refugee settlements once stood. Statues honoring wartime freedom seekers have been erected in Corinth, Mississippi, and in Helena, Arkansas; new parks were established at the site of refugee settlements in Mitchelville, South Carolina, and Camp Nelson, Kentucky; and Fort Monroe was declared a national monument by President Barack Obama, largely for its role in the wartime destruction of slavery. This local preservation work continues. And *Embattled Freedom* tells the story that connected these sites, the story of what it meant to search for freedom in the middle of a war, inside the space and bureaucracy and culture of the Union army.

﹏

The men, women, and children moving into these military-sponsored camps experienced their emancipation in slow motion. None of them became instantly and securely free upon setting foot inside Union lines, either because Union policies did not explicitly guarantee it — to be admitted into the Union sphere as a "contraband" was for a long time not the same as to be legally emancipated — or because little about daily life in the camps looked like freedom in any meaningful sort of way. This was not the immediate emancipation that an enslaved person may have dreamed about or that radical abolitionists had long advocated for them. Yet it also bore little resemblance to the gradual emancipations that had already taken place in other places, such as the British West Indies or even the northern United States in the decades after the Revolution. No formal system of apprenticeship replaced slavery during the Civil War, as in those other places, no clear end point was evident after which the men, women, and children would be recognized as free.[6] In fact, the end point, if one was even coming, seemed to keep moving with each passing day, as the fate of the refugees was beholden to the course of the war and to the Union army's ability to defeat the Confederacy. No one knew, as they set up tents amid those Union troops, if freedom would indeed come — or whether the war might end without their permanent freedom secured.

Civil War emancipation was thus a profoundly uncertain process. Those who lived and witnessed it cast about trying to describe it, to give it a name and therefore a meaning and logic. A visiting Quaker in the Mississippi Valley, noting the harsh circumstances that came with living in the camps, predicted that it would only continue "until the transition state from slavery to self-supporting freedom is passed through."[7] This was a "transition state" — a term that would be repeated over and over in the commentaries of army officials, missionaries, and refugees alike. Time in the camps was "their transition from a state of bondage and degradation to an unknown future," or simply "this transition state through which the Freedmen are passing."[8] Some looked for analogous transition states to describe this one, especially those that had occurred in the past. A missionary in Vicksburg observing a boat carrying 600 "poor destitute women and children" to that city grabbed on to an especially poignant precedent. "The sight and smell of that boat," he wrote, "reminded me of the 'middle passage,' described in the accounts of the slave-trade; women, children, horses and mules, all huddled together."[9] It was like the transatlantic voyage of over 10 million Africans to the Americas that played out over hundreds of years, only this time it would take place in reverse, as a passage from slavery to freedom.[10]

More commonly invoked was a biblical journey. "This transition state through which these people are passing is truly a wilderness of suffering," declared a white missionary in Virginia.[11] Life in the camps was like the Old Testament "wilderness" of Exodus: a period of hardship and deprivation experienced by the Israelites on their way out of slavery in Egypt and into the Promised Land. "It [is] said that God had set two hundred years as the extent of the bondage of my people," declared a black minister living amid the refugee community in Hampton, Virginia. "We may even be obliged to pass forty years more, in a half way wilderness state."[12] Enslaved people had long identified with the journey of the Israelites, seeing in their story a message of hope that one day their Moses would come and their period of enslavement would come to an end.[13] And now, having entered a "wilderness" of refugee camps during the Civil War, it seemed that the road to the Promised Land had finally been laid out before them, even if, as another missionary put it, it would be "rough and ruinous and full of perils."[14] This may explain why, even given the harrowing conditions and the uncertainty of their fate, the people kept coming and their journeys into the camps rarely slowed over the course of the war. It was an act of faith as much as a pragmatic search for protection.

Their uncertain, transitional position was expressed in other ways too, such as by the labels attached to the individuals themselves — "contraband," "refugee," or simply "vagrant" or "freedman." Each term, of course, was more than a label, but an entire category of meaning loaded with implications for policy and the sort of status these individuals would acquire once inside Union lines. Historians have grown accustomed to calling them "contraband," a term that, while rooted in General Butler's original language, succinctly conveys the unique transitional status they assumed during the Civil War. But that was not a term that the people tended to use themselves — it is very rare to hear a person emerging from slavery refer to him- or herself as a "contraband." And the word generated a great deal of vocal resistance at the time. The abolitionist newspaper the *Liberator* wrote in February 1862 that it "is not a proper term to be applied to human beings," while the *American Missionary* journal likewise objected to the fact that it "implies property in man." Although "no one word expresses their condition," the *Liberator* continued, it eventually settled on one: "Let them be called Colored Refugees, until we can obtain for them a recognized freedom and citizenship." The *American Missionary* concurred that "we prefer this designation of the people who are fleeing to our camps."[15]

This book prefers that designation too, inspired by the ever-present usage of "refugee" across the sources of the period, as well as by the term's acknowledgment of personhood over property. Some readers may not immediately recognize those seeking freedom in the 1860s as "refugees," however; in the post-twentieth-century world, in which the term refugee has received a precise definition from the United Nations, refugees are typically those who fear persecution and are thus forced to flee their countries of origin and cross national borders in order to obtain protection.[16] But what evolved with clarity in the twentieth century followed a century of fluidity in Americans' thinking about refugees. United States refugee policy was still in its infancy by the time the Civil War came, having evolved from the initial acceptance of only the religiously persecuted to a broadened acceptance of the politically persecuted too. Refugees from Canada after the American Revolution, some of them taking up residence in federally sponsored refugee camps in upstate New York, as well as both black and white refugees from Haiti amid its own revolution, already had forced the federal government to confront its willingness — and its obligation — to open its borders and protect the oppressed.[17]

By the time of the Civil War, that protection would extend to the persecution of the enslaved too. These individuals may not have crossed national borders as they sought protection from enslavement — whether or not they did depends on one's willingness to see the Confederacy as a separate "nation," something the Union and Abraham Lincoln himself were unwilling to do. But there was no question that they faced violent persecution of an all-encompassing sort in the antebellum South and the newly formed Confederate republic. And those in the Union most willing to help them found in "refugee" a term that evoked both their liminal status and their compelling need for protection.

Embattled Freedom thus positions these refugees from slavery, and the wilderness state of the camps into which they journeyed, more visibly in what historians now call the United States' "long emancipation" from slavery.[18] It argues that just as contemporaries viewed the journeys in and out of the camps as a distinct phase of the ex-slaves' extended journey to freedom, marking a distinct transition period in the decades-long battle to end slavery, it should remain so distinct in our recollections today. Yet to see this phase and to grapple with it requires slowing down the pace of the traditional emancipation narrative too. It requires setting aside the common temptation to foreground the January 1863 Emancipation Proclamation while quickly passing over what came before it or what transpired in its aftermath as "chaotic" or simply "mayhem."[19] This book instead takes the wartime chaos seriously, paying close attention to the way in which these journeys to freedom played out day to day and month to month over the course of the war. Only in this slowed-down, deliberate fashion can some of emancipation's most basic facets be seen, including its most central characteristic: that it was embedded in military conflict.

The United States was not alone in the Western Hemisphere, during what evolved into a century of slave emancipations, in witnessing the institution's collapse under the weight of war. Slavery ended in Haiti and, later, Cuba during revolutions, when the cause of the slaves' independence became part and parcel of causes of political independence. In the United States, however, it was not a revolution but a civil war that accelerated the turn to emancipation, and that proved, in turn, to be a different kind of war for ending slavery. The war effort to which the slaves' radical cause became fused was a fundamentally conservative one—saving a Union that had long enslaved them—which yielded, almost from the start, an imperfect fit.[20] It was the enslaved themselves who first looked for a fit, most notably those who set out for Union lines in the war's opening days. "They felt that their interests were identical with the objects of our armies," one superintendent working with the refugees noted while observing these early movements, and as a result, "this identity of interest, slowly but surely, came to be perceived by our officers and soldiers, and by the loyal public."[21] It happened "slowly," but not exactly "surely," because aligning the interests of the enslaved with the cause of saving the Union would take work— a great deal of work.

The story of how Abraham Lincoln managed to pull these causes together has been well told. The destruction of slavery ultimately proved itself to be a "military necessity" to save the Union, Lincoln concluded over time, thus transforming emancipation into an integral weapon in the army's wartime arsenal. Ending slavery, according to the Emancipation Proclamation, was "an act of justice, warranted by the Constitution, upon military necessity."[22] Union policy thus evolved to create what some have termed a "military emancipation," in which the task of freeing people was put into the hands of the army as it fanned out across the South. Yet military emancipation is, more often than not, described from the vantage point of Washington, D.C., and from the perspective of the commander in chief as well as other political officials in his administration and in Congress. Such depictions tell us a great deal about how the two interests were reconciled in the abstract, in principle as well as in policy, but barely glimpse the real work involved in bringing them together in daily life on the ground — and often take for granted that, indeed, the two would ever come together at all.[23]

To view military emancipation from the vantage point of the slave refugee camps is to see where the enslaved and the army *actually met*—where the people seeking freedom came face-to-face with the soldiers fighting to save the Union. Those people, and those personal interactions, mattered: to be joined by "necessity" was, after all, to be joined by something utterly practical in nature. Theirs was more than an ideological convergence or a joining of common sentiment; it was a practical merging too, one that played out every single day as soldiers and refugees had to figure out how to live and work and fight alongside one another. When an individual had to approach an army commander for something as basic as food, or had to find a space to erect a tent somewhere close — but not too close — to white soldiers, or had to relinquish that space the minute a soldier needed it, it became clear that the Union army was more than a force fighting for emancipation in the abstract. It was also an entire bureaucracy and culture within which freedom-seeking people had to maneuver themselves toward freedom, working constantly and daily to reconcile their needs with those of the Union.

Embattled Freedom accordingly pulls back from the political world of Washington, D.C., and zooms in on the material reality of the refugee camps. The daily encounters of refugees and the military, after all, largely turned on sharing the same physical spaces and sharing access to food, clothing, and shelter. These were the most important and crucial needs that all human beings carried into this war, and the attempt to reconcile them was wrapped up with the larger effort to reconcile the causes of emancipation and saving the Union. Sometimes the basic question of whether there was truly an "identity of interest" between ex-slaves and the army turned on the more immediate question of whether they could even coexist in the camps and share access to resources. With the insights of environmental historians, cultural geographers, and material culture specialists as a guide, then, *Embattled Freedom* turns attention to the physical dimensions of refugee camp life, to the spaces, things, and structures that were at the center of a refugee's encounter with the army.[24] And with this material world in focus, it asks a most basic question about Civil War emancipation: How did it *actually work* in daily life?[25]

A crucial answer lies in "military necessity." So often described as an "argument" or as the primary legal justification for emancipation, it is revealed here as an everyday governing logic surrounding those daily encounters between refugees and the army — a fluid, inconsistent, and contradictory logic.[26] An enslaved person's basic need for freedom may have remained relatively constant during the war, but Union military necessity never was; the army, despite its rigid command structure and bureaucracy, despite its culture of order and efficiency, was a complex and fluid organism. The people who commanded its departments brought into the system a vast array of beliefs about slavery and race; the tasks it confronted were wide-ranging, from feeding to housing to nursing to mobilizing and fighting; and the strategic imperatives it served varied greatly depending on local environments and enemy pressures, all of which changed over time. All of this meant that the calculus of "military necessity"—what military leaders believed the Union needed to achieve victory— changed constantly and was thus a moving target on which refugees pinned their hopes for liberation. Assertions of military necessity could at times collide as much as they could align with the ex-slaves' pursuit of freedom.[27]

Such moments of collision, felt deeply and tragically by the refugees, did not go unnoticed by Union officials. Secretary of War Stanton, for one, was well aware of these problems, and many others related to the conduct of soldiers, when in 1863 he tasked legal scholar Francis Lieber to draft a new code of laws governing the Union's conduct in war (a code that would go on to influence the Geneva Conventions). Lieber determined that nothing mattered more in war than the pursuit of a just end—in this case, the end of saving the Union without the stain of slavery. The most humane way to achieve that end, he contended, was to fight hard and vigorously, to fight a "sharp, short" war that might inflict suffering and death but would end quickly.[28] Away from Washington, D.C., however, out in the field where these issues were less theoretical and more immediate, officers, soldiers, and refugees alike wrestled with the implications of the Lieber Code. Was the just end of emancipation really served by hard war if those being emancipated were suffering and dying along the way? Might it sometimes be more humane, more just, to *rein in* zealous assertions of military necessity?

Those were questions hotly contested in the camps—and kept alive not only by the refugees themselves but by another group of individuals who emerged to assist them: civilian agents and teachers from Northern missionary and benevolent organizations. Many of them former abolitionists, both black and white, they were sent to the South at first by organizations like the American Missionary Association and the Society of Friends based in New York, Philadelphia, and Indiana. Over time, new secular organizations emerged, too, such as the Contraband Relief Commission of Cincinnati and the National Freedmen's Relief Association, based in New York, both founded in 1862, and the United States Commission for the Relief of National Freedmen, established as an umbrella organization in 1864. New journals and newspapers also emerged to report on daily life in the camps and to appeal for Northern assistance, with titles such as the *Freedmen's Bulletin*, the *Freedmen's Friend*, and the *National Freedman*. The organizations raised copious amounts of money, sending teachers, books, Bibles, and clothing into the refugee camps, an effort that left no doubt that there was a humanitarian crisis in the South that needed the nation's attention and relief.

These benevolent Northerners envisioned themselves as intermediaries in the camps, as self-appointed guardians who were there to prod army officials to remember the interests of humanity, and thus of individual refugees, when deciding when to move or where to go or how to distribute food. They sent appeals all the way to Washington, to Lincoln and to Secretary of War Stanton; they sent regular reports to daily newspapers and to their own journals. Some of them would even work their way into the army itself by assuming positions as superintendents of contraband and freedmen, working from within the military bureaucracy to stretch its authority further and further outward in the interest of humanity. But their work often came with strings attached, too, as was often the case with relief and reform efforts. Deeply ingrained expectations about the proper behavior and morals of newly freed people—ideas rooted in race, gender, and class—were channeled into nearly everything, from the provision of clothing to the establishment of schools. This, in turn, yielded an even more complex journey for those making their way through the wilderness, as the refugees brought with them their own ideas for how they should live as free people.

It was not uncommon to hear observers refer to the movement of these former slaves as a "stampede," a "flood," or a "rising tide." Newspaper articles, government reports, and even captions to illustrations of this wartime flight told of "swarms" that appeared at army camps, and of freedom seekers who "circulated much like water" and "rolled like eddies around military posts."[29] To W. E. B. Du Bois, writing in the early twentieth century, this wartime movement was a "great unbroken swell of the ocean"; more recent historians have continued to call it a "flood" and a "swarming."[30] Expressing awe at the scale of the former slaves' movement, these characterizations, then and now, have grasped at some way of understanding its size and force and have found it in environmental metaphors. To invoke floods and oceans and other sources of natural power is to convey succinctly that this wartime flight was something unstoppable, led not by a few individuals but by a truly spontaneous yet collective force that mobilized in multiple places at multiple times. To see this story as a "flood" or a "rising tide" has enabled Americans to see how it was that former slaves, scattered across plantations throughout the South, managed to exert so much force so quickly on Abraham Lincoln and his administration.

And yet the story told by these metaphors has also enabled us to maintain a certain distance from these refugees over time. To see the people as a "flood" or a "swarm" is to envision them in a faceless, and certainly nameless, kind of way: they are a collective more than they are individuals. To see them as this abstract force is to simultaneously — and perhaps inadvertently — still keep the individuals hidden in the background. Basic questions and facts about them are thus left unseen and unknown: Who exactly were these refugees? Where did they come from? And what did they experience? As consequential as they were, surprisingly little is known today about the individuals who set in motion the events that ultimately brought down slavery and secured freedom for all enslaved people.[31]

This book therefore set out to disaggregate the "mass" and to get to know them. It was a challenge little different from the one facing any historian trying to see the lives of those outside positions of formal power, who lived in less visible and conspicuous ways. With few rich personal narratives like those of Frederick Douglass or Harriet Jacobs to guide me, it might have seemed an insurmountable challenge — except that the Civil War marked a turning point in the textual archiving of African American history. Wars, after all, generate paper. And the encounters of African Americans with the army and the federal government left countless marks on the Union's paper bureaucracy, in the form of reports, orders, correspondence, and the occasional stab at a population census.[32] It was the first time that the federal government, in any systematic way, in fact, recognized enslaved people as individuals. For although the federal population census had long listed them by gender, age, and race, it had omitted their names; now, in the Civil War, as they emerged from slavery, they appeared in the documents by name and often with identifying information. As a result, there is today an enormous paper trail documenting the lives of individual refugees tucked inside thousands of boxes at the National Archives and Records Administration in Washington, D.C.

I set out to follow that paper trail. I went back over the same documents already familiar to military historians but this time read them differently: not so much as a formal transcript of military strategy and order, but as an informal, "hidden" transcript of slavery's demise and wartime disorder.[33] A black laborer mentioned in a quartermaster official's monthly report on the people he had recently hired; a provost marshal's list of ex-slaves arrested for selling whiskey to soldiers; a special order commanding an outpost's soldiers to stop admitting women and children into a camp. These sorts of documents came into being as assertions of military supervision and control—and they were that. But read from a different angle, the ex-slaves visible in them emerge as more than mere objects of that control but as individual subjects, too, maneuvering through the military apparatus to secure their freedom. Often the records noted a refugee's actions more than his or her words, however, but following their movements, it turned out, could be illuminating too.

The movements of Edward and Emma Whitehurst, Eliza Bogan, and Gabriel Burdett emerge most vividly in this book. None of them is well known today, none of them was well known at the time, and none had had their stories told before. But each of them piqued my curiosity when a particular document raised more questions than it answered and led me to search for them in other sources, such as missionary records, newspapers, censuses, and local property deeds and vital records. Like a genealogist reconstituting a family, I then worked backward and forward, connecting the dots of these individuals' movements, as well as those of their family members and other slaves from their neighborhoods. It was a process that played out differently along the lines of gender. Women are simply harder to see and to track in the federal records—and in army sources in particular. A military system and culture built for men and more accustomed to the presence of men reproduced that gender differential in its record keeping, leaving women, who were nonetheless present and consequential in the camps, less visible or unacknowledged altogether. Yet "archival fragments," as historian Marisa J. Fuentes has put it, do exist and can be read carefully in order to make visible women's actions too. And their resulting stories, like those of men, bring to life the refugee experience with a depth and a humanity that only the stories of individuals can.[34]

It was a thick stack of papers, a postwar claim for compensation filed by Edward Whitehurst with the federal government, that led me back in time to figure out how two enslaved people could establish their own store in a war zone. Their story anchors chapter 1, "Securing Work." It opens at the point where and when it all began, in eastern Virginia in May 1861, and follows the efforts of refugees like the Whitehursts to find work and to claim the privileges of free labor and, thus, economic independence. Next, a soldier's pension record from the 1870s that revealed intimate details about Eliza Bogan's family life prompted me to try to figure out how a mother of seven children fared in the most trying of circumstances. Her story winds through chapter 4, "Facing Combat," which moves to the Mississippi Valley beginning in 1863, at a time when the Union army accelerated its reliance upon ex-slaves to fight, quite literally, for their freedom. Finally, a wartime letter, one of the first ever written by Gabriel Burdett, made me wonder how this ostensibly secular military conflict opened up space for religious expression and freedom. His story is the basis for chapter 7, "Keeping Faith," and is set in 1864 in the place where slavery would die its last legal death, in the border state of Kentucky.

These three microhistorical chapters join together to form three narrative focal points in this book's structure, ones that, when read in sequence, carry the larger story forward across time and space. Each touches down in particular places and underlines a basic fact discovered by a federal commissioner surveying the scene in 1862: "that the condition of the colored Refugees varies very considerably in the different localities in which they are collected."[35] Wartime emancipation was a profoundly localized process, as anything embedded in military conflict is, beholden to local variance in strategy, resources, leadership, and the environment. To move our vantage point out of Washington, D.C., as this book does, and into these "different localities," is to see how the passage of time and the course of events could be interpreted so differently from place to place, as progress appeared in one location at the very same time it was impeded in another. It is to see that emancipation was not one process—but many.

Embattled Freedom, accordingly, does not unfold as a linear story. Emancipation itself was not a linear story, but instead a fitful journey of forward movements and backward retreats—as most journeys in war are. The movements of these refugees into Union army lines are more accurately thought about in terms of cycles: just as one person, or one group, made it inside Union lines, the process started all over again for another. Every day, the war brought a new beginning point for someone—and that same day might have brought an end, or a restart, for others. And all along, slavery itself, the thing to be left behind, continually impinged on the journey to freedom, either as the alternative to be avoided at all costs, or as the formative experience shaping the aspirations and strategies the refugees would employ in their new lives in freedom.[36] This is why this book's narrative stops at three points along the way, and in short interludes takes readers back into slavery in order to better understand the wartime actions of protagonists like the Whitehursts, Bogan, and Burdett.

Yet *Embattled Freedom* puts the individuals in the broader context, too, panning back and widening its analytical lens as it moves along, in order to look across the entire wartime South and survey all of the nearly 300 refugee camps I have identified. This broader perspective becomes evident in the five thematic chapters that are interspersed among the microhistorical ones, bringing the entire landscape of refugee camps into view. Chapters entitled "Finding Shelter," "Confronting Removal," "Battling Hunger," "Clothing Bodies," and

"Grappling with Loss" highlight, in particular, the basic material conditions of life inside the camps that transcended time and place. These chapters take up topics ranging from food and clothing to shelter and land, drawing attention to the most basic human encounters with the material world that were elemental to the freedom-seeking process. They reveal what it was like for individuals to live and sleep and breathe and eat inside these camps—what it was like to simply survive on a daily basis in order to have a chance at securing their freedom for the long term.

After all, there would be no freedom and no acquisition of citizenship rights without survival.[37] Other historians have written powerfully about the illness and death that plagued these camps, about the thousands who paid the ultimate price well before the war ended and their freedom was secured. It was a painful reality evident in all military camps across the wartime landscape, but one exacerbated in the encampments of African American people by a white medical establishment that at times neglected, and thus worsened, their plight.[38] This story winds through *Embattled Freedom*, too, but with its flip side—the story of the survivors—more fully in view. They were, after all, the majority. And to follow how they maneuvered through the military apparatus in order to make it out alive reveals a remarkable facet of emancipation's history: the basic urgency of building a new life—and simply living and surviving—inside a war zone.

"They will endure every privation for the sake of freedom," wrote one Union official in a report from Virginia in 1862, "and they seem too happy in their escape from slavery to feel very keenly any present and temporary suffering."[39] That was not quite right, as the refugees felt their suffering profoundly. But it is true that they did not always succumb to it either. They pressed on, sometimes for four years or more, in a journey through the wilderness of the Civil War that represented a unique period in the centuries-long journey to freedom and equal citizenship. It was a journey that took them deep into the heart of the most violent military conflict the nation had ever seen, deep inside its newly militarized spaces. It took them inside quartermasters' offices in search of work, into commissary warehouses in search of food, inside hospitals in search of care, and into court-martial commissions in search of justice. They sought places for themselves and their families inside the Union's military sphere because they believed that was the way to secure a claim to their long-awaited freedom. And yet, any freedom born in these circumstances would not be immediately and fully realized. It would be continually fought for and fought against, triumphant yet always under siege—it would be an embattled freedom.

Edward and Emma Whitehurst in Slavery

Edward Whitehurst had been working for freedom for a very long time. He knew that it would take work, and a great deal of it, for his emancipation from slavery was not going to come from a sudden change of heart on the part of his owner. To Whitehurst, the pursuit of freedom instead demanded money, and it demanded his participation in the very same market exchange that had enslaved him and millions of other people of African descent. If his ancestors had been sold into slavery, then he would have to buy his way back out again and purchase his own freedom. So he worked and he saved for much of his adult life. And by 1861, at the age of thirty-one, Whitehurst had accumulated a significant nest egg. "I had over $500 — in gold and silver when the war broke out," Edward recalled later. "[I] kept it in my trunk and with my wife" on their plantation on Virginia's peninsula. It was not yet enough to buy his freedom or that of his wife, Emma, but he was well on his way.[1]

Edward and Emma Whitehurst were unique to be enslaved *and* in possession of a trunk full of gold and silver — but they were not exactly alone either. It was one of the perverse realities of slavery in the United States. They were themselves property, at least in the eyes of their enslaver and of Virginia law, but they still managed to accumulate property too. And they did so openly, with their owner's permission, or at the very least, with his willingness to turn a blind eye to their savings.[2] This marked no crack in the foundation of slavery, or any symptom of its weakening, however, but was in fact a sign of something more insidious: the institution's ability to adapt, over and over again, to the changing realities of places like eastern Virginia. For slavery in the state had been undergoing a transformation during the Whitehursts' lifetimes.

The tobacco economy that had long powered slavery's expansion and brought the Whitehursts' ancestors to this part of the state was in decline, thanks to weakened markets as well as soils that could no longer sustain the plant's widespread cultivation. Landowners throughout the state turned elsewhere, diversifying the state's economy by increasing the cultivation of wheat and other crops, while also establishing industries devoted to the manufacturing of iron and the mining of coal and salt. They also discovered that great profits could be had from off-loading their now-surplus slave "property" to other parts of the South that needed it more, especially to the rapidly expanding cotton regions of the Deep South. Virginia planters thus refashioned themselves into traders and helped established a domestic slave trade that would pour hundreds of thousands of people into the cotton states, launching a massive redistribution of the South's enslaved population.[3]

The Whitehursts were never sold to the Deep South, but Edward, at least, still became enmeshed in a smaller-scale redistribution of enslaved labor across Virginia. Sometime in adulthood he began leaving his owner's property daily to go work for other men in the region as a "hired-out" slave. He may have gone to work for other farmers who needed laborers but could not afford to purchase a slave, or for local craftsmen and merchants in the nearby town of Hampton, whose growing enterprises in shipbuilding, oystering, and brick-making necessitated additional labor. Where exactly he went has not survived in the record, but Edward later characterized his work by noting, "I hired my time of my own master." With that turn of phrase Edward identified himself as a "self-hired" slave, part of a distinct subset of those hired out who sought their own employment and exerted some leverage, even just a degree of it, over the type of work and the working conditions they would accept. In return for his labor, a self-hired slave like Edward received wages that were divided between his enslaver and himself; he paid his owner a sum and then kept the rest to pay for his own food and clothing. Anything beyond that he could keep for other purposes, and if he worked in a situation that enabled him to work overtime, he could keep his "overwork" pay too.[4] And keep it he did—in the trunk.

That the Whitehursts had saved $500 from Edward's earnings by 1861 suggests he worked very long hours for days, weeks, months, and years.[5] At the same time, with no legal protections, Whitehurst also worked under extremely vulnerable conditions: vulnerable to being cheated out of his wages, vulnerable to the violence of an employer's whip, and vulnerable to his owner deciding, on a whim, to abrogate the entire deal and instead sell him to the Deep South. It was a precarious way to live that no amount of money in his trunk could obscure—even the money itself was vulnerable to being stolen at any time. As a self-hired slave, Whitehurst did not experience any kind of quasi

　　　　　　　　　　　　　　Edward and Emma Whitehurst in Slavery

freedom so much as he experienced things that would come to shape his future pursuit of freedom.[6] He had become a participant in the labor market, valuing and selling his own labor and earning compensation in return, while experiencing the market's fluctuations. He thus went through the motions of free labor even as he remained, profoundly and legally, enslaved.[7]

Although an estimated 40 percent of all enslaved people in Whitehurst's home county of Elizabeth City were hired out in 1860, the majority of them were men, like Edward.[8] Women were more likely to remain on their home plantations—and Emma Whitehurst appears to have been one of them. Her situation before the war is much harder to detect in the historical record, and the only clue that remains is Edward's postwar recollection that while he worked elsewhere, he left his trunk behind "with my wife." This implies that Emma, like so many other enslaved women across the South, experienced less mobility in her everyday life and was more confined to the space of her home plantation—and thus better positioned to safeguard the trunk on a daily basis.[9] Her days were thus likely spent laboring in the fields, perhaps planting and harvesting the sweet potatoes and corn or raising the hogs that had replaced tobacco cultivation on the property.[10]

The land on which she worked belonged to William Ivy, a striving white man who had gradually risen into the planter class. The son of a New Orleans sea captain of French ancestry, and a relatively new arrival to Virginia, Ivy first established himself as a surveyor before marrying into one of the oldest families in the eastern part of the state, the Parrishes. His marriage to Ann Parrish in 1848 allowed William to settle on a seventy-five-acre portion of her family's landholdings that stretched along the shore of Hampton Roads, the mouth of the James River, in an area known as Newport News.[11] This part of Virginia's coast was coveted real estate, not only for its access to markets but also for its historical significance: the area had witnessed naval engagements in both the War of 1812 and the Revolution, and even earlier, in the early 1600s, boats had sailed past this stretch of land on the way to Jamestown, including one ship that carried the very first African people to North America.[12]

By 1860, twenty-one men, women, and children lived there as William Ivy's property, and when combined with the other adjacent Parrish family holdings, that number rose to 100 enslaved people living and working in the Whitehursts' immediate vicinity. Together they formed an extended network of enslaved people that may have been linked by additional ties of marriage and family. Nearly half of them, a total of forty-five, were children under the age of twelve, raising the possibility, too, that Emma also spent some of her time caring for children—although surviving records never mention any children that she and Edward may have had. Maybe they did have children and their off-spring did not survive; on the same Ivy property, a woman named Susan lost five of her children in 1857 and 1858 to whooping cough, pneumonia, "worm fever," and being "burned," according to county death records.[13] These losses were a stark testament to the precariousness in which all enslaved people lived, to the way in which the Whitehursts had to simply survive before they could even imagine buying their way out of slavery and into freedom.

Yet any such imagining changed abruptly in May 1861. It would have been difficult for Edward and Emma Whitehurst to miss the alarm with which William Ivy, the Parrish men, and other white people in the region greeted the outbreak of war. "We did not know what it would bring," one of Ivy's neighbors in Newport News later recalled of the war's opening days, "but we feared every imaginable thing."[14] They were fearful in part because they knew this war would not be fought at a distance. Just seven miles around the bend of Hampton Roads was Fort Monroe, one of the few U.S. Army installations that would remain in Union control, even as Fort Sumter and other military posts in the South fell to the Confederacy (map 2). The sight of Fort Monroe — or at least its sounds reverberating across the water — offered a constant reminder that U.S. forces would not let the South secede quietly or peacefully. That was a troubling notion for these Confederate-sympathizing men ("intense Rebels," as a Union official would later refer to them).[15] So they quickly scattered: Ivy's father-in-law, Edward Parrish, gathered his family and some of his slaves and refugeed them inland to Henrico County, which surrounded the new Confederate capital of Richmond;[16] his eighty-year-old brother, John, remained behind to watch over their family property, believing, as rumor had it, that his older age would protect him and his property from seizure by Union troops.[17] William Ivy, however, decided to fight, and on May 14, 1861, at the relatively advanced age of thirty-eight, he enlisted in the Third Virginia Cavalry. Ivy's overseer also enlisted on the same day.[18]

Ivy had a lot to defend — his land, his slaves, his future. At the same time, the officer who enlisted him was Charles King Mallory, a neighbor and high-profile voice in Virginia politics and military affairs who served as the commander of the local militia and a delegate to Virginia's secession convention.[19] Mallory may have been persuasive in encouraging Ivy to enlist; at the very least, Ivy may have felt reassured by Mallory's example that leaving his property behind, both land and slaves, was a risky yet necessary step in order to defend it. What neither Ivy nor Mallory could have known at the point of enlistment, however, was that just nine days later, Mallory's own plantation enterprise

Edward and Emma Whitehurst in Slavery

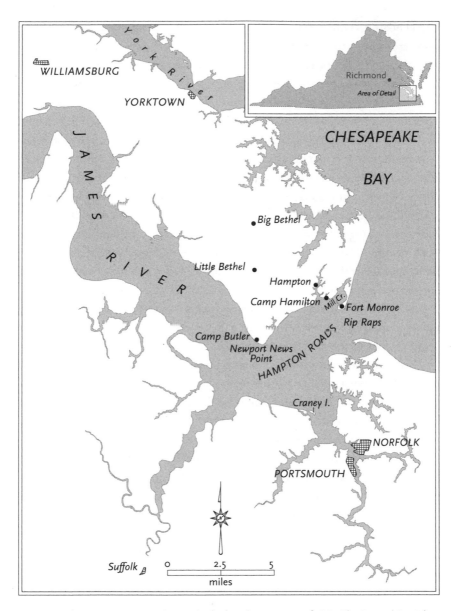

MAP 2. The Virginia Peninsula as it looked in the summer of 1861. The Ivy and Parrish properties were located very close to Newport News Point, about seven miles southwest of Fort Monroe. The Union army established additional outposts at Hampton, Camp Hamilton, and Camp Butler that summer, all of which became sites of refugee settlements. (Pauer Center for Cartography & GIS, University of Kentucky)

would begin to collapse; it was from his property that the first few freedom-seeking slaves approached Benjamin Butler at Fort Monroe on May 23.[20]

And that is how slavery began to disintegrate in the Whitehursts' part of the South—with the exodus of the planters. "The number of slaves who run away is not so great as the number of those whose masters run away," remarked a reporter in the region from the *New York Tribune*.[21] The departures of men like Edward Parrish, William Ivy, and Charles Mallory profoundly disrupted plantation power dynamics in eastern Virginia and opened up unprecedented room for enslaved people to maneuver. On the Ivy property, Edward and Emma Whitehurst no longer had an owner or an overseer to watch over their every move (with the exception of the elderly John Parrish). And it probably did not take long to get word about the Mallory slaves' successful departure for Fort Monroe. News traveled quickly across the region, courtesy of what one white observer called the "mysterious spiritual telegraph which runs through the slave population."[22]

Soon that telegraph brought notice that the Union army was coming even closer to the Whitehursts' plantation. On May 27, General Butler dispatched Union troops in the direction of Newport News. It was just four days after he had issued his precedent-setting "contraband order," allowing enslaved people protection inside Union lines. Now his troops sought to expand those lines beyond Fort Monroe as they marched onto the property of Parker West, located just one and a half miles to the north of where the Whitehursts resided.[23] Many years after the end of the Civil War, Edward Whitehurst reflected on the significance of this moment. "I was a slave at the beginning of the war," Whitehurst recalled in a sworn statement to U.S. government officials, "but I was free to all intents after the 27th day of May 1861." He explained that this was the date "when my master went off and left me," although that was actually nearly two weeks before, on May 14.[24] Still, he was right that May 27 was a turning point: the arrival of Union forces spelled an entirely new future for Edward and Emma—and their trunk full of gold and silver coin.

Edward and Emma Whitehurst in Slavery

} 1 {

Securing Work

The Whitehursts left the Ivy property soon after they got word of the arrival of Butler's troops. They traveled just over one mile, likely on foot, to the former Parker West plantation, which had just been renamed Camp Butler. And very quickly they could see that more than the name had changed: soldiers were busy clearing corn, oat, and potato fields to make space for tents, as well as digging earthworks and cutting and stacking the logs necessary to transform the fields into a fortified encampment (fig. 1).[1] Familiar faces may have greeted the Whitehursts too. Nineteen men, women, and children who had been enslaved on the West plantation had stayed there, among them Lewis and Tiny Boycan and their four children, Sylvia, Mary, Charles, and Dick. Others had come short distances from the neighboring Smith, Lee, and Sinclair plantations.[2] Union authorities allowed all of them to remain, per General Butler's orders.[3]

From them the Whitehursts might have learned that some of the Union soldiers in their midst seemed friendly. The man in charge of Camp Butler was Gen. John Wolcott Phelps, a forty-eight-year-old career army officer who, days before, had led the First Vermont Regiment in its successful occupation of the nearby town of Hampton. Phelps seemed to have been waiting for a moment like this, for his opposition to slavery had been growing steadily in the years before the war. He was an enthusiastic participant in the U.S. Army's efforts to stop Southern attempts to annex states in Central America and the Caribbean for the expansion of slavery in the 1850s; he was also outspoken in his belief that slavery was a "stain" and a "disgrace" to the republic. Later that summer, Benjamin Butler would describe him as possessing "a deep religious enthusiasm upon the subject of Slavery."[4] Phelps had no objection to Butler's contra-

FIGURE 1. "Erecting Stockade at Newport News by the Federal Troops,"
Frank Leslie's Illustrated Newspaper, June 15, 1861,. The scene as Edward and
Emma Whitehurst would have observed it upon their arrival at Camp Butler.
(University of North Carolina Libraries)

band policies; if left alone, he might have taken them in radical new directions. (Indeed, in the years ahead, he would.)[5]

One of the first people the Whitehursts would have met was another member of the First Vermont, thirty-four-year-old Lt. Roswell Farnham. He was the acting provost marshal at the camp, and General Phelps had charged him with greeting each incoming refugee. Only fragments of what was spoken in his initial meetings are visible on the pages of Farnham's personal diary, which doubled as an official record book. In carefully demarcated columns, the lieutenant recorded the names and ages of each individual, along with notes about any family ties that connected them ("wife of," "son of"). He also asked for and recorded another piece of information: the name of each person's owner, something that was required by Benjamin Butler for what the general termed "future use."[6] Butler planned to generate a "receipt" for each owner, as he would for any property taken from a private citizen, in the event that the Union eventually decided to return the "contraband" property or to compensate the owners for their losses.[7] So with the stroke of the pen by which Farnham recorded their owners' names, the Whitehursts were thus marked as property in the eyes of Union authorities. Farnham himself had no trouble referring to them as such. "I am very busy indeed," Farnham remarked on a subsequent page of his journal. "All the slaves in the country are running to our camp. . . . The owners are loosing property fast."[8]

Edward and Emma next submitted to an examination to determine how "able-bodied" or "serviceable" they were. This involved at least a visual scan

Securing Work

of their bodies; one reporter observing a similar scene at nearby Fort Monroe noted that an aide-de-camp "glanced his eye rapidly over the lot." But it may have also included touching and probing. The exam was a search for anything that might disqualify them from labor—for any bodily information that might help match their physical skills with the work demanded by the military.[9] It would have been a familiar process for Edward and Emma Whitehurst and the other refugees. Enslaved people had long been accustomed to seeing their bodies inspected and matched with the demands of white enslavers in the slave trade; Edward himself would have gotten used to this process while hiring himself out.[10] In this instance, both Whitehursts passed their examinations and were deemed "serviceable," and both were assigned to work in the camp hospital, which at this early stage was little more than a tent. Edward began working as a steward, which involved cleaning and burying dead bodies, and while Emma's exact assignment goes unmentioned, she likely assumed one of the two most common positions for women in the region's hospitals: a cook or a laundress.[11]

But would the army be any different from those who inspected them before? Any conversations with General Phelps might have signaled that something was changing; and yet, Lieutenant Farnham recorded them as property in his record book. Mixed messages were everywhere. "The most of them seem happy at the thought of escape," observed a *Pine and Palm* reporter at Fort Monroe just a few weeks later, "though the uncertainty of their future and the strangeness of the scenes through which they are passing impresses them deeply."[12] The various sights of the army encampment, full of unfamiliar white men in uniform, were only part of the "strangeness." It was undoubtedly stranger yet to be allowed inside Union lines and promised protection— and not be considered free at the same time. No one was able to clarify what would happen, or what their futures held. "They were somewhat perplexed by the contradictory statements of our soldiers, some of whom, according to their wishes, said the contest was for them," explained E. L. Pierce, Farnham's counterpart at Fort Monroe, "and others that it did not concern them at all and they would remain as before."[13]

Little was certain in those initial weeks and months except for the fact that the Union army wanted the refugees' labor and did not want them laboring for the Confederacy. Work was at the root of it all—the very thing that made their presence a "necessity" militarily. It was why these refugees were allowed into Union lines in the first place, and it was the basis for any kind of relationship they would forge with the Union army. But the Whitehursts brought with them another certainty: that their labor would amount to more than denying labor power to the Confederacy or contributing it to the Union. They would work to feed, clothe, and shelter themselves and their family and to build an independent livelihood; they would work to save money and acquire property. They would, in short, refuse to let up after spending so many years in slavery working and saving for their liberation. The journey of Edward and Emma Whitehurst through the refugee camps was thus guided in large part by their quest for economic independence — just as the journey would be for so many other refugees from slavery during the Civil War. But how well that ambition aligned with the military's need to secure the Union — that is, how well they could earn a living inside the military sphere — was not immediately apparent.

⌖

Union authorities at Newport News, as well as at Hampton and Fort Monroe, quickly identified a wide-ranging set of jobs for the new refugees. Two underlying characteristics would guide their choices: First, the positions were deemed necessary and important to the army's occupation and would therefore guarantee that the refugees were serving the Union's military interests. And second, the employment was work either that white soldiers were disinclined to perform themselves or for which they were deemed, for reasons that had everything to do with assumptions about race, comparatively less able to perform.[14]

Much of the work, after all, was hard, physical labor. The majority of refugees at Fort Monroe were put to work erecting fortifications and digging trenches, which meant, as a visiting *New York Tribune* reporter put it, "the soldiers are thus spared much of the lower drudgery of the works."[15] Or as Benjamin Butler himself explained, the refugees, assumed to be better suited racially to working in hot climates (as proslavery apologists had long argued), were "saving our soldiers from that labor under the gleam of the mid-day sun."[16] The initial group of refugees from the Mallory property who met with Benjamin Butler was assigned to assist stonemasons in the construction of a new bakehouse at Fort Monroe. Many others went to work for the quartermaster's department as stevedores, which meant loading, unloading, and coaling ships; as teamsters, driving teams of horses and hauling loads; and as members of the "Sand & Police Gang," a group of men assigned to "police" the grounds outside Fort Monroe and to bury "the carcasses of Mules and Horses lying on the beach."[17] Smaller numbers worked as laborers for the engineer department, building a railroad; as employees of the subsistence department, performing all tasks related to the issuance of food rations; or as workers for the ordnance department, carrying out the physical labor involved in managing the army's supply of cannon, muskets, and ammunition.[18] Anyone deemed too young or too small for such labor was more likely to be hired as a personal servant by an army officer.[19]

Some refugees also found themselves in demand to work as scouts and spies. Military authorities believed they possessed unique and invaluable knowledge about the surrounding landscape — and about the movements of the local Confederate population.[20] And by early June, just a few weeks after the first refugees arrived in Union lines, the army began calling on them to share this intelligence. Determined to extend its occupation of the region, the army had its eye on the Confederate outpost at Big Bethel Church, located nearly ten miles northwest of Camp Butler. General Butler thus ordered General Phelps to mobilize his Vermont regiment and set off to join soldiers from Massachusetts and New York, with the intent of waging a surprise attack at Big Bethel. Phelps took his orders and set about making sure that his raw, inexperienced Union troops, who were not at all familiar with where they were going, could get to their destination quickly and secretively. He first ordered his men to wear white armbands and have a password ("Boston") to avoid any confusion in distinguishing friend from foe. Next he tapped several refugee men to guide his troops on their expedition — and one of them was Edward Whitehurst.[21]

On the evening of June 9, Edward left Emma, as well as his work at the Camp Butler hospital, and set out with Phelps's troops. With him was Charles Smith, a longtime acquaintance who had been enslaved on a nearby plantation in Newport News.[22] Their task was to steer the soldiers of the First Vermont, commanded by Lt. Col. Peter Washburn, through the darkness of the night and into the village of Little Bethel, located three miles short of Big Bethel. Once there, Washburn's troops were planning to "make a demonstration," surprising the Confederates and distracting them, while the rest of the Union forces moved toward Big Bethel. That night, Whitehurst and Smith succeeded in guiding the regiment to Little Bethel. But once there, they heard something alarming — gunfire to the rear of the Vermont regiment. Lieutenant Colonel Washburn immediately assumed that it came from Confederate soldiers who must have outmaneuvered (and possibly outnumbered) his own, so he reversed the direction of his troops and sent them into retreat. Whitehurst and Smith, as well as the rest of the Vermonters, returned to Camp Butler.[23]

But the gunfire had not come from the Confederates, as it turned out. Soldiers in the Seventh New York Regiment, never informed about the system of armbands and the password, had mistaken another New York regiment for the enemy and opened fire. Later called a "sad mistake" by the Seventh New York's commander, the fifteen-minute period of friendly fire resulted in eighteen Union casualties and ruined the Union's attempt to surprise the Confederates at Big Bethel.[24] Alerted by the gunfire to the Union's presence, the Confederates had mobilized and opened fire on the now-confused Union troops and pulled out a victory. "Never since the invention of gunpowder was such a victory achieved," boasted the Confederate-sympathizing *Raleigh Register* in the battle's aftermath.[25] Edward Whitehurst left behind no record of his reaction to the Union's defeat in what was the first land battle of the Civil War. But it had to have been a sobering, deflating moment.

The setbacks only continued. Six weeks later, on July 21, came the Union's defeat at the battle of Manassas. It took place over 100 miles away in Northern Virginia, but the ripple effects of the battle were felt by everyone on the Virginia Peninsula, including by every refugee. Their lives were upended when Gen. Winfield Scott, general-in-chief of the Union army, responded to Manassas by ordering more troops to Washington, D.C., to shore up the capital's defenses, which were believed to be newly vulnerable. He sought the troops on the peninsula, which is why on July 24 he directed Benjamin Butler to send 4,000 of his men to Washington. It was a significant loss to Butler's command that required contracting the Union's occupation of the peninsula; on July 25, Butler ordered the evacuation of Hampton, just across Mill Creek from Fort Monroe, a move that, in turn, left Newport News and Camp Butler, and the refugees therein, newly isolated and vulnerable.[26]

Edward and Emma Whitehurst were forced to leave — and leave quickly. Confederate forces, under the command of Col. John B. Magruder, seized the moment provided by the evacuation to undo the damage wrought by the Union in the war's first three months, especially the damage done to slavery by Butler's "contraband" order. "If the negroes in the Back River region and on the James River can be surprised and captured at night or by day by small parties of troops," Magruder commanded one of his subordinates, "let them do it."[27] And sometime by August 2, Confederate forces did do it: they captured at least 150 men, women, and children who had previously fled slavery for Union lines, sending the men to work on Confederate fortifications and having "the rest delivered to their masters."[28] Reports later surfaced that some of those recaptured had been sent deeper into the South and resold into slavery. The Whitehursts, though, managed to escape that fate, fleeing Camp Butler just in time.[29]

But where could they go? Their options were narrowing rapidly as Union lines contracted across the peninsula. They had to remain physically close to the Union forces — that much was clear. And as those forces increasingly converged on Fort Monroe in order to board the ships to take them to Washington, it became apparent to the Whitehursts that following those troops and

FIGURE 2. "Stampede of Slaves from Hampton to Fortress Monroe,"
Harper's Weekly, August 17, 1861 (Library of Congress)

heading to the fort was their only option too. Hundreds of other refugees from Newport News, as well as from the recently evacuated town of Hampton, came to the same realization. And with that began a new exodus into the fort that was quickly dubbed a "stampede" by an artist for *Harper's Weekly* (fig. 2). In an illustration in the journal's August 17 issue, men, women, and children can be seen running—literally—in the direction of the fort, clutching baskets of food and sacks of possessions. The image conveys the urgency of their relocation to Fort Monroe, as well as the large numbers involved: a reported 2,000 arrived at the fort during this late-July, early-August migration.[30]

Edward and Emma Whitehurst thus hurried across the moat and into Fort Monroe during a moment of tumult. They had lost their shelter and their employment and were now surrounded by hundreds of others in the same predicament. The army itself was staggering in defeat and grappling with its reduced size—and now experiencing a change in command too. General Phelps left the region in mid-August with his First Vermont Regiment, which headed back to its home state to be mustered out while he was later reassigned to the Department of the Gulf.[31] General Butler's days in the region were numbered too.

Butler was feeling personally wounded by late July—stung by the order to remove the troops, which he interpreted as a rebuke for his failure at Big Bethel. He was also frustrated by signs that his slavery policy was not being followed by Union commanders elsewhere.[32] Then came word that the First Confiscation Act, congressional legislation that appeared to make Butler's "contraband" order the policy for the entire Union, actually fell short of his practices at Fort Monroe. The act authorized the Union to seize any property, including enslaved property, being used specifically for "insurrectionary purposes," while Butler allowed *all* enslaved property inside Union lines.[33] Protective of his position as a leader on slavery policy, Butler fired off a letter challenging the secretary of war, Simon Cameron, to take a bolder position on refugee slaves, even possibly freeing them outright.[34] But someone, likely Butler himself, leaked the letter to the press, which is how it also got into the hands of Confederate general John Magruder and reinforced his determination to stop the region from becoming "the harbor of runaway slaves and traitors." Magruder thus ordered his men to burn the town of Hampton on August 7.[35] "I confess myself so poor a soldier as not to be able to discern the strategic importance of this movement," a stunned Butler wrote to Gen. Winfield Scott the day after the burning, before requesting his relief from command in Virginia later that month. Butler was gone by August 17.[36]

A change in command was never a small matter for refugees from slavery. It had the potential to change everything, from employment and treatment to whether or not they were allowed inside Union lines in the first place. This was something that all refugees, no matter where they were, at any point in the war, would experience. For the Whitehursts, though, there was no other immediate option for confronting this upheaval than to wait it out and search for a new means of supporting themselves. Edward managed to secure a position fairly quickly, in a familiar capacity: as a steward at the old Hygeia Hotel, a landmark inside the fort that was now serving as a hospital. Edward later recalled that he "staid there a short time" and that his trunk got a bit heavier as he did so. As he explained, "When I was in Hospital service I managed to save a little all the time."[37] No evidence survives to indicate what employment, if any, Emma found at the fort. Perhaps she went to work as a servant to an army officer, an arrangement that was usually privately and informally struck, and thus made little visible imprint on surviving army records.[38]

Yet Emma and Edward had little intention of remaining in these new positions for long. They instead began laying the groundwork for a wholly different

Securing Work

means of support. As Edward later described it, they "went over near Hampton & in Hampton and started a store and Bake House" after just a few weeks at the fort.[39] Edward and Emma clearly decided to seize opportunity out of the confusion and upheaval wrought by war. But why specifically a store? Was it an extension of the work they had done while enslaved—did Edward work for a merchant as a self-hired slave? Or did Emma sell goods from their home plantation at local markets? The evidentiary trail is stubbornly elusive. However they got the idea to open their business, though, the moment marked a profound shift, redirecting their trunk savings in a wholly new direction in order to establish their economic independence and, thus, to secure their freedom.

They began by pulling together an inventory. Edward's first stop was to visit the sutler at Fort Monroe, a white man named John Moody, from whom he purchased various foodstuffs, likely flour and produce. He then took a big risk, making the eleven-mile journey back to the Parrish and Ivy properties in Newport News in order to collect items "from the farms I raised." It was harvesttime, after all, time to collect the fruits of what had been planted by Emma and the other enslaved people that previous spring. Edward also noted that he acquired "some in Baltimore" too, a vague reference that is not explained in any more detail but may suggest that he made a temporary sojourn to that city in August with one of the regiments leaving the peninsula for Washington.[40]

The Whitehursts then set their sights on burned-out Hampton, just across Mill Creek from the fort, no doubt encouraged to go there by the Union authorities who had begun reoccupying the town in the weeks following its burning. More and more refugees were returning too—an estimated 1,800 by December 1861—all of them greeted by the startling sight of a town in ruins.[41] Yet up against the lone chimneys that remained, they built new houses and other structures that could house people and businesses alike. The space claimed for the Whitehursts' new store was large enough to begin storing bushels of potatoes and barrels of flour and may have recreated the look of stores they had seen in Newport News. Edward's fellow guide in the Big Bethel expedition, Charles Smith, later chose to describe it as resembling a "country grocery store." Next to the store was a side yard where half a dozen hogs would be fattened up too.[42]

The store soon became a destination for fellow refugees and Union soldiers alike. The army's occupation of the region had shaken up its consumer market, sending many long-standing white storekeepers and consumers fleeing inland to escape the Union forces, while bringing new consumers into the area. The Union soldiers, in particular, had money, as well as needs and wants, and by establishing a store to sell food products, the Whitehursts found a way of making their interests serve the military's. But the store represented even more than additional income for the trunk. They became employers for the first time, hiring Edward from the Big Bethel campaign, Charles Smith, as well as another man named Thomas Ware.[43] And with the exception of needing to ask permission from the military to open the store—which was granted— they could operate fairly independently. The store allowed them to exercise a greater degree of control over their labor—over specific tasks, hours, and other daily conditions—than Edward had had as a "self-hired" slave. It promised them the economic independence that was propelling other refugees to establish "stalls" and "stands" that fall too, selling fruit and vegetables or the products of fishing, clamming, and oystering in nearby waters.[44] Others discovered that collecting Northern newspapers at Fort Monroe and then selling them to soldiers in military encampments outside the fort could be lucrative. Still others could be seen walking the streets of Hampton carrying baskets of eggs and baked goods.[45]

Edward and Emma made another pivotal decision that September: to get remarried. It happened as a result of their encounter with another new arrival in Hampton, Lewis Lockwood, a white Presbyterian minister and native of New York who showed up at Fort Monroe on September 3 as the first missionary sent by the American Missionary Association (AMA). Lockwood was an avowed abolitionist—outspoken, strident, and with little inclination to compromise—who had received permission from military authorities to take up residence in Hampton inside a building that formerly belonged to the Chesapeake Female Seminary.[46] Lockwood was confident, perhaps overly so, that he could make a difference in the lives of people emerging from slavery. On his first night in the region he took a walk around the fort, and after spotting a prayer meeting led by a black minister, Lockwood joined in and introduced himself. He reported back to the AMA that he was greeted warmly— and, firmly believing in his own powers, that his arrival "is what they had been praying for."[47]

The Whitehursts met Lockwood sometime soon after his arrival. Maybe they were at that initial prayer meeting, or maybe they attended the Sabbath school he subsequently established at the seminary. At the very least, Edward and Emma soon heard the missionary offer an impassioned plea on a subject he deemed "as thrilling as it is novel"—marriage. Lockwood discovered that the refugee couples around him "have been married only in slave fashion," which meant without legal or, in some cases, Christian sanction. That was a

Securing Work

reality of slavery that abolitionists like him had long found abhorrent, because, they believed, it required couples like the Whitehursts to live in sinful "concubinage." Now Lockwood finally had the chance to reverse this damage, and he offered to marry any couples who agreed to come forward. "Is it not your duty to become lawfully and Scripturally married?" he urged them.[48]

Not everyone thought that it was. Plenty of couples and families streaming into Union lines believed that they were married already and did not need the sanction of white civil or religious authorities in order to make their relationship any more true; some of them remained skeptical that any legal protections would follow.[49] But others were more persuaded by what they heard from Lewis Lockwood—and Edward and Emma Whitehurst were among them. Their names appear on a list that Lockwood kept as he moved between Fort Monroe and Hampton on September 29, 1861, administering marriage rites to a total of thirty-two couples. He did so with the sanction of military authorities, who were willing to assert federal power to supersede the Southern state laws that had long denied enslaved people the legal right to marry. And he set a precedent that missionaries and military authorities would follow all across the South, as weddings became commonplace inside Union lines throughout the four years of war. The Whitehursts, as they stood inside Fort Monroe to take their vows, were thus among the very first ex-slave couples to be legally married by federal authorities during the Civil War.[50]

Among the other couples married by Lockwood at the fort that September were several from the Whitehursts' old neighborhood in Newport News, including Edward's half brother, Immanuel Savage, and his wife, Susan.[51] The Savages had experienced a very different journey to that point during the war's opening months, although it was one more commonly experienced by the rest of the refugee population. Immanuel Savage had fled to Fort Monroe weeks before the Whitehursts, sometime in June, although little information has survived about the circumstances surrounding his escape to the fort, or when Susan arrived there too. What is known is that on July 1, while the Whitehursts were still working at the Camp Butler hospital, Savage was digging trenches at Fort Monroe, the most common occupation for men that summer.[52] He spent his days rising to the sound of a bell ringing at 4:00 a.m., the signal that he was to get up, leave his quarters, and report for duty. His name, and those of the other laborers, was called, his attendance verified, and then, with shovel or pick in hand, he headed off on a half-mile march to the fort's entrenchments, which he set about digging under the supervision of quartermaster officers. Along the way he answered at least two roll calls and took several breaks before being dismissed from duty at 6:00 p.m.[53] It was like he had become a soldier—fully immersed in the rhythms of military life.

But Savage only lasted in that position for two months. By early September, around the time the Whitehursts moved to establish the store in Hampton, Savage made a move too: the drum major of the fort's post band hired him to work as a cook. Savage acquired a more appealing line of work in the move, as cooking for the band involved less physical labor than digging entrenchments. His move also may have been driven by basic financial motives, as the cook position offered a 100 percent increase in wages: from the ten dollars per month he was promised for digging trenches to twenty dollars per month for working as a cook.[54] The latter wage would have been attractive for even more than simply being an increase, since it was a sum greater than the amount that white soldiers took home each month.

Other refugees similarly moved from job to job that first year. As one sample, take the couples married in September: among the sixty-four individuals included on Lockwood's list, the employment paths of fourteen can be tracked in that first year, and of them, nine were employed in more than one position.[55] Some stayed in their initial positions for as little as two to three weeks; others moved on after six to eight months. Some moved from hospital work to digging entrenchments; others went from working on the railroad to serving as a cook.[56]

They could move from job to job because the military's presence on the peninsula had opened up a new labor market there. Multiple army departments—the quartermaster's, commissary, engineer, and medical departments, in particular—found themselves competing for workers. And the army's overall demand for their labor grew quickly. Capt. Grier Tallmadge of the quartermaster's department explained this to his superiors when he refused to send the refugees to work on the Washington, D.C., defenses that summer. "With the present amount of work to be done in my Department," he wrote, "I cannot see that I can spare any negroes."[57] Outside observers, including a journalist for the *Pine and Palm* newspaper, similarly noted that demand was so great in the region that sending any refugees away would cause serious problems: "If, as reported, the Government has ordered the negroes to be sent to Washington," the reporter explained, "the Quartermaster, Commissary Department, and in fact the operations of the post, so far as labor is concerned, will be seriously embarrassed until their places can be filled." "It would be difficult to get along without them," the paper concluded, echoing the sentiments of Tallmadge, who later that fall wrote, "I do not know how the work here could have been carried on without these hands."[58] The Union army had become dependent on the refugees' labor in only a matter of weeks, and that dependence, in turn, could set the laborers in motion. It enabled them to move around to seek out greater compensation or a different line of work; they could exercise a degree of control over their labor that had been denied them in slavery. They could, in short, begin to glimpse their futures as free laborers.

But it was only a glimpse. William Giles, another man working alongside Savage that first summer on the entrenchments (and who also married his wife, Lucy, in a ceremony officiated by Lockwood), later explained that the pull of army demand was actually less powerful than a push factor in explaining his labor mobility: the refugees "were not paid." And for that reason, he "quit the work."[59] His experience turned out to be not the exception but the rule. As one government official put it the following year, "No wages appear to have been paid to the negroes" during that first year. "They received only rations and a scanty supply of clothing."[60] For example, the surgeons who supervised the work of Nancy Jones, a waiter and washerwoman who spent six months at the Hygeia Hospital, "told her frequently that she would be paid for said work by the Government," but by the time she determined to leave after six months of no pay, she received "the sum of Twenty five cents as a present." Her husband, Richard, likewise worked for the same surgeons and received nothing.[61] In another case, a man had received only rations and "a pair of shoes & a coat" after working several months for the government. This man had been a hired-out slave before the war and was "accustomed to make $6 a month over what he paid his Master." Now he was pulling in less than that—and almost nothing.[62]

The army was failing to uphold the promises it had made to the workers at the time of their employment. Each had been promised a wage, although those promises had been inconsistently made. Giles, for example, was promised wages of only one dollar per month to work on the entrenchments ("That was all the United States was paying," he was told), while Savage, engaged in the same work right beside him, was promised ten dollars per month by the same officer.[63] Some were promised wages below those which a white laborer would have received for the same line of work; others were promised wages at the same level. Another man who worked on the fortifications at Hampton was told he would be paid for his work "without mentioning any amount." (He left that work after three weeks.)[64] All were promised wages paid by the month, but none had those promises in writing, as there were no written contracts and, thus, no legal compulsions in place to guarantee the actual payment of wages. And in the absence of any overall system, any overall pay scale, any set of consistent standards, or any system for actually converting promises into cash, the burden fell to individual officers and supervisors to follow through with the payment of wages. And what incentive did these officials, especially those who may have been unfriendly to the cause of liberating enslaved people, have to actually pay them?[65]

Did the military *need* to pay the refugees for their labor? That was a key question underlying their employment that summer. The workers clearly thought so — and by promising wages, the army effectively acknowledged that it would not be able to attract laborers without some gesture toward compensation. But once the refugees were inside Union lines and put to work, was it in the interests of the military to follow through and actually pay? More profoundly, was the establishment of a free labor system in the military's best interests? Some officials argued that monetary wages were almost superfluous, even excessive, in a military setting, where sustenance — namely, food rations and shelter — and protection had value and were routinely provided.[66] There were other labor systems that could be instituted, after all, from apprenticeship, which had accompanied other emancipations in Northern states and in the British West Indies, to the indentured servitude that had taken root in Virginia back in the seventeenth century. Did the refugees fit more comfortably into any of these models? Or should a "contraband" be imagined as some other kind of laborer altogether?

Benjamin Butler had never addressed these questions in his initial deliberations over his order — he was more preoccupied with the question of *who* should be a "contraband" in the first place. On the issue of compensation, he deferred to Secretary of War Cameron, who, as he did on most matters related to the refugees, deferred the question. "You will employ such persons in the services to which they may be best adapted," Cameron had instructed Butler in late May, "keeping an account of the labor by them performed, of the value of it, and of the expences [*sic*] of their maintenance." The matter of settling that account "will be reserved for future determination."[67] That determination depended on the course and outcome of the war — and whether or not the Union decided to emancipate the refugees from slavery. To free them would require paying the refugees outright; to not free them would require sending their wages back to their masters, in a gesture that resembled hired-out slavery. The Union's intentions were still an unknown in that first year, however, even to those at the highest ranks of the federal government, like Cameron. For that reason, Butler dutifully followed Cameron's orders and told his subordinates to keep records — but he made no provision for actually distributing wages. Cameron, for his part, still indicated later that summer that payment would be forthcoming someday. "After tranquility shall have been restored upon the return of peace, Congress will doubtless properly provide for all the persons thus received into the service of the Union."[68] "Doubtless" was not enough of an assurance for those trying to scrape by on a day-to-day basis, however.

Butler's successor, though, turned out to have other ideas. Gen. John Wool, a seventy-seven-year-old New York native, had arrived to take command of the fort in August after a long military career that saw action in the War of 1812 and the Mexican War. In between, he had taken command of the removal of the Cherokee Indians to Oklahoma territory in the 1830s, a task he considered a "dirty assignment," though he was committed to military order and to doing his assigned duty.[69] He brought that same sensibility with him to Fort Monroe. Wool had little desire to inherit Butler's experiment with refugees from slavery—but two months after his arrival, increasingly frustrated with the disorder surrounding their labor, Wool issued a directive that would, for the first time, replace the various promises with established guidelines.

General Order No. 34, drafted in November 1861 in consultation with the heads of each government department employing refugees, divided the laborers into two "classes": Class 1, which consisted of "able-bodied" men over the age of eighteen, who were to receive ten dollars per month plus a food ration and "the necessary amount of Clothing," and Class 2, which consisted of "Negro boys from 12 to 18 years of age and sickly and infirm negro men," who were to receive five dollars per month plus rations and clothing. Yet the order also stipulated that most of the wages were to be deposited into a "contraband fund" to be managed by the quartermaster's department "for the support of those contrabands who are unable to work for their own support"—aged men and women, as well as children and any other refugees unable to find employment. Only one to two dollars per month would be paid directly to each laborer, and then only as "an incentive to good behavior." This, too, could "be witheld [sic] at the discretion of the chiefs of the departments."[70] Wool's new system thus left plenty of room to pay the laborers no direct wages at all—and actually seemed to perpetuate the system of promising wages without really paying them.

But in Wool's mind there was logic to his order that stood in contrast to what had been in place already. And that logic revealed itself in the term he used to refer to the working population: they were not "slaves," they were not "freemen," they were not "refugees," and they were not really "contraband," a term, one observer noted, "he does not like." They were "vagrants," or as he put it in one order, "vagrants or persons called 'contrabands.'"[71] Vagrants, in the eyes of a Northerner—in Wool's case, a native of Troy, New York—were impoverished people whose plight deserved contempt more than sympathy.

They were individuals out of work, rootless and roaming in search of hand-outs, primarily men who were neglecting their duties to support their families. Northern social welfare policies did not consider it the duty of the state to care for "vagrants" in institutions like poorhouses, or even with cash handouts; it was instead the state's duty to compel these men to get to work and support their families.[72] Wool brought this frame of mind with him to Fort Monroe, equating the refugees' labor mobility with idle roaming and instituting "an incentive to good behavior" to extract work from a population he assumed would not labor willingly. He also assumed they would not care for their families and handed the quartermaster's department the responsibility of making sure that dependent spouses, children, and parents were provided with rations and clothing out of the "contraband fund."[73] Wool's labor system was thus intended to reform "vagrants." Such a value judgment was not lost on the abolitionist press; one journal roundly objected that the term "vagrant" "indicates a degradation and status which the Refugees do not deserve."[74]

To Immanuel Savage, Wool's new system offered only the possibility, at most, of taking home two dollars per month out of his promised twenty dollars per month wage as a cook for the post band. That fell far short of what he expected. Also discouraging was the situation in which the orders placed his wife, Susan, and other women in the region. General Order No. 34 did not address female employees of government departments at all and did not set any pay rates for them, assuming they would either not work and remain dependent on a husband (in the spirit of vagrancy policies) or work as private "servants" for an officer and be paid by him directly. Those working as servants had had their pay set in a previous order—four dollars per month for women, eight dollars per month for men—all of which was to be deposited into the contraband fund.[75] The combined effect of these orders left women with no prospect of directly receiving any wages at all. There is no evidence of what Susan did after this point, but it is clear that Immanuel gave the new system six weeks. On December 18, he left his job with the post band after having "never received from the Government or from any person any pay whatever."[76] He also never appeared again on government labor rolls and at some point went to work at the Whitehursts' store.[77]

The Savages were hardly alone. In the period of late fall 1861 into the early winter of 1862, more and more refugees continued to abandon their government positions, thus refusing to become a captive labor force for the army. It got so bad that one quartermaster's department official "confessed" that "a large number have disappeared from the working ranks of the fort."[78] Some of the men joined women in "private service" as body servants, attracted, in part, by the knowledge that "superior inducements are offered by private than public service." It turned out that employers of servants had actually been paying wages, sometimes more than the military guidelines stipulated. Other refugees boarded ships and went to work for the navy, where Wool's orders did not apply and where workers, according to one government observer, tended to "have absolute control of the earnings of their own labor."[79]

The refugees thus exerted whatever leverage they could find in the region's labor market. If the government was not going to pay at the fort, they would move around, exploring all the pathways opened up by war, and find work that did pay. They refused to be slaves when they left their plantations; now they refused to be treated like "vagrants" when they left Fort Monroe. They instead managed to claim one of the basic prerogatives of a free labor system: the ability to quit and move on and search for better work.

The collective impact of that movement was felt and acknowledged by government officials. It prompted the quartermaster at Fort Monroe, the employer of the largest number of laborers, to write his superiors in Washington to appeal for the money necessary to pay the laborers. "They fully earn their wages working hard at all varieties of labor," Captain Tallmadge explained, but the actual payment of those wages was necessary "to keep and clothe all the negroes"; it was not a foregone conclusion, in other words, that he could "keep" them. Another quartermaster official, however, developed a different strategy for keeping the refugees working. Rather than dangle the carrot of paying wages, Sgt. John Smith of the Second U.S. Artillery, who had previously overseen Immanuel Savage's work on the entrenchments, opted for the stick: he cut off the issuance of food rations to anyone except those employed directly by the government. No "dependents" would receive rations paid for by Wool's "contraband fund"; instead, their only hope to have anything to eat was to become employed or to have an employee share their ration with them. "The poor & infirm find little or no mercy," noted one observer, suggesting that Smith's action was nothing more than a move "intended to drag or force men into government service."[80] Yet Smith's action only forced the refugees to mobilize in other ways.

❧

On January 5, 1862, two months after Wool's order and just after Smith's ration cuts, the refugees held a public meeting to discuss the problems at the fort. It was the very first time they did so. "The people could not help pouring forth their complaints," according to one report; men and women rose at the meeting, one after the other, to tell their stories. "I have from the first been in the service of Government, and have received but two dollars and a little clothing," one man explained. Another stood up to describe how "I have worked for Government since the 8th of July, and up to Christmas, have only received part of a suit and one dollar in money." Meanwhile his wife was ill and unable to work to support herself. "I want to be faithful to duty," this man assured the audience, "but it seems hard to see my wife destitute."[81] The personal accounts aired that evening made it abundantly clear that each individual was not alone, and that their stories, when knit together, revealed a systemic pattern of labor exploitation at the fort. It was not going to be enough for each of them to exert what little leverage they had by quitting jobs and moving on—they would have to exert collective pressure too. The meeting was just a start.

One refugee who understood this plainly was William Roscoe Davis, a forty-seven-year-old minister with deep roots in the region. Like Edward Whitehurst, he was a former self-hired slave, one who had also learned to read and write and had worked his way into the ministry at a local Baptist church. He knew well the hardships confronting the refugees: although his wife, Nancy, was safely inside Union lines with him, several of their five children had been taken away by their owner, to a place unknown.[82] He also knew that pressuring the army to pay wages would require bringing other voices into the fold—and he called on a particularly outspoken one, the AMA missionary Lewis Lockwood. With ties to some of the nation's most prominent abolitionists, and with a wide readership for the reports he had been publishing in the AMA's journal, *American Missionary*, Lockwood was well positioned to help draw attention from far beyond to the situation in eastern Virginia. He also happened to be frustrated with what he believed were overly sunny reports about refugee affairs appearing in Northern newspapers. "Is it not possible to get the current facts of the mission more constantly before the public in the daily & weekly press?" Lockwood fumed in early January.[83] He was not at all hesitant, then, to join Davis in an effort to get the "current facts" into the public eye.

Davis and Lockwood quickly hatched a plan: they would send Davis on a speaking tour of Northern cities. Four days after the mass meeting, on the evening of January 9, 1862, Davis left the region with the help of military passes secured by Lockwood and traveled to Philadelphia, where he then boarded an "express train" that arrived in New York City on the afternoon of the following day.[84] From there Davis went straight to the Plymouth Church, where the pastor was Henry Ward Beecher, one of the nation's most prominent white abolitionists (and brother of the novelist Harriet Beecher Stowe), and where an audience of 1,000 awaited him. "It was the first time he had ever addressed an audience of white people," reported the *New York Independent*. Davis sang, prayed, and spoke about the parable of the Good Samaritan, before telling his audience about the "past and present condition of his people in that part of Virginia." Accompanied by AMA missionaries, Davis then moved on to other churches in the city, as well as to those in Boston, Lowell, and Worcester, Massachusetts, and in Dover and Nashua, New Hampshire. At one point along the way his wife, Nancy, and two of their children also traveled north and joined him, for, as his grandson later put it, she grew concerned that he might never return to the South. The tour was a success. Davis's speaking engagements garnered extensive newspaper coverage — "Novel and Interesting Meeting," headlined one report — and appeared to have the desired effect back at Fort Monroe.[85]

General Wool, now feeling the glare of public disapproval, issued a new order on January 30, 1862, that sought to address the refugee situation. In General Order No. 5, he appointed a commission "for the purpose of making a critical examination of the condition of the persons known as Vagrants or 'contrabands.'" Wool charged the commission with the primary task of studying the labor situation, with the goal of making sure that both the "claims of humanity" and the "efficiency" of the army's work in eastern Virginia were being served. "It having been reported that the said class of persons, known as vagrants or contrabands, have not been properly treated in all cases by those having them in charge," Wool wrote in his order, "the commission cannot be too rigid in its examination in order that justice may be done to them, as well as to the public service."[86] With these words Wool charged the commission with finding a new way of aligning the interests of the refugees with those of the military. The question was, How?

Appointed to lead the effort were three white men with little past experience with slavery but plenty of experience with military procedure: T. J. Cram, the inspector general at the fort, as well as Maj. Le Grand B. Cannon and Maj. William P. Jones, both aides-de-camp working directly under General Wool. They were people whom Wool trusted — but who also managed to satisfy the missionary Lewis Lockwood. "I find it to be a Commission emphatically for the Colored people," Lockwood wrote excitedly after hearing the news. "Thanks and praise to God," he went on, "that through the exposures in the North such a Commission had been appointed as I find to exist. God has been unspeakably better than my fears."[87] His and Davis's gambit to take the problem to the Northern public had seemed to pay off.

The commission was the very first of a number of federal commissions sent into the occupied South during the war to examine refugee affairs. And it marked a decisive break from the improvisation that had characterized the military's response to the refugees up until this point in the war: now it would stop, study, think, and assess what to do next. The three commissioners got to work immediately behind closed doors, summoning everyone from heads of departments to refugee laborers into their office for interviews, a process that Lockwood was glad to hear had "startled" some quartermaster officials. He too was summoned, and he left his interview, in which he raised points about everything from labor to health care, pleased to hear that the commission was "determined in a discreet way to ferret out every wrong."[88]

Nearly two months later, on March 12, 1862, the commission submitted its report. It concluded that the current system at Fort Monroe was "highly objectionable, mainly wrong." Not only were the refugees owed a combined $10,000 in accrued unpaid wages by that point, but they also had been "defrauded" by Sergeant Smith, who, the commissioners learned, took the rations he withheld from refugees and sold them to sutlers for personal profit. Even worse, they discovered, Smith also whipped refugees to the point where they had visible scars; some were laborers he "unwarrantably assaulted," while another was beaten by Smith "for answering our questions." The report noted approvingly that General Wool had removed Smith from his post as the investigation unfolded — and replaced him with a new "superintendent of contrabands," a civilian and recently arrived missionary colleague of Lockwood's named Charles Wilder.[89] It was the very first time — but not the last — that the army would create a new, dedicated position within its bureaucracy to oversee refugee affairs. (Wilder later reported that one of the first things he noticed upon assuming Smith's old office were the "old fashioned Virginia instruments of torture, the overseers whips.")[90]

But the report did not stop with condemning Smith and concluded that his actions were part of a more systemic problem at the fort. Officials there had lost sight of what should have been guiding them more than any other consideration: military necessity. "The commission started with the general proposition that the military power has not only the right but it is among its highest duties to avail itself of any and all means within its control to perfect its discipline, render its position secure, or make it effective for an advance against an enemy," the report opened, "and for these ends it has the right to compel service or use from anything, animate or inanimate, which a military necessity may demand." But, the commission continued, compulsion could also turn around and undermine the military's interests. In this case, the army needed efficient and productive labor performed at the fort — but what incentive was there for government laborers to be "industrious" when they had no control over their earnings? Even if the two dollars per month had been forthcoming, the withholding of the rest of the wages for the contraband fund put these workers in a position of "*quasi* slavery." At the same time, what good did it do the government to try to keep women and children as a separate community and "compel them to be the recipients of its charity" from the "contraband fund"? Noting that laborers could and should take care of their families directly, the commission argued that "there is no necessity for any governmental charity to these people." There was a natural fit between the needs of the military and the needs of the refugees, it continued, but the neglect of the former had hurt the interests of the refugees too. The commission concluded that those interests could be aligned and served again by recognizing that "necessity is the only proper measure of the extent to which such [military] power should be exercised."[91] And it was a military necessity, above all, to make sure that "contraband" labor meant "free labor."

General Wool embraced the report. But he also knew that it marked a precedent-setting departure from the Union's current approach to refugees and might not be approved by his superiors. President Lincoln, after all, had already removed from command another general who he believed had gone too far—Maj. Gen. John C. Fremont, who in 1861 had ordered that any enslaved people owned by disloyal people in Missouri would be declared legally free. Wool, well aware of the Fremont episode, understood that it would take some persuasion to get the report's findings approved. He thus called on the assistance of two men who happened to be visiting the fort at the time: John Jay, an abolitionist lawyer (and grandson of former Supreme Court justice John Jay), and William E. Dodge, a New York businessman and less radical "emancipationist," as one of the commissioners, Le Grand Cannon, described him. Both men were at the fort to visit with their sons in the service there—and both were Republicans with the ears of the president and the secretary of war. Wool dispatched Cannon to read the report to each man in secrecy; both men, according to Cannon, responded "in the most enthusiastic terms, saying they believed it would solve the whole question of the negro's status." Jay and Dodge then agreed to accompany Cannon to Washington, where they delivered the report in person to the secretary of war, Edwin Stanton.[92] Stanton, who had replaced Simon Cameron at the helm of the War Department two months before, approved it on the spot. "I am disposed to entrust the subject to your exclusive control," he wrote in a letter to General Wool, but before doing so he decided "to submit the report to the President and receive his instructions."[93]

President Lincoln must not have objected, because within two weeks the report was in the hands of Congress and printed for mass distribution, while Wool set about implementing the report's findings at Fort Monroe. He first issued orders instituting free labor principles. The "contraband fund" was to be eliminated and wages were to be paid directly to laborers to enable them to support themselves and their families—wages to be determined by "individual skill, industry, and ability."[94] He also stopped calling the refugees vagrants (something evident in the report's title, *Africans in Fort Monroe Military District*, which, notably, also stopped short of calling them Americans). Free labor seemed to have come to the refugees at Fort Monroe. The new superintendent of contrabands, Charles Wilder, called the Wool report "a great advance upon the state of things previously existing at this place," and for this reason, Wool "should receive the approbation & support of all lovers of fair play & right dealing between man & man."[95] But as William Roscoe Davis, the Whitehursts, and all the rest of the refugees well knew, what came down in army orders did not always match what played out in daily life.

The Wool report refocused the region's officials on the guiding principle of "military necessity," but that necessity soon changed—and changed very quickly. In the same month that the report came down, Fort Monroe was becoming the epicenter of war in the eastern theater; roughly two weeks before the report's issue, the Whitehursts, the Savages, and all the other refugees witnessed the battle between the naval ironclads the *Monitor* and the *Merrimac*.[96] Then, by the end of March, Fort Monroe became the base for the upcoming Peninsula campaign, in which Union general George B. McClellan would lead his troops up the Virginia Peninsula from the coast in an attempt to capture the Confederate capital of Richmond. By early April, just two weeks after Wool's report, 400 ships arrived carrying over 100,000 Union soldiers. Lewis Lockwood remarked, in what had to be an understatement, that this was "an imposing sight" for the hundreds of people now refugeed at the fort.[97] The Peninsula campaign quickly changed the calculus of military necessity at Fort Monroe—and, as such upheavals are endemic to war, would reveal how inconstant a guide "necessity" could ever be for refugee affairs.

The arrival of such a large number of troops seemed to offer renewed opportunity for refugees to align their interests with the Union. A surge in the number of soldiers meant new customers for the Whitehursts' store. It also brought new possibilities for refugee employment, in serving those soldiers as they moved up the peninsula, working on the entrenchments, and carrying out other forms of heavy, manual labor as the campaign demanded. And as the troops moved up the peninsula toward Richmond, large numbers of people still enslaved in the interior of Virginia could now flee to Union lines for the first time. An estimated 1,000 more people, in fact, would subsequently make their way to Fort Monroe in what the superintendent of contrabands, Charles Wilder, termed a "great rush of Contrabands" that summer. Any information they brought with them about the landscape or about the movements of Confederates was also in great demand by Union officials.[98]

Yet the arrival of thousands of new soldiers also unleashed enormous new pressure on space and resources in the region. The refugees felt that immediately too. "The Contrabands have been notified repeatedly within the last three weeks," wrote one Union official in late March, "that they would have to vacate these buildings." Barracks, old houses in Hampton, tents in Newport News: anything that the refugees had occupied as living space was now fair game to be seized by the army to house the incoming soldiers, especially those who were sick and wounded. "Coloured people are being removed from almost everything suitable for Hospital purposes," Charles Wilder reported, noting that they were being issued orders to vacate their residences "at short notice."[99] More than a few were unwilling to leave; without anywhere else to go, and with children, infants, and sick family to care for, the refugees knew a protected space was essential to basic survival. Those who refused to go found themselves forced out anyway, however, as in the case of a dozen women threatened at the point of a gun to clean a building before vacating it for the soldiers.[100]

To Lewis Lockwood, this turn of events marked nothing less than a "crusade against the colored people." That it was a military necessity to make space for soldiers may have been understandable to some degree, but Lockwood also discovered that buildings were being ordered emptied even before there were enough wounded soldiers to fill them, and that "white squatters" in Hampton were allowed to remain out of fear of an "uproar." ("Yet there would be no uproar produced by throwing the poor colored people into terror!" Lockwood fumed.) "For all this there was no real military necessity," Lockwood concluded. "It was the result of a pro-slavery scheme, under cover of alleged military reasons, by which Genl Wool, who was at the time frightened almost out of his wits, was *duped*."[101] Here Lockwood pointed out the underlying problem with the Wool report's assertion that military necessity could serve the interests of refugees: "military necessity" was a rhetoric too intrinsically persuasive in a time of war, too easily taken at face value, and thus too easily bent to serve more nefarious racial agendas.

The pressure on space eased somewhat as the troops headed up the peninsula toward Richmond—but not for long. Despite reaching the outskirts of the Confederate capital by mid-May, McClellan's troops failed to reach their target and thus failed in one of the Union's best chances to end the war outright. Hampered by faulty intelligence as well as an overestimation of the enemy's strength and the general's propensity to waste valuable time reorganizing troops, the Union fell victim to a successful Confederate counteroffensive in the Seven Days' battles. By mid-July McClellan's weakened army staggered back down the peninsula again toward Fort Monroe. And although more and more refugees joined their ranks as they headed toward the coast, the troops' arrival back at Fort Monroe reworked the calculus of military necessity once again, upending life for the men, women, and children seeking refuge there.[102]

The Whitehursts encountered this firsthand on August 2. That Saturday morning an assistant provost marshal walked into their store with an order from his superior, Provost Marshal W. H. Baum. The assistant got right to it and ordered Edward, as well as one of his employees, Thomas Ware, to close the store immediately. If they failed to follow the order, he continued, they would be arrested and sent to the Rip Raps, a military prison located on a small island nearby. The official said little more, turned, and left, leaving the Whitehursts and Ware confused about why the store was to be shuttered. General Butler had authorized the store's establishment nearly one year before — so why was the military's highest police officer now so determined to close it under the threat of imprisonment? Why did the store suddenly represent a threat to military interests?[103]

Two days later, determined to get answers and, most especially, a reprieve, Edward Whitehurst and Thomas Ware paid a visit to the missionary Lewis Lockwood. They wanted to appeal the order up the army's chain of command, but they were not certain they had the authority to do so or that they would be listened to even if they tried. Just a year before, they were both restricted by Virginia law from offering testimony in legal proceedings against white people; and on their plantations and in their places of employment, the words of a slave rarely weighed as heavily as the words of a white person. But now the military brought with it a formal system of petitioning and deposition writing, which offered a means of responding to the provost marshal's order, although neither Whitehurst nor Ware possessed the literacy necessary to do so. So on August 4 they told their story to Lewis Lockwood, who then took pen in hand and sketched out the circumstances in one brief paragraph that described the events of two days before. It included no commentary — no direct request for action, no blame — but simply ended by noting that the assistant provost marshal issued the order "without assigning any reason therefore." After Whitehurst and Ware signed their names with Xs, Lewis Lockwood signed as a "witness," with an additional note that "the persons testifying above, are in my estimation, credible"—an endorsement that followed in a long tradition of white abolitionists vouching for the credibility of slave testimonies.[104]

The appeal worked. Four days later the provost marshal responded in writing and explained that his order was part of a more systematic effort to shut down stores in and around the fort. "I have had many complaints from Doct. McKay and Hunt about contrabands selling to sick and wounded soldiers," Baum wrote, explaining that his order served the interests of military surgeons determined to stop the commerce between refugees and soldiers.[105] But other military records from this period reveal that it may not have been the act of selling itself that was so problematic; the issue was a particular item allegedly being sold—liquor. Back in June, the provost marshal had launched a campaign to weed out the sale of alcohol by refugees to soldiers, ordering the destruction of a series of "booths" set up near the wharf at Fort Monroe. Inside the booths the provost marshal discovered thirty to forty men who had set up shop "for the ostensible purpose of selling apples," when really, officials believed, this was a front for selling whiskey to McClellan's defeated and wounded troops.[106] Record books from the provost marshal from that spring and summer likewise reveal that the sale of liquor to soldiers was one of the primary reasons for a refugee to be arrested and imprisoned.[107] It was an urgent matter of military discipline to stop this commerce, the provost marshal believed, and in his reply to Whitehurst and Ware, he denied that they had been singled out. "I do not allow any one *Black* or *White* to disobey those orders," Baum continued, "and if they disobey my commands I shut them up."[108]

But there was more to it. There was something else Whitehurst was selling that also ran afoul of the provost marshal: lumber. That summer he had taken to "getting Secesh lumber and riving it into paling for building and fencing," as he described it, leaving Thomas Ware to tend to day-to-day affairs in his store in Hampton. (His statement made no mention of Emma's precise whereabouts.)[109] Whitehurst realized that there was a growing demand for lumber in the region, as incoming soldiers set out to build new structures and as the refugees, forced out of their spaces, looked to rebuild again. But as he expanded his enterprise beyond food to include wood, he also encroached on a sphere that the provost marshal and other Union officials tightly controlled. "I do not allow any one to destroy buildings or take any property," Provost Marshal Baum explained in his reply, "without orders from *Headquarters*."[110] His record books likewise detail the arrests and imprisonments, sometimes for as long as thirty days, of other men doing that very thing that spring and summer.[111]

Military officials closely guarded what they assumed was their right to possess, and thereby regulate, any physical property in the region that Confederates once claimed belonged to them—including lumber. It was one of the prerogatives of an army's occupation of a place. The previous month, in fact, Congress had moved to strengthen the Union's claim to property with the passage of the Second Confiscation Act on July 17, which stressed how essential the possession of property was to the success of the army and, thus, to the Union. "That, to insure the speedy termination of the present rebellion," the act opened, "it shall be the duty of the President of the United States to cause the seizure of all the estate and property, money, stocks, credits, and effects of the persons hereinafter named"—referring to anyone who offered some kind of "aid" to the rebellion. A key passage of the act came in the declaration that under the president's authority, Union officials should "apply and use the same and the proceeds thereof for the support of the army of the United States." Any property seized under the auspices of this act was to support the army and its mission in this war—it was a military necessity, in other words, for the army to assume control of it.[112]

That same legal framework had, of course, enabled—and continued to enable—refugees like Edward Whitehurst to enter Union lines in the first place as "contraband." They were seized property supporting the army too. And in fact, the Second Confiscation Act had gone even further to stipulate how this particular form of property would be treated inside Union lines. Contraband men, women, and children "shall be forever free of their servitude, and not again held as slaves," the act declared, putting the promise of legal freedom into writing for the very first time.[113] But even as the Union essentially let go of its possession of human property after seizing it—indeed, the people were no longer to be seen as property at all under the Second Confiscation Act—it clamped down more firmly on other forms of property. And that is where the problem emerged: What happened when this newly liberated human property, people like Edward Whitehurst, claimed other forms of confiscated property for themselves?

Nearly every refugee who arrived in army encampments across the wartime South brought something with them—rare was the refugee who arrived empty-handed. This was evident in the illustrations by artists depicting the migration of people to Fort Monroe with baskets in hand and wagons in tow (fig. 2). They brought everyday essentials, such as the contents of their slave cabins, like the "feather beds, chairs, tables, pots, and pans" observed by a Quaker teacher in Norfolk.[114] They brought other things necessary to build a new livelihood, such as oxen, wagons, and horses. And they brought things that might make them money in the days ahead, which meant cotton in areas farther south and west or potatoes, beans, or other food harvests, like that which Edward Whitehurst had gone back to claim in Newport News.[115] They brought all of this property with them for practical reasons, but also because they believed it was rightfully theirs, the products of years of hard labor.[116]

Yet upon arriving inside Union army lines, refugees could count on losing much of that property almost immediately. Union authorities, empowered by the Confiscation Acts, made sure to seize it, or as official reports would describe it, to "relieve them" of property and make sure it was "turned over to Quartermaster."[117] One officer in the Deep South later explained to his men that their superior, Gen. Ulysses S. Grant, "denies the right of the negroes to such property, and regards it as the property of the United States to be turned over to the Quartermasters Department."[118] To deny that "right" meant to follow the letter of the law of Southern states, which had made it illegal for enslaved people to own property (even though slave owners, like the Whitehursts', sometimes ignored and flouted such laws). The Union simply followed in that spirit. Having deemed the refugees' furniture, livestock, and other effects the legal property of their enslavers, it was now, under the Confiscation Acts, the property of the United States government—refugee claims to ownership notwithstanding. "Generally, on reaching our lines, the picket officers relieve them of all stock," explained one Union official, and "in this way, the Government has been supplied with many thousand mules and horses."[119]

Union confiscation policies thus managed to liberate people and simultaneously strip them of the material things they needed to build a life in freedom. At times there was some leeway in the confiscation process, especially when a particular item possessed by a refugee was deemed of little value to the army. Union army regulations stipulated that only property to be used for "public purposes"—for "subsistence, transportation, and other uses of the army"—could be seized; other property taken for the "private" use of a soldier qualified as pillage and was punishable by court-martial.[120] Accordingly, one official noted that officers around him allowed refugees to keep property "unless pressingly demanded for military purposes."[121] But what was "pressingly demanded," or what served "public purposes," was a subjective judgment—and over time, the soldiers carrying out confiscation orders dispensed with such judgments and pillaged with abandon. They got away with it—because others around them were doing it too. "The Soldiers get their licens [sic] to practice all manner of depredations upon this long degraded people," a black AMA missionary noticed, "by seeing it done by officers in the army."[122] The soldiers had been socialized by the Union's general inclination to dismiss black property claims and to consider property claimed by refugees as "stolen"—taken either from their enslavers or from the United States.[123] Charles Wilder, the superintendent of contrabands at Fort Monroe, thus complained of soldiers "stripping them of whatever is found in their possession generally of little or no value to any one else" and doing so because the soldiers were "assuming that it was stolen."[124]

It was in this precarious context that the Whitehursts found themselves defending the store and their right to possess and sell property in early August. Always subject to seizure by rogue soldiers, and now threatened by provost marshal officials with imprisonment, the Whitehursts' entire journey to freedom seemed to be at stake. They had worked for years to accumulate property, in the form of money in the trunk, and then had continued to acquire more and to sell it as storekeepers in Hampton. They had achieved a degree of economic independence that freed them from the vagaries of Union army employment policies and enabled them to support themselves. They had probably even begun dreaming of the future. Perhaps it's no surprise, then, that they did not immediately shut down or abandon the store but were still there when the situation quickly took a turn for the worse.

It was on August 15, thirteen days after the provost marshal's order, when army wagons rolled up in front of the Whitehursts' store. Within seconds a "variety of squads of troops" from McClellan's retreating army began streaming out of the wagons, along with a few sergeants and corporals overseeing them, and headed inside. They grabbed everything they could find and left Edward and Emma, as well as Edward's brother, Immanuel Savage, Thomas Ware, and Charles Smith, nearly helpless to stop them. Edward appealed to a provost guard to stop the soldiers, but the officer "told me, 'You can't do any thing,'" and instead instructed them "not to make any resistance, as the soldiers were hungry, and would get something to eat." The Whitehursts could only watch as the troops then carried out an estimated twenty to thirty bushels of potatoes, two barrels of flour, forty pounds of butter, and two bushels of ginger cakes, as an officer commanded them to "hurry up and put [it] in the wagon." And they could only watch as the same troops seized six pigs from the surrounding yard, killing them on the spot in full view before tying them up and then loading them on the wagon. "They cleaned out the Bakehouse in one day," Edward later recounted, and with that the two loaded army wagons, filled with the entire contents of the Whitehursts' store, drove off, headed in the direction of the Union soldiers encamped in and around nearby Fort Monroe.[125]

Edward and Emma Whitehurst had lost everything. Edward had tried one last-ditch effort to save the business just before the soldiers left, asking the officers present to pay for the goods taken. One of the officers replied that "Uncle

Sam would pay us," as Immanuel Savage later recounted, although the officials provided no voucher for the items taken and no payment was ever made for the duration of the war.[126] For the officer to have suggested that Whitehurst could be compensated was an acknowledgment of his property ownership, at least in theory; but with no payment forthcoming, the transaction was in reality little different from all other property seizures. And those seizures only continued to escalate in the weeks ahead. As one missionary wrote later that August, "We are having dreadful times here. . . . The soldiers are nothing more than a mob. . . . The colored people are stripped of everything eatable."[127]

This included people who once worked alongside the Whitehursts back in Newport News. Similar reports emerged from the old Parrish property, which had been transformed over the last year into a refugee camp under the army's direction. John Oliver, a black AMA missionary who was working there, wrote to New York that the people around him had sixty acres under cultivation in 1862, which they planned to "live upon this winter" and to sell goods from in order to "perchus [sic] shoes and clothing for themselves." Yet in July, some of Gen. Ambrose Burnside's troops had come there and "destroyed nearly the whole of their early crop which they had industriously cultivated." Then, in August, "a part of Gen. McClellans retreating army were in camp here for two weeks, and while here they destroyed more than half their remaining crops which they hade still zealously worked." It was a double blow that left the people at harvesttime with little to show for their work and with little to support themselves over the next year. Oliver grew pessimistic, believing that "what is true in their case is also true throughout the union army where the slave has come into proximity with it." Or as another man on the Parrish property told him, "Good God, if this is the way we are to be treated we may just as well be in Slavery."[128]

That sentiment only intensified over the summer, as the practice of property confiscation bled quickly into the confiscation of human bodies too. "Send by the Steamer . . . five hundred contrabands," came an order from Gen. John A. Dix, who had replaced General Wool in command of Fort Monroe in June. Dix, an aging Democrat with a reputation as an antiabolitionist, was reluctant to inherit command over the fort's refugee affairs and felt immediately overwhelmed by the number of ex-slaves in the vicinity. Aware that General McClellan was looking for laborers to free up his white soldiers for combat roles, Dix turned to impressment, the long-standing military practice of compelling men to labor for the military without notice and without choice. Dix followed up his order six days later with another order for 500 more men— and he continued to issue more orders for men to be impressed into the army.

These orders meant separating the men from their families, sometimes "at the point of the bayonet," before sending them to McClellan's army as it moved from the peninsula to Washington, D.C.[129] Harrowing scenes resulted: women were observed to be "well nigh frantic" in the moments of their husbands' and sons' seizures, which often came after being "plundered" and "shot at" by soldiers and with no word of when they would be reunited again.[130]

"Persecution at Fortress Monroe" was how the *Liberator* newspaper headlined a report on the impressments. The paper pointed the blame at the change in command for making such scenes possible, arguing that "pro-slavery under-officers," who had never been content with General Wool's policies, were now taking advantage of General Dix's arrival in order to "hinder every good work undertaken for their [the refugees'] benefit."[131] The soldiers were "brutes" and no better than "the vilest of Southern Slave drivers," charged Superintendent of Contrabands Charles Wilder, who preferred the term "kidnapping" over "impressment."[132]

Some of the men sent away reacted with their feet: labor rolls from Harrison's Landing, where most of the men were initially sent before going to Washington, indicate that over 20 percent of the impressed men had subsequently, in the words of the clerks keeping the rolls, "deserted."[133] Meanwhile, the AMA missionary Lewis Lockwood headed to Washington, D.C., himself, to appeal to Secretary Edwin Stanton for intervention. The secretary, who had already demonstrated some sympathy for the plight of refugees, gave him "no satisfaction" in this instance, however, and instead told Lockwood "it was right to impress Cold. People &c." It was "right" because there was a military necessity for it.[134] And once their labor was deemed a military "necessity," it was no great leap to view their bodies as military "necessities," to be possessed and controlled at will.

❧

The aftermath of the Peninsula campaign that summer is more often told as the moment when military failure pushed Union policy more decisively in the direction of emancipation. Indeed, President Lincoln also traveled to Harrison's Landing—just before the impressed men were sent there—and what he observed convinced him that Union military necessity required a more decisive blow at Southern society, or a turn to "hard war," that meant striking directly at slavery. He then returned to Washington to draft his monumental Emancipation Proclamation. There's no denying that this was a pivotal moment for policy making—but there's also no denying that the fort's refugees experienced the campaign's end in a way that seemed like the causes of Union and freedom had come unraveled in their daily lives. The coming of the Emancipation Proclamation itself, in fact, would do little to change that.[135]

News about the proclamation arrived in eastern Virginia in late September, initially bringing welcome relief and hope to this population reeling from violent impressments, family separations, and unpaid back wages (a total of over $33,000 that fall, according to one official calculation). "We have rejoiced with you in the Proclamation of the President," was how Charles Day, an AMA teacher in Hampton, described the local reaction. "The people here (colored) seem to rejoice with joy unspeakable at the prospect of freedom at New Years."[136] In November they gathered in Hampton for a public meeting to begin planning a celebration for January 1, 1863, the day on which the proclamation was to take effect. The group adopted a series of resolutions: "1st Resolved—That the 1st day of January next be set apart as a day of Thanksgiving & rejoicing" was how it opened, with subsequent resolutions to begin worship services at noon that day that would last for twelve hours and would include a "special prayer . . . for the President of the United States & for our friends in view of what they have done for us." They also resolved to suspend their labor and "close our places of business that day" in order to pray with one accord "for deliverance from the yoke of bondage."[137]

Yet within three weeks of that meeting came devastating news: the Emancipation Proclamation would not apply to all people seeking freedom inside Union lines in the South. The president had identified specific regions to be excluded from the Emancipation Proclamation—and six counties in eastern Virginia were among them, including Elizabeth City County, the home of Hampton and Fort Monroe. Residents were alerted of this news via newspaper reports, although signs of the exemption had surfaced in the weeks before. General Dix, under pressure from Unionist men in the region who were "anxious on the subject" and wanted the exemption, oversaw a hastily organized special congressional election in December, which resulted in the election of Joseph Segar, a local landowner, to Congress. This meant that this formerly rebellious congressional district had returned to the Union and was now considered to be "loyal" again, so it was no longer a military necessity to emancipate slaves in the region. The exemption was granted. This was just part of what historian Eric Foner has termed an "unseemly scramble for exemptions" that took hold in the month before the proclamation's issuance, in which politics could change, overnight, the Union's calculus of military necessity.[138]

The refugees and their allies prepared for the worst. "We have fears of evil from the effect of the Proclamation," the superintendent of contrabands, Charles Wilder, reported to AMA officials in New York. No one knew exactly what the exemption would mean: Did it trump previous U.S. policy related to the refugees? Would the army stop admitting new arrivals in the region? Would it expel those who had already arrived? And could local slave owners, especially those claiming to be loyal to the Union, now come to the fort and reclaim their slaves? Those who had been "practically freed" over the last year and a half now seemed to be "in danger of being reenslaved," wrote another AMA teacher who feared the worst, prompting Wilder to call on the president to "define what may be done & what not & who shall do it."[139] Meanwhile local slaveholders in the region, according to another AMA teacher, had become emboldened by the exemption and were reportedly telling the enslaved "that no one on earth has the power to free them." As a result, "the slaves here are feeling the most intense grief from the effects of the proclamation."[140]

The president's order had only intensified the uncertainty that had always plagued the refugees from their first days inside Union lines. And that uncertainty was demoralizing, as Secretary Stanton learned directly, when a commissioner he dispatched that December to study the problems singled out this fact in his report back to Washington. "It may be regarded as one of the chief necessities for the comfort and happiness of the colored Refugees," LeBaron Russell wrote on December 25, "to be more definitely assured than they now are of their permanent freedom. They are still troubled by the idea of the possibility of their return to slavery."[141] It was nineteen months since Emma and Edward Whitehurst had entered Union lines. With their trunk emptied and their livelihood demolished, and now with their exclusion from the president's monumental order, their "permanent freedom" seemed less secure than ever.

}2{

Finding Shelter

The Emancipation Proclamation may have made people fearful in the recently Unionized region around Fort Monroe, while it supported the march toward freedom in other places still considered rebellious. But wherever it reached — or did not reach — the proclamation made one thing clear: place mattered. The president's January 1863 order, with its carefully worded passages listing which counties in Virginia or parishes in Louisiana would be exempted, or which border states would still be allowed to enslave, was closely attuned to geography.[1] It was a particular kind of geography, though — a fundamentally political one. The regions excluded were those deemed "loyal," and thus no longer (or never) in rebellion against the Union, and those determinations were greatly influenced by the lobbying of local political officials. The places where enslaved people could go in the hope of finding freedom, then, would be determined by the perception of political loyalty and disloyalty among the white people living there.

In this respect the proclamation was profoundly out of step with the course of emancipation already under way in the war's first two years — or with what might be called the military geography of emancipation. The collection of refugee camps established by the time of the Emancipation Proclamation hewed more closely to the army's movements across the South. The military's momentum had created its own geography of freedom, one determined by combat and conquest, and it fit poorly within the proclamation's political boundaries. This is why one-third of the refugee camps established over the course of the war — that is, one-third of the protected spaces opened up by the army — were in regions *exempt* from the Emancipation Proclamation (maps 3 and 4). Fort Monroe was just one of them.

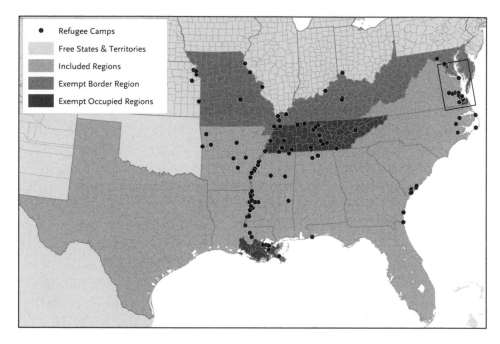

MAP 3. This map overlays the Emancipation Proclamation's included regions and exempted regions with the locations of the refugee camps. (Pauer Center for Cartography & GIS, University of Kentucky)

Legend:
- Refugee Camps
- Free States & Territories
- Included Regions
- Exempt Border Region
- Exempt Occupied Regions

President Lincoln was well aware of this conflicting geography—and had no real intention of fixing it. The significance of his proclamation, in fact, would come from its ability to do the political work of placating the loyal in exempt regions without stopping the military work of emancipation on the ground. Two policies already on the books would make sure of that. The Second Confiscation Act of 1862, which had declared "forever free" any enslaved person owned by those in rebellion against the Union, could trump the proclamation's exemptions in some, but not all, cases.[2] But even more significant, yet unheralded in history, was an article of war passed by Congress in March 1862 that had no name but simply declared that all Union officers were "prohibited from employing any of the forces under their respective commands for the purpose of returning fugitives" and that anyone caught and convicted of doing so would be "dismissed from the service."[3] This sweeping order explains why *none* of the camps in exempt regions would close when the proclamation came down and why there was no mass expulsion of refugees in its wake: once inside Union army lines, all refugees, no matter where they came from or whom they belonged to, could, if officials followed the letter of this policy, stay there.

Finding Shelter

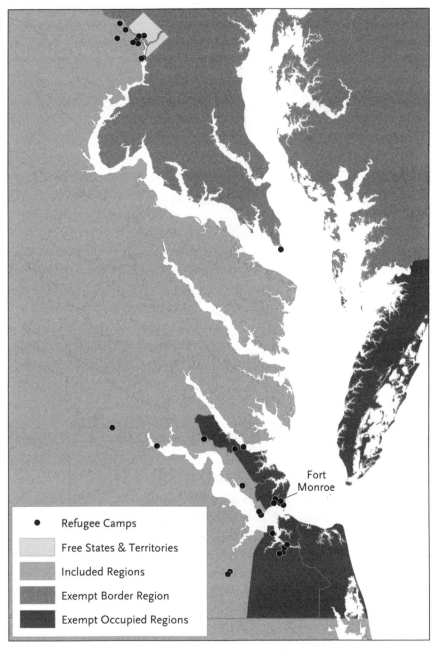

MAP 4. Close-up view of eastern Virginia that shows the camps located in exempt regions (Pauer Center for Cartography & GIS, University of Kentucky)

This included Edward and Emma Whitehurst and all the rest of the refugees around Fort Monroe, whose fears of expulsion, it turned out, never came true.

But how well could a fleeing slave see the Union's "lines"? That was the crux of the challenge ahead, as freedom seeking remained firmly tied to geography and to finding the right place to settle. It was one thing for policy makers in Washington, or army commanders in their headquarters, to envision those lines of Union occupation on a map: a curved line neatly bisecting Mississippi or a shaded region hugging the coast of North Carolina was not difficult to approximate on paper. But that was a far different perspective than what could be seen on the ground, in the everydayness of war. There the lines had no physical manifestation in the form of signs or fencing but were marked only by the scattered presence of Union troops (or the absence of Confederates). The Union army could never occupy *all* the space it claimed on a map, and Confederates constantly fought those boundaries anyway. For an individual packing up his or her children and heading into a war zone, then, a map's imagined boundaries between the freedom of Union occupation and the slavery of Confederate territory were an inadequate guide.

How would they know when they had made it? The sight of Union troops and their blue uniforms was an important first clue, but seeing, of course, was not the same as belonging. To know that one was actually anchored inside the Union's sphere of protection — that one had a place there — required something more reassuring, something more concrete. And that's what refugees from slavery found in shelter. In a tent or a cabin or a hut, they acquired a physical toehold in Union lines and, therefore, in the promise of freedom. It was in shelters that freedom could be seen, felt, touched, lived in, and experienced. But it was also where freedom could become endangered and lost, because the wartime transition from slavery to freedom was rarely a linear one, as the Whitehursts knew well. The crucial task of finding a physical place — and keeping it and not losing it — would thus be essential to achieving a metaphoric place in freedom during the war.

Refugees claimed shelters already in existence, or more commonly, and with the army's assistance, built new dwellings from scratch. They constructed an entire landscape of refugee camps — a cultural landscape of wartime emancipation — that staked a visible claim to freedom on a land previously devoted to enslavement and bondage. Scatterings of tents popped up along rivers and inside cities; planned villages with sturdier cabins were erected in isolated agricultural regions. And together the shelters and the camps represented more than a backdrop, more than a reflection of prevailing ideas and values about freedom, but were, in fact, constitutive of them. As enslaved people, military officials, and politicians alike contemplated the meaning of freedom, as well as where, when, and how it would unfold, shelter provided a focal point, channeling abstract principles into concrete, material forms. The construction of the refugee camp landscape thus amounted to nothing less than the construction of freedom itself.[4]

Finding the right shelter in the right place had always been pivotal to an enslaved person's pursuit of freedom. Before the war, runaways on the Underground Railroad had navigated Northern free states carefully, choosing particular routes and particular "stops" in places that were known informally to be safer than others. Yet the process changed once the Civil War came. Where before it was crucially important for these shelters to be concealed, or to enable freedom-seeking people to disappear and go unseen, in the Civil War the shelters came out of the shadows and into full view. Photographers documented them; soldiers and missionaries wrote home about them; and government documents sometimes included sketches and diagrams detailing how refugee shelters came to dot the wartime landscape. Most of the time there was little need for secrecy anymore. When it came to shaking off pursuers, either enslavers or Confederate patrollers turned guerrillas, it could be a boon to take up shelter in a visible space. Refugee slaves did not need to hide so much as openly flaunt their new ties to the Union army: to be seen inside, or in connection to, a Union army encampment was tantamount to being seen as backed by the power of the Northern army. It was to flaunt newfound leverage.

And from the start the army assumed the task of providing shelter to refugees. "The Quartermaster's Department will furnish all the materials and supplies necessary to shelter and protect the negroes destined to be located in this Camp," came one typical order from the Mississippi Valley.[5] It was to some degree a military necessity: How well would the refugees labor for the army if they were not protected from environmental hazards and disease? A shelter would protect them from rain and cold and other natural threats that could bring misery and illness, or hide them from Confederates ready to inflict injury. It would keep them healthy and thus ready to work.

Yet it was not just necessity that prompted officials to provide shelter to refugees — there was a certain duty at work too. "These people are in our care," Gen. John A. Dix wrote from Fort Monroe in November 1862, "and we are bound by every principle of humanity to treat them with kindness and protect them from exposure and injury."[6] Dix was no abolitionist and had no real track record as a humanitarian; indeed, he was the one responsible for the impressment of black men at the fort that fall. But he also could not ignore the fact that the army promised some protection to refugees, and if there was any form of protection that could not be overlooked, it was protection from gratuitous bodily harm. Shelter offered a tangible and visible means of fulfilling that most basic promise to the refugees. And, if the army's promise of protection had also meant shielding refugees from a return to slavery, then a tent or a cabin would erect a protective cover around each one, physically containing them in Union lines and sheltering them—literally, physically, metaphorically—from slavery.

There was precedent for this kind of assistance. The federal government already had an established track record, well before the Civil War, of providing humanitarian relief, including shelter, to people trapped by disastrous circumstances such as floods, fires, grasshopper plagues, or even the wars with the Seminole Indians, which left white residents of Florida displaced and in need of assistance. "Blameless suffering" or "blameless loss," as it was viewed, in which individuals had no control over the devastation they experienced, qualified a person for federal aid. Such acts of disaster relief were believed to be a fulfillment of the government's constitutional obligation to promote the general welfare—and represented the nascent origins of the federal welfare state. The provision of shelter to refugees in the Civil War simply extended this assistance to the "blameless," to those who were enslaved and now homeless in a war zone. But it also, notably, marked the moment when this kind of federal relief crossed the color line for the first time, including people of African descent among those deemed worthy of humanitarian aid.[7]

The expressed duty to provide shelter also had something to do with prevailing beliefs about military conduct in war. "Every military consideration is bound up in the bundle with the interests of humanity, with those of justice," Col. John Eaton, a Union official working with refugees in the Mississippi Valley, argued in 1863. "Shall we attempt to separate them in the management of these persons?" The answer, in Eaton's mind, was a resounding no. "There are certain laws of right, certain fixed principles of humanity" that must always be served by the military, he argued.[8] Here Eaton brought together two ideals at work in the American laws of war—military necessity and humanitarianism—two ideals that had often been in tension and still remained so in the new code of laws drafted by Francis Lieber in 1863. Yet just as the president managed to pull these ideals together in his Emancipation Proclamation, arguing for the military necessity of fighting for human freedom, so too did Colonel Eaton believe that offering physical care and assistance to freedom seekers was fully consistent with—and should be served by—the Union's military effort. Not all officials would agree with his formulation, however, and some would provide shelter only grudgingly, if at all.[9]

And in practical terms, the provision of shelter to refugees was not something for which the army was entirely prepared when the war began. There was no master plan, nothing in the U.S. Army regulations outlining how to distribute shelter to civilians. The logistics were daunting too. How could tens of thousands of refugees be sheltered in a way that did not siphon off too much of the man power and other resources needed to power the army? Even as men like Dix and Eaton argued that providing shelter was a military duty and necessity in the abstract, how could it be provided without turning around and undermining military readiness? The most common answer settled on by army officials was to adhere as closely as possible to the system in place for sheltering soldiers. The army already had established forms of soldier housing, as well as a supply and distribution chain overseen by the quartermaster's department that moved tents, lumber, and other housing materials out of Northern factories and mills and into army camps.[10] It seemed efficient, then, to fold the formerly enslaved into that apparatus as much as possible, which is why, upon arriving in a refugee camp, most could count on being assigned a tent.

They were "condemned tents," "unserviceable" tents, and "old tents," as various officials described them (figs. 3 and 4).[11] They were secondhand shelters that had already been used, and in many cases cast aside, by regular soldiers. In Nashville this meant tents retrieved from a convalescent camp "after having been a long time in use," as one officer noted.[12] They were dirty and ripped, possibly even contaminated after sheltering sick and wounded soldiers, and no longer acceptable for housing soldiers. But in the minds of some Union officials overseeing the refugees, the distribution of worn-out shelter was simply an example of "the most rigid economy" being applied to the management of refugee affairs.[13] And if tents could not be located, then open space in a military barracks might be shared with refugees, as was the case around Fort Monroe, where young and old, men and women, "huddled together in a long building at 25 feet by 150 feet with a ground and second floor, and not a single partition in the whole building," as an AMA agent described it.[14]

To be issued a tent or ushered into a barracks by a quartermaster official signaled to the refugees how embedded in the military apparatus their pursuit of freedom would be. Yet the shelter also carried the clear message that even as refugees might be treated like soldiers, they would rarely be treated *exactly* like soldiers during their time in Union lines. Their new beginning in freedom would take place in old, worn-out structures; it was something they would see

FIGURE 3. Refugee tents in Harpers Ferry, Virginia, in late 1862 (Library of Congress)

and literally feel every day. From Washington, D.C., came a report that the old army tents were so worthless that "some of the women remarked that 'the rain came in like a spring' and wet their beds."[15] "None of the tents being waterproof," reported a group of Indiana Quakers working in the Mississippi Valley, "everything within got 'soaking wet.'"[16] And from Nashville, in a camp without any trees near the tents, came reports that the shelter offered little of the necessary protection from the blazing sun.[17]

The army tents barely provided a roof over refugees' heads—and there was hardly anything below them either. "They live in tents," an AMA official in Virginia reported in 1862, "without floors of any kind."[18] The same was true for soldiers, although they could sometimes count on being issued rubber blankets for that purpose, and they had far freer access to nearby woodlands to build makeshift floors out of fence rails and logs.[19] Rarely were refugees given such access; as seen in Edward Whitehurst's case at Fort Monroe, they could

Finding Shelter

FIGURE 4. Sibley tents occupied by freed people in Richmond, Virginia, in 1865 (National Archives and Records Administration, 111-B-75)

even be punished for acquiring wood for themselves. This left them either to sleep on the bare ground or to improvise other ways of erecting floors, such as gathering the sticks and leaves of nearby trees. In the case of one Virginia camp, a nearby supply of brickbats became the source for a clean—but hard and uncomfortable—floor.[20]

The absence of tent floors was made all the more difficult by the positioning of refugee tents within the army encampment. In theory, and according to official army regulations, there was really no logical place for refugee tents in the highly ordered layout of the army camp. The 1861 rules were very specific in dictating that the basic organization should mirror the army in motion: "The terms front, flank, right, left, file, and rank, have the same meaning when applied to camps as to the order of battle," with infantry tents lined up first, in the front, and cavalry to the rear.[21] Refugees were never envisioned in 1861 to be part of the army in motion, so this, in turn, left little place for them in the camps at rest. Those working as paid servants to officers might reside close to their employers, but otherwise it was up to authorities to improvise, resulting in haphazard clusters of tents emerging in all different ways—and spots—in individual camps. Or at least that is how it seemed at first glance.

Over time, a de facto logic to the placement of refugee tents emerged with striking uniformity across the occupied South. They would be placed in the lowest-lying sections of an encampment: the places most likely to fill with water and mud upon a heavy rain or to be on the receiving end of contaminated water moving downstream. In Washington, D.C., in late 1862, refugees were placed in an area "not properly drained," leaving "ponds of water."[22] In

Helena, Arkansas, "the drainage in many cases was bad," according to a visiting Quaker, leaving the people not only mud soaked but also subjected to what government officials acknowledged was "putrid matter" and "effluvia" flowing from a nearby slaughter pen. On top of that was the problem posed by the nearby Mississippi River, which "frequently rises in the Spring to the height of three or four feet above the level of the ground where the camp is."[23] Horses could barely pass, with mud rising to knee level; soldiers sunk to their boot tops and had to pull themselves out by the straps; and Sanitary Commission agent Maria Mann relied on an army officer to carry her "several times in his arms through these streets of mud."[24] Few refugees, if any, received similar treatment, leaving them to walk in muddy streets and sleep and eat in mud-soaked tents, a situation repeated over and over in the occupied South, where military encampments were frequently established near the waterways that served as important military transportation routes.

A refugee waking up to a mud-soaked tent could not have missed the correlation between land elevation and one's position in the military structure; the landscape quite literally sorted the inhabitants spatially and reinforced the refugees' position at the very bottom of the camp hierarchy.[25] Take the refugees along the Mississippi River in Memphis, who arrived in the summer of 1862 and were immediately put to work in building Union defenses. An artist's rendering of their tents that appeared in *Frank Leslie's Illustrated Newspaper* months later depicted the tents "on the banks of the Mississippi," as the caption put it, a short distance from the steamboats moored at the river's edge (fig. 5). What the picture failed to capture was what lay behind the banks, or above and to the east of the refugee tents: the Chickasaw Bluffs rising to 200 feet above the floodplain. On top of the bluffs was Fort Pickering, where the soldiers' regiments erected their tents, far above and removed from the river waters.

The disparity in elevation could be explained, at least in part, as a function of military necessity: it was militarily advantageous for soldiers to stake higher ground in order to see and thwart approaching enemy forces.[26] The effect, however, no matter how justified by military need and convention, was to set up a racial disparity in exposure to the health hazards posed by cold, wet ground and contaminated water.[27] Relief workers arriving in these camps to assist the refugees frequently invoked the term "exposure" to describe the problem. "From this exposure they cannot avoid pneumonia, small pox and other diseases incident to camp life," wrote a group of Philadelphia Quakers visiting the Mississippi Valley in 1863, noting that their tents "shield them but very little."[28]

FIGURE 5. "The Camp of the Contrabands on the Banks of the Mississippi," *Frank Leslie's Illustrated Newspaper*, November 22, 1862 (University of North Carolina Libraries)

In the minds of the officials issuing the tents, however, all of this was a temporary condition, or something to be endured "in the interim," as an order from Nashville put it.[29] Just as soldiers — when they arrived in a place where they would be for an extended period of time, such as over the winter — embarked on constructing more substantial wooden cabins or huts, so too did the refugees pick up saws and hammers and begin building. And from that emerged a rough life cycle that would characterize the refugee camps all across the occupied South: what began as a collection of tents usually gave way to new huts and houses, and then, if military and environmental conditions allowed, to even more established "villages" and "towns." Some of those remained in place for the duration of the war.

Refugee men, especially those already employed by the quartermaster's department, sometimes found themselves on the receiving end of formal orders to build more substantial housing — orders that came with varying outlays of military resources to assist them. "Please let your Carpenter aid in putting up near Camp Hamilton sheds for about 150 women & children, families of contrabands in the employment of the Gov't.," General Dix at Fort Monroe ordered his quartermaster. But in a sign that, despite the abandonment of tents, some things would remain the same, he added, "Please also use for the purpose such lumber of poor quality as you have not absolutely nec-

FIGURE 6. Refugee housing at Helena, Arkansas
(Nebraska State Historical Society, RG3323-PH-6–12)

essary for public purposes."[30] Dix's words reflected the general hierarchy of
lumber distribution practiced by the government's sawmills: first came the repair of railroads and the building of bridges and fortifications; next came the
soldiers' need for more substantial housing, as well as firewood. Yet even that
need was rarely met adequately—soldiers were sent into the woods to fend for
themselves and left in their wake a "ruination of forests," as historian Megan
Kate Nelson put it. This left the refugees, at the very bottom of the hierarchy,
to obtain only the leftovers.[31]

   "Poor quality" lumber would therefore mean unclaimed logs gathered
from local woodlands, or wooden clapboard salvaged from ruined and burned-
out towns, or even a bamboo-like cane native to Mississippi, in the case of
buildings in Vicksburg.[32] In Young's Point, Louisiana, along the Mississippi
River, "the cabins are built from the fragments of steamboats, and drift-wood,"
observed one Union official.[33] Nearly anything that could be extracted from
their surroundings and appeared solid enough to withstand wind and rain was
fair game. The result was often a hodgepodge of housing styles, even within
one individual camp. The newly constructed housing at Helena, Arkansas

Finding Shelter

FIGURE 7. The Mill Creek, or "Slabtown," settlement in 1864 (Library of Congress)

(fig. 6), for example, featured rough-hewn clapboards of various sizes. Some houses contained windows, chimneys, or even covered spaces approximating porches, while others had none of those features at all. At the settlement in Virginia known as Mill Creek (fig. 7), just across a stream of the same name from Fort Monroe, pine slabs used previously for fencing were now put to use in houses of varying sizes and designs (and because of the building materials, the settlement eventually became known as "Slabtown").[34]

The task of building these structures could be urgent, especially if the winter months loomed, and this only compounded the need to improvise. The speed with which refugee housing appeared on the landscape, in fact, was notable enough to be remarked upon in the reports of Union officials and relief workers. It took a reported "few weeks" to build fifty houses in Corinth, Mississippi, in 1863; three months to erect 220 in Vicksburg in late 1864; and about six months to erect 240 in Tunnel Hill, Tennessee, in that same year.[35] But that was only in the places that could obtain lumber in time. Along the Mississippi River in Arkansas, refugees were left "to dig holes in the side of the hill," as one Union general observed, and live in what amounted to caves (or "cabins half underground," in the words of a local Sanitary Commission agent).[36] At least it was a hill, or in this case a ridge, that elevated the refugees above where their tents had previously languished in mud.

To the modern eye the structures built with leftover materials look dilapidated and desperate. That may have been how the photographers documenting them envisioned the scene; even the refugees themselves may have lamented the physical state of their structures. After all, they looked little different from, and, in some cases, arguably worse than, the cabins of their enslavement. Yet the structures were also little different from those that white soldiers built and lived in, a similarity that the refugees, as well as the soldiers themselves, would undoubtedly have seen too. The material similarity between soldier and refugee housing may not have conveyed racial equality so much as a narrowed disparity, or a shrunken distance, between the refugees' social position and that of the white people around them. After all, back on their plantations, slave owners deliberately created a visual disparity in the landscape between the cabins of the enslaved and the large, elaborate homes of the enslavers, in order to convey mastery, hierarchy, and status.[37] In the wartime encampments, though, that disparity was far less visible in the built environment—a sign to the refugees, perhaps, of what freedom could mean.

White observers saw a difference in this landscape too. There was something in the sight of refugees foraging for resources and working efficiently at building their own cabins that pleased military officials and missionaries alike. The refugees were "very busy" and "worked faithfully," they reported of the scenes, always emphasizing that the housing was something they "have built themselves."[38] Out of Clarksville, Tennessee, came a report that "all of the labor of the camp is performed, and the materials furnished, by the colored refugees themselves, thus giving them valuable experience in constructing their own dwellings and providing for themselves."[39] This particular response was more than a little tone deaf—while enslaved, the refugees had more than ample experience building and constructing dwellings—but it also echoed a more general enthusiasm among white observers for self-constructed homes. Home-building scenes enacted hopes widely shared among white officials that their assistance to the refugees would be only a temporary step on the road from the dependency of slavery to the self-sufficiency of freedom.

Army officials looked constantly for signs that the refugees were, or were becoming, self-sufficient. It was foremost among their preoccupations. To them it was partly a matter of reducing the expenditure required to provide for thousands of freedom-seeking people, although that was the least of their concerns. More pressing was the question of how ready—and how fit—former slaves would be for freedom and citizenship. Dependency, white Americans long believed, disqualified an individual from full citizenship rights: to be beholden to someone else for one's livelihood rendered one unable to be free-thinking and to have the free will necessary for the proper exercise of democratic political rights. This principle had long excluded those assumed to be "dependent," including slaves, women, and for a time, propertyless men, from full citizenship.[40] Now, in wartime, came a population of former slaves claiming a position for themselves as free people, and white officials grew practically angst ridden over whether, indeed, this population was, or could be, ready. "They never have learned to be self-reliant, and are not so," concluded three civilian commissioners dispatched by the secretary of war in 1864 to study the situation, in a report later submitted to the U.S. Senate. "They never had any care for the future, and therefore never learned to be provident for the future."[41] It was a distortion that none of the refugees themselves would have recognized in their lives, for the act of escaping slavery alone was emphatically a forward-looking act taken in the interest of protecting their own futures. And the extent to which slavery had rendered them utterly dependent, as the commission argued, was questioned by other white observers, such as the *Freedmen's Bulletin*, which contended that "heretofore they have supported their masters as well as themselves; and now that they have their masters off their hands, they will not fare worse."[42] Amid this disagreement, however, emerged houses and huts on the landscape, built by the refugees themselves, in a substantial, tangible demonstration of the resourcefulness and hard work associated with a self-supporting citizenry.

Yet as much as white officials may have wanted to promote self-sufficiency, they were wary of it too. Some feared what the refugees might do if left to their own devices and preferred that the path to independence be a controlled one, with limits and boundaries. This became apparent pretty quickly at Fort Monroe in mid-1862, when Gen. John Wool, newly committed to paying refugees wages following his commission's report, decided to compensate at least some of them with lumber. Issue lumber "[in] the amount of the wages due them," he ordered, so that "they may erect buildings for themselves."[43] Here Wool hit on what he probably felt modeled military efficiency by meeting the demands of shelter with the need to pay wages—all in one simple order. But it also modeled a form of labor and spending control, too, by dictating that any laborer at the fort *had* to spend his or her wages on a house and that to obtain a shelter at all required formal employment for the army. It was an order that would keep the refugees working—and working for their own support. Yet it never quite succeeded, either, as the payment of lumber was never enough to build a home, a missionary reported, requiring the refugees to purchase additional wood "from their own funds" too.[44]

In other instances, concerns arose that the refugees had taken too much license in the form and design of their structures. Take windows, for example, which failed to appear on many refugee houses. This was often a function of limited materials, as glass was not readily available in war-torn regions and not obtained by soldiers either. But at other times it was a deliberate choice. As a Sanitary Commission agent outside of Tiptonville, Tennessee, observed, "The inmates resist glass windows, contending that the door and chimney admit air and light enough."[45] This agent did not explain why they bothered to "resist," but perhaps it was simply the pursuit of something familiar, as windows were not always present in slave cabins either.[46] At the same time, as they lived with new faces, new officials, and new surroundings, not to mention with the enemy ever present in the distance, it is also not hard to imagine that refugees would want to limit how easily others could see and hear the goings-on in their lives. Unswayed by such desires, though, relief workers in Yorktown, Virginia, plowed ahead. "They need windows," declared an agent with the Friends Freedmen's Association of Philadelphia, and soon 250 window sashes were loaded onto a ship and sent down to Virginia.[47] It was an upgrade these Quakers believed "would have an elevating tendency," for otherwise the refugees would dwell in the dark rather than experience the light and air of freedom.[48]

Military officials and relief workers thus strove to channel the refugees' building energy in certain directions, to make sure that the housing constructed would do more than simply protect the refugees. It should help them transition out of slavery and into freedom—and to live in the way in which *they* envisioned free people should live. The clearest expression of this was in what might be called "planned settlements," places where white authorities took an active role in planning the layout and architecture of a refugee encampment before any building got under way. These were places where some white officials indulged their idealized visions for how the landscape of freedom should look—and took fewer and fewer cues from the designs of military encampments. The planned settlements, in fact, tended to eschew the word "camp" altogether, rejecting the term's associations with the chaotic and ephemeral in favor of "colony," or "town," or "village."[49] These spaces were to be less transient and more permanent—and were made possible by the relative distance these areas enjoyed from active military campaigns, which authorities believed offered them the relative luxury of uninterrupted time and space for formal, conscious planning.

Take the settlement located three-quarters of a mile down the Nansemond River from Suffolk, Virginia, established when the Peninsula campaign wound down in the summer of 1862. The camp became well known in missionary and government circles, attracting visitors who wanted to see this "model of cleanliness and order," as members of a government commission would put it the next year. What had once been an open field had become, within a year of the Union's occupation, a "town . . . laid out with great regularity," according to the commissioners. It had an open square in the middle, with streets running at right angles all around it, and on these streets sat orderly rows of refugee dwellings. There were seventy-eight houses in total, "built of small pines, laid up log-house-fashion," each averaging thirteen by sixteen feet in dimension. This was Uniontown, as it was called, a spot of Union ground in the middle of a Confederate state that would model the way in which freedom could come in a controlled and orderly manner.[50]

Beyond Uniontown there was Freedman's Village, which emerged on the former plantation of Confederate general Robert E. Lee and his wife, Mary Custis Lee, in Arlington, Virginia. Seized by the Union within weeks of the start of the war, and used subsequently to bury Union dead, the Arlington property became a refuge for freedom-seeking slaves from Maryland and Virginia, too. Here officials from the army quartermaster's department joined with representatives of the AMA to devise a layout "with streets regularly laid out and named, and a park planted in the centre," according to a report in the *Liberator* (fig. 8). A pond sat at the center of that park, and around it wrapped streets and other features named after prominent white men who supported emancipation. To the west were parks named after Abraham Lincoln and his ardently antislavery secretary of state, William Seward. A road called Hamlin Circle, named after the vice president, Hannibal Hamlin, formed the main artery along which two neat rows of fifty refugee houses, all of the same size, were evenly spaced. To the east of the housing were other buildings, such as a hospital, a school, and a chapel, as well as a home "for the aged and infirm." It was a plan, historian Joseph P. Reidy has noted, "designed to create an atmosphere of order, sobriety, and industry," the essential qualities of a self-supporting citizen. It was also one that, at least in the naming practices, reminded the refugees who was overseeing their transition to freedom.[51]

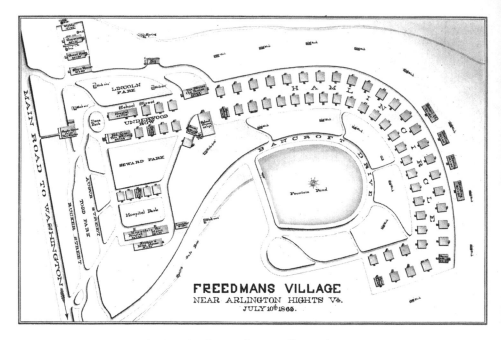

FIGURE 8. 1865 plan for Freedman's Village, Arlington, Virginia
(National Archives and Records Administration, Record Group 92: Map 110-4)

The names given to other planned settlements were similarly evocative of white leaders and their visions of freedom. Mitchelville, on Hilton Head Island in South Carolina, was named after the Union general overseeing its establishment, Ormsby Mitchel (fig. 9).[52] Acreville, on the coast of Virginia, was a place where each refugee received a one-acre plot of land, and those plots stretched along Whitall and Shipley Streets, named after two white abolitionists.[53] (Other places summed up their purpose with more general names like Freetown or Newtown.) No two planned settlements were alike, however; no common set of plans migrated from encampment to encampment, or from Washington, D.C., to local army headquarters. Yet there were basic spatial sensibilities shared across the planned settlements, most likely inspired by the Northern towns the men had left behind. In Uniontown, for example, Cpl. Charles R. Sikes of the First New York Mounted Rifles, the camp's superintendent of contrabands, dubbed the town's square Washington Square, a common name for city squares in Troy, Albany, and New York City, where his regiment was formed.[54] It may have seemed self-evident, even logical, to envision a new landscape of freedom like a northeastern town; their cities were the centers of free labor, of industry, of reform movements and change—a spatial frame of reference for envisioning how people can, and should, live as free people.[55]

FIGURE 9. Diagram of Mitchelville, on Hilton Head Island, 1865
(National Archives and Records Administration, Record Group 77: Map I-52)

Planners like Sikes believed that there would be no chaotic end to slavery in these settlements: the spatial order would bring social order. And one marked characteristic of all their plans was the clear lines and grid patterns that ordered the refugee housing spatially. These marked out footpaths, or "streets," that connected each house and enabled wagons, horses, and people to pass through unimpeded. That alone enabled a form of "order," but foremost in their minds may have been the easy passage of the military inspectors, whose task it was to survey and watch the settlements for "police and disciplinary purposes."[56] There would be a great deal of oversight in these planned settlements. The inspectors acted as the army's eyes and ears, watching this population for visible signs of "cleanliness, discipline, and good order," as one report put it, and they were known to arrest those found to be in possession of alcohol or "stolen" property.[57] The settlements' clear paths, with houses lined up at regular intervals, thus engineered these spaces in a way that made them inspectable. The naked eye had easy visual access to a collection of houses and could see, at a glance, whether anything seemed out of order. And this was an essential task in the eyes of those officials who believed that ex-slaves would not be able to transition to freedom without their control and guidance.[58]

But could their eyes see too much? Settlement planners, like so many white officials, claimed to promote a social order of self-reliant, free citizens, but the inspections could seem counterproductive too (and were undoubtedly reminiscent to the refugees of their lives with overseers on plantations).[59] To be watched was to have one's privacy infringed upon, one's autonomy as an individual threatened. So how could settlement planners talk about self-sufficiency on the one hand, and then impose such a rigid, invasive order on the other? Very easily, they believed, for the two impulses were easily reconciled. In their minds, what was most significant about their plans was less the streets and the inspection of them than the individual houses that lined those streets. Inside those homes families would be strengthened and supported, they believed, and nothing would do more to promote the right kind of citizenry than a well-ordered family.[60]

The family was at the center of their visions, for they claimed there was something deficient in the refugees' most intimate relations that needed their attention. Col. William A. Pile, an army chaplain from Missouri who visited camps in the Mississippi Valley in 1863, explained that "one great defect in the management of the negroes down there was, as I judged, the ignoring of the family relation." The problem, he claimed, stemmed from "the mixing up [of] two or three families in the same hut," or what he called "jumbling" and "huddling." It was understandable to some degree, in Pile's mind, since "the slaves of the South, as far as I have been able to ascertain, are almost wholly destitute of any accurate conception of domestic obligations." With that statement Pile betrayed a basic, racist assumption shared by other sympathetic white Northerners in the camps: that somehow enslaved people had no "conception" of what a family was or could be. It was a belief with no basis in reality for those streaming into camps with their children or aging parents in tow, who had maintained clear "domestic obligations" even amid the threats that slavery had long posed. Edward and Emma Whitehurst and others married at Fort Monroe were clear examples of that.[61] But in the minds of men like Pile, the refugee camps threatened only to worsen an already bad family situation. "The great weakness of the negro is in his social instincts," another superintendent likewise argued from the Mississippi Valley, and "this has been aggravated by being herded together in such numbers" in wartime.[62]

Some called it "jumbling," and to others it was being "herded"; the sight of large numbers of people crowding into small, confined spaces would loom large in the fears and imaginations of white officials around the camps. To them, crowding was a source of problems that could extend far beyond the domestic lives of black people, including into the realm of public health. "There is much sickness among them in consequence of the huddling together so many in so small a space," explained an army medical director in eastern Virginia to his commanding general in July 1862.[63] Other officials similarly associated high mortality rates to "places where they have been crowded together."[64] And indeed, nineteenth-century medical thinking increasingly associated crowding with illness. It was not that bodies in close proximity would transmit germs as they touched one another, for medical officials had not yet discovered germ theory. Instead they talked about "contagion," in which it was believed a disease could move from person to person simply through the air (with no real understanding of what, exactly, was transmitted between them).[65] Such beliefs only added to the push for refugee housing to contain windows—and explained the complaints that arose when the new cabins and huts were deemed "poorly ventilated" or "without proper ventilation."[66] Too many bodies in the camps were sharing air spaces considered too constricted for healthy, viable human habitation.

Yet crowding also raised the specter of something else that white observers long feared would accompany the end of slavery: insurrection. Even some of the most abolitionist-minded and progressive among them had long harbored fears of what ex-slaves would do once they became free. Generations of resentment and a desire for vengeance, coupled with what many whites believed was a predisposition for violence coursing through their veins, might, if given the opportunity, unite to launch a rebellion and the violent overthrow of white power. The association between emancipation and black violence was a long-standing one in white American politics, prompting some leaders to oppose emancipation altogether and others to propose that it could only be accompanied by the removal of the newly freed to a far-distant land, such as Liberia, in various colonization schemes.[67] Abraham Lincoln, however, although a longtime supporter of colonization himself, relied only on a special plea in the Emancipation Proclamation to "hereby enjoin upon the people so declared to be free to abstain from all violence."[68] Others supervising the refugee camps turned attention to the spatial problem of crowding that seemed too conducive to planning, plotting, and alliance making.

"They need to be enticed to set themselves apart in families," Col. John Eaton concluded in the Mississippi Valley, and with this "they will grow in domestic virtues and self-reliance."[69] And not just any family either: the nuclear family. As officials like Eaton idealized it, the mother-father-child family structure, ensconced in its own, private household, was an incubator of good social and political values; in it, future citizens developed the character and morals necessary to go out in the world and act as responsible citizens. Submission to family obligations, for example, was held up as a necessary demonstration of virtue and of one's fitness to be a law-abiding, self-supporting citizen in a free republic.[70] How else would these formerly enslaved people, already damaged by slavery, have any chance of acting responsibly in freedom without first forming nuclear families? White officials could see no other alternative; the nuclear family was foundational. "One of the first things to be done with these people, to qualify them for citizenship," Colonel Pile wrote from the Mississippi Valley, "is to impress upon them the family obligations."[71]

The military's sanction of weddings, like that of the Whitehursts at Fort Monroe, was already working toward that end. But some believed there was a spatial fix at hand to accomplish this task too: just as the landscape of a Northern town physically separated nuclear families into individual, private spaces, so too would the landscape of the planned refugee settlement. "Each family should be put by itself, as far as possible, in one hut, and the huts kept distinct and separate from each other," Colonel Pile concluded, for "the privacy of the family should be established, as far as possible, in all contraband camps."[72] And that is exactly what the diagrams of planned settlements like Freedman's Village reflected, with each square or spot on a map representing one private, nuclear family. The refugees, ideally, would not be organized spatially by rank or function, as the soldiers were in their encampments, but by families, as free Northerners were in civilian life. Officials in settlements like Uniontown and Freedman's Village thus set about issuing housing to individual family units, in some places including with the dwellings space for gardens in which families could cultivate their own food. The planned settlements would thus be anchored by the "properly-ordered, prosperous private dwelling," in the words of historian George Lipsitz, which was, and would continue to be, at least for white Americans, "the nation's key symbol of freedom."[73]

Yet refugees settling into places like Uniontown and Freedman's Village brought with them a different sense of space, one that did not associate living in nuclear families with freedom, or crowding with degeneracy. In fact, it was much the reverse. "Don't care if we *are* crowded," is what one refugee told relief worker Lucy Chase in Norfolk.[74] It was not that refugees like this one were willing to live with a lower quality of life — they simply defined it differently. If whites brought the spatial sensibilities of a Northern town to the settlements, then refugees brought those nurtured in the context of a plantation. There they

FIGURE 10. Family dwellings in the planned settlement of Mitchelville, on Hilton Head Island (National Archives and Records Administration, 165-C-362)

had also lived under a highly rigid ordering of space, one in which enslavers carved their patriarchal control into the landscape with clear boundaries, and, at its center, a large, grand house that left no doubt about the place and the person from which all power flowed. Yet, according to architectural historian John Michael Vlach, the enslaved routinely "countered the geometrically circum-scribed order imposed by their master's logic with what seemed like chaos" to white people, preferring landscapes with few overt boundaries and the clustering of people in close, common spaces. That was one of the ways in which they could undermine their enslavers' spatial — and thus racial — control: they developed communal living patterns in their quarters that prized sociability over the individual pursuit of status and power that had sent their enslavers scattering across the Southern landscape to construct their own plantation enterprises.[75]

The impulse to draw together was partly what drove refugees to the camps in the first place. There they would have a chance to build and restore social networks and to repair the damage wrought by enslavers who had broken up their families with the slave trade. "Mothers are having restored to them their children whom they never expected to see again this side of eternity," an AMA missionary at Camp Hamilton, near Hampton, Virginia, observed in 1862. "Wives are brought upon their knees in praise to God at the appearance of husbands, long ago torn from them and sold to the dreaded South."[76] This missionary mentioned only the nuclear family relations reunited in the camp, but cousins, aunts, uncles, grandparents, and many other relatives found one another in the camps too. That's because, in spite of the white officials' lamentations about damaged families, the emotional ties of family never disappeared under slavery, although those ties were far more expansive, and far more complex, than the nuclear families idealized by officials. Freedom, in the minds of refugees, promised to allow those extended family networks to share physical spaces, and to share all the social and emotional sustenance that this entailed.[77] What mattered was *who* was in the crowd—not how many. A "crowded" space could be very much a "free" space to a refugee from slavery.

And there were added pressures of war that made this sort of communalism even more desirable. Refugees faced new dangers in war zones: There were armed Confederates to contend with but also rogue Union soldiers, both of whom triggered fears about physical safety that could be alleviated, even in a small way, by knowing there were others close by who were ready to protect them. There was the danger posed by illness and disease that could be fought off more effectively (or at least more comfortably) with the care of those living around them. And then there was the additional danger facing those who had fled enslavers claiming to be Unionists, who could sometimes count on Union officials to send them back to slavery. In these cases, "crowding" offered anonymity, making it all the more difficult for officials to distinguish the enslaved of the Unionists from the enslaved of the Confederates. Close, physical proximity could thus offer multiple forms of security to a refugee from slavery: there was a degree of safety in numbers.

Nowhere was this more obviously expressed than in the refugees' migration into occupied cities. From Hampton and Norfolk, on the coast of Virginia, to Memphis, Vicksburg, and New Orleans, along the Mississippi River, the numbers of refugees soared, creating populations far larger than in any of the rural, planned settlements. Memphis, for example, witnessed the arrival of approximately 19,000 refugees by the fall of 1864; and in Norfolk that figure totaled 8,000.[78] The black population of Alexandria, Virginia, tripled to 8,000 during the war, while that of Washington, D.C., nearly doubled, from 14,000 to 27,000.[79] These same cities had been a draw for newly freed people before the war, too, thanks to the existence of social institutions like independent black churches and the promise of paid employment. This only continued in wartime, as cities offered possibilities for private employment—as barbers, porters, seamstresses, shoemakers, cooks, and waiters in hotels and family homes—that offered wages often higher than those paid by government positions.[80]

Yet the cities were also very much damaged spaces, with burned-out buildings, many without fronts or roofs, offering the only refuge for this rapidly expanding population.[81] "About fifteen thousand Freedmen are crowded into and around the city in shanties, smoke-houses, and other out buildings," came a Quaker report from Nashville, noting that in one house with a burned-out roof, "twenty colored families" were residing "with nothing more than an oil-cloth, or something of the kind, stretched over their beds as a shelter against snow and rain." And yet those families would not leave Nashville, the report noted, even as each one was reportedly paying eight to twelve dollars per month to rent the space (roughly one month's wages if they could obtain work from the army). Such were the "extortions" that residents of Nashville, either purportedly "loyal" whites or sometimes even other black people, were now charging.[82]

These refugees preferred the risk of extortion in the cities to the risk of en-countering the enslavers, patrollers, and rebels who roamed the countryside. "Not that they are averse to the soil—they love it," Professor William Wood-bury, an AMA missionary in Norfolk, explained to his colleagues surprised by the urban migration, "but they have just now a feeling of greater security in the city."[83] That feeling was well founded. Cities and larger towns were the most secure regions occupied by the Union army in the South, more so than the rural areas that could not be patrolled constantly by Federal forces.[84] The cities were heavily guarded by military patrols, and they were, in most instances, too formidable a target for Confederates to hope to reclaim. Militarily secure, the cities, in turn, offered a relative degree of security for the refugees' claim to freedom. And in these urban centers former slaves could experience the new privilege of moving freely through public spaces that were once associated with slave trading and the sale of cotton, tobacco, rice, and other commodities they had produced but had not profited from. In wartime they were no longer forced into urban spaces to be sold—but could freely enter the cities in the pursuit of safety from bondage.[85]

All those people crowding into cities offered more than added comfort and security, though: they also represented crucial sources of information, or in military terms, "intelligence," brought into the city from multiple points of origin, and sometimes, multiple states. AMA missionary Susan Drummond, writing from Portsmouth, Virginia, explained how this worked in the case of a woman who had resisted army efforts to move her to a rural camp nearby. The woman's husband and three of her five children had been "caried [sic] away and sold" since the war began, but "the hope of hearing something from her stolen ones induces her to remain in Town." Drummond explained this was a common impulse among the refugees around her, who, "not knowing how to read or write," have to rely on "verbal intelegence [sic] from each other by new arrivals in Town." The town or city became to refugees an information hub, a crucial nexus of oral information and communication that was all the more urgent to access in the chaos of wartime emancipation. "Hence," Drummond concluded, "so many wish to stay there although they have to wander about cold and hungry."[86] The information was too valuable to sacrifice for comfort; the more people they could gather around them, the more likely they would be to find someone who knew *something*.

Refugees could thus see freedom and progress in what white observers deemed disorderly "crowding," and for that reason, one AMA missionary in Virginia predicted, "there will be great reluctance on the part of the people to leave the city for any new or strange place."[87] The desire for physical safety, for reuniting family, and for the crucial information needed to secure both all worked to pull refugees together in concentrated ways in settlements across the occupied South. Yet urban living, and the impulse to congregate, cut against every other impulse expressed in the planned settlements to control the refugees' movements and to "order" their transition to freedom. Cities were disorderly spaces, in the imaginations of white missionaries and military officials, where people packed themselves into dilapidated spaces rather than being sorted neatly into individual houses. This push and pull never went away, for the tension between dispersal and crowding, between isolation and concentration, would remain for the rest of the war. After all, there was a lot at stake in the physical settlement of the refugee population: it was the spatial, and thus social, order of freedom.

} 3 {

Confronting Removal

"I object to massing the colored people together," declared the Union military governor of Tennessee and future president, Andrew Johnson, in 1863. "They should be scattered as much as possible among the whites," he continued, "because the influence of the whites upon them is beneficial, whereas the influences that surround them when congregated together are not calculated to elevate or improve them."[1] Johnson advocated for a form of racial integration that was of a highly paternalistic, white-supremacist form and certainly reminiscent of the plantation South. He did not elaborate on which "whites" were the best influences—apparently any would do—nor did his views engender the sort of unanimity he might have hoped for among other Union officials, many of whom preferred less proximity to black refugees rather than more. Yet they all considered the same question: How close to white people—to be specific, white soldiers—should the refugee settlements be allowed to get?

It was a question tied up in military logistics but one that also carried profound meaning for the transition to freedom itself. Where the refugees resided in relation to the army was tantamount to asking how they would relate to the army and to the Union cause—and to white people more generally. In spatial proximity there was social proximity, after all, and as the camps drew together people across racial, as well as class, gender, and generational, lines, it was no small thing to figure out how they should co-reside in space. It was, in fact, to confront one of the most enduring preoccupations in American race relations that would linger well beyond the Civil War: the search for particular residential patterns, for particular spatial organizations of people, that could control the interactions between the races.[2]

83

In the Civil War this became an especially pressing issue whenever military authorities sought to move refugee settlements around en masse, in wholesale removals from one place to another that were never entirely voluntary—and that at times resembled the devastating removals already experienced by Native people well before the war.[3] Though often prompted by immediate local circumstances, especially related to matters of wartime security, the removal efforts in the Civil War looked to the future, too, and they revealed a determination among white officials to seek what they believed was an ideal arrangement of people of different races across the vast space of the United States—and across its natural landscape. Particular environments and landforms, indeed, would play no small role in this effort to find the best fit between physical geography and racial order.[4]

Removal efforts might never have been attempted in the first place had women not comprised such a large proportion of the refugee population. Because what Union officials really had in mind when they thought about refugee-soldier proximity were particular refugees and particular soldiers in their midst: black women and white men. The refugee camps were new spaces that mixed races and genders (although white women, represented only by the occasional missionary or aid worker, remained a distinct minority, and in some places were nowhere to be seen). This was compounded in some regions where the army pulled black men away to the front as laborers or later as soldiers, leaving black women disproportionately dominant among the refugee population—and relatively alone to interact with any white men in their midst. In Holly Springs, Tennessee, in 1864, for example, 1,157 black women resided in a refugee camp along with 938 children, but only 228 black men were in residence there too.[5] At Vidalia, Louisiana, the year before, 600 black women and children lived with 70 black men, all of whom were categorized by the army as either aged or infirm.[6] That pattern was repeated across the South—and thus threw questions about race and gender to the forefront of the military's strategic thinking about the placement of refugee camps. Should black women and white male soldiers reside in the same places? How closely should they reside—or what sort of boundaries should exist between them? In their spatial coexistence, black female refugees and white soldiers thus triggered particular questions about gender, sex, and race in the new order of freedom.

This was a novel situation for some of the white soldiers. John T. Farnham, for example, a private in the 108th New York Regiment encamped near Uniontown, Virginia, in 1863, found the sight of a woman of color remarkable enough

Confronting Removal

to earn a spot in his private diary. First came the notation that "in a colored house saw cavalry man & black woman." The observation earned no further comment; the situation alone spoke for itself in Farnham's mind, either for the novelty of seeing a white man and a black woman together or for the intimacy implied by their position in the small "colored house." And it likely was a novel sight for a man who hailed from Monroe County, New York, where the population was 99 percent white in 1860. Then, about two weeks later, came his delight when he "saw colored half-blood woman with long black curls—splendid!"[7] Farnham's diary suggests he left it at that: fascination. But his comments also betray the way in which black women's bodies were on display in and around the refugee settlements, exposed for observation as well as for abuse and control.[8] These were places where a woman either worked for white soldiers or depended on them to defeat the Confederacy, leaving her body enormously vulnerable if one of these armed white men showed up at her door.

Across Hampton Roads from Farnham's Uniontown came reports in 1862 of a "horrid outrage from four soldiers" who appeared at a refugee home near Hampton "armed with sword and pistol." After forcing two men who lived there to leave, the white Union soldiers made their way inside "and then in turn violated a young woman who was there." One of the soldiers committed his rape "in presence of the family," and when the woman's father "uttered a groan" at the horrific scene, the soldiers "threatened to cut him to pieces." The events were later recounted by the woman's father and grandfather to AMA missionary Lewis Lockwood, who then advocated for the soldiers to be "identified and punished."[9] It is not clear if they ever were—but over time such incidents became too obvious, and too numerous, for military officials to ignore. Six months later, the assistant superintendent of contrabands at nearby Fort Monroe, Charles E. Brown, wrote to his military superiors about confronting "intruders" in the quarters of refugee women—the men were military guards who had left their official posts and were instead "interfering with the women." One of the guards followed a woman inside her residence, "annoying her and threatening her with the guard house, if she did not keep still." Brown, summoned by the husband of another woman nearby, confronted the guard, filed a report the next day, and two days later, the soldiers sat confined to the guardhouse, waiting to be tried by court-martial.[10]

Behind the euphemisms for sexual assault that appear in the records— "disturbance," "outrage," "illicit intercourse"—was a real effort by military officials to acknowledge and punish soldiers guilty of rape.[11] The case remanded to court-martial at Fort Monroe, in fact, would have been one of the earliest of its kind; it was later that year, in the spring of 1863, that the Union, through its new code of laws (the "Lieber Code"), first authorized the use of the court-martial process to prosecute soldiers accused of raping women. This enabled women, including African American women for the first time in their lives, to seek legal protections against rape, which they did by the hundreds. The court-martial trials acknowledged that sexual assault was a crime against women — *and* a crime against military discipline. To impose military order again in this case — to restore "the efficiency of the troops," as one Fort Monroe official put it — would thus simultaneously defend the bodily rights of black women.[12]

And along with prosecution came efforts at prevention too. The physical proximity between white soldiers and black women had made rape possible, even inevitable, officials believed, for it too easily allowed men "promiscuous admission" into refugee residences. Reports of rape routinely emphasized that white men were "intruders," violating not just the bodies of their victims, but also the domestic spaces in which the women and their families resided.[13] They violated the sanctity of a woman's marriage; they rendered black men, either fathers or husbands, powerless to protect the women; and they forced children, in some cases, to witness the brutal violence. Rape enacted a full-fledged assault on freed people's domestic spaces, and thus on their entire claim to a place in freedom. It also violated white officials' idealized vision of family homes as the essential spaces for nurturing the values and character they associated with freedom.[14] Rape was thus a spatial problem — made possible by the proximity of space, made all the more horrific by the violation of space — that required a rethinking of the way in which black women and white men co-existed in the camps.

This was a point with which even the least sympathetic white military officials could agree. Some of them did not see rape in their midst, preferring instead to view a black woman as the cause, rather than the victim, of a white soldier's lapsed discipline, or to interpret an assault as something more like prostitution — both assumptions fueled by racist stereotypes that black women were sexually promiscuous.[15] But even these officials could agree that the camps had a problem of proximity (or "a most loathsome intercourse between the army and these camps").[16] These reactions resonated with many other white Northerners at the time who harbored suspicions that consensual race mixing — or "miscegenation," a term coined during the war — would be the logical outcome of emancipation, thus diluting racial difference and undermining white supremacy. The problem of space in the refugee camps, then, channeled wide-ranging yet intensely felt beliefs about the sexually charged nature of race relations that would persist well into the future.[17]

The answer, officials increasingly concluded, was in separation — in placing physical distance between the refugees' homes and the soldiers' encampments. At Fort Monroe, Gen. John Dix ordered in 1863 that from that point on, "negroe [sic] quarters should be at a distance from the camps of White soldiers whenever possible, on account of the frequent intercourse between negresses and soldiers."[18] But how much distance should be between them? Col. John Eaton, grappling with the same question as superintendent of freedmen in the Mississippi Valley, surveyed the various camps under his jurisdiction and developed some measures of proper distance. Of Corinth, Mississippi, he reported, "Location good—half mile from any troops"; even better was a camp outside of Memphis with "no soldiers near," as the closest were two miles away. In some places, distance was only an aspiration: "As far as possible, separate from troops." And those that had not achieved any real separation at all suffered the consequences, such as the camp at Providence, Tennessee, that was "in the midst of town and troops—great evils resulting."[19] Achieving the ideal distance was tricky: proximity had always been associated with army protection, so how could some of that proximity be sacrificed without abandoning the army's duty to protect?

"In order to remove the contraband women and children from contact with the camps—a contact injurious to both," General Dix wrote to Sec. Edwin Stanton in December 1862, "they have been transferred to Craney Island."[20] This was Dix's answer in Virginia; Craney Island was a strip of land about a quarter of a mile wide and three-quarters of a mile long, located about ten miles south of Fort Monroe. Early in the war it had been a Confederate fortification; now, in Dix's imagination, it would become a protected island of racially segregated freedom. During a two-day stretch in late November 1862, the removal went forward as 1,000 black men, women, and children from Hampton, Fort Monroe, and Newport News boarded the steamer *Express* and set out across Hampton Roads.[21] They arrived to discover a nearly barren island containing old wooden barracks that could house roughly half of them; the rest, having just been removed from the houses they built for themselves on the mainland, would now have to start over again in tents.[22]

Over 28,000 other refugees joined the Craney Island migrants on island settlements across the South during the war.[23] Some of them settled on a string of barrier islands along the coasts of Georgia and the Carolinas known as the Sea Islands, which would be unique from the rest of the island settlements in the fact that the refugees on them were largely native to the islands already. All of the rest of the island settlements were like Craney Island: the deliberate creation of Union authorities seeking to resettle refugees somewhere distant from military operations. Refugees from the western states of Tennessee, Arkansas,

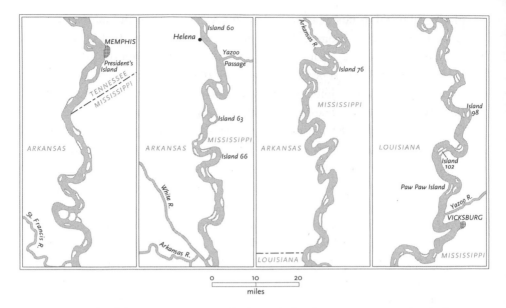

MAP 5. Eight of the Mississippi River islands to which refugees were removed and where new camps were established. Island No. 10, to the north of Memphis, is not indicated. (Pauer Center for Cartography & GIS, University of Kentucky)

Mississippi, and Missouri boarded boats headed toward a series of nine small islands in the Mississippi River, numbered sequentially going south from the point where the Mississippi intersects with the Ohio River—from Island 10, at a tight bend of the river between New Madrid, Missouri, and the Kentucky-Tennessee border, to Island 103, also known as Paw Paw Island, located sixteen miles above Vicksburg, Mississippi (map 5). Most of these islands were uninhabited at the start of the war and required shelters to be built there from the ground up by the refugees. That was after they were taken there largely by military force, as none of them had sought out the islands as a refuge for themselves.

Union officials across the occupied South envisioned the islands as the ideal solution to the problem of racial proximity. General Dix believed there was a natural fit between the isolation of an island and his desire to isolate the refugees from the "prejudicial influences" of white soldiers.[24] Officials in the Mississippi River valley likewise shared his concerns but also emphasized the problem of protecting refugees from roving Confederates. "Humanity said, place them were [sic] they will be protected from guerrillas," explained Col. Samuel Thomas in a report, and for that reason "islands were selected."[25] The commander in Helena, Arkansas, on the western bank of the river, also searching

Confronting Removal

around for a place to resettle the refugees whom he deemed to be "in danger," concluded that "the large Islands in the river appear to be the most suitable."[26] The islands' natural isolation, in which surrounding waters could take the place of military guards, would, they believed, protect refugees from the dangers of white soldiers everywhere, both Union and Confederate. The islands would also serve the additional purpose of dispersing urban settlements, since most of the islands were located near cities like Memphis, Helena, and Vicksburg. As one official in the Mississippi Valley put it, "The difficulty of access would be such that the colored people could be kept in camp and not be able to go so easily into the city."[27]

But even the island landscape required human intervention to ensure that its "natural" barriers would truly act as barriers. Waterways could of course be crossed, especially in the shallow areas, leading authorities to take measures to block easy trespass. "As the Contrabands are many of them refugees from Mississippi and Arkansas, you are liable to a raid from either shore to reenslave them," read one such order. "You will guard against attack by vigilance and defend your post to the last extremity."[28] The islands, then, would still have some soldiers on them — but a limited number, focused almost entirely on guarding the shores. They were to make sure to "prohibit any intercourse between the Island and the Eastern shore," as authorities on Island 60 were ordered.[29] In some cases this included explicit orders about the use of boats. The superintendent on Island 66, for example, was ordered not to prop his boat on the shore of the island but instead have it "moored in the Stream at a safe distance," lest it be taken and used to paddle away.[30] On Craney Island, General Dix's subordinates confiscated the small boats that a few of the refugees possessed.[31] Orders like these betrayed a concern not just that white soldiers might approach the islands — but that the refugees themselves might leave. And thus, a removal justified as an exercise of military "protection" could simultaneously enact far more serious and profound restrictions on the movement — and thus the freedom — of refugees.

The island isolation experienced by the refugees could indeed be profound. During the removal to Craney Island, AMA missionary John Oliver observed "a Mother . . . just passing with her daughter of 13 years upon her Shoulder, and a gard [sic] behind forcing her on."[32] The woman's reluctance, like that of other women, could very well have had to do with what she had to leave behind — not only her shelter but also the men with whom she may have shared it, such as a husband, a father, uncles, or brothers. Only men deemed "infirm" or "aged" were sent to the island, while "able-bodied" men were ordered to remain on the mainland to continue working for the army. Removal was an act that pulled apart refugee families, even those newly reunited after years or decades of separation. Military officials elsewhere may have supported, even promoted, the housing of these families together in planned settlements like Uniontown or Freedman's Village, but here the axe of military necessity fell hard and fast on such families — and the choice of some officials to wield it did not go unnoticed. "The separation of families," a disapproving Union official on the scene remarked, "is of itself a serious evil."[33] Compounding this were the significant numbers who died during the removal, making their family separations permanent.[34]

Yet the extent of the refugees' isolation was more than social or emotional. It was economic too. Separated from the wages of laboring men, the refugees on Craney Island also had little chance to labor for themselves. "The island is too small to give employment in agriculture," a report of New York Quakers in the region concluded.[35] General Dix had assured Sec. Edwin Stanton that he envisioned the refugees earning wages "in picking oakum, fishing, &c."[36] But this was hardly a sufficient plan. Picking oakum, which involved pulling fibrous threads piece by piece out of old rope, was the sort of hard labor to which inmates were often subjected in prisons and workhouses.[37] And fishing was a "limited resource," observed the local Quakers, compounded by the government's seizure of boats.[38] Without means of steady labor, the island's residents had no choice but to rely on the army for food and support. And this, in the mind of AMA missionary John Oliver, threatened not only their individual paths toward freedom, but the entire project of emancipation itself. "Craney Island . . . is the place to which all opposition at Washington to the emancipation proclamation will turn its eye," Oliver wrote in a public letter published in the New York *Anglo-African*. "The banding together of these people to be fed by Government . . . will retard its progress," he wrote, for surely Democratic critics "will not forget this place."[39]

The secretary of war did not forget about it. One month after the Craney Island removal, and after receiving a series of reports about it, Stanton dispatched LeBaron Russell, a Boston physician who was involved with sending Northern teachers to the South, to examine the situation. Russell's subsequent report agreed with Oliver and noted that "a persistence in this scheme must interfere with the growth of those ideas of self-reliance . . . which it is most important to cultivate by every means among these people."[40] Craney Island was simply too isolating — and the removal was too self-defeating for a federal government demanding that former slaves get on a self-sufficient path to freedom. In response, the island would be officially abandoned as refugee settlement by the end of 1863, although some refugees had already removed themselves by that point by seeking military passes from government officials and sheltering themselves with any family they could find still living on the mainland.[41] Union officials did not give up on island settlements—but officials would take some of the lessons of Craney Island with them into the future.

Around the time that Craney Island was abandoned, an island in the Mississippi River near Helena, Arkansas, known as Island 63 was "selected by the Secretary of War for a contraband camp, where it is hoped, by the cutting and sale of wood, they may become self supporting."[42] The island seemed ideal from the secretary's vantage point in Washington: it was heavily forested with cottonwood trees, which could be cut into supplies of wood and then sold to power the commercial and military steamboats traveling up and down the river.[43] With a special dispensation from a local commander that enabled boats "wanting to purchase wood" to approach the island, the refugees transported to Island 63 from Helena quickly got to work erecting huts for themselves and chopping wood for the riverboats.[44] They used the wagon teams they had brought with them from their plantations, something the quartermaster's department allowed in order to spare the government the expense of getting this enterprise under way. Men then headed out into the wooded areas to chop and haul the logs back into a woodyard, where women were waiting to unload and then cord it in preparation for sale. The same scene was repeated on six other Mississippi River islands by the end of 1864, and collectively, over 1,000 refugees on these islands produced over 60,000 cords of wood that year. Most of this was sold at below-market rates, although the army impressed some of the wood, too, which the superintendent of freedmen chose to refer to as a "clean gift from the negroes to the Government."[45]

Island 63 was considered a bright spot in the wood-chopping island chain, nicknamed the "Gem of the Mississippi" by Union officials boasting of its success.[46] Adj. Gen. Lorenzo Thomas sent word to Secretary Stanton that it had become "entirely self-supporting" by September 1864, which meant that refugees were now using the proceeds to pay for their own rations, tools, and wages.[47] Not only that, but the island had also become "self-governing," according to a visiting Quaker, by which he meant that the refugees had adopted "certain rules for themselves," which their white superintendent was charged with enforcing.[48] The island fulfilled many of the visions of white Union officials—it was isolated, it housed families together, and it made money—and for some, it was like a colonization dream come true (indeed, it would be referred to routinely as a "little colony" or "self-supporting colony").[49] Island 63 appeared to Union authorities to have perfected the island vision for freedom.

Except that eighteen months after its establishment, this "gem" of a settlement disappeared. It had gone "completely under water," observed a writer for the *Freedmen's Bulletin*, for the island that seemed environmentally suited to cultivate self-sufficiency had proven itself environmentally suited to disaster too. Humans likely played a role in bringing it on: the cutting of the island's trees may have rendered the island more vulnerable to flooding, and thus, what had been envisioned as a self-sustaining island of freedom was washed away in an instant by the very waters that were supposed to isolate and protect it. The Island 63 refugees, about 250 in total by this point, were put on a ship and ordered thirty-five miles north to Helena, which was itself flood ravaged but in the process of being rebuilt on higher ground.[50] Other camps along the riverbanks and on the islands were similarly evacuated in early 1865 thanks to flooding, which in some cases also had to do with the Union army's destruction of the levees.[51] The flooding made brutally clear how ephemeral the refugee camps could be, no matter how supported and ordered they were by the Union government and its officials. "How long these carefully planned enterprises are permitted to shield the poor unfortunate freedmen from oppression and want," observed an army chaplain in the Mississippi Valley, "depends entirely upon the chances of war."[52]

The "chances of war" involved environmental surprises like floods, to be sure, but more often than not it was a sudden turn in combat, and the recalculation of military necessity it prompted, that snatched away the refugees' settlements. Take, for example, those areas where the numbers of Union soldiers rapidly increased in advance of an upcoming campaign. The refugees at Fort Monroe had witnessed this just before the Peninsula campaign in the spring of 1862, when the vast increase in the number of soldiers created a new competition for space that the refugees almost always lost (or that "military necessity" always won). "We are having an *immense* influx of soldiers & everything goes by the board," an AMA missionary summed it up. "Coloured people are being removed from almost everything."[53] In Helena, Arkansas, visiting Quakers lamented two years later that "they get settled in a place, build a little hut, make a little garden, and in hundreds of cases have to leave immediately; they thus become discouraged."[54] Such removals were nothing less than "one of the most sanguine violations of human rights of which a Christian could be guilty," declared a missionary near Yorktown, Virginia.[55] They were also testaments to the force of military necessity, as the same army that could commit itself to the task of providing shelter could also take it away the instant soldiers appeared to need it.

The most severe "chances of war," however, were those inflicted by enemy forces that sought out and destroyed any refugee settlements they encountered. This happened in Tunnel Hill, Tennessee, in the fall of 1864, at about the time when 1,400 men, women, and children had just gotten settled. Located eight miles from Pulaski, in the south central part of the state, the camp was built on the property of a white man named Thomas J. Brown, who had fled his property with the arrival of the Union army. Brown's sixty-three enslaved people did not flee but remained behind to transform the land of their enslavement into one of emancipation, and by the summer of 1864, over 1,000 more joined them from other parts of Tennessee as well as northern Alabama. Together they built a village of 240 houses and planted cotton, corn, and vegetables to feed and support themselves in the year ahead. But before that harvest could be completed and taken to market, in late September 1864, Confederate cavalry led by Gen. Nathan Bedford Forrest set its sights on the camp at Tunnel Hill. The Confederates were only six or seven miles away when Union authorities sent a warning to the refugees and ordered them to leave immediately and make their way north to Union-occupied Nashville. Piling tools, looms, spinning wheels, and cotton bales into their wagons, the refugees set off on foot, on the backs of mules, or, in the case of children, in any remaining spaces in the wagons or simply in their mothers' arms. They wound their way through Middle Tennessee for three to four days before reaching Nashville, although some of the children never made it, succumbing to illness and fatigue along the way. Then, four months later, they were relocated again, removed from the city and settled on a plantation fifteen miles down the Tennessee River from Nashville.[56]

The refugees from Tunnel Hill had, for the most part, managed to flee and protect their bodies from assault. They had even protected some of their property. But the one thing they left behind, and that all refugees would be forced to leave behind when enemy forces came, was their shelter. Marauding Confederates wasted little time ripping apart and torching the structures at Tunnel Hill—and did so with consistency across the occupied South. From Plymouth and Washington, North Carolina, to Island 10 in the Mississippi River, to Huntsville, Alabama, no settlement in the path of the rebels was safe, not even the places that were the most planned and were envisioned to be relatively permanent, ordered spaces.[57] In early 1864 it was Corinth, Mississippi, called "the most satisfactory camp in the department," from which 2,500 refugees were evacuated after fifteen months of the camp's existence when Union general William T. Sherman's campaign to Meridian drew Union troops out of the region. ("The order fell like a bomb-shell among our contented people," a minister there reported. "But military orders are preemptory, and without a reason why, must be obeyed.")[58] Uniontown, the planned settlement in eastern Virginia, was destroyed after just over a year, when the nearby town of Suffolk became the target of a Confederate siege in April 1863, forcing the Union, including 1,300 refugees, to evacuate and leave behind the town's neatly ordered houses.[59] The rebels knew full well what the destruction of those shelters would mean to the refugees. These were practical losses but symbolic ones too: to have enemy forces destroy their new homes was to destroy their place in Union lines, to stop their journey to freedom in its tracks.

It was in light of this ever-present danger that both refugees and Union officials began looking outward, beyond the lines of the wartime South and its islands, for other locations that might welcome the mass resettlement of refugees. It took little stretch of the imagination to look northward to the free states, for that was, after all, the region to which enslaved people themselves had long moved through the Underground Railroad. This movement continued during the first couple years of the war, although this time army steamers retraced the routes of the antebellum journeys with an estimated "tens of thousands" of refugees. They moved largely through two official channels: from Virginia to points northeast, such as Philadelphia and New York; and from the Mississippi Valley to St. Louis or Cairo, Illinois, which both served as way stations, holding refugees in camps before dispersing them farther north into places like Keokuk, Iowa, or Chicago to work in industries or on farms.[60] These relocations did not just remove refugees from the South but also eschewed the spatial patterns that had been taking hold there; there would be almost no concentrated colonies or camps or villages established in the Northern free states, but instead, according to most plans, the refugees were to be scattered and integrated into existing communities, sometimes into individual households "with farmers families," as one order put it.[61]

Andrew Johnson may have once expressed support for such a dispersed arrangement—but that support was anything but widespread. Removals to the North were most popular among Union military officials, particularly local commanders, who were, at best, overwhelmed by the task of protecting refugees or, at worst, unwilling to make this work a priority of their military command. Plans to resettle refugees in the North thus removed a problem, an encumbrance, or as Gen. John Dix wrote from Fort Monroe, a "great source of embarrassment." Dix himself received authorization from the secretary of war in the fall of 1862, during the troubled aftermath of the Peninsula campaign, to open discussions with Northern governors about shipping refugees to their states. Dix drafted letters to nine state executives but focused his attention on

Massachusetts in particular, as it seemed, by virtue of the state's abolitionism and its antislavery Republican governor, John Andrew, to be a place amenable to taking refugees off his hands. Dix wrote Andrew directly, claiming his request was both a military necessity *and* a move animated by humanitarianism: the removal would protect refugees at the fort from any future Confederate attack by getting them out of the war-torn South.[62]

"I do not concur in any way or to any degree in the plan proposed," Governor Andrew replied. And that was from a man recently installed as president of the Educational Commission for Freedmen, a Boston organization that provided relief and support for newly freed people. To start with, Andrew did not buy the argument that refugees were unsafe in the South. "If you are attacked," he wrote to Dix, "let the blacks fight to preserve their freedom!" (In this martial spirit, Andrew would later raise regiments of black soldiers, including the famed Fifty-Fourth Massachusetts Regiment.) And Andrew's humanitarianism also drew him to the opposite conclusion from Dix's — that the lives of refugees would be *more* endangered, rather than less, by removal to the North. "The Northern States are, of all places, the worst possible to select for an asylum," he argued, for ex-slaves are "inhabitants of a Southern climate," possessing a "physical constitution" nurtured in warmth that could not withstand "the rigors of our Northern Sky." Andrew thus rejected the removal plan "precisely because I do not wish the Negroes to suffer."[63] There was something natural, something environmentally determined, about keeping former slaves in their native South, Andrew argued.

And in this belief Andrew was not alone among white Northerners. "They are as a people very sensitive to the cold," one missionary in Norfolk put it bluntly the next year.[64] Likewise, a published appeal of the Contraband Relief Commission in Cincinnati declared that the "laws of climate and their own constitution" made it difficult for blacks to endure cold weather.[65] Both statements reiterated a prevailing racist belief in nineteenth-century America, one often attributed to proslavery thinkers but nonetheless more widely spread among white people, even among abolitionists: that there was a relationship between skin color and weather tolerance, race and climate. Thomas Jefferson famously reasoned in "Notes on the State of Virginia" that the way blacks perspired made them "more tolerant of heat, and less so of cold, than the whites."[66] The belief that Americans of African descent were better suited to hot climates became a staple justification for enslaving them; the idea that they could not endure the cold temperatures of the North was simply its converse.[67] And it enabled men like Governor Andrew to imagine the North as "free" — but not open — to a new population of freed people.

This seemed like a crucial point to make for a Northern political leader with an emancipation agenda. The destruction of slavery became more palatable to white constituents like Andrew's if they could be reassured that it would not bring what they feared most—the mass migration of black people to the North. "Many people fear that if the slaves should gain their freedom, they would swarm at the North. Don't you believe it," Henry Ward Beecher, one of the North's most prominent abolitionist lecturers, summed up public sentiment back in 1861. "The black face was made to kiss the sun, and the North Pole is not suited to the skin of the blacks." To Beecher, popular beliefs about race and climate could offer reassurance to whites that freedom for the enslaved would not permanently alter the racial makeup of Northern society. And what he really meant was that they would not come north to compete for employment or to intermarry with white people, as was widely feared. They did not want to come, Beecher promised; and they should not come, argued John Andrew in his letter to Dix. Never mind that generations of enslaved people had explicitly chosen to flee to some of the coldest climates around, not just to the North but also to Canada, while fleeing slavery through the Underground Railroad.[68]

John Andrew would have been especially sensitive to these fears at the time General Dix reached out about removal plans. A November election was coming up, and Andrew, like other Republicans sympathetic to emancipation, knew full well that his opponents, especially the Democrats, would seize on military removal plans like this one as concrete evidence that the worst fears of the Northern white public were about to come true.[69] Northern politics thus doomed the military removal plans—and not just in Virginia, but in the Mississippi Valley too. In fall 1862, Sec. Edwin Stanton also yielded to the complaints by suspending removals from Arkansas to Cairo, Illinois; although the removals would resume in 1863 for a time, by the fall of that year he shut down the system altogether. Gen. N. B. Buford, the commander at Helena, became frustrated by the secretary's actions, noting that Stanton "refused" his latest request in November, "saying the Government intends to keep them South."[70] For good measure, state political leaders in Illinois, Pennsylvania, Wisconsin, and Minnesota proposed and debated new state exclusion laws that would outlaw the migration of black people into their states.[71] All of this largely curtailed the official transport of refugees en masse, although private organizations took up this work and individual refugees still sometimes found it possible to secure passes from local military commanders, who, of all Union officials, remained the most open to the idea of northern migration.[72]

Similar assumptions about race and climate wound their way into proposals to remove refugees to warmer places too. The superintendent of contrabands at Fort Monroe, Charles Wilder, once suggested Florida as an ideal location, while others looked beyond the nation's borders to British Honduras, Costa Rica, and Haiti. These were the sorts of places that advocates of colonization—the resettlement of newly freed slaves in regions beyond the nation's borders—had long imagined as a "natural" destination for people of African descent. Beginning in the aftermath of the War of 1812, with the founding of the American Colonization Society, such schemes appealed to those whites who feared what the end of slavery would bring and who could not imagine a postslavery social order based on racial integration and equality within the same geographic space. Physical distance would have to be placed between the races—and newly freed slaves would have to be removed elsewhere, far elsewhere. The Civil War revived this interest in colonization for a time, although with a new impetus behind it; it was, for its advocates, a safety valve, a practical outlet for what Union officials believed was an overpopulation of refugees. It was a relief for the army—in other words, they argued, a military necessity.[73]

The most serious efforts surrounded attempts to remove refugees to Haiti. This idea surfaced very early, within two weeks of Benjamin Butler's original "contraband" order in 1861, when the general received an appeal from Montgomery Blair, the postmaster general and an ardent colonizationist, urging him to consider the scheme. At the same time, James Redpath, a longtime antislavery activist and devotee of colonization, tried to persuade Secretary of War Stanton in those early weeks to send the "contraband articles," as he called them, to the island nation.[74] These early appeals did not gain much traction until later in the year, when President Lincoln endorsed colonization in an address to Congress in December, and Congress went on to appropriate funds for the initiatives the following year.[75]

African American opposition to colonization, however, had always been widely felt, citing deep attachments to the United States. "This is our native country," was how one group of free people in New York summed up that sentiment during the war. Frederick Douglass also spoke out against the wartime colonization efforts by attempting to blunt the argument that such removals were somehow "natural" or environmentally determined. "The negro has withstood under the most unfavorable conditions the rigors of this North American climate, for the space of more than two hundred years," Douglass argued in his *Douglass Monthly* newspaper in 1862. "If any people can ever become acclimatized, I think the negro can claim to be so in this country."[76] To remove refugees to Haiti would not fulfill any kind of natural destiny—and it was not the first inclination of black people themselves.

That is why it is all the more remarkable that some refugees did become interested in the idea of colonization in and around Fort Monroe by early 1862. It was at precisely the time when they had pushed back against unpaid wages and seized property—the same time when Gen. John Wool commissioned a study of their situation—and were thus disillusioned with the "protection" offered by U.S. authorities. Haiti seemed more attractive in that context, the AMA missionary Lewis Lockwood explained, and they became convinced "that there & there alone they will be free from annoyance." At this particular moment and place, colonization was a last resort—which is why, when Gen. John Wool then issued new orders in March 1862 to begin paying refugees fully for their labor, the interest in Haiti quickly died down.[77] A refugee's willingness to listen to a plan for removal to Haiti was a measure of his or her disenchantment with the Union army.

This could be seen again the following year at Fort Monroe, in the spring of 1863, after President Lincoln signed a colonization contract with two New York financiers, who were working with a shady entrepreneur named Bernard Kock. Kock sent two agents to Fort Monroe, including a free black man named William Watkins, whose mission it was to sign up refugees for removal to Île à Vache, an island off the coast of Haiti. It was an ostensibly voluntary effort— at least Lincoln wanted it that way—although it is hard to know for sure, in a military context where officials were eager to remove refugees, whether coercion played a role too. The agents were full of promises: that anyone who set sail for Île à Vache would first board a boat for Washington, D.C., where they would have the opportunity to meet the president; and that upon disembarking, they each would be given a fifty-dollar lump sum, a house, employment at a rate of ten dollars per month, and access to schools. The agents made an appealing pitch. The whole arrangement was presented "very prettily," according to Thomas Peake, a black resident of Hampton who wrote to AMA officials in New York seeking "the other side"—in other words, any known "disadvantages" to removal to Île à Vache. Peake suspected that the whole scheme sounded too good to be true. And he was right.[78]

Not long after 450 men, women, and children boarded a ship in April 1863, they realized something was not right. The boat failed to go to Washington, which was the first sign that the promises would be broken. "Soon after we had embarked on the vessel and sailed we had suspicions that we were deceived by our pretended friend, Watkins," some of those on board later recounted.

Any money they had brought with them was stolen by the crew of the ship, and upon arrival, they found themselves forced to sign unfavorable labor contracts, under penalty of being put in stocks and beaten. In the weeks ahead, living conditions in this hot, sandy, wet climate involved battling insects and disease, and within a year, 10 percent of the migrants had died (giving the lie to racist beliefs that they would thrive in a warm climate). Word made it back to Washington, though, in part through a petition sent by some of the Île à Vache migrants, and by February 1864 Lincoln ordered a government transport to pick up the refugees and bring them to Freedman's Village, one of the planned settlements in Northern Virginia.[79] This marked the moment when federal government–sponsored colonization schemes for ex-slaves would finally end, once and for all.

The failure at Île à Vache was merely the most dramatic—and deadly—attempt at the organized removal of refugees from the South. And it revealed, just like other efforts that directed ex-slaves to the Northern states, a basic fact about the refugees' own geographical attachments: that they were reluctant, if not entirely opposed, to being shipped off to unfamiliar, distant regions. They made this clear at times when the military found it necessary to use force to get them to move, as well as in conversations with officials, who frequently remarked on their preferences. "The most of them do not desire to go North," observed Benjamin Butler just two months after issuing his original contraband order.[80] "They do not seem inclined to scatter in the North" and "they do not want to move northward" appeared in the reports of various missionaries the next year.[81] Observations like these expressed some puzzlement on the part of those working with ex-slaves: Why would someone seeking liberation from slavery be averse to leaving the region associated with their bondage?

"Their local attachments are strong" was how the superintendent on Roanoke Island, Horace James, summed it up. "The climate and country they have always known are preferred by them to any other." Though James, while testifying before a federal commission in 1863, sought to reassure Northerners, once again, that ex-slaves did not want to come north ("Let all the Irish laborers rest assured of this"), he also tried to convey what seemed like a genuine and deeply rooted preference among refugees. "Although they regard the northern people as their true friends, and the southern people as their oppressors and natural enemies," he continued, "they will never leave the South if they can be protected here in the employment of freedom." But he stopped there, not yet able to explain *why* they were so unwilling to leave the South.[82] Others tried. "The negro is passionately attached to his home and family," observed a Northern Quaker visiting Virginia in 1862. And that "attachment to home" should be understood and honored by the Union. "It makes any scheme of forced migration a cruel addition to the outrageous injustice which the black race in this country has so long already suffered at the hands of the whites." Enslaved people had always been forced to migrate during the slave trade, whether across the Atlantic, or from the upper to lower South, or from plantation to plantation. Now, this writer urged, their freedom should require that white Americans respect their attachments to place and not force any more migrations.[83]

The South was their "home," in this writer's words, the place they had always known and where their families and communities had taken root, even in the most trying of circumstances. Former slaves may have sought distance from the particular places of their enslavement when running to Union lines, to be sure, but there was a limit to the distance they would accept. Moving too far away threatened to sever them from the people and the land to which they were attached; those same ties, in fact, likely played a role in keeping many other enslaved people from fleeing to Union lines in the first place.[84] Their preference for "home" and for the South could thus circumscribe the movements of refugees. And it raised a pressing question: How could they find a place in freedom, and be able to keep it and not lose it, while remaining in the wartime South? The answer: they would have to fight for it.

Eliza Bogan in Slavery

"They tell me I was born in N.C.," Eliza Bogan recalled many years after the war, "but I was brought to this country before I was old enough to remember it."[1] "This country" was the Mississippi River valley, specifically Phillips County, Arkansas, along the western bank of the river. She was taken there as an infant by her owner, an acquisitive planter named Josiah McKiel, who in the early 1830s had uprooted his thirty-three slaves and six members of his white family in order to stake a claim in the rapidly growing "Cotton Kingdom."[2] McKiel brought Eliza's sister, Hester, with him too. But the historical record is silent on whether their parents, who had already been forced across the Atlantic by the slave trade, went with them — or whether they were left behind.[3]

McKiel, for his part, left behind a reputation in Chowan County, North Carolina, a coastal section of the state along the Albemarle Sound. He was a political leader there, serving two years in North Carolina's House of Commons in 1826 and 1828, although little evidence survives to suggest his service was anything other than ordinary.[4] And it did not keep him from landing in a courtroom in 1829, standing before the justices of the Chowan County Superior Court. There he stood accused of excessive brutality against two enslaved men, identified only as "Dover" and "Isaac," whose labor he had hired out from a neighbor. The details of the incident — or incidents — did not make it into the court record, but the case clearly singled out McKiel as one of the county's most violent slave owners.[5] That was no small feat, given that it was in the same county, around the very same time, that one of the more notorious instances of brutality toward an enslaved woman took place and later attracted national attention. In the county seat of Edenton, Harriet Jacobs endured unrelenting sexual abuse by her enslaver, James Norcum, before escaping in 1835 and hiding in a crawl space for seven years. She eventually made her way to New York, where she wrote an account of her ordeal that stands today as one of the most important and widely read accounts of slavery written by a woman, *Incidents in the Life of a Slave Girl*.[6]

While Jacobs scored a long-term victory in the court of public opinion, it was McKiel who proved victorious in the Chowan County courts. As in so many Southern courtrooms, where the enslaved were barred from testifying against white people and where the enslaver's fate lay in the hands of his slave-holding peers, the result was nearly predetermined: McKiel was found not guilty.[7]

By 1833, McKiel moved his operation out of North Carolina and headed west. A new start, as well as a thriving cotton economy, awaited him in eastern Arkansas, along with "Great Bargains for Planters," as a local paper headlined lists of available land parcels.[8] Like the other white migrants streaming in from Virginia, the Carolinas, Tennessee, and Alabama, McKiel reestablished himself on the flat alluvial lands that fanned out to the west for miles along the Mississippi River.[9] And although McKiel's enterprise immediately had to weather two global financial panics in 1837 and 1839 that sent cotton prices plummeting, by 1860 his holdings eventually stretched out over 3,667 acres of land in Phillips County.[10] Excursions into the nearby river port town of Helena likely included stops at the slave auctions held on the courthouse steps (just across Main Street from "Planters Hotel"), since McKiel managed to nearly double his ownership of enslaved people to a total of sixty by 1860.[11] His journey to Arkansas thus proved to be nothing less than a cotton South success story.[12]

But behind McKiel's tremendous gain was the tremendous loss felt by each and every one of the people enslaved on his plantation. Eliza Bogan would have known that feeling well, as she came of age in Arkansas and was forced to become a field hand, carrying a sack across row after row of the McKiel cotton fields, all day long and into the night. She spent her days bent over, straining her back and irritating her fingers, picking boll after boll until they added up to her daily quota, which on some Mississippi Valley plantations could be as much as 200–250 pounds. Enslaved people like her had little choice but to comply or else be whipped, shocked, or branded at the hands of an overseer.[13] McKiel, though, dispensed with an overseer and preferred to take such matters into his own hands.[14]

Bogan lost even more over the course of the 1850s. Early in the decade she started a family when she married a fellow slave named Ben Houston and gave birth to their first child. A great deal of promise must have surrounded Bogan's transition to wife and mother—not the promise of freedom, but the promise of an emotional sanctuary from the toil and violence of her daily life. Yet that promise died quickly with the death of Ben Houston, whose passing is not explained in the historical record but is not surprising, given how slavery prematurely killed so many others; the estimated life expectancy for a slave by 1860 was thirty-two to thirty-six years.[15]

Sometime after Houston's death, Bogan then married Isom Patterson, a man enslaved on another plantation two miles away from the McKiel property. "I lived with Isom Patterson as his wife[.] I know it was a good while," she later recalled, although their relationship would not last either. "I lived with him long enough to have six children by him before Dr. Patterson took him away."[16] Patterson's owner moved him sometime in the late 1850s to Desha County, which bordered Phillips County to the south and was far enough away to effectively end the marriage.[17] "I was not divorced from Isom Patterson," Bogan stated, because "in those days there were no laws for colored people to get divorces."[18] But she no longer considered herself married either. By 1860 Bogan had given birth to seven children—and McKiel had gained seven new slaves—but she had also experienced great losses to her family.[19]

The loss of two husbands may have been cushioned by other relationships Bogan managed to forge in and around her neighborhood. She still had her children; her sister, Hester; Hester's daughter, Nancy; and the sixty other people enslaved on the plantation.[20] But just as important was the larger neighborhood in which the McKiel property was located, a set of five plantations knit together by various marriages and other blood ties among both the white and black residents. Thirteen other enslaved people lived on a property owned by Gideon Steele, a white man who had come to Phillips County from Alabama; four on the property of Florence Sullivan, originally from Indiana; and thirty-seven on the property of Monroe Bogan, a native of South Carolina.[21] Most significant to Eliza Bogan were the ties that bound the McKiel property to the seventeen enslaved people on an adjoining plantation owned by another Chowan County, North Carolina, native, Obediah Small.[22] McKiel and Small, in fact, were first cousins, although they had fallen into a "feud" around the time they migrated to Arkansas. "They had nothing to do with each other," Small's stepdaughter, Anna Banks, later recalled; by 1860, they "had not spoken to each other for thirty years or longer."[23] And they tried to impose the same sort of distance on their enslaved people, with an outright ban on slaves traveling between the two properties. One of the women enslaved by Small later noted that "none of Judge McKeal's slaves were allowed on the Small's place."[24]

And yet Bogan managed to marry a man enslaved on the Small property anyway. It was sometime around 1860 or 1861 when she first got together with Silas Small, who had been sold to Arkansas by a slave trader from Alabama, along with his mother, Indiana, and his sister, Celestia. (Small's father remained behind and would never be seen by them again.)[25] It's not all that remarkable that Small eventually found his way to the McKiel plantation, or Bogan to Small's, even with their masters' restrictions. Enslaved people across the South had always moved clandestinely across plantations, building neighborhood social ties that sometimes remained invisible to their enslavers. But it could be risky—and in Bogan and Small's case, did not go undetected.[26] "I'll tell you how it was," recalled Jerry Steele, a man enslaved on a neighboring plantation. "Silas got to running over to the McKeal place to see Eliza & his old master, Small, gave him two or three whippings for it."[27] Another man on the McKiel property likewise recalled when Bogan and Small were once "taken up" by the patrollers who roamed the county enforcing slave submission with the crack of a whip.[28]

Bogan and Small thus endured violent reprisals in order to exert the sort of control over their intimate, emotional lives that was lost in the end of Bogan's first two marriages and in Small's sale away from his father. Theirs was an aspiration shared by many other enslaved people across the South, who routinely risked punishment and death to sustain family ties. Such actions may not have threatened the fact of their enslavement exactly, but they did set some boundaries on their owners' control, something Bogan's and Small's masters tacitly acknowledged when they relented and allowed the couple to marry. Yet, in the very act of giving consent, and in also dictating that, as a field hand, Bogan would be allowed only a "little tea party" rather than a formal ceremony to mark her marriage, Josiah McKiel did not concede very much control over their lives.[29] And the marriage would remain divided across the two plantations; Small continued to live on his plantation, visiting Bogan on Wednesday evenings as well as Saturday nights through Monday mornings. Together they "made two crops on the McKeal place," Bogan later noted.[30]

Yet it was "just a slave marriage," as Bogan would term it in retrospect, rather than the marriage she envisioned was possible in freedom.[31] It was a *slave* marriage—vulnerable to being ripped apart on an enslaver's whim, without any legal protections from a state that refused to recognize its existence.[32] It was born amid a cotton boom, amid gains for the enslavers and losses for the enslaved, and threatened, always, by the specter of McKiel's violent control. Bogan knew well from her roughly thirty years as a slave that there was nothing natural about McKiel's assertions of power over her; his resort to violence, back in Chowan County and again in Phillips County, showed clearly that his

Eliza Bogan in Slavery

control was not a given but had to be fought for at every turn. It could also be fought against. Bogan might have spent the rest of her life fighting to protect her family from McKiel's grip, snatching more time together across the McKiel and Small properties and enduring the whippings that followed. But then the Union army came and brought another way to fight back.

} 4 {

Facing Combat

Eliza Bogan hesitated to approach the lines of the Union army. The first time she did so, in fact, was to find her husband and bring him home — back to their plantations and back to slavery. She set off one day in the fall of 1862, possibly with one or two neighbors at her side, and traveled a fifteen-mile path southeast toward Helena, Arkansas, that wound through woods and cotton fields before climbing Crowley's Ridge, 200 feet in elevation. From atop the ridge Bogan would have gained a panoramic view of the Union army's presence in the town below. Rows of tents lined the riverfront city's streets. To the west of town was the newly constructed Fort Curtis, with its four massive earthen walls and heavy artillery aiming outward from each corner. And distributed across the top of Crowley's Ridge were four batteries, some still under construction, that barricaded the city on the western side and kept it defended from Confederate attack (map 6). The Union's defenses had been thrown up quickly, over the course of three months, thanks in large part to the labor of men drawn from the local enslaved population, some of whom Bogan knew well: two men from her neighborhood, Frank McKeal and Jerry Steele, had been there since July, when the Union army first rolled into Helena. So too had her husband, Silas Small.[1]

The town was secured for the Union — but Silas Small's and his neighbors' places there, it turned out, were not. Changes in the military command had kept their situation unsettled. Back when the men first arrived in Helena, they encountered Gen. Samuel R. Curtis, the commander of the Army of the Southwest (and namesake of the fort), who had begun declaring any refugee who came into his lines "emancipated" beginning in early 1862 — before the March 1862 article of war and the July 1862 Second Confiscation Act had authorized

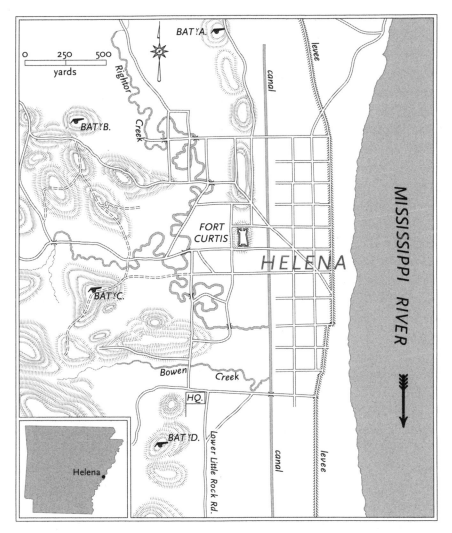

MAP 6. The river town of Helena, Arkansas, as it looked
in the fall of 1862 when Eliza Bogan first arrived
(Pauer Center for Cartography & GIS, University of Kentucky. Based
on "Map of Helena, Ark. and Vicinity, Showing the Location of
Forts and Batteries," 1865, Arkansas State Archives)

him to do so.[2] Yet by late August, after one month in Helena, Curtis left the city
when he was sent to take command of the Department of Missouri, and in his
place came Brig. Gen. Frederick Steele, a native of New York and conservative
Democrat with far less interest in emancipation. Steele was more concerned
with striking a conciliatory stance toward the Confederates in his midst and
acted quickly with that in mind. General Order No. 48, issued on September

18, reversed Curtis's efforts on emancipation and severely restricted the number of refugees allowed inside the lines. Only those formally employed and working on the defenses would be permitted to stay in Helena, Steele ordered, while the rest would be "put outside of these lines, and allowed to return to the plantations whence they came."[3] Over 500 women and children were then expelled.[4] And thus, where his predecessor had once been out in front of Union policy on slavery, Steele now positioned himself defiantly behind it.

This "Slave-Catching General," as one newspaper critic called him, soon became "notorious" for his "violations of the new article of war and the Confiscation act."[5] But that was not all. On Steele's watch wages also went unpaid, to a total of $50,000 by the end of December 1862, and even the laborers allowed to stay inside the lines found little in the way of food, clothing, or medical care.[6] The "hospital for colored people . . . has none of the comforts and necessaries of a hospital" and was instead "miserably provided for," wrote seven Union chaplains in an "Appeal for the Contrabands at Helena, Ark.," a public condemnation of Steele's policies that subsequently appeared in Northern newspapers like the *New York Times*. As a result, the chaplains wrote, "many of the sick there are dying daily."[7]

News eventually wound its way back to Eliza Bogan's neighborhood that Silas Small might be among those "dying daily." He, too, had fallen ill—and when Eliza heard that, she headed into Union lines and tracked him down. "I persuaded him to come home to my house on the McKeal place," Eliza later recalled of finding Silas in Helena. She nursed Silas briefly following their return, until "his mother sent for him and took him from my house saying that she and the white folks . . . would take care of him."[8] It seemed like a backward move for a freedom-seeking person, but for a woman who had already lost two husbands, Eliza's fear of Silas losing his life must have weighed most heavily on her mind.[9] Survival could trump the immediate pursuit of emancipation. And yet, even as Silas apparently agreed, he also needed to be "persuaded" by Eliza to return to his plantation too, revealing that his view of the Union army—of its intentions and its willingness and power to liberate him—was in no way clear-cut or settled.

What Silas Small likely knew, as he labored to build the defenses and as he witnessed the influx of over 10,000 soldiers into Helena, was that the Union army also posed a formidable threat to this part of the South. Never before had the Mississippi Valley's cotton planters seen their physical control over the land and people so directly challenged, and never before had enslaved people seen such force mobilized to combat their owners. That was the inescapable fact about the Union army that no refugee could miss, even as they grappled with unpaid wages and the violence of impressment: they shared a common enemy. Bogan, Small, and many others from their neighborhood realized this and would eventually join the Union army's combat apparatus in a variety of roles, not just as laborers, but as enlisted soldiers, as occupiers of land, and as regimental laundresses and nurses. They would fight back against their enslavers with the resources of an army behind them. And they fought mightily, in battles large and small, sometimes face-to-face with their own enslavers, because they knew as well as anyone that the promise of freedom meant little until the war was won.[10]

January 1, 1863, was supposed to mark a turning point for a place like Helena. But the Emancipation Proclamation came and went that day with little change in the region, even as it included Arkansas within its jurisdiction. "The virtue of the President's Proclamation had little hold upon many officers & soldiers" was how Samuel Sawyer, one of the seven chaplains behind the "Appeal," put it later that year. Although the proclamation had coincided with yet another change in leadership—General Steele was promoted and left Helena in early January, and Sawyer, the chaplain, was appointed the city's first superintendent of contrabands—all sorts of "abuses" still greeted incoming refugees.[11] "There is not a cordial feeling here among officers or soldiers on the subject of emancipation," observed Maria Mann, a newly arrived agent with the U.S. Sanitary Commission (and the first female agent to be sent into the South). Many officers were "proslavery," and "the barbarities from *our soldiers* are unparalleled," including their efforts to assist local owners in catching slaves. At a time when the Emancipation Proclamation aligned Union interests with the refugee slaves more closely in the abstract, Mann concluded that, in Helena, "so few friends have the negroes among the Officials."[12]

The situation, in a region where the proclamation was supposed to be transformative, did not escape the notice of President Lincoln. In the weeks after its issuance he received complaints from commanders in the Mississippi Valley, such as Gen. Stephen A. Hurlbut in Memphis, who called the over 5,000 men, women, and children refugeed in his area a "weight and incumbrance" for the Union forces.[13] Their numbers in other areas along the river valley were growing rapidly, too, as the Union army continued to advance down the river that winter and spring. There were over 3,000 at Corinth, Mississippi, by March; 1,250 who arrived in a twelve-day period at Lake Providence, Louisiana, in February; and 1,700 at Grand Junction, Tennessee, by April.[14] The numbers seemed like a growing distraction and burden to the forces who believed that gaining control of the river was their primary and most essential task. Cyrus Boyd, a private in the Fifteenth Iowa Regiment that moved to Lake Providence, Louisiana, that winter, explained how quickly the white soldiers' sense of being overwhelmed could then give way to race-fueled frustration and resentment. His comrades had begun responding to incoming refugees with "cries of 'Kill him' 'drown him.'" "The prejudice against the race seems stronger than ever," Boyd concluded.[15]

Now, four months after the proclamation's debut, in April 1863, the president, along with the secretary of war, Edwin Stanton, set in motion a new campaign of sorts—a campaign of persuasion intended to force compliance with the principles and the spirit of the Emancipation Proclamation. They selected Brig. Gen. Lorenzo Thomas, the adjutant general of the Union army, to lead the effort, and in late March sent him out of Washington and into the Mississippi Valley. There he was to tour all the Union's military encampments "and explain to them the importance attached by the Government to the use of the colored population emancipated by the President's Proclamation." Thomas, according to Stanton's orders, was to urge the "use" of refugee slaves not only as heavy laborers for the army—but as soldiers, too, just as the proclamation had authorized. It would be his task to begin forming the first black regiments in the Mississippi Valley, commissioning officers, recruiting men, and guaranteeing that the new regiments were well supplied.[16] And on April 6, after stops in Columbus, Kentucky, and Memphis, Tennessee, he arrived in Helena, where nearly 7,000 soldiers, officers, and laborers gathered inside Fort Curtis to hear what he had to say.[17]

Thomas minced no words. To those in attendance he declared "that he had the power to strip the shoulder-straps off any man who opposed" the proclamation, a Sanitary Commission agent later reported. "And what was more he meant to do it."[18] But it was not just the stick of demotion that Thomas wielded to persuade his listeners; he also dangled the carrot of victory. He had been urged by Secretary Stanton to remind the troops of the military necessity of emancipation—that ending slavery was part of "the declared purposes of the Government in using every means to bring the war to an end."[19] And that, according to Thomas, proved to be his most effective argument. Later in the day he telegrammed Stanton with an update and claimed that the speech "has infused new life into the troops, and they say, now they see that the rebellion will be crushed."[20] For some of those in attendance, Thomas's personal appeal made a far more compelling case for the link between ending slavery and winning the war than the abstract language of the proclamation had ever done.

Facing Combat

Others who observed the scene were quick to agree that Thomas's speech finally brought the turning point to Helena that January 1 had failed to deliver. The plan to enlist black men in the Union army "was heartily approved by all present," wrote Pvt. George Flanders of the Fifth Kansas Cavalry in a letter to his mother. Other letters noted that the soldiers "enthusiastically cheered at almost every sentence of the short address"; Minos Miller, of the Thirty-Sixth Iowa Regiment, described how another officer asked the soldiers to remove their hats if they favored Thomas's speech, "and in a second . . . every head was bare."[21] No doubt any man who hesitated would have felt pressured to participate in such a public display of support; still, the gathering persuaded others that, as Sanitary Commission agent William Allen put it, "in one night the whole spirit of the post changed." But it was not just a change in spirit; it was a change in practice, too, as General Thomas went ahead and commissioned officers for a new black regiment that very day, and recruitment for what would become the First Arkansas African Descent (AD) began the next. A week later, after traveling deeper south, Thomas himself declared that "the prejudices in this army respecting arming the negroes are fast dying out."[22] He was overly optimistic, however; other reports from the valley still took note of lingering resistance among white soldiers to the idea of enlisting black men.[23]

Yet Thomas's journey down the Mississippi Valley did transform, at the very least, the way in which enslaved people in the region could fight for their freedom. They had always been fighters, to be sure: fighting to survive the dehumanization of slavery, or in the war now ravaging the nation, fighting with axes and shovels, and with their flight from their plantations, to swing momentum defiantly toward the Union. In some ways the coming of formal enlistment in the army might have seemed like an incremental step forward rather than a radical new leap. As Union officials initially put black soldiers to work building and protecting fortifications, rather than in frontline combat, the weapon in the new soldiers' hands sometimes remained the same. And they were promised roughly the same wages as they had been promised as laborers: ten dollars a month. But something still had changed. The backward momentum of refugee affairs in Helena was now stalled; the uncertainty that surrounded the changing local command was now clarified by the Union's move to pull enslaved men more tightly into the Union's war machine than ever before. Black men were now given the uniforms they were once denied. Their names, ages, birthplaces, and physical characteristics were recorded on the Union's muster rolls, the first time the federal government acknowledged their individual names. They were not fighting alone now, as they always had, or in ad hoc groups of fellow slaves. Their fight was now unmistakably embedded in the powerful machine that was the Union army, with no less than the president of the United States commanding them.[24]

By the end of 1863, 21,000 black men in the Mississippi Valley had enlisted in the Union army.[25] And among them was Silas Small. It took just four days after General Thomas's speech, on April 10, for Small to make his second journey into Union lines at Helena, and once there, he enrolled in Company E of the First Arkansas AD.[26] His arrival so soon after the regiment's formation suggests he was an enthusiastic enlistee. But given the way his first journey into Union lines had ended, his deliberations about whether to stay or enlist must have been more complex. His mother, Indiana Kelly, later described his enlistment this way: "Soon after he got well the rebel soldiers came into our neighborhood and my son got scared and went off to the Yankees and enlisted as a soldier."[27] The Union army, in her account, offered a perfectly timed escape, a relief from the ongoing terror of Confederate violence. But surely it also crossed Small's mind that enlistment offered a more powerful means than ever before to fight back against the regime of white violence that had long confined him, and his family, in slavery. And it no doubt influenced him that at least seven other men from his neighborhood were enlisting that same week: Jerry Steele and Frank McKeal, who had gone to Helena with Small originally; John McKeel, another enslaved man on the McKiel property; Guilford Sullivan; and Charles, Lewis, and Dennis Bogan.[28] This time they went to Helena for good—although that was not the case for all new enlistees. Just three days after Small enlisted, one of the officers of his new regiment was found to have been "engaged in pressing negroes into the service and receiving bribes for their release"—bribes paid by local slave owners.[29] It was a sign of how uneasy the alliance still was between former slaves and the Union army.

~~~

It was not just men who were newly mobilized by Lorenzo Thomas's tour through the Mississippi Valley. The general also opened a path for women's mobilization, a path that wound through the region's cotton plantations. The Union had had its eye on cotton from the earliest days of its occupation of the Mississippi Valley, not so much as a target for destruction but as a commodity to protect. Northerners, after all, were already dependent on cotton in all sorts of ways, from the New York financiers and merchants who trafficked in the international cotton trade, to the New England textile mills that processed the raw material, to the consuming public that had grown increasingly enamored of cotton fabric in the antebellum period. Union officials were well

Facing Combat

aware that in order to keep the Northern economy humming, not to mention the worldwide cotton trade (through which the United States exported 80 percent of its cotton production in 1860), producing the crop was urgent, as long as the profits sustained the Union's interests rather than the Confederacy's.[30] This meant that the army in the Mississippi Valley would be tasked with more than holding the territory it conquered; it would also be tasked with facilitating the cultivation of that land and getting the cotton to market. The cotton trade was therefore deeply entwined with the Union army's strategy for holding and occupying the valley, something Thomas well understood as he traveled the valley in April 1863.

"Men should be employed with our Armies as laborers and teamsters . . . [or] mustered as soldiers," Thomas had written Secretary Stanton at the beginning of his tour, and "the women and children placed on the abandoned plantations to till the ground."[31] Thomas devised a plan for the Mississippi Valley based in large part on a system already in place along the coast of Virginia near Fort Monroe, on the South Carolina Sea Islands, and in West Tennessee and southern Louisiana: the relocation of women and children out of refugee camps and onto nearby plantation lands now held by the Union. There, the women and children (and men deemed unfit for military service) would be paid to harvest cotton for the very first time. Women were to receive five dollars per month; men over fifteen years old, seven dollars per month; and children between the ages of twelve and fifteen, half of what adults of their respective gender received. Children under twelve were not to be employed.[32] Their work was to be overseen either by men who migrated south from Northern states, who leased the properties from the government, or by local planters identified as "loyal" by Union officials. Both were to pay the workers' wages and were bound by the army to "feed, clothe, and treat humanely all the negroes thus turned over" (although the cost of clothing was to be deducted from the laborers' already-low wages).[33] Any land not in the hands of these loyal men was to remain under the direct administration of government officials and be turned into what were called "Government Farms" or "Home Farms," or in the case of those that housed mostly the aged and infirm, "Infirmary Farms."[34] Profits from the cotton sold went either to the lessees or to the U.S. Treasury (which in South Carolina in 1862 reaped a reported $500,000).[35]

Overseeing the plantation operation was a man named John Eaton, a minister from New Hampshire already working as an army chaplain. That summer Gen. Ulysses S. Grant commissioned him as a colonel and appointed him the superintendent of freedmen for the Department of the Tennessee and State of Arkansas, which meant he was in charge of all refugee affairs in the valley between Memphis and Vicksburg. Eaton later recalled his "shock" and "consternation" when given responsibility for such a large geographic area and for so many people; he termed it "an enterprise beyond the possibility of human achievement." Yet Eaton took his orders and got to work, and over the next two years he would become one of the loudest advocates on behalf of refugee affairs in the army's command structure.[36]

The plantation plan served an unmistakably strategic purpose for the Union army. Those sent to plantations were not just going to "till the ground," as they had done in slavery; their mere presence on the farms now assumed a new military importance for the Union. Thomas had his eye, in particular, on plantation lands along the western bank of the Mississippi River — on the lands near towns like Helena. As Thomas explained to Secretary Stanton in a subsequent proposal on April 12, he intended "to locate on and near its banks a loyal population, who will protect (instead of destroying, as is now done) the freedom of commercial intercourse on this great 'island sea.'"[37] Refugee women and children would be positioned precisely on lands that were crucial to the Union's hold on the river; without that western bank, the Union would not be able to protect the ships that would be so essential for transporting cotton or supplying the troops for the Vicksburg campaign. Already those ships had been plagued by attacks from guerrillas given access to the river by Confederate-sympathizing landowners; now that much of that riverfront land was falling into Union hands, women would be dispatched to create a plantation buffer zone between the river and the Confederate territory in the interior. And to protect them, in turn, from any Confederate threats in their midst, Thomas ordered that the new regiments of black recruits be sent into the region to garrison the plantations. Women, in Thomas's plan, were not just going to labor for the Union but *occupy land* for the Union.[38]

The plan essentially reenvisioned the antebellum plantation as something more akin to a fortified village. This was a long-standing tactic in the history of military occupation, in which civilians took up residence in, cultivated, and literally occupied lands, all the while armed and ready to beat back any enemy forces. It was the sort of tactic resorted to in 1842, in the U.S. Congress's passage of the Armed Occupation Act, which enabled civilian men (and their families) to take hold of lands in Florida and improve and cultivate them, while armed and prepared to fight any Indians who challenged their control.[39] It would be seen again later during twentieth-century occupations.[40] Although the women on the Civil War's plantations were not armed themselves, their husbands, fathers, sons, and brothers and other formerly enslaved

Facing Combat

men were. And they would be especially effective in that role, in the eyes of General Thomas, for the "Negroes, being acquainted with the peculiar country lining its banks, would know where to act effectively."[41] They knew where Confederates lurked or could anticipate how the terrain would be exploited by rebel marauders. "By lining the river banks for miles in breadth with a loyal population, self-supporting, and contributing to the revenue, to render secure these water-courses," Superintendent Eaton summed up the plan, the refugees would thus "co-operate in making successful our military operations."[42]

Women were envisioned as critical to that cooperation, and thus critical to the military success of the Union in the Mississippi Valley—a sign of how their position was evolving in the eyes of Union authorities. Even as General Butler, back at Fort Monroe in 1861, argued for the military necessity of allowing all refugees in Union lines, including women, or as members of Congress in the Confiscation Acts or President Lincoln in the Emancipation Proclamation had included the emancipation of women as a military necessity in the abstract, it was difficult for all Union officials on the ground to see the arrival of women in refugee camps as anything other than a burden. With the exception of those women who obtained the limited jobs open to them, as cooks or as laundresses, women had never fit easily into the army's apparatus, and on a day-to-day basis they had little opportunity to demonstrate the "military necessity" of their presence in Union lines. Their arrival might have subtracted crucial labor from the Confederacy, but what did it add to the Union? To some historians, the answer has been very little, leading to the conclusion that Union policies paved the way for a "martial" road to freedom for men, while leaving women behind and on the margins of this great battle for emancipation. But that is not how General Thomas saw things, for his plans attempted to mobilize women (and even children) into military service for the Union.[43] And "that pleases us," a refugee woman reportedly stated about the government farm system in Virginia; "that makes us of some account."[44]

On a day-to-day basis, women's plantation labor, even if it was now under the supervision of a Northern man or a government official, may have seemed little different from the slavery they tried to leave behind. Some worked in the very same fields they always had and were subjected to the same sort of compulsions to work long hours and produce high yields as they had been with their owners. But even as the work itself was materially the same, Thomas's plan attempted to change the meaning and purpose attached to it in a time of war: women's labor would now serve the military's interests. He made this change most visible to the laborers, perhaps, in his effort to replace plantation order with military order. The whip, for example, which for so long compelled the labor of the enslaved on the plantation, was explicitly forbidden on leased plantations.[45] Any conflicts between employer and employee were instead to be settled by the army's ostensibly neutral third party—the provost marshal system. The military police, which had long overseen the arrest and incarceration of disorderly personnel, would now also adjudicate problems related to wages, hours worked, and treatment. The provost marshal officials were assigned to separate districts in the valley, each charged with riding on horseback from plantation to plantation within his district, examining the books and the labor arrangements and hearing the complaints that inevitably arose. "Planters had often to be reminded, that they were not working slaves," Superintendent Eaton observed of the system.[46]

The Union now offered enslaved women like Eliza Bogan a firmer toehold in Union lines. Or, at the very least, it became harder and harder for officials to refuse them a place. The landscape of refugee settlement was expanding vastly across the Mississippi Valley, with the government-supervised plantations alone encompassing as much as 400,000 acres by the following spring.[47] Even the least sympathetic Union soldier, who may have recoiled at the congregation of women and children in an army encampment or in a city, had little trouble accepting that a black woman should take up residence on one of these plantations.

Still, Bogan did not immediately leave the McKiel property. Her sister, Hester, would later look back on the moment as a time when the two debated the question of whether to go, to the point where their conversations grew heated. "Eliza wanted to go," Hester explained years later, "but I ding donged her so much about it she did not follow him."[48] Hester did not explain why she opposed Eliza's desire to join Silas Small in Union lines, and why, at least at first, Eliza listened. Maybe it had to do with her seven children? Eliza may very well have wanted to take her children with her—if they had not already been sold away from her—for that was what so many other women did when they headed into Union lines. Refugee camps across the South housed large numbers of children, so many that they sometimes comprised close to half of a camp's population. In the Mississippi Valley that spring and summer, for example, children numbered 600 of the 1,400 people at Clarksville, Tennessee; 1,559 of 3,657 at the Corinth, Mississippi, refugee camp; and 891 of 1,708 at Grand Junction, Tennessee.[49] The numbers reveal that more and more families had decided it was safer to risk escaping with children than it had been before the war, when fears about children's safety discouraged many women from

Facing Combat

running away.[50] Hester, though, may have believed that it was still too dangerous to bring children into a combat zone.

Or maybe it was a matter of security at home. Could Bogan have left safely
and securely without incurring the wrath of Josiah McKiel? Or without leaving
others behind, vulnerable to his anger and violent outbursts? The answer to
these questions was a resounding no for many other enslaved people across the
South, evident in cases upon cases of violent reprisals suffered by family members who remained behind on plantations after others fled. The answer might
have been no in Eliza's case, too, given McKiel's long history of brutality against
enslaved people, and given that he fit almost perfectly in the role of the acquisitive yet aggrieved cotton baron, desperate to save his disintegrating empire.

Yet McKiel turned out to be more complicated. He claimed to be loyal to
the Union, *not* to the Confederacy, and he made his loyalty known loud and
clear to his neighbors. He had a habit of carrying a copy of the U.S. Constitution around with him in his pocket, subjecting residents of Phillips County to
arguments about the illegality of secession, so conspicuous in his actions that
a report about it made its way into a Philadelphia newspaper.[51] McKiel's loyalty
may have been deeply felt—but it also may have been pragmatic, for an outward attachment to the Union could go a long way toward saving his property.
The Union's new plantation system, reinforced by President Lincoln's Proclamation of Amnesty and Reconstruction in December 1863, allowed lands to
remain in the possession of men deemed "loyal," as long as those men agreed
to abide by the terms of the system, including an acceptance of slave emancipation and the payment of wages to all laborers.[52] Perhaps Hester felt that their
freedom was better secured by remaining on the plantation and asserting their
new leverage to obtain wages from McKiel.

Eliza remained on the McKiel property for another month before finally
resisting Hester's arguments and leaving for good. "When all the people in
our neighborhood left the plantations to go to Helena, Ark.," Hester later explained, "she went too." "All the people" included another woman from her
plantation, Matilda Yount, as well as Silas's sister, Celestia, from the neighboring Small plantation, both of whom also had husbands enlist in Silas's regiment.[53] Eliza then "staid with the army until after the war" and would not see
her sister again for over two years.[54] There is no evidence that she saw her children either, for her subsequent actions were unlikely to have involved children, and they go unmentioned in recollections of her time in Union lines.
Perhaps Eliza planned to rely on Hester and other women who remained on
the property to care for her children—the same people she may have always
relied on for child care when she worked in the cotton fields. Or maybe Josiah

McKiel may still have been lurking, whip in hand, making it unlikely that multiple children could slip off quietly with their mother, as Eliza headed toward Helena.

Eliza thus took an enormous risk when she went to Helena, not knowing if she would ever return to her sister and her children, and not knowing if she would be able to be with her husband in the months and years ahead. It was not a risk that a woman who had experienced so much loss in her life already would have taken lightly. But it was the sort of risk that many, many other freedom-seeking people also took when they thrust themselves deeper and deeper into the Union army's orbit. They chose to join the fight — to become a part of it and to shape it — rather than have it unfold around them. Eliza would join that fight, too, learning quickly that, no matter how much her owner may have claimed to reject the Confederacy, the Union's fight to victory was still far from over.

~~~

Freedom-seeking people in the Mississippi Valley thus immersed themselves in the Union army's combat apparatus throughout the summer of 1863. In Helena, the newly recruited men of the First Arkansas AD, joined by another new regiment, the Second Arkansas AD, set about drilling and learning the ways of the military, while women and children either settled into the refugee camp in town or were dispatched to occupy 8,000 acres of nearby plantation land seized by the Union.[55] Their service to the Union in the year ahead involved more than occupation, however. In the war-torn Cotton Kingdom, where freedom-seeking people like them had just assumed new leverage as combatants but where most cotton-hungry planters were Confederates who had no intention of giving up, the powder keg of antebellum plantation violence now exploded in multiple directions. The war in the valley would become raw, venomous, and hard fought — and former slaves, men and women alike, would be crucial actors in that fight.

The region was transformed into the epicenter of war by the summer. The city of Vicksburg, located 200 miles south of Helena on the eastern bank of the river, had been the target of the Union's campaign that year. If successful, the capture of Vicksburg would hand the remainder of the Mississippi River to the Union and leave the Confederacy divided in two. Throughout that winter and spring Gen. Ulysses S. Grant, commanding the Union's forces in the West, searched for routes into Vicksburg, and after several failed attempts to approach the city from the north, maneuvered his troops for an approach from the south and east. By the time Eliza arrived in Union lines in Helena, Grant's troops had successfully occupied a position south of the city, on the eastern bank of the river, after a victory at Port Gibson. From there they prepared to lay siege.[56]

Along the way, Grant's campaign had siphoned off white Union troops from the riverbanks and replaced them with the newly recruited black regiments to take over the crucial work of guarding newly seized plantation land. Silas Small and the other soldiers of the First Arkansas thus received word in early May that they were being sent 150 miles directly south from Helena to Lake Providence, Louisiana, on the western bank of the river (map 7). Lake Providence had been serving as a staging area for Grant's troops, with tens of thousands of men headquartered in the region earlier in the year. But when those troops marched toward Vicksburg, they left behind several thousand refugees on plantations that were newly vulnerable to Confederate troops intent on destroying the cotton harvest and capturing the people. It would now be the job of Silas Small and the First Arkansas to fend off these Confederate attacks and to protect the refugees.[57]

But this meant, of course, that Silas and Eliza had to separate once again. They had been living together in Helena in Silas's tent, but now Eliza was to be evicted as Silas and his comrades packed up their gear for their journey south.[58] Eliza was not alone in her dislocation that summer: the rest of the refugees in Helena were in flux and on the move too. Their settlement was being relocated two and a half miles to the south of town, in the direction of the plantations, in order to seek, according to Sanitary Commission agent Maria Mann, "better location, better water, & lands for gardens." The army committed itself to helping refugees construct new houses there, with chimneys, doors, and two windows each, a design that promised to protect them from heat and cold but not necessarily the wet ground. The houses "will have floors in time," as Mann put it. It was to this settlement that Eliza would have moved after Silas's departure, although it hardly proved to be a refuge from the ravages of war.[59]

At 3:30 a.m. on July 4, 1863, Eliza would have been awakened by the sound of a shot ringing out from Fort Curtis. It was not the sound of celebration for the nation's birthday, but a signal—a warning—that Confederate troops had arrived on the outskirts of Helena and were preparing for a direct attack on the Union defenses.[60] Confederate general Sterling Price was at the head of the assault, in which scattered rebel troops converged in an attempt to expel the Union; more important, the attack was meant to divert Union attention from Vicksburg. Price and his troops had the numerical advantage in this fight, since so many Union troops, such as Silas Small's First Arkansas AD, had been sent down the river. But it did not matter. When the fighting commenced, the

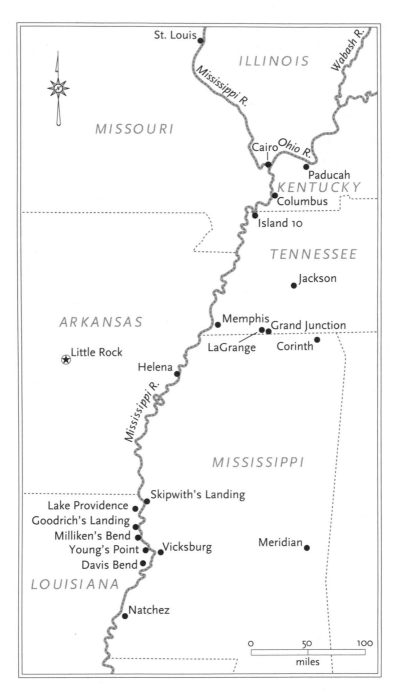

MAP 7. Map of the Mississippi Valley, indicating Helena's location in relation to the other places, such as Lake Providence, where the First Arkansas AD moved. All locations on the map were sites of refugee camps. (Pauer Center for Cartography & GIS, University of Kentucky)

FIGURE 11. A refugee woman and young child in a tent at Helena
(Nebraska State Historical Society, RG3323-PH-6-10)

Union forces, ensconced in the four batteries atop Crowley's Ridge, drove back each Confederate advance, and by the end of the day, they sent the Confederates back into the interior of Arkansas.[61]

The Confederates had failed not just in Helena. On the very same day, Vicksburg fell to Grant's forces, and as monumental as that was in the West, news of the Union victory at Gettysburg the day before began to make its way into Helena too. All of it was cause for celebration—but especially Helena's role in the series of victories. Several days later, on July 8, the Union troops gathered in Fort Curtis to cheer their commander, Gen. Benjamin Prentiss, as he thanked them, in turn, for their victory. "Victory crowned our National banner on the nations birth day," Prentiss declared. "The annals of the nation will record the Battle of Helena as one of the most noble and successful efforts in maintaining its integrity."[62] This time the cannon at Fort Curtis was fired in celebration.[63]

Yet amid the pomp, the refugee settlement in which Eliza resided lay in ruins. What was a cause for celebration for some was a moment of desolation for others—a devastating reminder of how imperfectly the Union's interests aligned with those of freedom-seeking refugees. In the course of the battle, members of the Confederate Thirty-Fourth Arkansas Infantry, streaming in from the south and west, had made their approach to Helena along Lower Little Rock Road, the same road extending south from town along which the new refugee settlement was located.[64] That made the settlement an easier target for the rebel troops, who quickly set about torching nearly everything recently built by refugee men and women. "On the 4th July last the rebels burned [the settlement]," the superintendent of contrabands, Samuel Sawyer, reported, including "cabins to accommodate five hundred contrabands & nearly all the property in the camp." A schoolhouse, which Sawyer described as the "first free school" ever built in Arkansas, was among the ruins, along with a chapel.[65] Other reports noted that "most of their clothing & effects" were burned too. Stripped of their possessions and shelter, the refugees, in the wake of the battle, did not rush to celebrate but instead were ushered into town again and "packed into the three churches & empty cabins."[66]

As hundreds of people crowded into the small buildings, local surgeons warned that the conditions might soon breed an "epidemic" of fatal illness.[67] Union officials then tried to quickly relieve the problem by turning to a familiar strategy—removal. Four orders issued from July 12 to August 8 outlined the process, such as the one directing the superintendent of contrabands to "forward a boat load of contrabands under his charge to St. Louis Mo., as soon as transportation can be procured." There they would be moved into a refugee settlement taking shape in the abandoned Missouri Hotel, before being placed with employers throughout the city. Or, they might be sent even farther north to make their homes and livelihoods in any number of upper midwestern towns.[68] Either way it was a sign to the refugees in Arkansas that they had lost their foothold in Helena. The city "will not be a place to colonize this long while," wrote Maria Mann before gathering her belongings and heading back to Massachusetts that summer.[69]

Eliza Bogan, now "packed" inside a building with too many others, in addition to reeling from the violence inflicted by the rebels and fearing the onset of illness, could not have been blamed for feeling decidedly unfree in this seventh month after the Emancipation Proclamation went into effect. The prospect of migrating to St. Louis did not necessarily change those feelings. Missouri may have been a Union state, but it was also exempt from the Emancipation Proclamation. And no matter how "free" Union officials promised it would still be, it was even farther from everything she knew—from her children in Phillips County and from her husband, now in Louisiana.

Yet to remain in Helena offered the likelihood of being sent off to a nearby leased plantation. And that may have seemed little better. During the first year of the plantation system, refugees discovered that any hope of converting the plantations into successful free labor enclaves was quickly dashed. The lessees, one sympathetic Union official discovered, often proved to be nothing more than "adventurers" and "hangers-on of the Army," who "cared nothing how much flesh they worked off of the negro provided it was converted into good cotton."[70] Wages often went unpaid, or in some instances, the monthly wage was either prorated for time actually worked or eaten up by exorbitant deductions taken for very minimal clothing provisions, leaving laborers with far less in their pockets. The workers also had little choice over who their employers would be, for military authorities assigned them to plantations and denied them the ability to test the market for their labor.[71] Even worse was the reliance on physical force and violence. "Looking for 'experience' in the management of blacks, and in the making of cotton," Superintendent Eaton wrote of the Northern lessees, "some of them have employed, as they should not, on any terms, have been allowed to do, old overseers." Although banned by the army from using the whip, the overseers were turning to "blows, and kicks, and cuffs" instead, maintaining the regime of violence that had long undergirded slavery. Much of this should have been stopped by the provost marshal officials, but they found themselves overloaded with districts too large to manage and showed up on plantations too infrequently (and at times proved too vulnerable to bribes from the lessees).[72] Eliza might as well have returned to the McKiel plantation; the government-supervised ones seemed little better.

But Eliza did not return to the McKiel property. Nor did she stick around to be sent to a leased plantation, or to board one of the boats headed to St. Louis. She instead decided to move in the opposite direction. "[I] got on a boat and went down the river and found the regiment at Goodrich's Landing," just south of Lake Providence. That was how Eliza later described her next move: she had decided to go searching for her husband and his regiment.[73] It was an extraordinarily risky decision, but one animated by the same impulse that had led her to retrieve Silas from Helena in 1862 and to follow him back into the city in 1863. How she made this particular trip is unclear; perhaps a sympathetic military official secured her a spot on a navy gunboat, or maybe a commercial steamer allowed her to stow away with the cotton bales heading to New Orleans. However she found her spot on a boat, water transport would have been much safer than making her way into Louisiana by land, where along the way she would have encountered Confederate forces. She also may have found some degree of safety by traveling in numbers. The two other women from her neighborhood with whom she had gone to Helena — Silas's sister, Celestia, as well as Matilda Yount — also traveled to Louisiana at the same time.[74] The three women found their way to Goodrich's Landing, where the First Arkansas AD was encamped, but it must have taken little time once there to learn that Company E was not with the regiment. Silas Small and his comrades had gone missing.

⌐┐

The task of protecting plantations turned out to be no peaceful garrison duty. Just one week before the battle of Helena, Silas and Company E were still present with the regiment. They had been assigned to protect a collection of six leased plantations in the region, 4,000 acres in total, and had taken a position in a fort located ten miles south of Lake Providence on what was known as Mound Plantation. The fort was built at the top of an old Indian burial mound, which rose 80–100 feet in an open field, giving the troops an elevated position from which to see (and, they hoped, repel) any approaching Confederates. Surrounding the bottom of the mound was a trench two to three feet deep dug by the soldiers, and in that trench, watching and waiting with rifles in hand, was the First Arkansas AD — including Silas Small.[75]

Small had a frontline view when a combined force of Arkansas and Texas troops approached the mound on June 29. Determined to destroy the cotton cultivated on Federal plantations and capture any refugee slaves, the Confederates had set their sights on the fort. To capture it would knock out the Union defenses and then render the surrounding plantations vulnerable to their incursions. Silas may have realized that the garrison on the Indian mound was an open and vulnerable target for the incoming Confederate forces that outnumbered his own. Maybe he also realized that, without any artillery at the top of the mound and with only heavy timbers to roll on top of those who tried to climb it, the black troops were at a serious disadvantage. Certainly the Confederates realized it and, upon their approach, demanded the surrender of the Federal forces. The white Union officers commanding the black troops quickly complied.[76] "The entire company was captured at Mound Plantation La after an unsuccessful engagement of six hours June 29, 1863," an assistant adjutant general later reported.[77]

Silas Small's very first encounter with Confederate troops while in uniform had ended; his first chance to fight the white South, backed by the power of the U.S. Army, was dashed. He did not have the chance to earn the sort of gratification that his comrades at nearby Milliken's Bend had earlier that month when they successfully fended off Confederate forces.[78] His battle ended far worse. In their surrender, the white officers of his regiment requested that their Confederate counterparts treat them as prisoners of war, but they only asked this for the officers — leaving Silas and his fellow privates surrendered to the rebels without condition. If they were not to be classified as POWs, then what were they exactly? Their Union service records subsequently labeled them "missing in action," but it was the Confederates' classification that would matter most to the men in captivity. Ominous signs of what the Confederates were thinking surfaced immediately after capture, when an estimated twelve to fifteen men died as the Company E soldiers left the mound with the Confederate forces. At the same time, the rebel troops ransacked the surrounding plantations worked by refugees, leaving the quarters and cotton gins destroyed "and the negroes captured or driven from the plantations and scattered."[79]

To the Confederates, a black man in uniform was not a soldier, nor a combatant, but a rebellious slave, one who had committed treason against his master. About that most Confederate partisans agreed. Yet the question of how to treat those rebellious slaves once captured generated different answers and sometimes conflicting responses. There was an official Confederate policy, one issued by President Jefferson Davis in December 1862 and later reinforced by a resolution of the Confederate Congress, ordering that any captured black man be sent back to the states to be dealt with according to state law. In most cases this meant he would be punished with death, as slave rebels had been before the war, usually by hanging. Yet the policy emanating from the Confederate capital was not always directly and evenly applied on the ground, in part because some Confederate commanders never knew what the policy was in the first place. Others willfully subverted it by executing black soldiers on the spot. And then there was Secretary of War James Seddon, who in April 1863 devised another plan by ordering black soldiers to be kept in the possession of the Confederate army and made to perform hard labor, such as digging fortifications.[80] The army would thus reenslave the men, restoring their subordination to white men while simultaneously benefiting from their labor.

That is what happened to the men of Company E. Their service records reveal that after arriving in Confederate lines they were scattered and put to work at various outposts in Louisiana. Charles Bogan, from Small's old neighborhood, later recounted how he was put to work in a convalescent camp near Clinton, Louisiana, and charged with erecting a "cabin" for smallpox patients there.[81] Bogan had been taken over 150 miles to get to his new work assignment; others in his company were put to work closer to their point of capture, about half that distance, in Monroe, Louisiana. It is not clear exactly where

Silas Small was sent, however, although very likely to Monroe too. Yet, despite being separated and reenslaved across Confederate Louisiana, the Company E soldiers had not seen the last of one another.[82]

If they were going to be reenslaved, then they would respond to their bondage in the same way they had before: by escaping. "Escaped and reported within the Union lines August 9, 1863," was how one service record put it.[83] John McKeel, a man formerly enslaved with Eliza, "escaped and reported within Union lines and rejoined his regiment" on September 1, 1863, along with at least one other man from their plantation.[84] Charles Bogan likewise abandoned the smallpox hospital and returned to Union lines on September 4.[85] The word "escape" appears throughout the service records of the Company E men, including those of every one of the men from the old neighborhood who had enlisted alongside Silas.[86] They did not all escape on the same day—some in early August, others at the end of the month—but beyond this the historical record is elusive. How did they do it? How did they escape the fate of so many other black soldiers? And how did they pull this off at roughly the same time, from different points of departure? The evidence points to some degree of coordination among the men, but little more.[87] Certainly the men, having already escaped one set of captors when they first enlisted in the Union army, were becoming experienced at eluding and outfighting their enslavers. That fight would only continue.

～～

Silas returned to camp at Goodrich's Landing to the sight of his wife among his regimental comrades and their tents. Silas and Eliza were surely relieved to see each other again, although the emotional strain of the previous weeks' battles likely weighed on them too. Both had confronted the war with a new intimacy, from Eliza's nearly frontline view of the fighting in Helena, to Silas's exchange of gunfire and his capture at Mound Plantation. Both, though, survived and were able to continue envisioning a future of freedom. Perhaps it crossed their minds that they could run off and head north to a place like St. Louis and begin building that future on less conflict-ridden ground. But Eliza and Silas made a different choice. They did not retreat but instead doubled down, throwing themselves deeper and deeper into combat in the aftermath of their reunion. As Eliza would describe the moment: "I joined the company at Goodrich Landing."[88] She did not mean "join" in any general sense of togetherness; in her mind she had, in that moment, become an actual member of Silas's company. As she explained it, she "was sworn in as the wash-woman for Co. E" and "then staid [sic] with the regiment three years."[89]

Facing Combat

Popular memory of the Civil War has afforded little room for women as members of a company or regiment. Women were not officially enlisted as soldiers, they did not shoulder guns, and they did not wear the distinguishing uniform of a combatant. But with Eliza's language as a guide, such definitions of regimental membership seem too restrictive and miss the complex ways in which a woman could become embedded in, and develop a sense of belonging to, the combat apparatus.[90] Eliza took some sort of oath to the First Arkansas, one that may not have been officially required or sanctioned by the army and was perhaps a local convention, but one that was meaningful enough to be remarked upon years later: she was "sworn in." Army regulations made a place for these women, too, stipulating that "four women will be allowed to each company as washerwomen." And each woman, known also as a "laundress," was to receive a daily food ration from the army, and each was to be paid either by the month or by the piece, a process to be overseen by a company's captain.[91] The army took the position of washerwoman — and its responsibility to it — seriously enough to also outline procedures for how a woman could obtain her food rations should she become separated from the company. She was, as the regulations specifically termed it in one passage, a "company woman."[92]

"I washed clothes for him," Eliza later wrote about her work for Silas. "I washed clothes for pretty much all the soldiers" in Company E.[93] It was physically taxing work that was more easily avoided by the middle-class white women who came south to work with the Union army; they tended to be placed in established hospitals, working as nurses. Washing, as well as cooking, meanwhile, tended to be the domain of working-class white and black women, including those formerly enslaved.[94] This was because the work was so draining, involving the constant, monotonous ritual of soaking, scrubbing, and pounding clothing dry, which damaged the skin on their hands and threatened to strain elbows and shoulders. The sight and smell of sweat, blood, and other human fluids soaked into the uniforms compounded the drudgery and exposed women to infection and disease. And for laundresses like Eliza who were attached to a particular regiment, all of this occurred while on the move and required lugging washtubs and scrubbing boards from place to place.[95] As Eliza washed for "pretty much all" of the company, then it was 114 men whose clothing she contended with along the way.[96]

Eliza, like all regimental laundresses, took on this exhausting labor while at the same time exposing herself to innumerable physical dangers. As she marched with the regiment from Goodrich's Landing, Louisiana, to Haynes Bluff near Vicksburg, Mississippi, that fall, she enjoyed little to no protection from the same hazards of combat confronted by the men. And on top of that

FIGURE 12. Army laundresses with washtubs like those that Eliza Bogan would have used. This photograph was taken at a Union encampment at Yorktown, Virginia, in 1862. (Library of Congress)

were the dangers of sexual assault at the hands of vengeful Confederates or even of Union men.[97] Though Company E records are elusive on specific instances of rape, an order issued by the regimental commander in February 1864 suggests that something troubling enough of this nature had occurred in the camps of the First Arkansas to prompt a response. "The presence of women in the camps tends to demoralize officers and men, interferes with discipline, and is a Scandal and injury to the service," the order from Brig. Gen. Isaac Shepard began. Shepard was more inclined to see women as the cause, rather than victims, of any disorderly behavior, leaning back on racist assumptions about black women's sexuality. General Shepard thus cracked down on the presence of women for the sake of military "discipline," mandating that "all women not in actual employ and under pay in their several camps are at once dismissed and removed out side the lines to localities intended for their accommodation"—in other words, to a refugee camp. The order also reduced the number of women who could be employed by a company—from four to two—but added that "it is earnestly recommended to all officers to dispense with even these and employ males instead."[98]

Facing Combat

Company E did not follow this last recommendation, however, and kept Eliza in its employ as a laundress. Eliza herself clearly wanted to stay. Certainly the promise of wages, a first in her life, was compelling, and although those wages were often inconsistently paid, she did earn enough to loan money in five-dollar increments to various members of her extended family later on in the war.[99] She also earned something else. The February 1864 order, in an attempt to implement more oversight over the employment of women, had required that names of remaining laundresses be forwarded to headquarters so that "certificates of employment" could be issued to them in turn. "Without these no colored female will be allowed to remain in any camp or quarters," the order explained.[100] Eliza must have received one of these certificates, which undoubtedly meant more than simply substantiating her employment: it was a written acknowledgment that the U.S. government recognized her position in its military and, thus, codified her own martial route to freedom as a "company woman."

Undoubtedly important to Eliza's desire to remain in the Company E camp was the state of the alternative — those places "intended for their accommodation," or the refugee camps and leased plantations. In the weeks and months following the conclusion of the Vicksburg campaign, as the Union assumed control of the entire Mississippi River, the numbers of refugees continued to swell, and Union officials responded by expanding their efforts to move refugees out of camps and onto leased and abandoned plantations along the river. But life in the plantation settlements proved to be no less turbulent than it was in the regimental camps.

This owed largely to one key fact: the fighting never stopped in the Mississippi Valley, even as the war's center of gravity shifted east and turned toward Atlanta in 1864. Irregular Confederates — guerrillas — sustained the fight along the river and continued to lash out against Union occupation. Their targets, though, were not primarily the Union army and its encampments, nor the navy's boats sailing down the river; instead they set their sights on the plantations and the lessees, and especially the refugee laborers. As historian Daniel Sutherland has put it, "The rebels no longer had a legitimate chance to defeat the navy or run the Federals out of the Mississippi River valley, but they continued to exact a toll in lives and property."[101] The federal government's plantation system, after all, represented everything that Confederates feared: the coming of free labor and the payment of wages to black people, as well as a loss of control over the land and over the people they had long forced into submission. Never mind that the reality of the federally controlled plantations was often far from a free-labor utopia. Confederates still feared that the plantations, the backbone of white Southern supremacy, were slipping from their control.

The guerrillas' retaliatory attacks would go down as some of the most vicious of the entire Civil War. "Planters and laborers, defenseless women and children, have been murdered," railed Superintendent of Freedmen John Eaton in 1864. "The ferocity of these guerrilla massacres has rivaled everything in savage warfare short of cannibalism."[102] At Young's Point, Louisiana, to the west of Vicksburg, guerrilla raids in April 1864 were "daily occurrences," according to one report, and "the poor blacks are carried off as trophies."[103] Those captured "run the great risk of being carried off into slavery again," according to a Union official across the river; other reports told of captives taken to slave jails, forced to spend months without fuel to warm themselves or food to survive.[104] A particularly devastating raid at Young's Point came on a day when the guerrillas captured twenty-nine refugees and forty-six horses, along with a doctor and the lessee of the plantation. The rebels shot two of the refugees, and "several others were scandalously abused" (a reference, very likely, to rape), before the doctor and the lessee were taken "some distance" and forced to remove their clothes. They too were shot—and the doctor's ear cut off.[105]

It was gruesome violence intended to send a message. The sights of mutilated bodies and of "blood flowing from their lacerated backs," as a Union official described it, or of a child being shot while held in his mother's arms, would instill a visceral fear in anyone connected with the government plantation system across the Mississippi Valley.[106] Any Union sympathizer living along the river, but especially the black refugees, had to live with the "terrors" of knowing that guerrillas "lurked in swamps and cane-brakes near the river, ready at any moment to pounce."[107] Just a rumor, or a vague sight or sound, of guerrillas nearby was enough to send refugees and their white allies into the woods or in the direction of a Union gunboat, looking for a place to hide.[108] "The fear of the guerrillas creates a general unsettlement in the camps" was how visiting Quaker Samuel Shipley described the scene in Helena, where raiding parties launched five midnight attacks on the leased plantations over a two-week period in March 1864.[109] "Unsettlement" was an understatement for the terror inflicted by such raids; as Superintendent Eaton observed across the valley, "Panics and stampedes have been of continual occurrence."[110]

This was exactly the sort of violence that Union officials like Adj. Gen. Lorenzo Thomas had tried to prevent by assigning black regiments, such as Silas Small's First Arkansas AD, to guard leased plantations upon their enlistment. Union officials understood that the presence of regular forces was essential to the success of the plantation system. "The scope of these operations depends entirely upon the movement of the armies," Superintendent Eaton argued, and upon the "protection for this industry" provided by the presence of troops.[111] Around Helena, the commanding general recognized the urgency of dispatching troops to plantations, writing, "I have to protect them, or the Governments plans are frustrated."[112] The refugees did not just need Union troops to score a victory in this war, these officials recognized; they needed those troops to make sure they *survived* the war and could enjoy the fruits of that victory. They needed the sort of protection that came from armed forces scaring off raiders by their very presence (one Union official in Louisiana noted the "wholesome dread guerrillas have of a regular force"), or from those forces fighting back when guerrillas approached. And yet, in the spring of 1864, many plantations up and down the river did not get anything close to adequate protection.[113]

To some degree the geography of the plantations proved very difficult for sustaining military protection. The plantations were usually located miles away from the more heavily garrisoned cities like Vicksburg or Memphis, and from the riverbanks patrolled by Union ships.[114] Allowing this to happen, Superintendent Eaton declared that summer, was a crucial and self-defeating mistake. "Had locations been selected —not as some have insisted, upon a civil basis, but in accordance with military ideas," Eaton wrote, "losses of life and property would have been greatly lessened." The lessees had been too "moved by hopes of large gains" and had chosen their lands accordingly, Eaton explained, when considerations of military protection should have been paramount in locating the plantation operations at the outset. Now the plantations were instead scattered in remote areas, some further isolated by swamps and bayous, leaving them "exposed to guerrillas."[115] Over time this forced some lessees to contract their operations. Others who came forward to demand more military protection rarely got it; they were nothing better than a "carping grumbling throng of men," according to Eaton, for believing that "all military operations [should be] devoted to the safety of their plantations and the making of their private fortunes."[116] Eaton was more inclined to applaud the decisions of black lessees, who comprised a small but notable segment of the lessee population, to locate in safer regions, eschewing cotton cultivation altogether in favor of vegetables. "The black man was the only one in whom was left a shred of reasonable prudence," Eaton sighed.[117]

Yet the lessees' choices did not deserve all of the blame. For at the very same time they tried to get their enterprises up and running, the Union's military strategy underwent a monumental shift that rendered the plantations more vulnerable than ever to guerrilla terror. It happened in the winter and spring of 1864, when the Union army began drawing significant numbers of troops away from the Mississippi Valley to mount new campaigns to the east. Gen. Ulysses S. Grant had been elevated to the command of all Union forces, leaving the West in the hands of Gen. William T. Sherman, who in February moved 20,000 troops over 100 miles east into the interior of Mississippi, to Meridian, where they tore up an extensive railroad network and destroyed locomotives.[118] It was a preview of what would come by September, when Sherman guided over 100,000 troops farther east to Atlanta in an ultimately victorious and pivotal campaign that left the city in Union hands and launched his march to the sea.[119]

The Union troops heading east would liberate thousands more men, women, and children from slavery in Georgia and the Carolinas—but they left in their wake thousands more in the Mississippi Valley, who were now more vulnerable than ever to capture, torture, and return to slavery. "Irregulars grew more active across the Western theater" as a result of such removals of troops, historian Earl Hess has explained, "seemingly unafraid of the small Union garrisons left behind as Sherman maximized troop strength on active fronts."[120] Those small garrisons were largely black troops, like Silas Small's First Arkansas AD—now renamed the Forty-Sixth U.S. Colored Troops (USCT)—which Sherman declined to bring with him out of a desire to rely on more seasoned soldiers—and out of his own personal disdain for black troops.[121] But this, in turn, made the undermanned black regiments targets, too, as seen most horrifically in April 1864, when Confederate cavalry forces, under the direction of Gen. Nathan Bedford Forrest, overwhelmed the small garrison of black troops at Fort Pillow in Tennessee, capturing it and then massacring over 300 unarmed black soldiers after they had surrendered.[122]

White officers complained about the insufficient numbers of troops in their midst. Brig. Gen. N. B. Buford, the latest to assume command at Helena, declared a month before the guerrilla attacks in his area that this "little handful of troops of mine" was inadequate to protect refugees. Even worse, it was "the only force on the Mississippi now in the state of Arkansas," and "there is no force in the State of Mississippi between Memphis and Vicksburg." He asked that 300 cavalry and 500 infantry be sent to him at once.[123] The reduction of troops also sent refugees, as well as the lessees, fleeing the leased plantations in search of more protected ground, especially in cities. "There has been a general stampede from all the camps near the river between here and Helena, in consequence of the removal of all federal protection," reported an official on

Facing Combat

Paw Paw Island. "Hundreds in the country were frightened from their homes and labor, through fear of guerrillas, upon the withdrawal of our troops from the outposts," reported another in Vicksburg, and as a result "have sought and found refuge and employment in the city."[124] Vicksburg's black population increased nearly tenfold over the course of 1864, from 1,100 in December 1863, to 4,554 in September 1864, to 12,000 by February 1865. The influx of refugees also sent Memphis's black population rising, from 6,000 in December 1863 to around 22,000 by February 1865, while Helena's, although never that large, doubled in the first half of 1864, from 1,700 in January to 3,308 in June.[125]

The Union's plantation system, meanwhile, never recovered. "There is scarcely one of them all which has escaped guerrilla atrocities," Superintendent Eaton observed, and "the greater proportion of the whole number have entirely and finally broken up." He foresaw no possibility for the plantations to be sufficiently protected, for to do so would require "making military operations subservient to the cotton raising interest; which is not the intention of the Government."[126] The troops would remain in the East to finish out the defeat of the Confederacy—leaving the West vulnerable for the duration of the war. It did not help the plantations either that in September 1864 the cotton crop was nearly destroyed by an insect known as the "army worm." "After braving all the perils of guerrilla warfare; after months of hard work," wrote one Union official, "it was hard to see the whole crop snatched away."[127]

~~~

It was now over a year since the Emancipation Proclamation first drew refugees from slavery into combat, but the fight in the Mississippi Valley had changed dramatically. The guerrilla attacks along the river in 1864 amounted to nothing less than the war stripped to its most violent essence. The war was not just a battle between the Union and the Confederacy in the valley: as the two regular armies moved on to other battlegrounds, spaces opened up in their wake in which slave owner and former slave, white and black, now came face-to-face. The plantations and all the refugee camps were fast becoming their own battlegrounds.

No matter how much the refugees were forced to pick up their children and flee, though, they also prepared to fight back. Black soldiers were ready, of course, but civilians also armed themselves for a fight. Union officials' writings from this period are rife with discoveries of refugees "well armed with revolvers." At Young's Point, across the river from Vicksburg, Maj. George Young of the Sixty-Third USCT reported that "many of the negroes . . . have arms."[128] But such incidents were a source of concern for white Union officials, who preferred regulating black civilians' access to weapons. At Helena, for example, Gen. N. B. Buford ordered his subordinates "to visit and search all contraband houses, cabins, tents &c. in and around Helena Ark. to search for Guns, Pistols and ordnance arms," which he reflexively assumed had been "stolen" from Union authorities.[129] In cases like these, provost marshal officials seized the weapons in the name of protecting military order but were undoubtedly also driven by the same race-fueled concerns about black insurrection that had previously moved Southern states to outlaw the possession of guns by the enslaved.[130]

Yet those who armed themselves revealed that personal security was a paramount, if not *the* paramount, concern as they pondered their next moves in 1864.[131] And this was no less the case for Eliza Bogan. She could have left the Company E camp, as some Union officials preferred, and taken up residence in Vicksburg or back in Helena, but such a move would have still run the risk of her being sent out to an insufficiently guarded plantation. Eliza again chose proximity to Silas instead: "I staid right with Silas Small in the barracks."[132] Of all her options, it was her husband's camp that promised some degree of security, for in the same proximity to soldiers that Union officials associated with scandal and demoralization, Eliza likely saw safety and emotional comfort and familiarity. This made her one of the more fortunate women, though, as Union officials in Vicksburg reported that spring that "the colored soldiers have complained most bitterly about the way they have been treated, by their wives being taken away from them and sent they knew not to what camp or plantation."[133]

Bogan's choice revealed the irony of seeking personal security by going deeper and deeper into a war zone. The company was on the move again in early March 1864 during Sherman's Meridian campaign, ordered to move up the Yazoo River in an attempt to divert the Confederates' attention from the Mississippi city. "I was with the company on this march," Eliza later recalled. "The regiment had a fight, on that march, at Roche's plantation—at the Gin House. Sixteen colored soldiers were killed & the gin house was burnt down."[134] Eliza also witnessed the liberation of more refugees from slavery during that campaign—an estimated 4,500, according to Union reports—who loaded themselves onto wagons and wound their way into Vicksburg.[135] Yet she also witnessed Silas's fall in this battle. It did not come from gunfire—but once again from illness. Silas had contracted measles in the weeks before the march up the Yazoo River, but according to Eliza, he "was just getting so he could stir about when the regiment marched." Yet the march then took a toll. "He was taken sick on the march & was put in the ambulance & carried to

Vicksburg & was placed in the hospital," which was nothing more than a tent. Eliza then moved into the tent with Silas and went to work nursing him back to health.[136]

It was not unusual for a laundress to become a de facto nurse. In regimental camps all across the warring South, where there was little in the way of formal medical care to rely upon, no surgeon in camp, and no real hospital beyond the tent, it was often up to "company women," like Eliza, to take on nursing duties.[137] And refugees had always, even while enslaved, tended to their own health care rather than rely entirely on an inadequate and neglectful white medical establishment.[138] The army's medical system was changing by 1864, however, with the appointment of a medical director and inspector of freedmen to oversee much of the Mississippi Valley. The number of surgeons treating refugees subsequently increased from eight to thirty-two total, but these efforts could not reach everyone, most especially those on the remote leased plantations and in the regimental camps like the Forty-Sixth USCT's.[139]

Eliza might have been prepared to deal with the danger of measles. One year before, and not long after their first arrival in the regiment's encampment in Goodrich's Landing, Silas's sister, Celestia, had fallen ill with the disease too—and quickly succumbed to it. Eliza probably witnessed the death of her companion firsthand, an event that must have taken no small toll on this interdependent network of Phillips County refugees.[140] During Celestia's illness they would have seen the rash take hold of her body, and possibly a high fever, bloodshot eyes, and a hacking cough too. Through the illnesses of the other men in the company who succumbed to smallpox, rheumatism, measles, and other illnesses identified in a company register of deaths only by symptoms like "diarrhea," they would have seen up close how quickly disease could snuff out the pursuit of freedom.[141]

Eliza thus set to work caring for Silas. And she had help: at her side in the hospital tent was a man from their old neighborhood named Dennis Bogan, another member of Company E, whose relationship with Silas she described as like "partners—I mean theirs close friends. They were pretty much always together."[142] (Another woman in the company likewise noted that "Silas and Dennis Bogan used to run together more than most of the soldiers did.")[143] Dennis routinely visited the tent after Silas became sick, offering companionship as well as the emetic that Eliza administered to help purge Silas of his illness. Dennis, in fact, proved resourceful in tracking down and obtaining various medicines—and for that Eliza was grateful. "I used to go to Dennis to get him to get niter for Silas from a lady that was about a mile from Barracks," she later explained. But as they tended to Silas and got to know each other in the tent (Eliza explained she only "knew Dennis Bogan by sight before the war"), they did not know that something astonishing had transpired back in their old neighborhood—something that would forever shake the region and reveal, with startling clarity, the degree to which the war in the valley had become a fight between former slaves and slave owners, black and white.[144]

～～～

Those who remained in Phillips County had endured unrelenting waves of violence—just as nearly everyone did in the Mississippi Valley. Eliza's owner, Josiah McKiel, was seized in the summer of 1863 by Confederate guerrillas "for the purpose of hanging him," according to newspaper reports, as a punishment for his public Unionism.[145] He was later released unharmed, however, and the next year went on to get himself elected as one of four delegates from Phillips County to a state convention overseeing Arkansas's restoration to the Union.[146] The reports did not bother to mention how the guerrillas treated the black people who remained on McKiel's plantation, including Hester, her daughter, Nancy, or Eliza's children. But it is hard to believe they were spared. Still, the guerrillas' attack on the McKiel property was not the most shocking incident of violence that the neighborhood would witness that year.

A couple plantations over resided Dennis Bogan's owner, Monroe Bogan, whose reliance on the whip was growing in proportion to his desperation. Monroe Bogan was a twenty-eight-year-old who had only recently established himself as a planter and slaveholder in Phillips County. Like other white men in the neighborhood, Monroe had migrated west from South Carolina in the 1850s and arrived in Arkansas by 1859, bringing with him many of the thirty-seven slaves he would own by 1860, including eighteen-year-old Dennis.[147] He quickly developed a reputation in the neighborhood as an especially "cruel" and "exacting" master, denying his slaves rest on Sundays and whipping someone nearly every day. Sometimes he replaced the whip with other nearby objects, like a chair; women he whipped "in the most indecent manner."[148] Yet Monroe felt his control slipping as the war dragged on, particularly after April 1863, when Dennis took off and enlisted in nearby Helena, along with two other men he claimed to own, Charles and Lewis Bogan.[149]

The dynamics of slavery had forever changed on the Bogan property, as was true on most Southern plantations. Here was a weakened slave owner, desperate to hold on to his enterprise, who now had slaves around him who could see that change was coming but were not yet part of it. It was a combustible mix. It exploded on the Bogan plantation on December 15, 1863, in the early morning hours, when one of the enslaved men still on the property,

West Bogan, discovered Monroe just outside his cabin. It was not their first encounter that day. That one took place even earlier, after West refused Monroe's order to work and was subsequently caught "running to town," into Union lines at Helena.[150] Their second encounter was then witnessed by a woman named Maria Bogan, who was nursing her infant at the time. She realized something was happening only when children came running into her dwelling, shouting, "Master is trying to whip West." Maria then went to the door just in time to look outside and see West strike back with an axe. She quickly turned and shielded the children—and herself—from the scene. It was a grisly one: her master was hit on the head and neck at least twice and his head was "nearly severed" from his shoulders. Monroe Bogan was dead.[151]

West finally had his chance to enter Union lines. He dropped the axe and ran to Helena, where he quickly got himself hired by the quartermaster's department. But his employment did not last long. Less than two weeks after his arrival, Union authorities arrested him on the charge of the "awful crime of murder" and locked him up in the military prison.[152] The officials, in occupying Helena and its environs, had instituted martial law and given themselves wide latitude to maintain order among the civilian population, and this included bringing a murder case like this to trial. And thus, two months later, in February 1864, following a court-martial trial in which he could not testify on his own behalf, West was found guilty and sentenced "to be hanged by the neck till he is dead." It was a devastating outcome—especially so for a man like West, who may have viewed the Union as an ally in his fight for freedom. Now these defenders of the Emancipation Proclamation were going to kill him.[153]

As West Bogan awaited his execution in Helena, Dennis Bogan, back in Vicksburg and most likely unaware of the events that had transpired on his old plantation, continued to assist Eliza in nursing Silas Small back to health. Eliza, for her part, continued to envision her future with Silas, one that would involve transforming their marriage into more than "just a slave marriage." Special Order No. 15, issued by Adj. Gen. Lorenzo Thomas on March 5, 1864, in Vicksburg, had authorized Superintendent Eaton to oversee the ordination of ministers and the issuance of marriage certificates, just as the Union had done at other places, like Fort Monroe.[154] Over 1,400 couples had their marriages recognized by the government over the next seven months, but as Eliza later explained, she and Silas were unable to join them. "We had set a time to go," she recalled, "but before we did he took the measles and died."[155] Silas had deteriorated rapidly, succumbing to the disease on April 6, 1864, a week after his return from the Yazoo River campaign.[156]

Small died just as authorities back in Helena were growing uneasy about executing West Bogan. That spring and summer, Maj. Gen. Frederick Steele, the same unsympathetic commander who had expelled refugee slaves from the town back in 1862 and who now commanded the Union's operations throughout Arkansas, found reason to question West Bogan's death sentence. He suspended it and instead allowed new reviews of the case to travel up and down the army's military justice chain of command. The move was prompted by a complaint from Chaplain John J. Herrick, who had represented Bogan at the trial, that he was never allowed to introduce evidence of Monroe Bogan's "despicable and cruel character" during the proceedings. This led some officials to question whether the charge of "murder" was even correct in the first place, since there seemed to be no "intent to kill" and thus clear self-defense was at work. Others, including the highest-ranking official overseeing the court-martial proceedings, Judge Advocate General Joseph Holt, soon reframed the events entirely by shifting the blame off West Bogan's shoulders and onto Monroe Bogan's. The crucial, most telling detail in Holt's view was Monroe Bogan's attempt to whip his slave in the first place; this, concluded Holt, was something "he had no right to do," thanks to the "changed relations of the white and black population of the Southern States."[157]

Relations had changed, Holt argued in a written appeal to President Lincoln about the case, because the Emancipation Proclamation had changed them. The president's January 1863 order did more than alter the meaning of the war in the abstract; it did more than authorize the freeing of slaves in rebellious territory or the enlistment of black men in the Union army. It changed the meaning of each and every daily encounter between master and slave on the South's plantations. To hold a man in slavery, and to impose on him "ceaseless toil and cruel punishments," as Monroe Bogan did, Holt explained, was, in the aftermath of the proclamation, "in violation of law and right." Therefore, it was to be expected, even justified, that a man illegally enslaved would do what it took to free himself. The axe West Bogan wielded had rightfully changed from an "implement with which he was quietly going to his unrecompensed toil," Holt concluded, "into a weapon of revenge."[158]

The judge advocate general essentially condoned killing, even slave uprising and rebellion, as a means of implementing the Emancipation Proclamation—exactly what so many of emancipation's opponents, as well as some of its supporters, had long feared would accompany slavery's end. Holt's judgment was befitting of his record for punishing Confederates swiftly and firmly, and for advocating emancipation wholeheartedly, but it was not a position ever before espoused by the president, to whom he sent the case for a final ruling. Lincoln had already urged freed people, in the Emancipation Proclamation, to "abstain from all violence." But he also followed those words with the caveat "unless in necessary self-defence," which gave him room to agree with at least some of Holt's reasoning. The president said nothing about the case publicly, but in July 1864 he added his signature to the trial record beside the simple notation "sentence disapproved."[159] West Bogan's life was spared by the president of the United States.

In many ways Holt's and Lincoln's ruling had simply acknowledged what was already ongoing in the Mississippi Valley, where freedom seekers had to arm themselves and fight back against their enslavement, or else be beaten and killed before securing their freedom. It acknowledged that what was once called slave insurrection was now a necessary means of implementing emancipation—that in this war there was little difference between West's killing of his master and a Union soldier's killing of a Confederate guerrilla during a surprise raid. The outcome of West Bogan's case thus underlined a basic truth for everyone, even Eliza Bogan: freedom did not come on January 1, 1863, nor did it come with the arrival of Union troops in Confederate Arkansas the year before. It would come when those seeking freedom fought their way out of bondage—and that fight was still far from over.

} 5 {

Battling Hunger

Sometimes the gravest battle involved fighting hunger. Eating was, of course, along with sleeping, a most basic human need that could not be set aside on the journey to freedom. Hunger would imperil the very physical act of making one's way into Union lines; nourishment could energize refugees to press on and walk mile after mile, across creeks and swamps, through forests and fields, and into a Union camp. And yet, as the men, women, and children on this journey left their plantations behind, they also left behind accustomed food supplies — the rations doled out by their owners, or the gardens they tended on their own time, or the nearby streams in which they fished. Sometimes it was not difficult to hunt and forage on the trek into Union lines, or if the journey was short, to survive on what could be carried on their backs or in their wagons. But at other times, the extended journey became a painful, tortuous period marked by the ravages of hunger.

One woman who walked alone for twenty-three days on her way to Yorktown, Virginia, in 1864 grew "so faint with hunger," as she later described it, that she approached a remote cabin and asked a woman and "dying child" inside for help. "We also are nearly starved," they told her, before producing "a morsel of corn bread" to share among the three of them. The refugee woman survived and later told of feeling "bitter sorrow" at having taken bread from the child.[1] But her act exemplified the desperation widely felt among this population on the move. Those refugees who could not resort to even these measures were observed arriving inside Union lines "famished with hunger," "faint and sick from hunger," and "emaciated," in the words of observing missionaries.[2]

The existence of hunger, even outright starvation, exposed one of the more grim realities of wartime emancipation. If liberation from slavery meant, at its core, the liberation of bodies that had long been confined and exploited by others, then it was going to require more than simply removing one's physical self from the site of enslavement to experience the bodily self-determination associated with freedom.[3] The refugees' emancipation, after all, took place in a war, one that stressed and destroyed bodies on a scale never before seen in American history. Scarcity of food was only part of what threatened them. The war also turned on the infliction of wounds, scars, and mortal combat; then there was the collateral damage inflicted by rampant disease that swept through military encampments. At the same time, refugees from slavery entered a military sphere in which armies depended on the regimentation of bodies to form a well-oiled combat machine, issuing orders to men about what to eat and what to wear and where to march and move. War required a continued fight for bodily control and survival against harsh odds — and that fight became especially visible in the basic effort to eat.[4]

~~~

One of the first things refugees learned as they entered Union lines was that food supplies were not abundant or freely distributed but instead regulated by the army's war-making machine. Food had become a weapon in this war, an element of Union strategy in particular that involved breaking down Confederate resistance by slowly, gradually starving the Southern population. The Union, especially with its turn to "hard war" by 1864, made war on the South's food production, tearing up agricultural fields and the transportation networks necessary to distribute foodstuffs. It also aimed directly at food supply chains when looking to conquer cities like Vicksburg, where the Union's siege involved blocking the roads and railroads necessary for carrying food into the city from the surrounding farms. In that case, according to historian Mark M. Smith, the Union created nothing short of an "artificial famine." Conversely, in other occupied areas, the Union handed out rations to Confederate civilians, aiming in part to weaken their loyalties to the Confederacy by creating a dependency on the Union. Food had always, across time and place in history, offered strategic leverage in wars, and in the U.S. Civil War the Union exploited this to great advantage.[5] The refugees had played their part in starving out the Confederate South by abandoning their plantations and the food cultivation that took place therein. But to keep themselves from starving, too, they would have to navigate the Union army's grip on the food supply.

The army's subsistence department positioned itself as the supplier of their food. And it assumed that role beginning at Fort Monroe with Gen. Benjamin Butler, who made the issuance of food rations a nearly automatic response to the arrival of "contrabands." Just days after admitting the first into Union lines, Butler wrote to his superiors, "I have therefore determined to employ ... the able bodied persons in the party, issuing proper food for the support of all."[6] Food came nearly first in Butler's mind: he may have overlooked the payment of wages to the refugees, but attending to pressing physical needs was a different matter. It was a self-evident part of the "protection" promised to the refugees by the military—so much so that very little public debate surrounded the army's provision of food to refugees during the war. "They have a right to some kind of assistance," a federal commission argued in 1864 in a nod to basic human rights, "and the government alone has the means and ability to furnish it." But it was more than a degree of humanitarianism that put the army in the position of food provider. "It is a military necessity that they should be fed from army rations," the *Freedmen's Bulletin* summed up a widely held belief. If it was important to keep this population working and fighting for the army, then it was in the military's interest to keep them fed and, thus, able bodied.[7]

The daily allotment of food, known as a "ration," resembled the one issued to soldiers. The two basic components of the soldier's daily ration, as stipulated in the official army regulations, were meat (twelve ounces of pork or one pound and four ounces of beef) and bread (one pound and six ounces of "soft bread or flour" or, in its place, one pound of "hard bread" or one pound and four ounces of cornmeal). Besides the protein and the starch, soldiers had to share a collective supply of beans or peas, rice or hominy, and coffee, sugar, vinegar, soap, salt, potatoes, candles, and "when practicable," molasses.[8] Orders from local commanders related to refugee rations varied from this only in quantity. The meat, according to 1864 orders from the subsistence department, was to be two ounces less than that given to soldiers; the bread, flour, or cornmeal ranged from six to eight ounces less. Similar reductions were taken for nearly every item issued, and in addition, children under fourteen years old were to receive half of what adults received.[9] In type and variety, then, the food may have been roughly the same as what soldiers received, coming from the same suppliers and traveling the same distribution networks, but the smaller amounts were the first indication that a refugee would not eat exactly like a soldier. And even that was only if these orders were followed in the first place.

The reality of food distribution turned out to be far graver and more precarious than anything dictated by these orders. No matter how carefully army regulations stipulated the measurement and variety of food rations on paper, this was war, and the disruptions it wrought could limit food supplies for days or even weeks. Serious food crises plagued Union encampments, affecting soldiers and refugees alike, most notably when Confederates disrupted Union supply lines or when Union troops picked up and moved rapidly, temporarily cutting off their connections to food supply channels. Shortages resulted, and what eventually made it into the mouths of soldiers and refugees could be spoiled, infested with insects, or in the case of the hardtack biscuits frequently issued with meat, stale and nearly inedible from years of sitting in storage. No one ate well in an army encampment; hunger was familiar to all, as were diarrhea and other ailments brought on by an insufficient diet.[10] To a Sanitary Commission agent assigned to Helena, Arkansas, in 1863, the situation was downright appalling. "The food is anything but healthy," Maria Mann wrote home to her aunt in Massachusetts, "bread especially." The meat was nearly inedible, too, for the beef, she wrote, "don't taste of it," and the pork was "more shocking try not to look at it."[11]

Poor management by officials compounded these problems at times, although when it came to feeding the refugees in particular, deliberate neglect and abuse played a role too. "The 'contraband ration' is smaller, less varied, and inferior to the ample allowance issued by Government to her soldiers," complained a Western Freedmen's Aid Commission report.[12] The problem stemmed first from clerks whose distribution of food failed to conform to orders. In Nashville, for example, Michael Deaver, a private with the Thirty-First Ohio, admitted to a group of visiting federal investigators in 1864 that "*the quantity issued I guessed at.*" Despite the orders' stipulation of exact measurements of food, Deaver claimed he never was given "*any direction as to the manner or quantity of my issue of supplies.*" He kept no record books "nor any writing or memorandum of the quantity or kind of supplies I receive or issue." This was remarkable, given that the army's regulations on the issuance of food were so detailed as to include thirty-eight different forms on which clerks were to record their work. Deaver, however, instead waited to see if the refugees "complain," and if so, "the next time I issue more." It was sloppy distribution at best—or deliberate neglect at worst. The Nashville investigators leaned toward the latter in their report, pointing to the food shortages, in addition to inadequacies of shelter, to conclude that "this colored refugee camp has been, and is, grossly neglected in all things necessary to the reasonable care and comfort of its inmates."[13]

The army's ration system required the proper functioning of its chain of command in order to put food in mouths. But that was precisely the problem, in the mind of Maj. E. L. Wentz, testifying before the American Freedmen's Inquiry Commission from Virginia in 1863. Refugee rations "are dealt out to them by subordinates, among whom there is a great deal of dishonesty," Wentz reported, and as a result "they do not give the contrabands near what they are entitled to."[14] Their dishonesty stemmed from a lack of sympathy for the refugees and their pursuit of emancipation, but also from the pecuniary gain that they themselves stood to enjoy. Rations, after all, were greatly valued and could be sold for profit, something that at times put soldiers' rations in jeopardy too.[15] That is what got Sgt. John Smith at Fort Monroe removed from his position in 1862, when Gen. John Wool's investigation found he had withheld rations and then sold the surplus to local sutlers for a personal profit of $550.[16] And it is what prompted forty-five refugee men on Roanoke Island to appeal to Gen. Benjamin Butler for help in 1864. "Knowing you to be a Gentleman of justice and a friend to the Negro race in this country," they began their query, before explaining that soldiers had been selling their rations to "secech citizens" in the region, and as a result, "it is no uncommon thing to see women and children crying for something to eat."[17]

Neglectful and corrupt practices only begin to explain why refugees all over the occupied South were crying for food. There was another systemic problem too. Designed only with the needs of young male soldiers in mind, the ration system, even when issued properly, was not adequate nutritionally for the diverse population of individuals crowding into the camps. "We have old people and very small children that need something different," came a report from Huntsville, Alabama, in early 1865, "especially when sick." Likewise, a report of the Western Freedmen's Aid Commission argued that "the sick, who are found in every camp, need other food than these rations, and ought to have a diet adapted, in some degree, to their condition."[18] The army's system had the potential to adapt to such needs: when soldiers became ill, for instance, it was not unheard of for hospital workers to secure other kinds of sustenance, in some instances selling a soldier's ration locally in order to purchase alternatives.[19] But such adaptations were only sporadically made for refugees. Civilian relief organizations occasionally stepped in to fill the void with appeals, like one issued by the Northwestern Freedmen's Aid Commission to followers in Chicago to "send us all the Pickled Cabbage, Sauerkraut, Potatoes and Onions you can procure. The SCURVY is making its appearance and cannot be checked while we feed on army rations."[20] But these organizations more commonly shipped plates, cups, and forks instead—essential items for consuming food that could be shipped long distances without concern for spoilage.[21]

The ration system may have been flawed in both design and implementation, but in the eyes of military officials, there was also no reason to revise it: the system was not supposed to support the refugees for very long anyway. This was to be temporary relief—in other words, a form of charity—a very different kind of food provision than that provided to soldiers. A man serving the nation as a member of the army or navy received food as compensation for his service; it was something he *earned*. But the men, women, and children taking up residence in the camps were not believed to have earned their rations so much as they *needed* them. Yet need, officials believed, was a fleeting condition, brought on in their case by an emergency. If the need lasted with any length, however, it became something other than the "blameless" condition that had initially obligated the federal government to provide food (as well as shelter). That assistance could thus be withdrawn, leaving the refugees, in contrast to the soldiers, unable to count on food rations for the duration of the war.[22]

It did not matter to most officials that the refugees had experienced similar journeys out of slavery, or similar challenges in forging a life in freedom during a war. They did not assume that all freedom seekers were equally needy—or even needy at all. "New comers are, without exception, objects of charity," stipulated orders from Fort Monroe, and for that reason, for them "aid is furnished at once."[23] But it was the refugees who had been in the camps for some time already who officials believed were ready to support themselves. In this respect, the army ration system came to resemble long-standing poverty relief policies on the state and local levels that had always distinguished between the "worthy" poor (the truly needy, or the "blameless") and the "able" poor (those deemed able to work). In antebellum cities, for example, it was not uncommon for the "able" poor to be identified and purged from the relief rolls, in the interest of reducing dependency and fostering the idealized qualities of independence and self-support associated with democratic citizenship.[24] The same impulse simply carried over into the wartime distribution of refugee food rations. Yet, in this context, to distinguish the "able" from the truly needy required getting to know the refugees, and this, in turn, gave rise to an intricate process of study and classification.

Names of individual refugees began to appear in ledger books kept by government clerks. Oversized and resembling the books that were ubiquitous in army camps, recording every enlistment, military order, arrest, admission to a hospital, and so many other day-to-day happenings, the ledgers were intended to record each single disbursement of food in the refugee camps too. Each entry listed a recipient by name, along with the circumstances behind his or her food issue, separated into columns. Omitted in these records was any notation of an owner's name, a small but meaningful indication of the refugees' changing status: they were no longer categorized as the dependents of enslavers. But the process of determining their "need" also betrayed an underlying fear that they might become dependent on the federal government instead.[25]

The information recorded alongside these names emerged from an inquiry that brought refugees face-to-face with government officials. In places closest to active combat, these meetings could be brief and haphazard; in places more settled and distant from the battlefront, a more formal system took shape. In eastern Virginia, for example, there were three steps to that inquiry. The first typically involved a visit from one of the subordinates of a superintendent of contrabands to a refugee's tent or cabin in order to conduct, in the words of a Virginia official, a "careful investigation" of their "situation and circumstances."[26] Near Fort Monroe in 1864 this duty fell to two men, "one white and the other colored," appointed for their ability to get to know the refugee population. One of them was Thomas Peake, who was familiar to some of the region's refugees already. Peake had been born a slave in eastern Virginia but was emancipated before the war at the time of his owner's death. Peake thus did not have to flee to freedom after 1861, but he established himself inside Union lines anyway, along with his wife, Mary, who was herself born free. The Peakes soon emerged as leaders among the refugee population around Fort Monroe and Hampton, with Mary establishing the first school in the region in September 1861 and Thomas working as a spy for the Union army. Though Mary succumbed to tuberculosis less than a year after the war began, Thomas continued to work on behalf of the Union and the refugees, becoming one of the outspoken voices when, for example, wages were not forthcoming.[27]

Peake possessed exactly the sort of social knowledge that Union officials felt was essential to the food-distribution process. "I visited the houses & those that I found—being acquainted with the place, being a native of the place— that needed rations," Peake later described, "I would give a little note . . . saying that they needed rations."[28] Peake's appointment was an admission of the imperfect, unscientific process involved in determining need. There were no clear-cut determinants, and the army issued no directives outlining exactly the standards by which need should be determined. It would be up to the officials meeting with the refugees to make such judgments, and those who could elicit the most information, like Thomas Peake, were perceived to have a better chance of making sound decisions. Peake not only relied on his own firsthand impressions, but he also "would inquire from the neighbors around" the refugees, asking how others in the community perceived the subjects of his investigation. How "self-supporting" were they? Or could they become so? This kind of subjectivity had the potential to encourage abuse and fraud, but Peake simply described his sources as "some persons I was acquainted with that I thought would do justice by the govt."[29]

Peake's "little note," referred to also as a "ticket," marked an individual as needy. But it did not mark the end of the information-gathering process. The ticket holder next took the slip to the superintendent of contrabands, Charles Wilder, and in that second meeting, the higher-ranked official personally observed who had been awarded rations, possibly engaging them in another round of conversation before signing his approval on the ticket. He also determined how much food the bearer would receive — one ration or two? Finally, the ticket holder then made his or her way to the local commissary office, where the paper would be redeemed for the rations, uncooked and handed out in bulk (fig. 13).[30] The rations were to be distributed every ten days over the course of one month, and for as long as three months, depending on the officials' determination.[31]

Among those whose names appeared in the ledger books in Virginia in 1864 was Mary Brooks, a mother of two children, who took up residence in Hampton while her husband enlisted in Company B, Fourth USCT, and went off to fight in the Petersburg campaign that summer; she received two rations to share among the three of them. Also receiving food was Phillip Bright, an unmarried and "infirm" man, referred to by government clerks as an "Old Man native of this Place"; he received one ration. Fanny Holt, a widow in Newport News with three children, including one son in the Union army, received one ration, while Elizabeth Wilder, also a widow, received three rations to share with the four children living with her, while two other sons were off fighting in the army.[32] Far more women than men earned lines in the ledger books. A sampling from November 1864, for example, shows that of 3,794 people in and around Fort Monroe who received rations, 1,783 were women, 1,942 were children, and only 69 were men. This meant that men received only 2 percent of the rations distributed that month, even though, according to a population census taken the following month, they comprised 27 percent of the total refugee population in that area.[33] The same proportions played out month after month, in regions beyond Virginia too.

Only "infirm" or "old" men, like Phillip Bright, were likely to show up on the ration lists. The rest of the men, no matter how badly they needed to eat, no matter how much they had to rely on the army's supply chain to obtain food, would have to earn their food. Men were thus expected to enlist in the army almost immediately upon arriving in a camp or to find employment quickly as an army laborer; they would then be paid with wages — and rations. Food for refugee men thus became a form of compensation for work, just like it was for

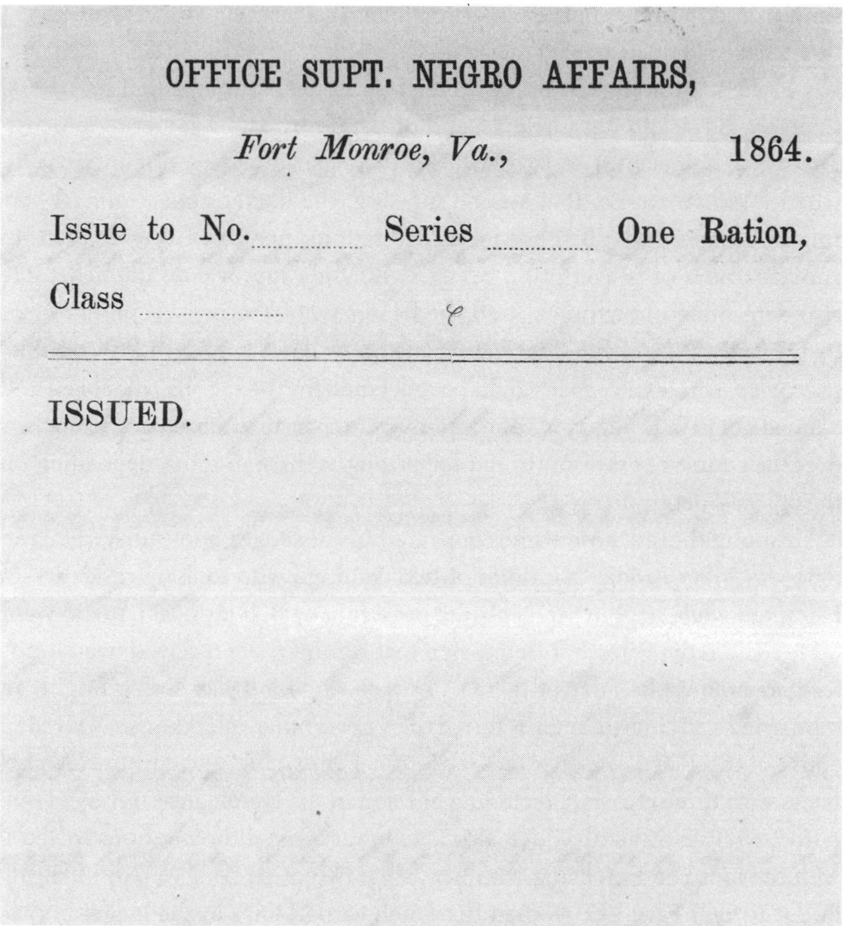

OFFICE SUPT. NEGRO AFFAIRS,

Fort Monroe, Va.,   1864.

Issue to No.＿＿＿ Series ＿＿＿ One Ration,

Class ＿＿＿＿＿   ₵

_____

ISSUED.

FIGURE 13. A ration "ticket" that recipients of rations had to
bring to the commissary office in order to receive food
(Charles Wilder to Major General Ord, January 23, 1865, Letters Received, ser. 12,
M619, reel 429, Record Group 94, National Archives and Records Administration)

a white soldier, which also meant, in turn, that it could be a harsh instrument
for coercing labor and service out of them. "If any able to work are found loitering in the camps," an official in Vicksburg explained in 1864, "they are either
given labor in the department; or their rations stopped; compelling them to
find labor somewhere else." Never mind that someone "loitering" may have
quit work because of the chronic lack of payment of wages, as so many men
did around Fort Monroe at the war's beginning, or because he did not want to
become separated from his family, which many positions, especially those of a
soldier or an impressed laborer, required.[34]

Battling Hunger

It was less difficult for officials to classify women and children as dispro-portionately needy and "blameless" and therefore requiring more protection. That was, after all, the sort of patriarchal assumption that had long guided law and policy in the United States, as well as social welfare policies in their home states and cities.[35] Yet the army did not aim to create a permanent roster of female charity cases either. The efforts to employ women on leased plantations in places like the Mississippi Valley, or in hospitals and quartermaster's de-partments, or as personal servants all evinced a perfect willingness to see black women continue working as they always had and earn their own food. And at the same time, a closer look at what appeared next to the women's names in the ledgers reveals a deliberate effort under way to ensure that their food sup-port—and the women's dependence on the federal government more gener-ally—would only be temporary too.

After noting the date, as well as a woman's full name, the clerk recorded her camp of residence, number of children, and her "class" and "series." "Class" referred to how many rations had been issued to her, with a 1, for example, representing one adult who received one ration, while a 6 indicated an adult and five children who received three and a half rations to share. More telling was the letter that indicated her "series": an A was for "Soldier's Wife"; a B for "Sailor's Wife"; a C for "Widow"; a D for "Infirm"; or an E for "Husband out of the Department." Not only did this column underscore that this was really a process for women primarily—only one of the categories, "Infirm," could be applied to men—but all of the other designations revolved entirely around the woman's marital status. She was either a wife or a widow in the eyes of the federal government. The reason for this, beyond reflecting basic assumptions that male officials had about the duty of women to marry, was revealed in the last column, variously labeled "Remarks" or "Husband" or "Military." In this column the clerks jotted down such notations as "Co. C, 1st USCC," or "three sons in army"—anything that could help officials identify the name and loca-tion of a husband or other male provider.[36] This was essential information, for if a husband (or son) was alive and could be located, then the cost of a woman's rations could be deducted from his pay. This would, in turn, shift a woman's dependency away from the government and onto the shoulders of a man.[37]

Here again the military recognized—and exploited—the strategic value of food. This particular system may not have gained the Union any military ad-vantage over the Confederacy, but it did exert social pressure on those seeking protection from the Union. This pressure was similar to the pressure surround-ing shelter, especially in places where Union officials had designed planned settlements around private family homes, disaggregating the larger, more complex social networks to encourage the smaller, nuclear families associated with American citizenship. Now the ration system would mold *how* those families, ensconced in their private homes, could become self-supporting. Men were to work for wages and support the women and children dependent on them: that was the proper social order of freedom in the eyes of white, Northern military officials. And that belief had already played no small role in the army's push to legally marry refugee couples during the war.[38]

Yet this expectation bore little resemblance to the families streaming into refugee camps. These were individuals whose biological families had long been torn apart by enslavers and the slave trade, and whose kin relations had gone unrecognized (and unprotected) by state law. For generations they had adapted and formed other kin relations with those who were not blood relations but who were every bit family in their minds and hearts. And then, once war came, the Union army, while supporting families' reunions inside the camps, simultaneously threatened those relations once more by separating families with policies like impressment. The families could not, therefore, be easily categorized into discrete, nuclear structures, with husbands supporting dependent women and children. Their social networks were too diverse, sometimes too shattered; even the men assumed to be natural providers could not always step into that position, especially if the military failed to pay them wages, or abruptly evacuated a camp and sent them moving again with no guarantee of employment at the other end.

The food rationing system was thus about far more than meeting basic nutritional needs. It exerted the leverage of food to bring about social change — and to bring it about very quickly. Rations were not issued indefinitely but instead for periods of only one, two, or three months in length. Once that period ended, a refugee could expect a return visit from an investigator, who would approach his or her case "as an entirely new one" and start the entire process all over again.[39] With new investigations held regularly, officials believed that it could take as little as a month, or perhaps as much as three months, for a man and his family to move from dependence and into the self-support associated with freedom. After that one-to-three-month period, a refugee was more likely to incur suspicion that he or she was no longer needy, or no longer "blameless" for his or her suffering but instead "blamed," and thus no longer entitled to rations. The refugees were therefore put on a clock, expected to cycle off government food support at a pace that was downright astonishing for a population trying to build new lives after slavery.

Yet the underlying impulse to squeeze a diverse and ever-changing refugee population into a rigid system defined by columns and "classes" never went away. They could, at the very least, be seen and counted this way. And for that there was an overwhelming practical need: the army needed some way of counting how much food was consumed and, therefore, how much more would be needed in subsequent months.[40] Food relief fast became an enormous expense, no matter how hard the army tried to purge individual people from the relief rolls. Superintendents of contrabands routinely turned to their clerks' ledgers to calculate totals and sent aggregate numbers to their superiors in Washington. In an 1864 report from eastern Virginia, for example, Charles Wilder computed the total value of refugees' rations issued that year at $130,902.42; his counterpart at City Point, Virginia, Lt. Col. Horace Porter, reported $412,534.52 the same year. Notably, they offered no estimates, no round numbers, but aimed to be exact, right down to the penny.[41]

Their precision conveyed control and reassurance that Wilder and Porter were on top of the numbers and, thus, on top of the system and the people within it. Numbers, after all, were powerful and meaningful. By the mid-nineteenth century, "the prestige of quantification was in the ascendant," as historian Patricia Cline Cohen has put it, with statistics assuming a persuasive power never before seen in American culture and politics.[42] And in the middle of a war that was upending the American social order in a revolutionary and unprecedented way, the impulse to count and aggregate and wrap one's mind around the size and scope of the freedom-seeking population was profound. In addition to filling ration ledger books with names, there were full-blown attempts to enumerate a "census" in camps: Fort Monroe conducted one in February 1862, for example, as did New Bern, North Carolina, in April 1863; Helena, Arkansas, in November 1863; and Murfreesboro, Tennessee, in February 1864.[43] The process was never an especially precise one and involved sending detailed soldiers (as well as the occasional missionary) into refugee tents and cabins to elicit identifying information. But it proved difficult to gather complete information for a population that so often was on the move.

Regardless of the veracity of the numbers themselves, the process of counting and categorizing the refugee population lent an air of order to an otherwise disordered wartime upheaval. The result, on the pages of ration books or census returns, broke down what seemed to anxious white officials like a mass of crowded, undifferentiated people into knowable individuals who could be tracked over time. And this was reassuring to a superintendent of contrabands like Charles Wilder, who wanted to know if his work was, indeed, working. Wilder believed his primary purpose as superintendent was "to make the Negro self-supporting and place him in a condition to remain so," and there was no better indication of self-support, he believed, than in the source of one's food. He routinely calculated what percentage of the refugee population received rations and liked what he saw. "That seventy eight percent of the adult colored population in his district — all of whom less than four years ago were in slavery — are now independent of assistance," Wilder argued in late 1864, "fully shows its success."[44] Others, as he did, routinely counted up and reported on those who were "independent" versus those who were "drawing rations," a determination meant to illustrate, in a convincing way, how well the military was guiding former slaves into a future of freedom.[45]

〜〜〜

No matter how forward-looking the food policies may have seemed to the Union officials implementing them, to the refugees the food-rationing system was utterly familiar, more of a relic of their past than a sign of change to come. In slavery they had endured a rationing system, too, as their enslavers relied on a food distribution system that rarely met their full nutritional needs — or their tastes. Yet the enslaved had never tried to rely on rations alone, knowing that the woods around them could be hunted, or that the lake and river waters nearby could be fished, or that the land around their cabins could be cultivated with fruits and vegetables. In what spare time they had, if they had any at all, the South's enslaved people worked to supplement their plantation rations as a matter of basic survival for themselves and their families.[46] This impulse never left them as they made their way into refugee camps.

Faced with meager rations once again, combined with the army's push to limit their duration, the refugees knew that they would have to fend for themselves in order to survive, just as they always had. Yet their escape into freedom also set them back temporarily, wrenched as they were from the local environments they had come to know so well — the woods, rivers, and gardens where they had long found reliable food sources.[47] Where could they find food now? And find it quickly — and in abundance? For those who had traveled hundreds of miles, moving from rural plantations into cities, or from the hinterland to the coast, the journey to freedom was an environmental migration that required learning anew about the land around them. And it was not easily done, for there were often hundreds, if not thousands, of other people trying to do the same thing at the same time in the same places. Union soldiers, most especially, were also unwilling to rely solely on government rations and set about hunting and foraging too. And, as they were most likely the first to arrive in a given region, they sometimes cleared out the berry bushes and local crops before the refugees even arrived.[48] "Not a hen in Helena," Sanitary Commission agent Maria Mann observed as a result, "soldiers long ago annihilated them."[49]

Battling Hunger

More often the difference between survival or not came down to a garden. The refugees would have to produce food for themselves. Raising chickens, hogs, and other animals was very difficult, for any livestock brought into the camps was usually seized by the federal government. They instead looked to fruit, grains, and especially vegetables, starting with whatever seeds they brought with them or could find nearby — or could be sent to them by benevolent organizations. The Western Freedmen's Aid Commission, for example, sent fifty-four boxes of garden seeds to the South during a five-month period in 1863; the Friends Freedmen's Association of Philadelphia likewise issued a call for "a quantity of seeds," especially beans, peas, and seed corn, to be sent to Virginia the next year.[50] The gardens that resulted ranged from larger, communal vegetable gardens on the leased plantations to what were described by white observers as "little garden patches," or "a very small garden plat," next to individual shelters, as was most common in the planned settlements.[51] At Young's Point, Louisiana, the refugees created a series of gardens on either side of a levee.[52] From the harvests came more wide-ranging flavors than those provided in their rations, as well as nutrients that were sorely lacking but so necessary to prevent illness.

To establish a garden, however, required holding fast against the momentum of war. A garden required time, care, and stasis: everything threatened by the campaigns and battles that moved troops at a moment's notice and emptied camps of soldiers and refugees alike. It necessitated residence in one place during the long planting and growing seasons, something that was difficult for a man or woman who arrived in a camp too late to plant — or for those who were forced to evacuate before harvesttime. The relatively fixed position of a garden also made it a sitting target, not easily removed or protected when word came of approaching troops. "The soldiers of the neighboring garrisons have been deterred, neither by discipline nor principle," a report from the Mississippi Valley described marauding Union troops, "from appropriating the entire product of their labor."[53] And then Confederate soldiers did the same, turning the gardens of refugees into spoils of war.

A bountiful garden, when it survived, promised to push a refugee beyond basic subsistence. The men and women gardening at Young's Point in 1864, for example, did not just eat the fruits of their own labor but also filled bushel baskets with their harvests and took them across the river to Vicksburg, where they encountered, as one Union official put it, "a good market for vegetables." In other cities — in any areas with large concentrations of refugees and Union soldiers, and in some cases Confederate-sympathizing white civilians too — the demand for fresh produce offered refugees the chance to earn money from their labor in the gardens. Sometimes they sold to army sutlers; other times they supplied stores, like Edward Whitehurst's at Fort Monroe; other times they sold right out of their own baskets and wagons. With the proceeds from these sales, refugees could then turn around and purchase meat and other more desirable food, such as fresh-baked bread, enabling themselves and their families to continue supplementing and diversifying the rations obtained from the government.[54]

Those who gardened beyond subsistence were attuned to the vagaries of the wartime market in food, however volatile. Take the report from Acreville, Virginia, that described the settlement carefully divided into one-acre family lots. "In most cases a vegetable garden has been enclosed about the house, and successfully cultivated," the report explained, "and the balance of the lot devoted to Indian corn."[55] Or the report from Huntsville, Alabama, that described the camp's acreage divided into four sections, with 280 acres devoted to corn, thirty acres to cotton, seven acres to sorghum, and the rest to a "large vegetable garden."[56] Both places devoted greater attention — and acreage — to corn production, a move that responded directly to wartime demand. Corn was necessary to feed and fatten livestock; it was also the basis for cornmeal and corn bread, both of which were scarce in army rations but greatly desired. "Corn meal is most needed," came an appeal for expanded rations in Virginia.[57] Another official in the Mississippi Valley likewise discovered in a rough survey of refugees that "every" single person, "with one solitary exception," preferred to have "corn bread and bacon" in their rations. He explained why: "This is the food which they have been accustomed to all their lives," he wrote, "and on it they thrive and have good health." Hardtack and beef and other substitutes, in contrast, had made them ill. Yet cornmeal was difficult to transport over the Union's supply lines from any distance, as it was "liable to heat and becomes musty in a short time."[58] It needed to be produced and consumed locally, which is exactly the need refugees could meet, converting fields into corn and grinding meal in abandoned mills. Some of it was sold to the army, in turn. By 1864, the *Freedmen's Bulletin* report noted from the Mississippi Valley that "a great part of the meal used [in rations] is made by the people."[59]

Military officials viewed the rise of this fresh produce economy as a sign of the growing self-sufficiency of the refugees — and another signal that they could discontinue rations, in turn. Officials back at Young's Point, for example, while keeping track of the rations issued to the sellers of produce, ordered that "the first gain from their labor is to go to the liquidation of this debt."[60] Any harvest from the gardens, in other words, would result in a reduction in rations and, presumably, an eventual termination of government food support altogether. Likewise, over in Virginia, William Badger began cutting rations in half when he noticed refugees were supplementing their food supplies. "Some lived where they could get oysters or greens," he reported, "& we would take advantage of that."[61] There were exceptions to this, though. On some of the leased plantations of the Mississippi Valley, officials wanted to keep refugees growing cotton and discouraged the cultivation of vegetables, which in turn kept plantation laborers dependent on army rations.[62]

Refugees were also not free to buy and sell as they pleased in Union-occupied areas: army officials saw much to be concerned about in these burgeoning markets, especially the potential for sales to dissolve into conflict. Signs of trouble appeared all around them, from soldiers ransacking stores, as the Whitehursts had experienced near Fort Monroe, to inflationary prices that unleashed violence and theft. Officials in Helena, Arkansas, responded with an order in August 1864 requiring any sellers coming into the city to pass through a provost marshal's "examination" first. Their sales then had to conform to a strict price range, from two to three dollars for a bushel of potatoes, to fifty cents for a peck of tomatoes, to ten to twenty-five cents for a head of cabbage. And anyone who failed to comply would be fined and have his or her produce confiscated. The order was intended to ensure that "both soldiers and civilians may be amply supplied at a reasonable price." This, in turn, would help reduce conflict and theft and would ensure "that Marketing may with security be brought from the country into the city." For good measure, though, the order made sure to assign a provost officer to escort any wagons coming into Helena.[63]

The volatility surrounding food was a testament to its value and to the ever-present demand that raged across the wartime South. And at times these contestations over food spilled over into deadly violence. Two refugees in Hampton, for example, had their fifteen-year-old son delivered to them with a bullet hole in his head in September 1862, the victim of a nearby white landowner who accused the son of stealing his corn. This case drew together the Union's court-martial commission, which pronounced the white man guilty of manslaughter. He was sentenced to six months' hard labor.[64] The white man may have been punished—but his light punishment belied the fact that the Union felt black people taking food, even from Confederates, were guilty too. In central Kentucky later in the war, a Union officer issued an order encouraging white "citizens" in the vicinity to "shoot any and all negro Soldiers who should be found upon their premises" taking corn. Not long afterward some of those soldiers were discovered on a white man's property gathering up corn, sweet potatoes, and jars of blackberry jam, whereupon a conflict ensued and a soldier killed the white landowner. In that case, the soldiers were sentenced by a court-martial commission to be hanged by their necks for their crime.[65]

Cases like these did not take into account hunger as a possible mitigating factor explaining why the people in Virginia and Kentucky went searching for food on the properties of Confederate sympathizers. Nor did the officials involved acknowledge that the army largely tolerated, and sometimes officially authorized, this kind of foraging by white soldiers.[66] Or that those doing the foraging might have considered the food the product of their own labor, as Edward Whitehurst had earlier in the war when he returned to his plantation to gather up the harvest. The unevenness of the punishments meted out in these cases instead exposed the underlying role that race played in determining when and how the army asserted its control over the food supply. And thus refugees, even those who enlisted, found themselves less able to move freely across the farms and woods of the South to gather the resources that awaited them there.

It was another way that their basic bodily need to eat had become entangled in—and constrained by—the army's war-making machine. Not surprisingly, in some places refugees made it known that they would prefer to receive cash from the government—one dollar and fifty cents weekly, as was proposed in eastern Virginia in 1863—rather than food rations distributed by the army. This way they could stretch the money and purchase their own food, making sure for themselves that they got the quality and the quantity and the taste they so desired. But officials in Virginia demurred, with one superintendent claiming that prices were too volatile in the local markets and could leave refugees in an even worse position than their current one.[67] The idea, therefore, never took off anywhere in the occupied South.

And the struggle to control for oneself how (and what) to eat thus never went away. The refugees may not have been the direct objects of the Union's overall military strategy to impose food scarcity on the Southern population— that was reserved for Confederates who did, indeed, increasingly go hungry as the Union army waged war on the South's food production in 1864 and 1865.[68] But ex-slaves nonetheless struggled with the Union's control over the food supply in their own ways—over access and prices and determinations of "need"—and that remained a constant for the rest of the war. They would continue to try, persistently, to wrest some control over feeding their bodies away from military oversight and control. And they would do something similar when it came to clothing their bodies too.

} 6 {

Clothing Bodies

The bodies of refugees were closely watched, as each man, woman, and child made their way into army encampments. Artists documented the torn dresses, ill-fitting pants, and various hats and head wraps that they wore into the camps; missionaries who wrote letters and reports home left little to the imagination when describing their clothing, or lack thereof. The refugees were "*naked*," "half-naked," "unclothed," or "wretchedly clad," wearing "filthy rags" or nothing more than a "ragged piece of carpet," as various religious and benevolent workers put it.[1] "Thousands of poor liberated negroes are flocking to our borders," opened a report by New York Quakers in 1864, "many of them having scarcely a rag to cover their nakedness."[2] Few to none were naked in a literal sense, but they looked and dressed very differently from the white, middle-class soldiers, teachers, and relief workers who were taking notice of them.

Sometimes they had nothing more than the one set of clothes on their backs. On their plantations, their owners had doled out few garments to start with: maybe two changes of clothing per year, with one pair of shoes.[3] Some owners made it worse when the war came by cutting off supplies to the enslaved, out of recognition—and out of spite—for the fact that emancipation was becoming a reality. "Nine hundred came yesterday, all ragged," reported Mary Forster Collins, a Quaker working in Norfolk, Virginia, in May 1864. "Their masters had not given them clothes, some for a year, others two years."[4] And then, much of the clothing they did have could not survive the trip intact, as it was damaged along the way by wading through water, or by climbing through dense underbrush, or by the need to make bandages for the injured among them. "The few clothes that they could carry, in their hurried march from the plantations," concluded a relief worker in the Mississippi Valley, "should be thrown aside as entirely useless."[5]

The war continued to threaten their access to clothing. The inconsistent payment of wages made it difficult to purchase garments and fabric once inside the camps, and then battles and campaigns that forced sudden evacuations sometimes meant leaving newly stockpiled clothing behind. Epidemics, like smallpox in 1863, further threatened the clothing supply by requiring, as in New Bern, North Carolina, the burning of all clothing in addition to bedding and shelter.[6] Thus, it was at times impossible for refugees to keep themselves adequately clothed without relying on the assistance of others. In contrast to the provision of shelter and food, however, the army would be of limited help in this instance. While the military issued uniforms of deceased soldiers to male laborers, as well as newer uniforms to enlisted soldiers, it did not provide clothing for all the rest of the refugees, especially women and children. Doing so would have required establishing whole new supply operations, which seemed to fall too far beyond the realm of military necessity.[7] "The government will, so far as it is possible, issue them army rations for food, and provide them such nominal shelter," the Northwestern Freedmen's Aid Commission summed up, so "the chief deficiency, therefore, is in the lack of supplies, which, for obvious reasons, the government cannot furnish; namely, *clothing for women and children.*"[8]

Benevolent groups thus stepped in to provide clothing relief, supported by a promise from the army to provide shipping free of charge on government transports.[9] Both religious and secular organizations across the Northern states responded, launching a large-scale clothing campaign that sent thousands upon thousands of garments to the South. The effort attempted to meet refugees' most basic need for clothing in order to preserve their privacy and dignity and to protect them from all sorts of environmental hazards, such as insects, rain, and frigid temperatures. But this assistance also came with conditions, with competing ideas about *how* those bodies should be clothed. And this meant that a refugee's survival into freedom would involve not just obtaining articles of clothing—but asserting the right to decide for oneself how to do so.[10]

Word spread quickly into the North about the deficiencies in clothing. "Very interesting letters have been received today from Fortress Monroe giving a painful picture of the extent of the distress there and asking for clothing," recorded one group of Philadelphia Quakers in 1862.[11] "The want of everything

Clothing Bodies

like clothing is alarming," concurred another report two years later.[12] This was an emergency—one that any person reading such reports, no matter how far removed they were from the camps and from the South, needed to help relieve. And, urged an appeal in the *Friend* in 1863, it "is not any ordinary aid which we are now called upon to furnish our share to." "This is a case where *all the means which all the members of our Society could afford to contribute*, would be inadequate to relieve all the suffering."[13]

And so it came in boxes and barrels. Shirts, dresses, undergarments, pantaloons, and shoes were folded and stuffed inside shipping containers and transported from their points of origin in Northern towns and cities to receive a second life in the refugee camps of the South. The volume was at times staggering: 771 boxes and 285 barrels of garments were piled high on steamboats and shipped from Cincinnati to the Mississippi Valley during a five-month period in early 1864; by April of that same year, an additional twenty-five tons of men's, women's, and children's clothing made the journey by railroad from Chicago to the same region.[14] The mass shipment of clothing relief had started in the spring of 1862 and continued month after month throughout the war, bringing (primarily used) clothing to tens of thousands of refugees. Organizations boasted about the numbers in their annual reports: the Contraband Relief Commission of Cincinnati reported shipping over 30,000 garments and 355 pairs of shoes to the Mississippi Valley by the end of 1864; the Western Freedmen's Aid Commission listed over 69,000 garments sent in the same period; and the Friends Freedmen's Association of Philadelphia reported sending over 56,000 garments, primarily to Virginia, by April 1865.[15] And these are just glimpses of the totals.

The effort to send clothing south cast a wide geographic net, pulling in used garments, as well as money to manufacture new clothing, from the far corners of the nation. The assistance came all the way from a schoolhouse in Springfield, Wisconsin, where students raised three dollars and twenty-five cents; the congregation of Trinity Church in Aurora, Illinois, which sent eighty-seven cents; and the town of Hastings, Minnesota, where residents collected and sent one package of garments.[16] Representatives of the National Freedmen's Relief Association, meanwhile, headed west to San Francisco to appeal for aid in May 1864.[17] And thus the relief efforts created vast links across the warring nation, connecting places that may heretofore have seemed disconnected. Of the twenty-seven and a half boxes and barrels received in a ten-day period in 1862 by Fort Monroe's superintendent of contrabands, Charles Wilder, for example, three had made the trip from North Brookfield, Massachusetts; one box from Castleton, Vermont; and one box and two barrels from

Westerly, Rhode Island (which earned the notation "valuable").[18] Throughout 1864, the Western Freedmen's Aid Commission gathered garments and shoes across fourteen different states and then turned around and distributed the items to nineteen refugee camps in and around the Mississippi Valley.[19]

Garments and monetary relief sailed in from Great Britain too. These shipments largely followed the paths of long-standing, international collaborations among the Quakers in particular, most notably those forged in efforts to abolish slavery across the Atlantic world. But the wartime plight of refugees stirred the British Quakers to a renewed sense of duty. "Our nation has largely shared in the sin of American Slavery," came a statement from the London Yearly Meeting in early 1865. "We do not forget that it was Great Britain that planted slavery in your States."[20] The British Friends also took some responsibility for slavery's perpetuation. "They have toiled without remuneration and without hope, to supply Lancashire with cotton, and to build up the *commercial greatness of our country*," argued a circular issued from Birmingham. "Can there be found in all Britain a single man, woman or child, who has not benefited by the cheap clothing of cotton, wrung from their ill-required toil?"[21] New committees formed, such as the Birmingham and Midland Association for the Help of the Refugees from Slavery in America, and fundraising events, like an Islington "soiree" featuring a visit from the American abolitionist Levi Coffin, resulted in thousands of dollars in donations, as well as boxes of clothing, sent to Philadelphia with duties waived by the U.S. government.[22] Close to half of the money collected by Quaker women in Philadelphia in 1863 and early 1864, in fact, came from Great Britain.[23]

Clothing relief also reconnected former slaves who had previously migrated into Northern states with the plantation districts they had left behind. In Philadelphia, a longtime destination of freedom-seeking people, twenty-seven women who had once been enslaved in Harpers Ferry, Virginia, began cutting and sewing new garments to be sent back to Virginia. They worked in a room donated by a white Quaker woman and were supported by the Women's Aid Committee of the Friends Freedmen's Association. Within a week of getting started, the number of women involved jumped to seventy, and then to 140 by the end of the first month. Together they produced shirts, pantaloons, skirts, and petticoats by the hundreds, totaling 1,400 that first month, a rate that remained fairly constant in the months ahead.[24] In the eyes of the Friends, the new manufacturing enterprise was a model of benevolent efficiency, offering relief both for refugees and for the freedwomen who "received employment" from the effort.[25] But for the women making the clothing, who saw a garment leave their hands in order to be clothed on the body of someone still trying to escape slavery, the meaning had to have been far more profound.

It was part of a reversal that took place in the commodity flows that had long guaranteed the enslavement of millions. Typically, a cotton boll picked under the threat of the lash by a slave in Mississippi was ginned and bound in bales before being loaded on a steamboat and shipped north to the textile mills of New England. There it was spun and then woven into fabric and either sent to market for direct purchase by a consumer or seamstress or loaded onto a train and taken to a workshop to be cut and sewn into dresses and pants. The garments then made their way into the private homes of consumers, into their wardrobes, and onto their backs. But now those garments, after having been repeatedly worn, were packed again, folded into a box or barrel and put aboard a train, or possibly a steamboat, to head south. The original cotton fiber, with its origins in slavery, would now return to the South as part of the effort to lift people out of bondage. It was perhaps the most liberating role played by cotton in the nineteenth-century South.

— ~ —

Large numbers of Americans who had never participated in any form of abolitionism before, who may not have been especially sympathetic with the cause of the enslaved, now pulled shirts out of their drawers and dresses from their closets to send to the refugees. As the numbers attest, it was not very difficult for organizations to generate this vast assistance. The emergency need for clothing—the need to clothe the "naked"—appealed to the most basic humanitarian and Christian impulses that could, at least temporarily, transcend social boundaries of race. "Wherever these appeals have penetrated," noted a report in the *Friends Review*, a "quick feeling of sympathy" resulted.[26]

For the Quakers, who were among the most ardent providers of clothing relief, the need for clothing stirred another sense of duty too. "Shall they be left in tatters to disgrace the government which has freed them?" queried a columnist in the *Friend*. "Friends are loyal; they cannot fight to sustain the government," this writer continued, in a nod to the Friends' pacifism, "but they can promote the general good by caring for these people."[27] It was not just particular individuals who needed the Friends' contributions; the entire nation and the federal government would be well served by making sure that the process of emancipation did not create needless suffering. Clothing relief, and the visible emergence of enslaved people from "tatters," could enable the Union to show that it had successfully moved people out of bondage and into a better state of freedom—countering the long-standing claims of Confederates that the enslaved would only be worse off in freedom. And, for others beyond the Quakers who could not fight—for reasons having to do with age, gender, or disability—this sort of relief work also offered a means of simply getting involved in the war effort and demonstrating one's loyalty to the Union cause.

Yet that duty and sympathy could also be felt and acted upon from a distance, and that was undoubtedly crucial in generating a high-volume response. Clothing relief afforded average Northerners an opportunity to perform their duty to the less fortunate without having to get too close to the people or to the places where the suffering reigned. And this, in turn, likely assuaged other deeply held fears. To relieve the refugees' needs in the South could diminish, at least to some degree, the ex-slaves' impulse to move again. It might even extinguish any calls by military authorities to remove them to the North and into its local communities. After all, if properly provided for in the South, why would they need (or want) to move north? Each shipment of money and clothing was thus an investment in containing refugees in the South, reinforcing the efforts of politicians to halt the removals of refugees to Northern states. And it was a pattern that would persist well into the twentieth century's refugee crises. As geographer Jennifer Hyndman has noted, destitute refugees "become less mobile as humanitarian aid is able to cross borders more quickly."[28]

White Northerners inside the refugee camps, however, approached the issue from a much different vantage point and with less enthusiasm. They grew to dread altogether the burden of providing clothing relief. W. S. Bell, an AMA missionary who, along with his wife, had arrived in Norfolk, Virginia, in 1863 to work as a teacher, had only the educational and spiritual welfare of the refugees foremost in his sights when he first arrived. He set to work opening schools on a series of government farms in the region, including one on the property of Governor Henry Wise of Virginia, but he soon found himself preoccupied with the unwelcome task of material relief. Bell complained to AMA leaders in New York that "the giving out of clothing is the hardest *task* in our missionary life." It was not what he expected, nor how he wanted to spend his time with refugees in the wartime South.[29]

Bell was not alone. Fellow AMA missionary Abisha Scofield, working at Camp Nelson, Kentucky, was a Congregational minister who had spent the years preceding the war delivering impassioned attacks on slavery. Sermons, verses, scripture: that is what he had always contributed to the fight against slavery.[30] Now, however, in early 1865, he stood before the ex-slaves at Camp Nelson as a purveyor of clothing. "It is not quite the labor I came here to do," Scofield conceded, but he hoped mightily that "the way will thus be prepared

Clothing Bodies

for instruction."[31] Bell and Scofield, like so many others, learned quickly upon their arrival in the South that their primary aim to preach to former slaves, and to teach them the basics of reading and writing, would have to be put on hold. There were too many "more pressing physical wants of the freedmen," or "present bodily wants," or "immediate physical wants of the suffering and destitute," as representatives of various organizations put it.[32] It was crucial to prevent the bodies of the refugees from "perishing," an editorial in the *Friend* explained in 1864, before there was any chance of rescuing their minds "from the ignorance and degradation in which they have been kept throughout their life of cruel bondage." Or as Sanitary Commission agent Maria Mann asked rhetorically from her vantage point in Helena, "Will their moral & intellectual elevation ever commence until their physical natures are improved[?]"[33]

Yet the work of distributing physical relief was more easily discussed in the abstract than actually performed. "It is not the *giving them away*" that was so troubling about handing out garments, Bell explained, but instead "the effort and anxiety of mind which one undergoes in trying to give them away *properly*." It was "proper" to give clothing out to the neediest, Bell wrote, but wholly improper to provide this sort of charity to those who might otherwise take care of themselves. This, he explained in a statement that echoed the central preoccupation of military purveyors of food relief, risked creating a new form of dependency and thwarting the refugees' transition to self-sufficiency and citizenship.[34] "The distracting question, to give or not to give," summed up Quaker Lucy Chase, "is always staring at me, and frightening me out of patience, if not out of wits."[35]

The refugees seemed to white relief workers anonymous and undifferentiated as they crowded themselves into the camps in large numbers. "We don't know them always and cannot tell whether they are needy or not," W. S. Bell explained from Norfolk. "We talk to them, to draw them out and discern, if we can, their real condition," he recounted, "but they are so secretive and untruthful that it is impossible for us to come at the truth in most instances, only as we may guess at it."[36] Even the most humanitarian-minded missionaries could share the doubts of their military counterparts issuing food, as well as an apparent unwillingness to consider that any "secrecy" exhibited by refugees was in fact an assertion of privacy (something continually intruded upon in these repeated inquiries about need). The distributors of clothing, both in Bell's Virginia and elsewhere across the South, instead went beyond conversation to put their eyes to work in determining need too. "It is made the duty of our teachers to visit the freed people in their huts and tents," explained a Western Freedmen's Aid Commission report, "and by personal inspection ascertain their real condition and wants." Even a few glances, it suggested, could size up physical needs quickly, unmediated by the words or sentiments or beliefs of the refugees themselves.[37]

Those deemed "really in need of clothing," as a report of the Indiana Friends put it, were then given a ticket, in effect a promissory note, which spelled out what garments they would be given.[38] In some places these tickets, merely slips of paper, acted as necessary "testimonials," in the words of the Northwestern Freedmen's Aid Commission's *Freedmen's Bulletin*, "from officers in charge of the camp, or from other responsible people." No refugee would receive clothing without a "responsible" authority vouching for his or her need first. Once that ticket was in hand, the man, woman, or child could then take it to a storeroom and redeem it for the garments listed.[39] Those who did not receive a ticket were expected to visit a store or otherwise find a way to purchase the goods for themselves.

New stores increasingly catered to that purpose. Similar to the army sutler's store, where soldiers purchased clothing, food, coffee, utensils, and other supplies, stores geared specifically for a refugee clientele became a pet project of missionaries and relief workers across the South. Sometimes the clothing donations flowing in from the North were diverted to stock these stores — a source of consternation for some of the donors, who preferred to see their clothing distributed for free — and at other times missionaries and relief workers invested significant sums of money to get the enterprises off the ground. In Hampton, Virginia, Quakers from Philadelphia raised $6,000 to open a store in early 1864, utilizing half that sum to purchase goods to sell and the rest to construct the building.[40] Soon, clothing and shoes, in addition to cooking utensils and food supplies, lined the store's shelves (although tobacco was nowhere to be seen, for the Friends concluded that would be "improper").[41] After they established a second store twenty miles away in Yorktown, the Friends reported $3,000 in weekly revenue between the two enterprises by early 1865, for a total of about $150,000 in a span of ten and a half months. The sum — which surprised even the Friends — soon prompted them to reduce prices and to invest any leftover profits in a "Contingent Fund" to cover any future losses.[42] Similar enterprises emerged in the Mississippi Valley later that summer in what the *Friend* would call "the store movement."[43]

The point of the "store movement" was not to turn a significant profit. "The stores are intended only for the blacks," the *Freedmen's Friend* tellingly revealed, for any white person who wanted to shop there had to have a "special permit from the military authorities."[44] This was because "the object of establishing stores," according to the Friends Freedmen's Association of Philadelphia, was "the improvement of the negroes, they should be made self sustaining."[45] The stores promised to transform the refugees from recipients of charity into consumers and, thus, the missionaries believed, to harness the allure of consumption in order to instill certain virtues, such as hard work, saving, and prudent decision making, that were considered essential to free labor and good citizenship.[46] That potential prompted a convention of seven freedmen's associations in 1864 to pass a resolution encouraging stores "as a means of stimulating industry and of teaching the freedmen the value of money." At the same time, the stores themselves, under the missionaries' watchful eyes, would provide protected spaces for such lessons, as they would be shielded from price gouging or unfair duties (or "imposition," as the Friends put it).[47]

Never mind that many refugees were already seasoned consumers — and even proprietors too. That was evident in nearly every town and encampment where refugees sold the products of their gardens or purchased food to supplement their rations. And it was evident in the store that Emma and Edward Whitehurst had established independently two years before. Some of the Philadelphia Friends conceded as much but still saw a pressing need to reintroduce the refugees to commerce under their tutelage. "Though the poor, oppressed — but now unfettered — negro is not entirely blind to self-interest," noted the *Freedmen's Friend*, "there is reason to fear that his present desires, rather than future needs, regulate his actions."[48] There was a right way and a wrong way to operate as a consumer, the article suggested, and in the context of specially established stores, under the guidance of white Northern proprietors, "with an occasional word in season from our storekeepers," the former slaves would leave their supposedly impulsive buying habits behind.[49]

Refugees must have strongly disagreed with such assumptions — but they did not hesitate to patronize the stores either. The first store to open in Hampton, Virginia, in 1864 was reportedly "watched eagerly" for three days prior to its opening, as the contents of the store arrived to fill its shelves. At noon on the day of the opening, a "crowd" gathered expectantly at the door of the store, waiting to go inside. "The two attendants were taxed to their utmost for the remainder of the day," the *Friend* later reported, "in meeting the demands of their customers." The sales that first day totaled $544; Quaker observers believed the refugees had "saved, it may be for weeks, in view of this opportunity."[50] The Friends had their own self-interested reasons to trumpet their store as a success. But the refugees, too, had every reason to patronize it, no matter how much it attempted to regulate and circumscribe their purchasing. For just as benevolent Northerners were uneasy about prolonging the bestowal of charity, so too were its recipients eager to provide for themselves. They would "rather pay for their clothing than have it given to them," explained Harriet Jacobs, a former slave turned teacher working with a group of New York Friends in Alexandria, Virginia, "and they value it more."[51]

Yet the stores were only part of the strategy by which missionaries and benevolent workers tried to make something as essential and everyday as clothing prepare former slaves for freedom. They also set their sights on the manufacturing of the clothing to be sold in the stores. It was not enough to instill a work ethic or a propensity for good financial decision making, they believed; it was also necessary to instill certain habits of industry, and in particular, the skill to construct clothing from scratch. They set up sewing rooms inside the refugee camps, or what were also described in various places as an "industrial school," a "tailoring school," and a "knitting school."[52] All were to provide industrial education—practical, hands-on learning that would prepare the refugees for future employment while meeting the immediate needs of the refugee population. Sometimes the "students" in these schools were paid for their work in wages, like the 225 "poor colored women" in Helena who received twenty cents for each afternoon of work. Others were to be paid simply with knowledge.[53] It was hoped, as a report in the *Friend* summed up, that such work would "show them how to provide for themselves."[54]

As with the stores, however, the missionaries and relief workers once again overestimated how new this education would be. It had long been a task of enslaved women to construct many of the garments distributed on plantations. Some women spent the days of their enslavement spinning, weaving, cutting, and sewing garments; others had to squeeze in this work after a long day of working in the fields.[55] Manufacturing garments was entirely familiar work to many women emerging from slavery, something that some missionaries eventually conceded. "We occasionally find excellent seamstresses among the women," came a surprised report from Baton Rouge, Louisiana, in 1864, and soon the aid workers began drawing on that skill.[56] At Yorktown, Virginia, that same year, Quakers began employing black women as teachers in their sewing classes, paying them two dollars and fifty cents a month to teach from 3:00 to 5:00 p.m. six afternoons per week.[57] Yet the Friends still stopped short of relinquishing the entire process of camp manufacture to the women. There was one step in the process, cutting, that would remain the province of Northern cutting rooms in Philadelphia and New York. It was a step believed to require the most skill in clothing manufacture, as it established the foundation for quality construction and well-fitted garments.[58] The cut pieces were then sent south into the camps, helping to ensure, as one Quaker put it, that the camp sew-

Clothing Bodies

ing rooms would instill the "Yankee way" of sewing, rather than the "Ole Virginny" way (by implication, a more haphazard, imprecise way).[59]

‿╼‿

However one obtained it—by donation, by purchase, or by manufacture—the clothing received by the refugees was, in the eyes of the missionaries, transformative. "There is a decidedly improved look already in the persons of the women & children," an AMA missionary in Virginia summed up approvingly.[60] Missionaries eager to lead the refugees beyond their wilderness of suffering—to be their Moses—looked constantly for signs of progress. And clothing was especially useful in that regard: in the replacement of "the rags of the slave" with sturdy, Yankee-made attire, or in a covering up of the "naked," a change became instantly visible in a way that was not always possible with other types of relief, such as food. The bodies of the refugees, in an instant, could appear to have shed their past of enslavement and suffering and take on the appearance of freedom (by, quite literally, wearing the clothing once worn by free people). Their entire journey—their journey out of the wilderness—could thus be made visible on the body.[61]

That was the visual power of clothing. Nineteenth-century Americans believed wholeheartedly that clothing was an important, visible marker of status and social position, but one that was changeable rather than fixed or static, and thus open to transformation. In an era, for example, when cities were growing rapidly and people from widely divergent walks of life converged and mixed themselves up in new ways, the desire for reinvention could be satisfied in part through clothing. New attire allowed an individual to transform him- or herself, to assert a new social identity or at least strive for one. "The seductiveness of fashion," writes sociologist Diana Crane, "lay in the fact that it seemed to offer a person the possibility of becoming in some way different, more attractive, or more powerful."[62] Some of the white benevolent workers may have experienced this firsthand back home in the North, marking their rise in class status through the purchase of items of clothing that signified gentility and refinement. They certainly brought this belief in the social power of clothing with them into the refugee camps, as they were quick to see—and to believe—that a change in clothing had signaled a change in the status of the refugees. It was thus a highly validating process, a source of self-satisfaction.

Yet these benevolent Northerners were not always so comfortable with the transformation. It was one thing to usher in a change in the condition of clothing, from ragged to new, but it was a whole other thing to witness a change in style as well. "It troubles me to see their fancy for long dressed . . . hoops & other new points they are able to reach in our style of dress," wrote Sanitary Commission agent Maria Mann from Helena, Arkansas. In her view, the refugees, particularly the women, were beginning to look too much like her — like a white woman of means from a Northern city. That they could do this had much to do with the central role that donations played in clothing the refugees, for it was largely the clothing of middle- and upper-class white women that made its way into the boxes and barrels headed south. There was little else for the refugee women to choose from. Yet Mann saw too much meaning conveyed in "our style of dress" to be content with letting this practice continue. "Their own style is so appropriate," she contended, "so suited to their form, color, condition."[63] Mann's letter thus betrayed a common anxiety that often accompanied the transformative power of clothing: that it could trigger too much change too quickly, wrapping a person's true, inner identity in an inauthentic cloak and thus threatening to blur the social boundaries of race that Mann believed should still exist after slavery.[64]

If the material expression of such differences were erased, then would those differences cease to exist altogether? Clothing relief, so wrapped up with visual cues of status, thus could not be disentangled from the deeper, underlying contestation over racial boundaries that accompanied the destruction of slavery. Like many other white abolitionists, Mann was entirely committed to ending slavery but stopped short of envisioning full equality for black people; some differences, like race, seemed too natural and too necessary in the new order of freedom. That accounts for the near-reflexive complaints coming from white officials whenever garments of a certain quality or style flowed into their camps. Two barrels from Boston were deemed to be "too good in texture & style of making" by Mann to be of any use in Helena, while another shipment to Virginia was declared "too fine for our use" by a frustrated Quaker, who envisioned a more favorable alternative by requesting garments be made from "negro cloth."[65] A fabric manufactured in Northern textile mills specifically to be sold to Southern plantations during slavery, "negro cloth" was distinctive for its coarse texture made of lower-grade fibers — either wool, cotton, or linen — and for its bland appearance that unmistakably marked an individual as a slave.[66] Similar appeals simply asked for items made of "coarse" fabrics, as in a Sanitary Commission official's request that "none but coarse heavy shoes and clothing should be sent."[67]

The recipients of clothing made from "negro cloth" or similarly less desirable fabric would seem to enjoy no change in the visible markers of their status. In this moment of profound and wrenching social transformation, as

Clothing Bodies

they passed from enslavement into freedom, they would still, on the outside, look like slaves. But that is not how Northern relief workers claimed to see it, for they, eager to demonstrate their effectiveness at guiding the refugees through the wilderness, tried to attach new meaning to "negro cloth" and to other, simpler styles of dress. It would become a badge of efficiency and frugality—and thus of good consumerism. Maria Mann, in Helena, wrote home that "I preach economy" in her dealings with refugee women and their clothes, complaining about the "wastefulness" that she perceived in their "passion" for "showy goods and finery."[68] That "finery" was what white women like Mann wore routinely and donated as castoffs—yet it became "showy," in Mann's eyes, when draped on the body of a black woman. In just a few words Mann recast a threatening assertion of social status on the part of black women into something "wasteful" that demanded her correction. When one woman purchased a "very small cheap hair net" and "a hoop skirt, a poor one," for four dollars and fifty cents, Mann forced the woman, in her presence, to return the goods for nine and a half yards of calico and three yards of unbleached muslin in order to make her own plain garments. Mann also pressured another woman to return "a tinsel belt" valued at one dollar.[69] Under the cover of promoting good consumerism, Mann managed to police the boundaries between black and white women's dress and perpetuate dull, simple styles for black women.

It was no coincidence that Mann focused her attention almost solely on women's clothing—and not men's. The army uniforms routinely issued to soldiers and male laborers left little room for variance in men's clothing and thus imposed something closer to a material uniformity across racial lines for men. "The men and the boys wear what other men and boys wear," an appeal for clothing donations for civilians likewise explained it in 1863.[70] And this only amplified the significance of women's clothing. It meant that women's bodies would become far more variable barometers of social change than men's and would generate more interest and observation among those working in the camps.

Maria Mann once approached an officer in Helena and asked him "to gather all the women together"—notably *not* the men—so that she could address them at once "on points of dress." She then announced a new system, whereby any new dresses that arrived for the refugees or fabric sent there to be turned into garments "would be measured off for them to suit me in length." Her style judgment would rule, and all skirts, she continued, would "contain only five breadths" of fabric—a modest width that was less than that already seen in dresses streaming into the South.[71] Mann's plan would purportedly conserve fabric—but in effect, the refugee women would not be entitled to wear full skirts like those worn by Mann and other white women in the North.

There was a lot at stake in the width of a skirt, Mann believed. "Perhaps you & Auntie & your friends . . . will say I am laboring at the nonessentials," she wrote home that spring in a letter describing her work, "but it is in such ways, my forte lies, in preventive planning."[72] She would prevent the sort of social chaos that even the most sympathetic of white abolitionists sometimes feared would accompany freedom; she would ensure that freedom was ordered in a way that preserved a degree of white privilege and made it visible on the bodies of black women. The refugee women who gathered to listen to Mann's lecture on fabric may not have agreed with the substance of her talk, or with her vision for their skirts, but there was one general point with which they wholeheartedly agreed: clothing was no mere "nonessential."

It was instead one of the "small rights" of freedom. Other rights, like voting and property ownership, would assume a more conspicuous position in the broader pursuit of freedom after slavery, but other rights that involved intimate, everyday matters, such as what to wear or how to wear it, were no less meaningful. These were the kind of rights, in the words of historian Thavolia Glymph, that "make for a 'whole life' " — "that get people through the day, that make it possible for them to partake of those larger rights."[73] Clothing, in particular, was at the heart of their quest for self-determination — mainly, the right to own and control one's body. This was a significant achievement for any person seeking freedom, whose life in bondage had been marked by the loss of ownership over one's body. And it was especially profound for women, who had endured the exploitation of their bodies not only for productive labor but for reproductive labor as well. It was no small matter, then, to reclaim control over *all* aspects of one's body, including the everyday matter of how the body looked and felt when dressed.

Women had asserted this right even while enslaved, when they went to great lengths to seize some control over their appearance. After being given allotments of clothing from their owners, constructed from "negro cloth" in a style that could only be described as uniformly shapeless and androgynous, some women worked late into the night to alter their clothing in a way that added color and individualized style. They made buttons and beads, dyeing them with the help of berries and tree barks gathered from local woods; they hooped their skirts with grapevines; and they made necklaces out of dried fruit. Some pieced together one particularly nice outfit for religious services or parties, while others wove and sewed new garments around unique patterns and designs. Such alterations were no less than efforts "to make their bodies spaces of personal expression and pleasure," as historian Stephanie Camp put it, and thus profoundly at odds with the bodily domination wielded by their enslavers. To put on a dress altered with dyes and beads was nothing less than an act of resistance—an act of reclaiming one's body, and regaining one's individuality—against the entire regime of slavery.[74]

Women carried this impulse with them into the war, as they entered the camp stores and tried to purchase tinsel belts and hoopskirts. These were purchases intended to distance themselves from slavery, and from the bland uniformity and the lack of individuality that characterized the clothing of their enslavement. They were guided not by a desire to look like, or try to be like, white women, as Maria Mann feared. After all, after being enslaved by them, they had every reason *not* to respect and covet the tastes of white women.[75] Refugee women were instead more concerned with not being a *slave*, and not looking the part of a slave. Those big, full skirts that Mann believed were too excessive—and too threatening—were, in fact, something that enslaved women had long sought on their own time and in their own alterations. Those who spun and wove fabric on the plantations and made garments in their off time often went for a more generous cut to the skirts that were longer and fuller than the shapeless frocks provided by their owners.[76] The result may have been a dress that, materially, resembled the full skirts of white women, but the meaning black women attached to it and thus their motives for seeking it were different from those assumed by Maria Mann.

The desire to distance themselves from slavery prompted some women to outright reject a shipment of newly made dresses sent from Philadelphia in 1863. The dresses were made out of a thick gray flannel, a fabric that resembled "negro cloth" more than it did the cotton dresses they preferred. "The negroes have a repugnance to wearing them," reported Helen James, a Quaker working in North Carolina, "especially those who have been for sometime free. They *will not* buy them." The only women who would wear such dresses were those newly arrived inside Union lines, who were desperate for some clothing relief; over time, however, with the accumulation of wages and the ability to shop in the local store, they made their real preferences known. "The reason why they dislike this material," James explained of the flannel, "is because they have worn it as slaves."[77] But not everything worn in slavery was so quickly cast off. Maria Mann, for example, found herself dumbfounded when the sunbonnets she sewed for women out of curtains sent from the North became something "which they discard generally."[78] It may have been because the women preferred to continue wearing head wraps, which they had long worn in slavery as a "unique expressive form," according to historian Stephanie Camp.[79]

Refugee women thus made choices in ways that would honor the humanity that had been threatened by their enslavement. Maria Mann may have once complained that they "choose the outside, the showy," rather than make undergarments a priority, but what she considered "showy" could be to them a gesture of respect and dignity.[80] Take the clothes chosen for burying dead children. "They say, 'We want them to look pretty,'" is how Maria Mann quoted one such grieving mother, whose choices struck the Sanitary Commission agent as too excessive, when an old "flannel skirt" would have sufficed.[81] But something "pretty," to this mother, was more than the superficial gesture Mann feared: it was a way of honoring the shortened life of the child and the family into which it was born. It was about reclaiming a very basic, human ritual—mourning the dead—that had been threatened by slavery. That same impulse led some refugees to seek out finer clothing for events like weddings, too. In Virginia, while one Quaker woman assured a man about to get married that his "patched pantaloons" were perfectly fine for the ceremony, the man was not so sure. "Well I reckon we'll be mo like *people* if we's married," the woman quoted him as saying, "an it'll be much mo indecent." His clothing may have been fitting of his former status as a slave, but now, in partaking in the ritual of marriage, it seemed "indecent." Decency, and respect for his new status, led him to select instead a "light colored Friend's coat" and a pair of trousers from a recent shipment from West Chester, Pennsylvania.[82]

Against many odds, refugees in some places attempted to extract clothing relief from these primarily white, Northern organizations, pooling their money and resources to form their own aid societies inside militarized zones. It happened in Norfolk, Virginia, in late 1862, with the founding of a "regularly organized society," as an AMA missionary described it, which had collected five barrels of clothing and forty dollars for "relieving the poor." In nearby Portsmouth in May 1863, the "more fortunate" black residents formed a Human Aid Society that met weekly in a local Methodist church and vowed to "take care not only of ourselves, but also of our poor brothers who have no work, and nothing to eat or wear."[83] These efforts were few and far between, however, requiring the stability that only distance from military upheaval could provide, as well as the payment of wages that would provide some refugees with the means to assist others. Far more likely, perhaps, were more informal relief efforts, from the sharing of clothing within a family or across an encampment, to the lending of sewing skills in order to alter donated clothing into something useful and desirable. This work was not visible enough to make it into the historical record, however, making it impossible to capture fully the extent of the refugees' own clothing relief efforts.

Whether it came from the far Northern states or from the refugees' own hands, the immense volume of clothing sent into refugee camps throughout the war offered a measure of the suffering absorbed by bodies on the way to freedom. There was no instant liberation upon their exit from slavery, for, as with food, to clothe one's body required withstanding the upheaval of war and the expectations of missionaries and military authorities alike. That was life inside the wilderness of the Civil War.

Yet the process of relieving physical suffering involved more than the provision of material relief. The suffering of bodies also provoked an inward reckoning, as refugees, and sometimes those assisting them, tried to explain it and reconcile it with their visions of freedom. And that was a matter of the spirit—of faith and religious worship. "Most of the sufferers we saw had found refuge in religion," explained a report from Quaker women in Virginia, because in their faith were "consolations to overbalance all their afflictions."[84] Likewise an AMA missionary concluded that "they have strong faith in the Lord, and are very patient in their sufferings."[85] But the religious beliefs and practices of the refugees turned out to be more complex than that—and could not always so easily overwhelm or make understandable their physical suffering.

Gabriel Burdett in Slavery

Gabriel Burdett was a child when he first began envisioning how freedom would come. His mother encouraged him. It was she who told him, in a conversation he later recalled at an abolitionist reunion in 1874, that "sometime they would be freed." She did not know when it would happen—just that it would, "sometime" in the course of his life. Burdett never forgot his mother's words during his thirty-four years as a slave in Garrard County, Kentucky, for it was no small thing to be liberated from the belief that he was destined to be enslaved for life. He thought a lot over the years about how exactly his full, physical freedom would come, because, again, his mother encouraged him. In that same conversation she predicted it would not be an isolated affair that liberated them; their freedom would come instead in the wholesale destruction of slavery everywhere in the United States. It would come "either by England or France, or some foreign nation."[1]

Had Burdett's mother predicted a war, like the Revolution or the War of 1812, in which Great Britain had offered freedom to enslaved people in exchange for their service in its military? Or a revolution brought on by the enslaved themselves, as in the French colony of Saint-Domingue (Haiti)? The record of Burdett's 1874 remarks does not say. Yet he held on to her message and grasped it tightly, keeping his eye on the promise of liberation for years to come. He prayed, he searched, and he prophesied too. But he eventually grew unwilling to believe that their freedom would be won by the actions of people outside of the United States, an ocean away from where he toiled as a slave. He came to believe instead that liberation would come from a higher power, working through the hearts and minds, and the faith and prayers, of those who lived inside the United States.

Gabriel Burdett became a Baptist minister sometime by the 1850s, when he was at least twenty years old. He likely got started in much the same way that other enslaved ministers did, preaching in secret meetings in woods or ravines or in other secluded spots on a plantation, in what has been called the "invisible church." Burdett may have led secret meetings among the twenty-six other people enslaved on his plantation, perhaps meeting in the woods along Sugar Creek, where his owner, Hiram Burdett, owned over 400 acres of land. Or maybe his meetings were even larger, including the enslaved from other white Burdett family properties that adjoined Hiram Burdett's. It was in meetings like these, beyond the watchful eye of their owners, that the enslaved of Garrard County could freely pray and sing, seeking consolation while imagining the future, in services that likely blended elements of Christianity with religious beliefs and rituals inherited from West African cultures.[2] It was also where they mourned the dead and held their own weddings; Burdett himself married Lucinda Huffman, a woman enslaved on a neighboring plantation, in 1855, in a ceremony conducted by another enslaved minister named John Burnside.[3]

No matter how secret it all was in the beginning, or may have continued to be, at some point Burdett's ministerial role became visible to white people in Garrard County—particularly to the elders of the Forks of Dix River Baptist Church. The Forks Church, as it was known, was a white church in its governance, first organized in 1782 by a group of white Virginians who migrated to central Kentucky after the Revolution (and who included among their number the family of Gabriel's owner). Sometime in the early decades of the nineteenth century, as the evangelical revivals of the Second Great Awakening brought thousands of new members into Methodist and Baptist churches, the Forks Church opened its doors to enslaved people too—or really, to white owners bringing their slaves with them. It happened in such numbers that when the church constructed a new building in 1849, it included a "slave gallery," a segregated area either in the back or in a loft space, from which the enslaved would watch and listen to the white pastor's preaching. By the 1850s, the enslaved sitting in the gallery comprised 200 of the Forks Church's 500 members. Among them were Gabriel and Lucinda Burdett, along with many other people from their plantations, including Gabriel's brother, Elijah, also owned by Hiram Burdett, and Elijah's wife, Clarissa, who was enslaved nearby.[4]

To the men and women sitting in the gallery, evangelical Protestantism may have seemed appealing for its emphasis on the inward conversion experience of the individual and the spiritual equality of all souls. That was what drew many thousands of enslaved people to evangelicalism throughout the South during the antebellum decades, as they embraced the empowering notion that they could choose to be saved and thus affect their own fate. Yet, from the galleries of Southern churches like the Forks Church, the enslaved also heard white pastors striving to contain the leveling impulses of their faith by preaching submission and inequality too. They heard ministers deliver sermons about the Bible's sanction of slavery and about how their salvation—the salvation of *both* black and white—depended on the harmonious functioning of the institution. They heard lessons about the godliness of a slave's submission and about the Christian benevolence of their enslavers. They heard, in short, a proslavery Christianity that attempted to curb any subversive impulses among the enslaved while pushing back against the abolitionist threat emanating from the North. Its core message, that slavery was God's will, would remain a cornerstone of the white South's overall defense of the institution.[5]

The numbers of enslaved congregants at the Forks Church grew so large that sometime by 1859 the church decided to let the enslaved attend their own separate services, to be conducted by men identified as spiritual leaders among them. "Bro. Gabe is privileged to occuppy [*sic*] the church on the after noon of the 1st Sabbath in each month," the church records from April of that year noted Burdett's appointment as a minister, "except when occupied by the whites."[6] The move, which appeared to grant Burdett and the black congregants a degree of independence over their worship, was a peculiarity of the Baptists, who, with a tradition of respecting congregational independence, were more likely than other denominations to allow separate services when black congregants pushed for them. The Baptists also allowed the establishment of separate black churches in the antebellum period, which is how at least seventeen African Baptist churches appeared across Kentucky by 1860.[7] But this was toleration with limits, as black ministers in white churches were still heavily supervised. In some places they were told exactly what to preach, down to the scripture passages, and were expected to act, essentially, as mouthpieces of white proslavery Christianity. Some black preachers, subject to intimidation and force, complied.[8]

But the Forks Church elders were mistaken if they thought Gabriel Burdett would be so controlled. They gave him a very confined space for preaching, and it is likely that he continued to hold "invisible" church meetings on his own, beyond the confines of the church, as many other black ministers did. The religious worship of the enslaved was never fully absorbed by white churches, historian Albert Raboteau has explained, which meant that their religion "was both institutional and noninstitutional, visible and invisible, formally organized and spontaneously adapted."[9] Five years after his appointment to the

Gabriel Burdett in Slavery

Sunday services, Gabriel Burdett began to push back against his confinement inside the Forks Church. His sermons began to change — and white church elders took notice. "We are informed that Bro. Gabriel on the evening of the 1st Sunday of this month," the church's daybook recorded in June 1862, "used publicly very objectionable language casting reflections & Slurs upon the church & evincing a disposition to claim higher privileges than can be granted or tolerated." The records do not say what the "Slurs" were exactly, but it was serious enough, in the eyes of white authorities, to dispatch two church leaders to visit with Burdett and seek "satisfactory acknowledgements" of his transgressions. His punishment for failing to satisfy them would include the revocation of his ministerial license — and the ominous threat to "cite him to our next church meeting."[10]

It takes no stretch of the imagination to conclude that Gabriel had strayed from the proslavery message of the church. Here was a man whose mother had instilled in him the belief that freedom was coming, even as he remained physically enslaved. So how could he accept and preach the idea that his enslavement was somehow natural and divinely ordained? Enslaved people across the South may have feigned adherence to such ideas while sitting in the slave galleries, but they still drew sharp distinctions between the Christianity of their masters and their own "true" Christianity.[11] "All the pro-slavery doctrine which preachers and masters pressed upon them, as from the Bible," a Northern minister visiting the South that same year observed of black religious leaders, "their very instincts, reason, and religion rejected."[12] Burdett simply rejected it in the very place where it was supposed to be most protected.

Yet something else may have emboldened Burdett to speak up and claim "higher privileges" at that particular moment. Turn back the church daybook to the previous fall and there appears a simple notation that church services were moving to the nearby Mt. Hebron Baptist Church "in consequence of the church being occupied by the sick soldiers from Camp Dick Robinson."[13] The Civil War had come to Garrard County and to the Forks Church. It had not come in the flash of battle, or in a large-scale campaign, but instead it had moved slowly and gradually into a state that had attempted to remain neutral during the war's first six months, before openly aligning with the Union. The Union army established a recruiting depot in Garrard County named Camp Dick Robinson, after the property's owner, which was located just two miles up the road from the Forks Church. The space between the camp and the church soon appeared to narrow, however, when the numbers of sick and wounded overwhelmed the camp and were sent to the church instead, turning its pews into hospital beds.[14]

That is what Gabriel Burdett saw of the war in its first year: the sights and sounds of suffering and, very likely, of death too. The arrival of the wounded disrupted the physical space of the Forks Church—an event of no small significance. For Burdett worshipped in a religious culture that attached significant meaning to geographic space, with religious beliefs and practices closely linked to particular places, like church buildings and cemeteries and neighborhoods, and to the people congregated within them. These sacred spaces "represent articulations or extensions of the adherents' faith," geographers of religion have noted; to unsettle these sacred spaces, as the Union army did, was to disrupt the dynamics of religious worship altogether. And it was into that disruption in 1862 that Burdett stepped with his "objectionable" sermon.[15]

What Burdett thought would result from his forthright challenge to the proslavery church is lost to history. But what is clear is that the incident did not immediately trigger his flight to freedom. Burdett instead accepted his punishment from the church when the leaders visited, and they, in turn, "being satisfied with his acknowledgements," dropped the matter.[16] Burdett continued to preach under the supervision of the Forks Church elders for another full year. He did not go to Camp Dick Robinson, and he did not reflexively attach himself to the Union army. But he had already grasped the potential of the war and the military to disrupt the religious landscape of the South and make room for his pursuit of religious freedom.

} 7 {

Keeping Faith

The Union army showed up on the Burdett plantation one year later, in midsummer 1863. It did so with little fanfare — no regiments appeared en masse, no significant marching or gunfire could be heard. Only one man, and possibly a few soldiers, set foot there one day: George Denny, a thirty-eight-year-old resident of Garrard County who may have been familiar to Gabriel Burdett already. He was a planter and slave owner in the county, with twenty-five enslaved men, women, and children to his name; during the secession crisis and the early years of the war he represented the area as a state senator.[1] Denny was by all accounts loyal to the Union and had been seizing ways to profit from the Union army's presence in central Kentucky. First he secured a contract to sell 5,000 bushels of corn, at one dollar a bushel, to a nearby quartermaster.[2] Now he arrived on the Burdett property as a hired agent for the army, seeking enslaved men to take to Camp Nelson, a new military installation located ten miles up the road in neighboring Jessamine County.[3]

The camp was a supply depot, established with the intent of supporting Gen. Ambrose Burnside's Army of Ohio as it moved south into Tennessee later that year. To get those troops supplied, however, a series of new military roads needed to be built first, which led Union officials to issue an order stating that 6,000 enslaved laborers were to be impressed for the work. The orders affected a fourteen-county swath of central Kentucky and targeted all "male negroes" between the ages of sixteen and forty-five. In a nod to the planters' interests, no more than one-third of any man's slaves were to be taken, to guarantee that impressment would not "hinder and materially injure" the cultivation of crops.[4]

A ledger book kept track of each man impressed under these orders in Kentucky. And thanks to George Denny's efforts that day, the name "Gabriel" appeared on its pages. Next to his name, in a column labeled "Owner's Name," was "Hiram Burdett"; after that was a mark clearly etched in a column labeled "Slave." The "Free" column remained blank.[5] That explains why Burdett would earn no wages for the long hours he then spent "constructing roads, chopping timber, &c." Instead, according to labor rolls, Hiram Burdett would claim the thirty dollars each month for the services rendered by his slave. Gabriel Burdett thus entered the Union army's orbit for the first time not as a freedman, nor as a "contraband" or any other murky designation, but as a slave.[6]

This happened six months after the Emancipation Proclamation went into effect. It was also two full years since Edward and Emma Whitehurst were offered protection as "contraband" inside the Union lines at Fort Monroe — and around the same time Eliza Bogan left her plantation for Helena.[7] And yet, in a sign of how the momentum of emancipation could simultaneously start and stop across different locations in the South, enslaved people in Kentucky still had virtually no place to go to seek freedom inside this Union state that was exempt from the proclamation. Anyone who challenged that exemption was forcibly expelled from Union encampments, and sometimes jailed and returned to their owner, by Union army officials.[8] Other freedom-seeking slaves left the state altogether, crossing into Ohio and points north, or farther south into Tennessee, sometimes enlisting in another state's regiments.[9] No refugee camps for Kentucky's enslaved people would be formally established in the state until the war's final year, which meant that one could only enter the Union army's sphere as a slave in 1863, as Burdett did.[10]

Kentucky had avoided many of the political and military pressures that still advanced emancipation in other regions, like eastern Virginia, that were exempt from the proclamation. This had much to do with the Bluegrass State's loyal Unionism — and with President Lincoln's determination to make sure that it remained on his side. "I think to lose Kentucky is nearly the same as to lose the whole game," he famously wrote early in the war, while working assiduously to placate the state's Unionist politicians, many of whom were slaveholders and firmly proslavery in sentiment. The exemption of Kentucky from the Emancipation Proclamation was only part of this effort.[11]

The president also took steps to make sure that the army would not become a force for freedom anyway, as it had in eastern Virginia. He appointed native, slave-owning Kentuckians to positions of military command, such as Gen. Jeremiah T. Boyle, an owner of thirteen slaves in 1860, who commanded the District of Kentucky at the time of Burdett's impressment.[12] The War Department also garrisoned the state with native Kentucky troops, and it filled other army positions, like impressment agent, with men personally invested in

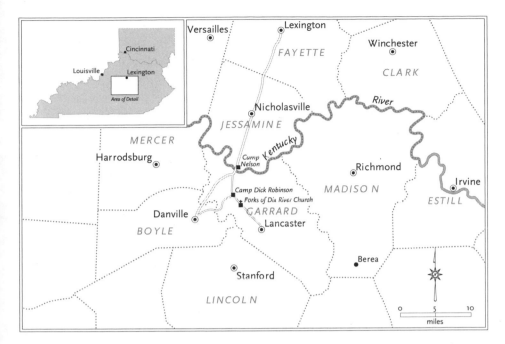

MAP 8. Gabriel Burdett's route through central Kentucky that extended from Garrard County, just north of Lancaster, past the Forks Church, and across the Kentucky River into Camp Nelson (Pauer Center for Cartography & GIS, University of Kentucky)

slavery, like Denny.[13] All of this paved the way for army officials to openly flout the one federal policy that still should have forced their hand on emancipation: the March 1862 article of war banning Union soldiers from returning slaves to their masters.[14] "I want men of my command to have nothing whatever to do with negroes," General Boyle announced in June 1862. "This must be understood."[15]

Gabriel Burdett had no real choice but to climb aboard the army wagon rolling out of Garrard County. As he traveled down the Lexington and Danville Turnpike—the same road on which the Forks Church stood—he would have passed the church and seen it recede from view as he moved closer to Camp Nelson (map 8). At the time, that moment might not have seemed so significant. But Burdett would never again preach at the church. His impressment physically removed him from Garrard County and from the church and its watchful elders. He was no longer under their control. But now Camp Nelson stood before him, an unfamiliar and decidedly secular place for preaching and praying. The army may have unsettled the church landscape of Garrard County, but would it also, in turn, support the sort of religious freedom he was seeking? Burdett's journey through the army camp would test that question.

His quest to worship openly—to find space, both literal and figurative, for the free expression of his beliefs—would thus be central to his liberation from slavery and to the destruction of slavery altogether in Kentucky.

The army wagon carrying Gabriel Burdett crossed over the Kentucky River, lined on both sides with limestone palisades that rose to an elevation of 400 feet, before arriving at Camp Nelson. The cliffs' natural defense kept the camp well protected from roaming Confederates (it was the "Gibraltar of Kentucky," as a Louisville newspaper once put it). And the rolling bluegrass farmland fanning out from the river was now dotted with barracks and warehouses—which would eventually number over 300 in total—storing food rations, clothing, and other equipment. Six large workshops housed blacksmithing, shoeing, and woodworking, while other buildings contained sutler stores, taverns, cookhouses, and mess halls. Tents were scattered about to shelter soldiers; a large two-story white mansion served as quarters for the officers. Yet anything resembling religious life at the camp would not have been immediately visible.[16]

The Union army had done little to foster a thriving spiritual life inside its encampments across the South. To some officials it was doubtful whether religion met any true military necessity; others were skeptical about how well a person's spiritual integrity could be maintained amid the drinking, swearing, and gambling that occupied men in camp. The army employed chaplains to minister to its soldiers, to be sure, but the degree to which local commands respected or supported their work varied from place to place, and a "polite indifference," in the words of historian George Rable, generally prevailed. Some soldiers grew outright disdainful for what they believed were "poor"-quality chaplains, who were sometimes recruited more for their political than spiritual qualifications.[17] Yet, as long as their religious services did not impinge on the needs of the army, they were generally allowed to proceed unimpeded inside an encampment.

That indifference extended to the religious worship of ex-slaves across the occupied South, since the Union army was far more concerned with their physical labor and needs than it was with their spiritual well-being. The order books of local commanders, in which everything from food rations issued to days worked was tracked in individual entries, were notably silent about religious affairs. Refugees may have been told what to eat and where to sleep—but they were given no such orders about praying and preaching and worshipping. Religion turned out to be the least regulated aspect of the life of an ex-slave inside a Union encampment.

The earliest arrivals into Union camps found they could claim space for worship without much interference. The places may not have been marked physically, since actual church buildings or chapels were few, and existing churches in Southern towns and rural neighborhoods that came under Union control were sometimes taken by the army for other purposes (as when the Forks Church was used as a hospital). The religiously devout instead claimed other spaces for their purposes—next to a building, or under a tree, or inside a tent, or in the corner of a barracks. Amid the army's quasi indifference, the most unassuming place in a camp could become marked as a sacred space, and this eventually earned the notice of others around them.[18] One white Union soldier observed an open-air religious meeting at his encampment near Louisville in 1863 and noted that these meetings were held "every evening yes every evening after their work is done." Each time, "they spend from one to 3 hours in talking singing & praying."[19]

The sounds of voices—the songs, the prayers—became a noticeable and remarked-upon part of a camp's soundscape. "It is one of the most striking incidents of this war to listen to the singing of the groups of colored people in Fortress Monroe," a visiting journalist reported during the camp's first summer. "Every evening they sit and sing, to the edification of all the neighborhood," he continued, and when "the lights are put out, and the night is comparatively still, the voice of prayer, loud and earnest, interspersed with fervent responses, may be heard within." Reports in letters home, and in newspapers and magazines, included transcriptions of the words that were overheard, thus disseminating the voices of refugees far beyond the camps themselves.[20] In a more notable example, the lyrics of the spiritual "Go Down Moses" appeared in print for the very first time when Lewis Lockwood, the AMA missionary at Fort Monroe, arranged for its publication in New York in 1862 under the title "The Song of the 'Contrabands.'"[21]

In the very act of being observed—of being *heard*—religious ex-slaves made an aural claim to space in the camps. That they could be so readily heard, and often seen, was significant, for it meant that they were now worshipping freely without hiding. The invisible church was becoming visible. And as it did, particular themes—particular antislavery themes—could be heard loudly and clearly. One black minister in Virginia, identified as Mr. Carey, was overheard exhorting at a prayer meeting in late 1861: "O Lord, we believe that you have come to deliver your people. O trample the secessionists under foot, bless the Union cause, and right every wrong. Bless the President, the Congress Hall and the Senate. Help them make laws that shall be for the good of the Union, and the freedom of thy oppressed people. Oh Lord, I pray. Bless the army and the officers."[22] It was exactly the sort of politicized preaching that would have earned someone like Gabriel Burdett a reprimand in a proslavery Christian church.

But inside the Union camps there were no such reprimands. Sentiments like these now aligned with the politics of the white men around them, and especially with the providential beliefs of the religious among them. They too saw God's hand in the bloodshed of war—and in the progress of the Union. Some of them viewed the war as God's punishment for sins like slavery, while others saw in it something more purposeful, a deliverance from the nation's sins.[23] This providential faith offered understanding—a reason for a soldier to be hopeful and expectant amid unprecedented violence and death, or in the case of the refugees from slavery, amid the insecurity of their position on the road to freedom. "I am assured that what God begins," another black minister reassured his followers, "he will bring to an end."[24] "God," summed up another, "is working in a mysterious way to fulfill his counsels of liberty for the oppressed."[25]

But were God's ways so mysterious? Ministers among the refugees continually turned to biblical precedent, to the Exodus story of the Old Testament, to make sense of their current predicament. "There must be no looking back to Egypt," William Thornton, a minister who had also worked as a carpenter when enslaved, told those gathered for a meeting in Virginia in 1862. He likened their old plantations to the place of the Israelites' enslavement—and their time in the army encampments to the biblical wilderness, where the Promised Land was not yet visible and where they did not know how long they would remain. But, according to Thornton, ex-slaves also could not passively wait for deliverance. "Israel passed forty years in the wilderness, because of their unbelief," he explained. "If we would have greater freedom of body, we must first free ourselves from the shackles of sin, and especially the sin of unbelief." His followers must believe in God and live according to his laws first. They must have "faith, patience, and perseverance," Thornton urged, or they would never leave the wilderness. "Unless we repent of the sin of unbelief and other sins," another black preacher in Virginia put it similarly that month, "we may even be obliged to pass forty years more, in a half way wilderness state."[26]

Black ministers thus imagined the military camps as places to convert the doubters and to sustain the believers, which, in turn, would help bring about the long-sought "freedom of body" described by Thornton. Salvation and emancipation went hand in hand.[27] But as they got to work holding prayer meetings and Sabbath services, large-scale revivals did not instantly wash over the encampments either. Many, if not most, ex-slaves remained skeptical, if not outright indifferent, to Christianity and sometimes to religion more generally, as they streamed into the camps. Scholarly estimates suggest that as few as 10 percent, and perhaps not more than 38 percent, of enslaved people were practicing Christians by the eve of the war.[28] Ministers like Gabriel Burdett were thus in the minority—and had their work cut out for them as they established their ministries inside the military encampments.

They also were left to wonder: If the refugee camps were analogous to the biblical wilderness, then who, or where, was Moses? Though ministers and refugees in other places sometimes came to see President Lincoln assuming that role, especially after his issuance of the Emancipation Proclamation, things were too uncertain in Kentucky to make that connection.[29] They did not automatically view the president, the Union army, or any of its leadership in a Moses-like role. The army's indifference to worship had opened up space for their religious freedom, to be sure, but that indifference had another side too and could unleash the force of military necessity in ways that also tested their faith and devotion. The federal government, after all, still considered men like Gabriel Burdett to be legally enslaved. It thus remained to be seen if the Union army was indeed God's army.

Gabriel Burdett started preaching sometime during his first year as an impressed laborer at Camp Nelson. The exact details of when, where, and how he got started have not survived in the historical record.[30] But he likely noticed right away that the social makeup of his congregants was not quite the same as before. He had come from a plantation of twenty-seven total enslaved people and had presided over a congregation of 200 black people at the Forks Church; now Burdett faced as many as 592 men—the total number impressed and located at Camp Nelson by the summer of 1863.[31] The numbers had grown, but still one crucial element of the religious community to which he was accustomed was missing: women and children.

His wife of now eight years, Lucinda, appears to have remained on the property of her enslavement, along with the two young children she and Gabriel had had in the intervening years: a six-year-old girl named Mary and a four-year-old boy named Smith.[32] So had all the women and children, as well as men deemed physically unable to perform hard labor, throughout central Kentucky. The army had impressed only "able-bodied" men to work on its military roads; to bring in anyone else seemed to step too far beyond the realm of military necessity. The army was firm in its resolve to exclude women and children, as one of the men impressed with Gabriel learned firsthand. Robert

Burdett, who had also been working on the Hiram Burdett property as a hired-out slave at the time of his impressment, attempted to go back to his original owner's property that summer to find his wife. He was quickly caught, however, by the slave catchers unleashed by his angry, Confederate-sympathizing owner. Thrown into a local jail, Robert faced the prospect of being sold to the Deep South, until the Union army intervened and brought him back to the camp. It did nothing to rescue his wife, however.[33]

Impressment thus split up families. And as families often anchored religious worship, it split up religious communities too. There would be no families to pray together at Camp Nelson, no children to guide and instruct, no young or female voices to enrich the singing of hymns. A significant part of Burdett's invisible church would not be made visible at Camp Nelson — at least not yet.[34] But over the next year, the ever-changing calculus of military necessity, while keeping the camp closed to women and children, would open new doors too. It would bring a new opportunity for Burdett to choose, for the first time, whether he wanted to remain in the camp — and whether he wanted to anchor his religious worship inside the Union army's sphere at all.

The most significant change came in March 1864. That month brought an abrupt end to impressment, as Union authorities, realizing that the military roads would not be completed in time for the Army of Ohio's spring campaign, declared the practice "revoked" and the men "returned to their owners."[35] Gabriel Burdett, Robert Burdett, and many others did not immediately return to Garrard County, however, and one month later, in April 1864, came a near reversal. Union authorities decided not only that the army needed the men's labor after all, but that it needed black men to labor as enlisted soldiers specifically. President Lincoln had just struck a deal with the state's proslavery Union governor, Thomas Bramlette, promising to make sure the enlistments did not hurt Union slaveholding interests, by limiting recruitment only to men whose owners consented to the enlistment, paying those masters $300 in compensation, and sending any recruited men out of the state for training to spare white Kentuckians the sight of former slaves drilling in the uniform of the United States.[36]

It proved to be an untenable system. A wave of violence quickly followed across the state, as substantial numbers of owners objected, rather than consented, to enlistment. Yet enslaved men fled to enlist anyway, and military officials, unsure about whether or not their owners' consent had been given, routinely defaulted to sending men back to their owners. Camp Nelson thus

Keeping Faith

became "a hunting ground for fugitives," observed the quartermaster, Capt. Theron E. Hall, who had a frontline view of the situation. "It has been an almost daily occurrence for some squad of men to be employed in hunting slaves and detaining them to their masters," Hall wrote, and in many cases those captured were "tied together" like a "slave gang" and prodded along by armed soldiers.[37] Other reports surfaced of owners severing the ears of men they retrieved with the army's help or, in one case, of two men "fastened to trees in the woods and flayed alive."[38]

The brutal violence pushed the Union's hand. Not only did it threaten military order, but it also exposed the Union's complicity in acts of inhumanity that, according to the laws of war, could not be ignored.[39] Two months later, in June, the army dropped the requirement that owners must consent to a man's enlistment. "All who present themselves for enlistment," stipulated Adj. Gen. Lorenzo Thomas's Special Order No. 20 on June 13, "will be received and enlisted into the service of the United States."[40] It did not matter how their owners felt about it—and those owners would no longer be compensated for their service. "The matter of their enlisting is optional with themselves," one officer explained the new policy. "If they desire to enter the U.S. service they can do so—if they desire to remain at home and work for their masters they can do so."[41] As with all other Union soldiers, the men would be freed upon enlistment. This meant that the very first path had opened to legal emancipation for an enslaved person in the state of Kentucky.

The freedom that Gabriel Burdett long imagined, that his mother had predicted, now stood before him. He had a path through the wilderness—if his owner did not find a way to stop him. Years later Burdett recalled that Hiram Burdett showed up at Camp Nelson in this moment and attempted to use "persuasions" to get him "to desert from the Union army." Hiram could not rely on the army to return Gabriel Burdett to his property anymore; he could only try to persuade him to make another choice. But Gabriel, wielding all the leverage over his ex-owner that the change in Union policy now afforded him, chose the opposite route—he enlisted in July for a three-year term with Company I of the 114th USCT. He then went even further and signed on to be a "recruiting agent" for the army too, working to encourage other men in the region to choose enlistment.[42] Robert Burdett, as well as Gabriel's brother, Elijah Burdett, and 14,000 other men in the state followed suit and enlisted over the summer of 1864.[43]

To be a recruiting agent was extremely dangerous work. "Masters hold on to their slaves as Pharaoh did to his bondsmen," a sympathetic white observer wrote two months later, describing efforts to stop black men from enlisting.

"Some masters use personal violence; and others offer bribes."[44] Even worse was the escalating violence surrounding those who would be left behind, including the women and children in Gabriel's own extended family. "When my husband enlisted," Clarissa Burdett later recalled, "my master beat me over the head with an axe handle saying as he did so that he beat me for letting Ely Burdett go off." Clarissa was married to Gabriel's brother, Elijah, and the man who beat her was Smith Alford, the same owner who had previously thwarted Robert Burdett's attempt to retrieve his wife from Garrard County. It did not matter to Alford that Clarissa's husband technically belonged to — and was lost by — a different owner, Hiram Burdett; the prospect of now losing Clarissa was enough to fight over. "He bruised my head so that I could not lay it against a pillow without the greatest pain," Clarissa reported of an act that would become distressingly familiar across the state as desperate slave owners found in violence one of the only means of putting a stop to black recruitment.[45]

As Gabriel Burdett assumed his duties as a recruiting agent, bringing in only men and leaving women and children behind, the pattern of family separation established by impressment arguably deepened and worsened. There is no evidence of where his wife, Lucinda, and their two children were at this point, although nothing suggests that they made their way to Camp Nelson in this moment, and even if they did, they would have been turned back. The Union repeatedly expelled large numbers of women and children who attempted to follow men enlisting at Camp Nelson that summer and early fall.[46] Gabriel Burdett thus felt personally the army's limitations as an agent of emancipation. But he chose to join it anyway and immersed himself deeper inside its apparatus. Rather than work from without, he would work from within. He had decided to set to work making sure that the Union army did God's work and that Camp Nelson would become a space for the spiritual and physical freedom of all.

It helped that black enlistment brought another population into Camp Nelson that would forever change Gabriel Burdett's religious work: agents from the American Missionary Association. Over the next year at least eight teachers and ministers arrived, mostly white and mostly hailing from the Midwest and other Northern states.[47] Committed to emancipation and determined to offer spiritual guidance to people making the transition from slavery to freedom, the AMA agents appeared to share much in common with a man like Burdett. But they were strangers too: the organization was unfamiliar, and the fact of white religious figures espousing antislavery Christianity was a novel one for the former Forks Church member. It would take time to get to know these new arrivals.

Burdett first met John G. Fee, a man with deep roots in Kentucky and its slavery debate. The son of a slaveholder from Bracken County, along the southern bank of the Ohio River, Fee had grown disenchanted with slavery at an early age and, much to his family's dismay, sought an education across the river at the Lane Theological Seminary, a well-known abolitionist institution in Cincinnati, Ohio. He was ordained a Presbyterian minister in 1844 and subsequently became a strident abolitionist, espousing an antislavery Christianity that would distinguish him as one of the most radical of slavery's white opponents in Kentucky. In tracts with titles such as *Non-Fellowship with Slaveholders the Duty of Christians*, Fee argued that true Christians could not worship with those who perverted their faith in the defense of slavery, a stance that put him at odds with his fellow Presbyterians and prompted his departure from the church. Fee went on to envision the model Christian church as a nonsectarian one, firmly committed to antislavery principles and to racial equality. He spent much of the 1840s and 1850s, with the assistance of the nonsectarian AMA, working to establish independent churches in Kentucky where white and black people could worship together on an equal basis.[48]

Burdett probably heard about the antislavery minister's exploits while back at the Forks Church. In 1855, Fee had traveled to Garrard County to hold two public debates with a local attorney on the subject of colonizing black people in West Africa, something he opposed. His stance got him run out of the county by a mob of nearly forty men. Burdett may have heard about that incident, or maybe four years later he heard about Fee's most radical move yet: the establishment in 1859 of Berea College, twenty miles to the east in neighboring Madison County, which Fee envisioned as the first racially integrated institution of higher learning in the South. Fee's efforts came to a halt later that year, however, when mobs in Kentucky, whipped into a frenzy by the news of John Brown's raid on Harpers Ferry, Virginia, grew increasingly threatening toward Fee — and forced him to leave the state and seek exile in Cincinnati. It was only the news of the Union army's willingness to enlist black men in the summer of 1864 that brought Fee back to Kentucky again.[49]

Fee and Burdett met sometime soon after the missionary's arrival at Camp Nelson. There was much for the former slave turned soldier to like in Fee. Both were antislavery Christians, both were willing to speak out in defiance of the state's proslavery churches, and both had been previously silenced by white Kentuckians for doing so. They shared a religious mission. But Burdett was a slave whose pursuit of freedom involved the pursuit of independence from controlling white church elders, while Fee was attached to a primarily white missionary organization that set out to bring former slaves under its wing. How well those visions could be reconciled would be at the heart of the encounter between them — and between all black religious leaders and white missionaries who encountered one another in refugee camps across the occupied South.

On August 8, 1864, Fee reported back to AMA leaders in New York that "there is one man here of wonderful preaching talent — meek, gentle, childlike."[50] That was how he first introduced them to Gabriel Burdett. It was a puzzling but not altogether surprising thing to say. A penchant to be "meek" is not obviously indicative of "preaching talent," and certainly Burdett had displayed no such propensity to be meek during his tenure at the Forks Church. Had Burdett toned down his manner in the face of these new white people? Possibly. Or maybe Fee wanted to imagine an ex-slave preacher in this way. A "meek" and "childlike" person is a teachable person, and that, after all, was precisely what the AMA was looking for in places like Camp Nelson. They were in the South to teach, to cultivate, and to liberate those who they believed were confined "in the ignorance of heathenism," as an AMA agent in Virginia once put it, and to "give them the blessings of a christian education."[51]

Fee believed he had discovered a rising talent among the black soldiers, who would benefit from the tutelage of a white minister like himself. "I teach him," he wrote in that same letter back to New York.[52] The same paternalistic impulse was shared by other white religious Northerners, who found themselves impressed by the vigor of black preachers but skeptical that they had the knowledge and discipline to be sanctioned by their organizations. Black worship services relied too much on a "great deal of bodily excitement," one white missionary observed with discomfort ("I do not believe in jumping, dancing, or rolling on the floor," he added). Others saw too much superstition at work, or too much enthusiasm.[53] The second AMA missionary to arrive at Camp Nelson after Fee, the Reverend Abisha Scofield, an abolitionist from upstate New York, declared them "peculiar" worshippers in their preference for "*earnestness, directness* and *simplicity*." Scofield, however, relieved to find them also "soundly orthodox" and firm believers "in God and the Bible," also decided that it was more effective to accept some aspects of their religious culture. "If you speak to them in a round about Rhetorical Method they will not hear you."[54]

Burdett, as Fee and Scofield would tell it, learned quickly. And three months later, in October 1864, they granted him a more official position. "We . . . ordained a colored brother who is an able preacher of the Gospel and will we think be greatly useful to his suffering fellow free men," Scofield wrote back to New York. "His name is *Gabriel*, and I can assure you that he blows the Gospel trump with rare eloquence and power."[55] Burdett had been "ordained." It was an unusual move: the AMA did not typically ordain ministers, leaving that task instead to particular denominations. What Scofield more likely referred to instead was ordination by the independent church that John Fee had started before the war in Berea that had now taken root as the Church of Christ at Camp Nelson.[56] This nonsectarian church was established to be resolutely antislavery, and now, with the ordination of a former slave like Gabriel Burdett, it could boast of fulfilling Fee's original vision for racial equality too.

It is difficult to know how enthusiastically Burdett sought out the sanction of these white religious leaders. Other black ministers and congregants in refugee camps resisted that sort of supervision. "They seem to prefer their own colored ministers to us," an AMA missionary in Virginia once reported; others wrote back to New York concerned to find refugees "partial to their own race" or inclined to "prefer a colored preacher." Some missionaries attributed this to a "clannish" quality among them or to simply "preference, which like many human preferences are not founded on wisdom."[57] But another AMA missionary saw more logic in refugees' inclination and tried to explain it to AMA leaders. "They have been obliged to listen to white ministers provided, or placed over them, by their masters," a woman identified only as Mrs. Woodbury explained from Norfolk, "while they have had men among themselves whom they believed were called of God to preach." Now, inside the wartime camps, "to have white preachers still placed over them is too much like old times to meet with their approval."[58]

Yet there is no evidence that Burdett resisted the ordination by the white organization either. One clue to the contrary, in fact, came in a postwar letter, in which Burdett declared that the new church at Camp Nelson had embodied the truest form of religious freedom for ex-slaves. "The Colored people in this state were once all members of the white Slave holding Churches," he wrote to an AMA missionary, yet the Camp Nelson church emerged as "the only independent church in all of the land." Its independence came from its nonsectarianism — something he had come to value alongside John Fee. "I have never been able to see how we could be independent with out coming out entirely from all of the old slaveholding Churches," he wrote, "and form an independent church entirely a part from all of them."[59] The Camp Nelson church seemed to offer Burdett the freedom from slaveholding governance he had been seeking ever since his reprimand from the Forks Church. And this might have made his ordination, even if it came at the behest of two white ministers, seem more liberating than confining.

There was also the practical benefit of Burdett joining forces with men associated with the AMA. The organization brought access to resources he did not have before, such as the vast fundraising network that enabled the shipment of clothing and other supplies into the South, as well as important contacts with the white military establishment. The missionaries' whiteness, and the familiarity and comfort that bred, coupled with the backing of their churches and organizations, had given them a certain entrée with military officials that eluded someone newly out of slavery, like Gabriel Burdett. Sometimes white missionaries became military officials themselves as superintendents of contrabands or freedmen, positions which in some cases came with military commissions too.[60] At Camp Nelson, John Fee struck up a partnership with the quartermaster, Capt. Theron E. Hall, who, it turned out, hailed from the same town in Massachusetts where Fee had given a public lecture back in 1859.[61] "I know you, all about you, and have for years," Hall reportedly announced when Fee first approached him at Camp Nelson.[62]

Their relationship had an immediate impact on Gabriel Burdett. With Hall's assistance, Fee explained, "I had him detailed for our school room." No longer would Burdett work as a recruiting agent. It would now be his official military duty to work with the AMA in teaching and preaching to the soldiers around him; his religious and military services were becoming more tightly fused.[63] In this position he would be even better placed to influence the army and make sure it could support his religious mission. He stayed in this role even as the rest of his regiment left Camp Nelson and headed to Virginia that winter.[64]

❧

Burdett, Fee, and the other AMA missionaries quickly got to work that summer and fall. They held regular worship services for the USCT soldiers — daily prayer meetings, services on the Sabbath — but their attention focused increasingly on setting up schools. They knew that schooling, and especially the teaching of reading and writing, offered the necessary foundation on which their religious mission could be built. It was an urgent priority that all missionaries and ministers brought with them as they fanned out across the South.

This aspect of their work fit well with the military's needs too. "Hall wants all the non-Commissioned officers taught to read & write as soon as possible," Fee explained of the quartermaster's request that schools be established at Camp Nelson.[65] From the army's point of view, schooling was essential to groom these men to become leaders in a military system that was profoundly dependent on the written word. They had to be able to read and sign all sorts of reports, orders, and letters. Without the ability to comprehend written texts, ex-slaves could not detect the falsified orders or passes waved by slave catchers to justify taking them out of a camp, and they could not read the real orders from Union officials verifying they had a right to stay. The men needed access to an entire flow of written information generated by the army to help ensure their protection in the war.

At Camp Nelson, Fee and Burdett followed Captain Hall's directive and began with the noncommissioned officers. They erected two tents and inside them, on July 13, established the very first formal school at the camp, which they named the Camp Nelson School for Colored Soldiers.[66] Their haste was deliberate. "When regiments are liable to go within two or three weeks time, it is very desirable to act immediately," Fee explained to his AMA colleagues. "Place these at once under teachers," Fee wrote of the noncommissioned officers, "& teach these to help others in the regiment."[67] The regiments would then become traveling learning communities, with the lessons of the Camp Nelson school radiating outward across Kentucky and the South in the weeks and months ahead. Over time, as privates remained at Camp Nelson for a significant amount of time, they too joined the noncommissioned officers inside the school.[68]

Fee and Burdett had little trouble attracting students. Nearly 700 of the 4,000 soldiers at the camp that summer attended class sessions during the month of August. The numbers required that twice-daily sessions be held, and at times the numbers of men outstripped the space provided by their tents, with one single session attracting as many as 150 men.[69] The rate at which they attended school was not unusual, for most refugee camps hosted schools and the rates of attendance could be just as high in those places. That same year in Virginia, for example, in Fort Monroe and Hampton, 23 percent of the refugee population (or 1,762 men, women, and children) was enrolled in a total of eighteen schools.[70] In Helena, Arkansas, five schools emerged by the first half of 1865 that 15 percent of the population (or 520 refugees) attended.[71] Estimates for the Mississippi Valley, minus New Orleans, put the proportion at 12 percent attending school in 1864.[72] New Orleans, meanwhile, boasted 55 percent of the population of refugee children in school in early 1865.[73] These rates of enrollment appear even more significant when it is considered that only an estimated 2 percent of the African American population in the United States was attending school in 1860.[74]

White teachers were struck by their pupils' progress. "All my scholars are learning very rapidly," came one report from Fort Donelson, Tennessee, while others elsewhere wrote home about "the rapidity of their progress" and their "rapid improvement in reading and writing."[75] It was, in fact, the most common refrain in teachers' letters. John Fee claimed to see "astonishing progress" just five days after the establishment of Camp Nelson's school.[76] One missionary in the Mississippi Valley likewise reported that it was "truly astonishing to witness the rapid progress they have made" and attempted to quantify their rate of growth. "In some instances, they have learned the alphabet in fifty-five minutes," he contended, "and in forty-eight hours have been able to read short sentences." Perhaps this was true, but it was also likely that the missionaries were exceptionally eager to see a transformation among the refugees.[77] It offered one more indication that the former slaves were making their way through the wilderness — just as the provision of clothing had — and thus one more indication that the missionaries were succeeding in their efforts to lead them.

Yet these statements also exposed some low expectations that white teachers brought with them into the camps, something that the most self-aware among them eventually acknowledged. "I did not put a sufficiently high estimate upon their ability to provide for themselves and their susceptibility to elevation," confessed Rhoda Smith, a Quaker teacher in Virginia.[78] Surprised statements like hers really amounted to expressions of racial awakening. "I must frankly say that their rapid progress has entirely robbed me of the vague idea of the inability of the colored race to become an educated people," an AMA missionary in Virginia reported back to New York. And if anyone wondered if the "partially white" were more "apt to learn," something that had been frequently asked, he was ready to demolish that assumption. "I can say that some of the blackest are among those who make the most rapid progress."[79] These discoveries revealed a degree of unlearning that went on inside the schools too — an unlearning of racist assumptions that even the most sympathetic white opponent of slavery could possess.

Few white teachers acknowledged the most crucial reason for the refugees' academic progress: that they had already begun learning well before they stepped inside the camps' schools. John Fee tacitly noted this in his August report, one month after the school's establishment at Camp Nelson, which labeled 350 of the 692 students as those "who read and spell," while 300 of them were pupils "who write."[80] "Most of these knew their letters," Fee summed up his initial assessment of the students, "quite a number could spell a little, and some few could read."[81] For half the student population to be able to read already was an astonishing figure — and it prompted Fee to the quick conclusion that "no slaves in the nation are superior in intellectual development to these

Kentucky ex slaves."[82] But that missed the mark, for enslaved people everywhere, beyond Kentucky and across the South's refugee camps, brought with them a long-standing history of schooling.

Well before the Civil War, enslaved people had seized any secret means at hand to learn how to read and write—often alongside their "invisible" religious worship. They clandestinely obtained books that they would struggle over on their own time, established secret schools in their quarters, and traded goods with poor white people in exchange for being taught letters. There were plenty of strategies employed by the enslaved to acquire even rudimentary reading skills, even without formal instruction. Some learned to read limited passages and then memorize them; others relied on the reading skills of others to listen to biblical lessons, which were then committed to memory and passed on orally. Reading could be a collective affair, as an ex-slave minister in Virginia described of his religious meetings, in which attendees pooled their skills so that "when one could not make out a word, another could." And then there was the power of spirituals, too, to convey through song various Old Testament themes and elements of the scriptures [83]

It all had to be done in secret, for their owners well understood the threat to slavery posed by black literacy. These skills enabled the enslaved to overcome some of the practical barriers to freeing themselves, such as reading the sign, map, or newspaper that could guide a runaway into a free state. Literacy also enabled them to prepare themselves for a life in freedom, by accessing the political information necessary to vote, or by reading the labor contracts on which the free labor system depended. And, most alarming to white Southerners, it could enable the reading of abolitionist pamphlets, or the Constitution or the Bible, and the forming of ideological arguments against slavery.[84]

This goes a long way toward explaining why half of the men in Fee and Burdett's school could read from the moment they arrived—and why Burdett himself was probably among them. The only evidence of his literacy that survives is in a letter written by John Fee to his AMA colleagues in which he notes, "I taught him to write in form his first letters" once he arrived at Camp Nelson and that "he has learned all since he came into Camp."[85] Fee was quick to take some credit for Burdett's progress, but only for teaching Burdett to "write"— he did not mention reading. That was something Burdett had probably taught himself while still preaching in his old neighborhood and at the Forks Church. He thus picked up his self-teaching where he left off once he arrived in camp— just like many other men around him.[86] Fee himself noticed several companies of black troops "pouring [sic] over their primers or first readers" while "resting from drill."[87] The former slaves' invisible world of reading and writing—like religious worship more generally—was becoming visible.[88]

⌣⌣

That those troops at Camp Nelson had primers in their hands signaled another change taking place behind military lines, one triggered by the arrival of Northern missionary organizations. Groups like the AMA brought not only experienced teachers but also, crucially, money and access to the material goods that were so essential to extending and enhancing the learning process. Books in particular, but also slates, alphabet cards, writing instruments, and maps— all the tools of learning that had long been a struggle for the enslaved to obtain or, if they possessed them, a necessity to hide—could now be freely obtained and passed. Boxes and crates thus flowed into the camps from cities like Cincinnati, New York, and Philadelphia, taking up space on military trains and ships at no cost, alongside the shipments of clothing.

To open a box is to see this world of learning with particular clarity. One box sent from the Women's Aid Committee of the Friends Freedmen's Association of Philadelphia, to be distributed to a school at Fort Monroe in 1863, for example, was fairly typical. According to its inventory, it contained four boxes of steel pens and a half gross of penholders, as well as 104 "copy books" in which to practice writing letters and words. Also inside were two dozen arithmetic books and one dozen *First Lessons in Geography*, the latter purporting to be used in schools across the nation, from New York and Chicago to St. Louis and Philadelphia. With a book like this, the refugees could see what students elsewhere were learning, from the very basic facts ("The Earth is round like a ball") to the more startling and racist interpretations (of the people of Africa: "They are very ignorant and degraded" appeared below an illustration of primitive, nearly naked people wielding spears).[89] School supplies, indeed, were evocative of Northern assumptions about what and how a former slave should learn.

In addition to the instruments of reading, writing, geography, and arithmetic, the same shipment included "6 doz. Spools cotton—1 lb. colored skein cotton—one gross colored tapes—2 gross buttons—1 gross pins—8 pairs scissors—½ lb. patent thread—1 piece gingham—one piece unbleached muslin— remnants calico & drilling—2 undergarments cut out."[90] Book learning did not have to detract from the industrial schools already being established inside the camps to get refugees sewing their own clothing. "We consider it feasible to unite study and sewing," was how one white teacher explained the melding of the two, "so we hang out A B C cards upon the wall, and keep heads and fingers busy."[91] If this proved a physical impossibility, however, then in some camps night schools were established that met only after refugees completed a full day's work as soldiers or laborers. Day sessions in these camps were largely for children, with night schools serving "mostly grown people, who after toiling all day, come eager to learn to read."[92] The night sessions lasted from one to two hours, varying, as one Virginia teacher put it, "in proportion to the degree of fatigue they have undergone during the day," as well as based on the availability of lamps to illuminate their studies.[93]

"12 Hymn books" filled out the box from Philadelphia, also signaling how embedded religious education was in the study of reading, writing, and geography. "I always open the school or class with a chapter from the gospels," reported a Quaker teacher in Virginia.[94] At a nearby school, another Northern teacher reported that in the morning, "school is opened by the repetition, in unison, of the Ten Commandments and the Lord's Prayer, the recitation of a few short answers in a simple catechism, and a short prayer," while in the evening the adult learners began with a reading of a chapter each from the Old and New Testaments.[95] For this reason religious publications were always in demand by teachers. The very first request that AMA missionary Lewis Lockwood sent back to New York after arriving at Fort Monroe in 1861 was for 1,500 "Sunday-school Primers, with pictures," in addition to "A.B.C. Cards, with pictures attached."[96]

Hymnbooks in classrooms also reflected the tight links that refugees themselves made between religion and literacy. "There is great ambition to be able to read the Bible for themselves," observed Lucy Chase, a teacher in Virginia.[97] It was an oft repeated characterization of what ex-slaves desired most upon entering a camp classroom — "to read the Scriptures for themselves." The teachers gladly complied by making sure that thousands of Bibles were also packed into the boxes and sent into the South during the war.[98] To them, the flow of Bibles from north to south was confirmation that the former slaves were willing, and ready, to be converted to Christianity, if they had not been already; to those receiving the Bibles, however, it was a sign of something even more meaningful. "O how I longed for the day when the Bible should be a free book," William Roscoe Davis, the black minister in Hampton, Virginia, who toured the North in 1862, exclaimed when inside Union lines.[99]

The Bible had become a "free book." Where Southern states once cracked down on the distribution of Bibles to the enslaved, they could now be freely obtained and freely passed inside the camps.[100] The Bible was something that could now be held, possessed, and owned for oneself without fear or surveillance. To touch the Bible freely was to control one's experience with the text, to determine how quickly or slowly or how often one read, or to choose what passages one read in the first place. It was a meaningful intellectual, but also sensory, experience; a Bible in hand invested one's religious worship with particular emotions. In the middle-class homes from which many of the white Northern teachers came, after all, the family Bible had become an object of reverence, passed down through the generations. It was a keeper of family history, with genealogical notes, and sometimes photographs and pressed flowers, affixed to its leaves, invoking emotions about family and the passage of life.[101] For the former slaves now touching Bibles of their own, the experience was no less emotional, although for different reasons. Reverend Davis in Virginia described how he "kneeled down by my book" the first time he obtained a Bible, praying that "God would teach me to read it—if only a little." To him the Bible was a physical embodiment of God's word and wisdom; to kneel before it was to exhibit reverence and submission.[102]

In the sight of an ex-slave carrying a Bible in hand, or in the sound of hymns streaming from the schools, no one inside the refugee camps could have missed the physical imprint that schooling and religious worship made in the camps. Yet nothing made these pursuits more conspicuous than the actual classroom spaces themselves. Dissatisfied with the improvised learning spaces carved out by the refugees on their own—under a tree or inside an ex-slave's shelter—Northern teachers made it a priority to establish separate, dedicated buildings for educational purposes. Using whatever ties they had with local military commands, the organizations secured empty military barracks and lobbied their Northern headquarters for funds to construct new buildings altogether. At Camp Nelson, John Fee's initial meeting with Quartermaster Hall resulted in the construction of a new building, eighty feet long and thirty feet wide, built by refugee laborers using the army's sawmills.[103] In other places teachers obtained permission to take over occupied structures once belonging to Confederates, such as former president John Tyler's house in Hampton, Virginia. "Little did the ex-President think that his house would ever be used for such a purpose," noted one AMA missionary.[104]

A postwar AMA report noted that "almost anything in the shape of a building was extemporized into a room for schools."[105] But there had to be a building: a roof and walls were essential, the teachers believed, for keeping out the heat or wind or rain that threatened to disrupt the proceedings, and for generating the order to which they were accustomed inside Northern classrooms. There needed to be a wall or a door to paint black, one teacher explained, "so as to serve for blackboards" or on which to hang portraits of men they revered, like Daniel Webster or George Washington.[106] There needed to be a solid surface on which to hang maps or other written texts that could be pointed to as needed in a lesson. A "Miss Humphrey," teaching in Memphis for the AMA, told of hanging "choice passages of scripture" on the wall of her school, to which she pointed with "a rod which had formerly striped the back of my best pupil." An old slave rod had been refashioned into a learning tool in her classroom, albeit one that still structured a certain kind of order. Schedules and the ringing of bells and the lining of benches in rows or semicircles also worked to create schools in which learning was ordered, rather than illicitly and haphazardly pursued.[107]

The physical landscape of schoolrooms may have signified progress toward freedom, but in war it also was an index of security. In regions well protected from enemy troops, and thus where refugees could count on staying put for months at a time, boxes of supplies could readily flow into barracks made available by army authorities. In occupied cities like Memphis or New Orleans, as well as in planned settlements like Uniontown or Mitchelville, schools became a prominent feature of the landscape. But when enemy troops beckoned, or when the calculus of military necessity changed for any other reason, schools were among the first structures sacrificed, and teachers, as well as students, sometimes found themselves sent off to distant campaigns, breaking up schools in their wake. The military's support of refugee schooling thus revealed itself to be conditional—easily sacrificed to the call of military necessity or to the violent incursions of enemy guerrillas.

The most vulnerable schools were on the leased plantations of the Mississippi Valley, where the establishment of formal schools was "entirely neglected" in the first place. In part, this had to do with the lessees' single-minded focus on cotton production. "On the part of the greater number of the planters," Superintendent of Freedmen John Eaton reported, "there does not appear to be any disposition to educate the blacks."[108] Lessees did not invite Northern organizations to set up on their property, nor did those organizations desire to send teachers or supplies to places swarming with rebel guerrillas. But this only meant that formal resources did not make it to the plantations, for the ex-slaves themselves made sure that schooling itself never disappeared. Black teachers, working alone and without any outside support, instructed refugees with whatever means they could find—in the open air, on the piazza of the main house, or in their cabins.[109] Their plantation schools had to be nimble, able to move in an instant at the threat of a guerrilla attack, with supplies improvised from found materials: roof tiles taken from rebel forts were used as slates, broken slate fragments sometimes approximated pencils, and "large grapeshot" simulated the shape of the earth when teaching geography.[110] Any book that could be found among nearby soldiers and officers was put to use, "scarcely any two of them alike" in some schools.[111]

Schools thus absorbed both the tumult and the stasis of military life — something Gabriel Burdett and John Fee learned firsthand back at Camp Nelson. By early November 1864, their school building was becoming inhospitable in the early winter chill, thanks to a lack of heat. Several appeals to military officials to provide them with a stove were met with what seemed like empty promises, which led the men, along with AMA missionary Abisha Scofield, to find an old condemned stove in the area and install it themselves, replacing its broken pipe with a newly purchased one. They went into a nearby forest and cut wood for themselves, but returned one day to find the building occupied by soldiers who had been arriving in increasing numbers in preparation for a campaign into Virginia. "We found our benches outdoors, the stove broken, and the wood nearly gone," Scofield reported to AMA headquarters upon his return. "Our room had been converted into barracks." Scofield was concerned that "the officers seemed not to care" and that "we were not respected." They were then forced to close the school.[112] One of the most important spaces claimed by the camp's religious leaders was now lost, which threw the question of how well the army supported their mission back out in the open again.

~~~

The loss of the schoolroom turned out to be only the beginning of a tumultuous month for Gabriel Burdett and every other ex-slave at Camp Nelson. Although the reelection of Abraham Lincoln to the presidency in early November may have inspired some optimism, slavery still remained largely intact for most African Americans in Kentucky. The death of Burdett's enslaver that fall only made that vividly clear: in the settlement of his estate, Hiram Burdett's heirs, unwilling to concede the reality of emancipation, sold all eight of his remaining slaves, including two children, to other white people in a public sale on November 9, 1864.[113] That there were people willing to buy them nearly two years after the Emancipation Proclamation was a testament to some white Kentuckians' determination to see slavery persist well into the future. And at the same time, as Gabriel Burdett rose to lead his congregants in worship services at the camp, he was undoubtedly reminded by the sea of male faces before him of the way in which the Union army had opened a path through the wilderness only for some — and left many others far behind.

Women and children had continued trying to claim a place for themselves in the camp throughout that fall, squeezing into soldiers' tents and other wooden shelters, sometimes with the encouragement of friendly white officers willing to ignore army policy. But that, too, came to a screeching halt on the unusually cold morning of November 23. Nearly 400 women and children who were congregated in the camp awoke that morning to the sight of armed guards carrying out the orders of the camp's commanding general, Speed Smith Fry, to expel them from the camp. It was the ninth such expulsion of women and children since black enlistment began. Told they would be shot if they did not comply, the women and children quickly boarded a series of military wagons—six to eight in number, according to one eyewitness—and huddled close to one another, bracing for bitter temperatures that hovered at sixteen degrees at 7:00 a.m. The wagons then set off down the road toward the nearby town of Nicholasville, about six miles from the camp, with the aim of getting the occupants beyond the lines of Union pickets. In their wake, Fry's soldiers tore down and then torched their shelters, eliminating the families' claims to space inside the camp.[114]

Among those in the wagon that morning was a family Gabriel Burdett knew well from Garrard County. Mary Ellen Burnside and her two children had entered Camp Nelson to be with her husband, John Burnside, the same minister turned soldier who had married Gabriel and Lucinda Burdett nine years before. Like Gabriel, John Burnside had gone to Camp Nelson as an impressed laborer first. He then enlisted in the 124th USCT, while Mary Ellen and the children remained on the property of their owner, William Royster. There they lived in "constant dread," as John later described it, for Royster was suspicious that Mary Ellen was feeding the Union information about his son, a Confederate raider, and he threatened to "scatter them to the four winds of heaven" if he found out this was true. John Burnside eventually received assurance from a sympathetic enlisting officer that he could bring his family to the camp with him—which he did in September 1864, whereupon they "earned their living with hard work." They lasted only two months before the expulsion came.[115]

Burnside set out that evening to find his family. He followed the path of the wagon and eventually found them in a wooded area, "thrown out without any protection or any home," enduring the cold temperatures while it "rained hard."[116] An old meetinghouse provided shelter for part of the group, although rain fell steadily through the roof. No refugees had any food to eat, and there was only one fire to deliver heat to the entire group. All were newly vulnerable to the slave catchers who were likely to find them soon. One woman had no choice but to deliver a child in the freezing temperatures.[117] Another woman, suffering from a painful case of neuralgia, was now separated from the five sons she had gone to for protection at Camp Nelson after her husband was whipped to death in a neighboring county.[118] Burnside, along with several other men who had gone searching with him, immediately returned to Camp Nelson to press their case.

They dictated their stories in a series of affidavits taken by Capt. E. B. W. Restieaux, an assistant quartermaster who had overseen the labor of impressed men in the previous year and who was known to be sympathetic.[119] Restieaux immediately passed the affidavits to his superior, Capt. Theron E. Hall, who wasted no time circulating their contents beyond Camp Nelson. He appealed to Gen. Stephen Burbridge, in command of the District of Kentucky, that same day, seeking the reversal of Fry's expulsion order. He then sent a "strong letter" to the abolitionist senator Benjamin Wade of Ohio, asking that he share it with the secretary of war. Hall finally went outside the bureaucratic channels, too, and worked to influence public opinion by drafting a letter under the pen name "Humanitas" and sending it, along with one of the affidavits, to the *New York Tribune*. The paper published it on November 28, now five days after the expulsion, and from there the letter and affidavit traveled to other papers across the North under titles such as "Cruel Treatment of the Wives and Children of U.S. Colored Soldiers." Meanwhile, Hall sent 200 food rations out to the suffering families.[120]

It was "cruel" treatment. That was the message emanating quickly from Camp Nelson—a message (and a word) so potent that it set military officials reeling. General Fry tried to defend his actions as being fully in line with military precedent and orders. The act "was under the circumstances one of necessity," he argued in a letter to Captain Restieaux, and there was "no violation of orders." He felt he was only following the order sent down by the adjutant general the previous summer, which was to "discourage as far as possible negro women and children coming into camp."[121] But Hall, Restieaux, and other military officials at Camp Nelson saw things differently, for in Fry's order they saw something entirely unnecessary and, thus, a profound violation of the military's laws of war. It was an "atrocious cruelty," Hall wrote in his "Humanitas" letter, and cruelty, the author of the Union's laws of war, Francis Lieber, had argued, was at odds with the principle of military necessity. Cruelty represented nothing more than the "unnecessary infliction of pain, pain for its own sake to satisfy the lust of revenge or a fiendish hatred," Lieber spelled out in the code, and thus was out of bounds in the army's conduct of war.[122] There was no way, then, to justify Fry's expulsion of the women and children as a military necessity.

With the turn of events aired so publicly—and nationally—the pressure was on Union officials to reverse course. "You will not expel any Negro women or children from Camp Nelson but give them quarters and if necessary erect buildings for them and allow back all who have been turned out," came an order from General Burbridge.[123] Then, over in Washington, D.C., Quartermaster General Montgomery Meigs, having read the "Humanitas" letter in the *Tribune* (and probably unaware that his own subordinate, Hall, was behind the letter), ordered an investigation to make sure no quartermaster officer was "at fault" in the "unparalleled atrocities" at the camp.[124] Secretary of War Stanton likewise supported Burbridge's actions and ordered a permanent shelter established for refugees at Camp Nelson. That marked a significant blow to slavery in Kentucky, as it now opened the doors to *any* enslaved man, woman, or child wanting to enter the camp.[125] And on December 13, Senator Henry Wilson of Massachusetts went further and introduced a new bill into the Senate, an act "to encourage enlistments and to promote the efficiency of the military forces of the United States." It promised to declare all wives and children of Union soldiers "forever free," removing all doubt about their status in Kentucky.[126]

Back at Camp Nelson, 250 of the original 400 expelled refugees returned. By February an estimated 800 more women and children had taken shelter there, and now, as in so many other encampments in the occupied South, food rations were forthcoming and boxes of clothing began to arrive from Northern cities like Cincinnati.[127] The women and children initially took up shelter in military barracks and what benevolent workers described as "huts of very rude construction and small size."[128] But illness and death, much of it triggered by the events of late November, swept through the barracks: a reported 102 of the 250 refugees previously expelled had died by late February.[129] This, in addition to "noise feuds disease and disgust," as John Fee described the quarters, led AMA officials, as well as refugees themselves, to push for something less chaotic and more orderly.[130]

By the spring it came in the form of what was called the Refugee Home, a village of nearly 100 cottages lined up in rows, each sixteen by sixteen feet in dimension and made to house up to twelve people. Fellow refugees built the cottages and were, this time around, paid for their labor and provided with materials (fig. 14).[131] Camp Nelson had become something like the planned refugee settlements that had taken root elsewhere in the South, with each new cottage anchoring a place for refugees inside the Union's military sphere. Overseeing the Refugee Home would be Theron E. Hall, who resigned his position as quartermaster to become the superintendent. And working alongside him

FIGURE 14. Refugees and their cottages at the new Camp Nelson Refugee Home
(Camp Nelson Photographic Collection, Special Collections
Research Center, University of Kentucky)

was a newly appointed assistant superintendent drawn from the ranks of the
black soldiers — Gabriel Burdett.[132]

The dynamics of military necessity now pulled the army more closely behind the mission of Gabriel Burdett, John Fee, and the other missionaries and
teachers at Camp Nelson. To some of Burdett's AMA colleagues, the establishment of the Refugee Home was a sure sign that the military was now, once and
for all, doing the work of God and would lead all refugees, including women,
through the wilderness. The new superintendent, Theron E. Hall, called it a
"triumphant result" and saw in the arrival of women and children the work of
a higher power. "Give to God the praise," Hall wrote to AMA officials in New
York. "It is His work."[133] John Fee reacted similarly. "God opens the way," he
wrote, seeing in the turn of events a new chapter of their mission. "There are
many doors now opening to me in this state," he explained in February, and
"I thank God for the privilege."[134] There was little doubt that Camp Nelson had
become a space in which their religious mission would be secured by army protection rather than impeded by indifference or outright exclusion.

His appointment as assistant superintendent of the Refugee Home now
made Gabriel Burdett one of the highest-ranking black officials involved in
refugee affairs in the South.[135] But he assumed his new position with some
trepidation. That winter he took pen in hand and aired his concerns in a letter
to John Fee, who was traveling to Berea in early January. It was the first letter
Burdett wrote that would survive the war (and John Fee would send it to New

Keeping Faith

York "to show the progress of the writer"). "I would like verry much to see you and here your advice on matters at this time," Burdett wrote on January 20. "I myself have no room to complain for I am well and doin well but som things do not please me, for I love peace and union and I have lived long enough to know that if men do not love each other they do not lov God and if they do not love God they will not werke for him."

Men around him were putting earthly strife before their higher devotion to God, Burdett observed. "How vane it seames to me to see men strive one against another as thoug they knew not that thare was a God who ruls the Heavens and the earth." Burdett did not specify who these men were exactly. Perhaps he was talking about the Union and the Confederacy in a general sense and making what amounted to an antiwar statement in his gesture to "peace and union."[136] Yet the recent turn of events had only inflamed long-simmering internal strife among white officials at Camp Nelson too.

Just after the expulsion, for example, General Burbridge had removed and then reinstated General Fry as commander, while Fry turned around and arrested his most public critic, Theron E. Hall, for "ungentlemanly behavior," only to release him eight hours later.[137] Hall, in turn, incurred the resentment of AMA officials, who did not see him as the right man to serve as superintendent of the Refugee Home. Hall had "taken the entire possession of the contrabands in camp," Abisha Scofield complained, and seemed to be sidelining the religious leaders.[138] Declaring Hall "artful and ambitious," and chiding him for his "seldom" church attendance, John Fee grew to regret not seeking the superintendent position himself.[139] Burdett thus found himself caught between his AMA colleagues, Fee and Scofield, on the one hand, and his new military superior, Superintendent Hall, on the other. Clearly some of the underlying tensions between religious and military leaders had not fully disappeared in the aftermath of the expulsion.

Burdett did not believe he had the luxury of celebrating or fighting, as these white leaders seemed to be doing. He was one of the refugees, too, with family members still in slavery and people close to him still suffering immensely. Nothing in the record suggests that Lucinda and their children had made it inside the camp yet. Burdett thus closed his letter to Fee by urging the missionary to come back and "see yourself how things are going on." And he hastily added, almost as a postscript, that "thare has been much sickness and many deaths here since Dec. 24/64. thare has been 43 deaths and still they die." Illness continued to take the lives of large numbers of refugees well into the spring, with 468 of the 2,782 admitted into the Refugee Home dying between January and May 1865. That is what worried Burdett most, although he tried to maintain some perspective. "But we cannot complain," he closed in a nod to the reality of war, "for death is abroad in the land."[140]

Burdett saw the suffering every day as he got to work in the Refugee Home. He saw it even as the new cottages were established to house individual families, and even as, most monumentally, Congress passed Senator Wilson's legislation and President Lincoln formally signed into law on March 3 the bill to free the wives and children of black soldiers. The law permanently secured the position of women and children at the camp—and made freedom a reality for an estimated total of over 72,000 people in the state.[141] But they still had to get to Camp Nelson or to any Union encampments in the state to realize that freedom, and that is where things got difficult. White Kentuckians zealously guarding their hold on enslaved people saw their grasp slipping and continued to lash out violently to regain it. Those refugees who made it out of their farms and plantations and into Camp Nelson brought with them harrowing stories that the clerks in the Refugee Home—possibly Burdett himself—noted in a record book:

> NANCY "Master beat her and her children with anything at hand."
> JULIA ANN "Master told her to go off. Kept her best clothing. Put her in jail for asking for food. Told her to go to Lincoln and get it."
> FLORA "Mistress drew a gun and threatened to shoot her, for speaking for the Union cause."
> SOPHIA "Master had threatened to shoot her because her husband had enlisted."
> JULIA "Master threatened to give her 150 lashes. He is a *preacher*."

"The old oppressors," an AMA official explained, "enraged at their loss, strike at the nation's black defenders through those dearest to them."[142]

The stories were at times deeply personal for Gabriel Burdett. Perhaps he was the one who recorded the continuing ordeal of Clarissa Burdett. "On Wednesday last March 22," she testified about her owner, "he said that he had not time to beat me on Tuesday but now he had time and he would give it to me." This was the same man, Smith Alford, who had already beaten her over the head with an axe after her husband, Elijah (Gabriel's brother), enlisted in the Twelfth United States Colored Heavy Artillery the previous fall and who had tried to sell her brother Robert Burdett to the Deep South. "He then tied my hands threw the rope over a joist stripped me entirely naked and gave me about three hundred lashes. I cried out," she recounted. Alford was especially enraged that Clarissa's niece had left for Camp Nelson already; he demanded that Clarissa go get her, vowing to "be jailed before one of his niggers would go to Camp." "He then caught me by the throat and almost choked me then continued to lash me with switches until my back was all cut up." Clarissa Burdett then fled, literally running for her life, with the injuries visible on her back as she arrived at Camp Nelson. But she had to leave her four children behind. It was impossible to get them away without inciting Alford's wrath, but it also seemed impossible to return, knowing that her master "would whip me" and "would not let any of my children go." Clarissa asked the Refugee Home officials for help.[143]

Clarissa's position was all too familiar to the staff at the Refugee Home, who heard many other stories of women forced to leave behind a nursing infant or a child restrained by a master at gunpoint.[144] The army may not have been keeping them apart anymore—but the task of enforcing the new law and helping families come together was also at times overwhelming. Still, Clarissa and many others recognized, they now had the apparatus of the state, of the army in particular, behind them, and it could be put to work in reuniting their families. Possibly at Gabriel's behest, her case garnered the attention of the army's command at Camp Nelson, and within two weeks came an order to "arrest and hold subject to orders from these Head Quarters, Smith Alfred, who is charged with inhumanly beating Clarissa Burdett a colored woman."[145] Alford was subsequently arrested and fined by Union authorities.[146] Clarissa thus reunited with her husband, Elijah, and their children—all now legally freed—at Camp Nelson in early April 1865.

It was nearly four years into the Civil War by this point, nearly four years after the Whitehursts and other enslaved people in eastern Virginia began seeking freedom at Fort Monroe. Yet from Gabriel Burdett's vantage point, the enslaved of Kentucky had not yet made it out of the wilderness. There were more women and children inside the camp, to be sure, broadening his spiritual community and establishing the camp as an even freer space for religious worship. And within that field Burdett assumed new religious duties that March when he performed his first three baptisms ("He had not baptized before," John Fee noted).[147] His religious work was expanding rather than contracting at war's end.

But Burdett could not remain focused on his mission either. In April came word that his regiment, the 114th USCT, had fought in the victorious Petersburg campaign in Virginia, which led to the fall of Richmond and ultimately the surrender of Gen. Robert E. Lee's Army of Northern Virginia at Appomattox.[148] The war seemed to be over. Except that on April 27, 1865, came the news that "Priv. Gabriel Burdett 114th U.S.C. Infty. is hereby ordered to proceed to Lexington Ky . . . for the purpose of being mustered into service."[149] Burdett was to rejoin his regiment in Virginia as it prepared to depart for Texas, in order to secure that western state for the Union. By early May, Burdett left Camp Nelson with a military pass in hand, traveling first to Lexington and then to Cincinnati, before heading east to meet his regiment in Virginia.[150] Military necessity had asserted itself yet again, this time forcing Burdett to abandon the church, the school, the congregants, the newly baptized—the entire world of religious freedom he had steadily built over the last two years. He was headed into combat for the first time. But first, he headed to Fort Monroe.

} 8 {

Grappling with Loss

Gabriel Burdett arrived at Fort Monroe in late May 1865 and met the rest of his regiment there. The 114th USCT had been among the first troops that marched into the Confederate capital of Richmond back on April 3, a movement that epitomized the radical social upheaval wrought by the Civil War. Black men, mostly former slaves, had marched in the uniform of the United States to secure the fall of the Confederate capital—the capital of slavery and secession. Burdett may have missed that stunning moment himself, but even as he moved around freely at the fort at the same time that Jefferson Davis, the now-former Confederate president, sat confined in one of the fort's casemates as a prisoner charged with treason, he, too, demonstrated how dramatically the war had turned things upside down.[1]

Had Burdett looked beyond the fort's stone walls during that time, he would have seen a landscape drastically transformed over the previous four years too—transformed by refugees from slavery like Edward and Emma Whitehurst. The Whitehursts had remained in the region over the last three years, ever since the looting of their store. They had little money left after that loss but managed to scrape by for a time, selling a horse to raise needed funds and borrowing money from another freedman when Edward became sick and had to pay hospital fees.[2] But eventually they moved out to a Union-occupied plantation that bordered the city of Hampton, where they rented land from the government at two dollars per acre, as well as a surplus military horse for a sixteen-dollar deposit.[3] They never opened another store. Around them several thousand other people established themselves on similar plots of land, having enjoyed relative isolation from military action since the Peninsula campaign, which enabled them to build new shelters, churches, schools, and stores, with some hope of staying there. By early 1865, superintendents in the region's Department of Negro Affairs reported that the majority of refugees were self-supporting; Gen. Benjamin F. Butler, who had resumed command at Fort Monroe in November 1863, was beginning to establish a new public school system.[4] The once transient refugee camps were showing signs of becoming permanent settlements.

Burdett did not stay there long, however. With the 114th USCT, he boarded a steamer on June 6, 1865, and headed first to Mobile, Alabama, for a quick stop, before arriving one month later in Brownsville, Texas, at the border between the United States and Mexico.[5] There Burdett may have glimpsed other USCT regiments streaming into the region too, including Eliza Bogan's Forty-Sixth USCT, which sailed in just four days before his. One year had passed since Bogan watched her husband, Silas Small, succumb to measles; in the intervening months, she continued to work as a laundress for the Forty-Sixth USCT, as it moved from Louisiana to Memphis to New Orleans and now to its last stop, the coast of Texas. There she camped with the regiment on Brazos Santiago, a sandy island with little vegetation or firewood that was surrounded only by salt water and hot sun. The summer would pass without adequate supplies of fresh vegetables or fruit; an estimated half of the soldiers in the region would suffer from scurvy. The island quickly transformed the Forty-Sixth USCT's fight from military combat to a war against disease. The fight had changed but it was not over.[6]

As his path crossed with the Whitehursts' in Virginia, and then with Eliza Bogan's in Texas, Gabriel Burdett's postwar journey allowed him to see up close the various ways in which former slaves had become immersed in the bureaucracy and spaces of the Union army—from those who worked on the occupied farms of Virginia, to those who served in the regimental camps as far away as Texas. But even as it seemed like the interests of former slaves and the Union army had become more closely fused by war's end, with all of them celebrating the defeat of the Confederacy and the defeat of slavery, it would all soon unravel again. And Burdett would see that, too, up close.

The Union's military victory proved to be a proverbial double-edged sword for the newly freed people. On the one hand it secured the legal end of slavery—but it also led to the withdrawal of Union troops from the South and, thus, to the loss of military protection. Nearly 80 percent of the Union army went home between April and November 1865, while those who remained (an increasing proportion of which were black troops) moved on to previously unoccupied areas, like Burdett's and Bogan's regiments did in Texas. This rapid demobilization revealed that the calculus of military necessity had changed once again, and this time it would prompt the biggest upheaval yet in the lives of a population that had already experienced constant change throughout the war. No longer was their labor needed. No longer could their spaces be justified. Where the refugee camps were once "a war measure," as one military official in Kentucky described them, "an instrument in the hand of the Hon Secy of War with which he harassed and worried the enemies of the Gov.," now they could no longer be seen as such. Nearly all refugee camps would be emptied as the army demobilized over the coming year. And thus, the places where refugees from slavery had found their foothold in freedom, the places that had never been fully secure but had made their emancipation seem more likely, were taken away. In victory there would be loss for the refugee population — a great deal of tangible, material loss.[7]

At war's end the landscape of refugee camps stretched far and wide across the occupied South. Many had come and gone over time, but by the war's last year, over 200 still had roots planted along the region's coast and rivers and on the grounds of once-prospering cotton, hemp, sugar, and rice plantations. At least half a million people had taken up residence in these spaces, marking a movement — and a redistribution — of people that was as rapid as it was concentrated. People once scattered across distant farms and plantations had come together in unprecedented numbers. The dense concentrations of people were readily evident in the built landscape, in the form of 525 new buildings constructed on a 180-acre farm near New Bern, North Carolina, known as the Trent River settlement, for example, or in the 1,000 new shelters built in one small section of Alexandria, Virginia.[8] Individual farms along the Atlantic coast or in the Mississippi Valley now housed far more people than they ever had in slavery. The Taylor farm, for example, located fourteen miles outside Norfolk, saw its population increase from eleven enslaved people in 1860 to 1,000 refugees living inside 200 newly built cabins.[9] In Mississippi, the "Dr. Langley" plantation in Issaquena County increased from sixty-one enslaved people to 264 refugees; the six plantations at Davis Bend, including one that had belonged to Jefferson Davis, now hosted 10,000 ex-slaves.[10] Together these spaces offered a glimpse into a remapped future for the South, one in which concentrated communities of black people replaced the dispersed settlement patterns of the plantations.

Many things had made this resettlement possible over the course of the war's four years, but nothing was more foundational than the availability of land. The war literally opened up space through the abandonment of land by fleeing rebel landowners, the confiscation of land by occupying Union troops, and the transformation of land by freedom-seeking people. Men, women, and children in the refugee camps built an entire scaffolding of new lives on the lands occupied by the Union, from houses to churches to schools to gardens. Always aware of the fragility of their efforts, though, as military campaigns and floods and marauding guerrillas moved in and destroyed their camps, they knew how easy it was to lose their hold on the land. And never far off from anyone's mind was what would happen next: How secure was their hold on this land for the long term? What would happen when the war ended? Would Union victory guarantee they could stay or move to other, similar settlements?

No one had clear answers about what would happen next—not even the laws and policies of the United States. The federal government had gained legal title to all land "confiscated" during the war, but that was a fairly small portion of the total property occupied by the army, and President Lincoln was not inclined to maintain ownership of it. He believed, as Congress stipulated in a joint resolution in 1862, that legal title to these lands had been forfeited by the rebel owner only during his or her lifetime, meaning that it would have to revert back to the owner's family after death. The situation was even murkier for "abandoned land," the property that Confederates left behind as they fled from the Union army and took refuge in the interiors of their states, which was the majority of the Union's holdings. No legal mechanism was in place to determine how the Union could take possession of abandoned land, or when and how those lands might be returned to their original owners. This meant that, strictly speaking, the Union's occupation of abandoned lands was something more like "temporary custody," with a great deal of uncertainty and disagreement over what should happen next. That ambiguity would envelop the refugee camps, too, as the vast majority of them were built on abandoned lands.[11]

Before the end of the war, before its end was even in sight, some official efforts emerged to clarify the situation and to secure this land for the freed people's settlements. Most well known is the work of Gen. William T. Sherman, who by January 1865 had acquired a vast, multistate swath of abandoned land during his march to the sea, and who afterward heard from a group of black ministers in Savannah about the importance of claiming that land for their freedom. Sherman thus issued Special Field Order No. 15, which reserved 400,000 acres along the South Carolina, Georgia, and Florida coasts to be carved up into forty-acre parcels, each to be granted to freed people. The head of each household would be given "possessory title" of each plot of land, leaving it up to Congress to decide the ultimate legal fate of the property. Congress itself acted two months later in March 1865 with the establishment of the Bureau of Refugees, Freedmen, and Abandoned Lands ("Freedmen's Bureau"), which was given custody of all the confiscated and abandoned land acquired by the United States during the war. In its founding legislation, the bureau was empowered "to set apart, for the use of loyal refugees and freedmen, such tracts of land within the insurrectionary states as shall have been abandoned, or to which the United States shall have acquired title by confiscation or sale, or otherwise." Each freed person would be granted up to forty acres to rent for three years, with the option of purchasing that land outright during that period.[12]

Other local, private efforts supplemented these government initiatives. One month after Sherman issued his order, Charles Wilder, now superintendent of Negro affairs at Fort Monroe and its surrounding area, attended a government auction in Virginia and successfully bid $4,500 in private money on four farms settled by refugees. It was part of a plan he had hatched over the previous year, when he began raising funds from wealthy, sympathetic Northerners.[13] Wilder felt "great anxiety" at the prospect that refugees "should be deprived of the little interest and rights they had in the lands, where they had been permitted to erect their huts," so he planned to divide the land and sell it at "cost," allowing each buyer time to pay in full. It was a move to preserve the refugee settlements that had already been established in the area—to secure "to the negroes undisturbed occupation of their huts and gardens." Each of the four farms had given rise to entire villages of houses, schools, churches, and stores during the war. One of the four farms, the Mallory place, in fact, was the same property from which the very first refugees entered Union lines at Fort Monroe in May 1861.[14]

Another of the four properties was the Sinclair farm—a 600-acre tract where Edward and Emma Whitehurst were now renting land. A "great many colored people" resided there, too, Whitehurst later recalled, or an estimated 4,500 men, women, and children on both the Sinclair place and an adjoining farm known as the Shields farm.[15] The lands now hosted five churches, "built by ourselves since the Rebellion," as some of the residents described it, as well as a "store of our own" and what a government report termed a "contraband hospital." "Our settlement on Sinclair's farm is laid out in streets with order and regularity," the residents noted, and "contains many buildings of comfort and convenience, and some even of elegance." Not only that, but the lands "will this year yield better, richer and heavier crops twice told than was ever known before under the system of slavery."[16] To have the farm purchased by Charles Wilder would ensure that the settlement remained permanent, becoming its own thriving town rather than a plantation again.

But that was precisely what some of Charles Wilder's fellow Union officials found objectionable. The new commander at Fort Monroe, Maj. Gen. Edward Ord, who arrived to replace Benjamin Butler that spring, was a veteran of hard-fought campaigns in Vicksburg and Petersburg, as well as a recent witness to Gen. Robert E. Lee's surrender at Appomattox. A Union man through and through, he never wavered in his commitment to seeking military victory, but he was also never convinced about the importance of emancipation, or even of the black soldiers in his command, toward securing that end.[17] Ord did not want to oversee the kind of social program Wilder had in mind and immediately ordered the superintendent to turn over the lands he had just purchased. But Wilder refused, prompting the general to remove him from his position as superintendent and have him arrested on a series of trumped-up charges during the spring of 1865.[18] Ord accused Wilder of embezzlement, claiming the superintendent had defrauded the freed people around him; he also accused Wilder of speculating on the farmland for his own personal gain. A court-martial commission eventually found no basis for any of Ord's claims, however, and Wilder was quickly acquitted (and reinstated to his position as superintendent).[19] Ord lost the trial, but his determination to put the brakes on preserving land for freed people would be upheld by his superiors.

That March, around the same time that Ord was arresting Wilder, President Lincoln suspended the sale of confiscated land across the South, effectively halting other similar, private efforts to purchase land for freed people. Lincoln was thinking about reunion — about the war coming to an end, and about the urgency of doing nothing to damage the prospects of stitching the Union back together.[20] He knew that the land once fought over, the land that had supported the destruction of slavery by housing the refugee camps, was now deeply entwined with the task of reuniting the nation. Following the surrender of the Army of Northern Virginia, white Southerners would begin streaming back to their lands, fully expecting to have their property rights respected and demanding to resume their planting midseason. Lincoln, though, would not live to oversee the fraught process of sorting out the competing claims on the land. Following his assassination on April 14, the refugees, like so many other Americans, were left to mourn his loss and to wonder how differently the process might have played out had he lived.[21]

Lincoln's successor, Andrew Johnson, then took up the issue with zeal. His Amnesty Proclamation, issued on May 29, 1865, promised former Confederates "restoration of all rights of property, except as to slaves," as long as they took an oath of loyalty to the United States. The largest landowners (with property valued at more than $20,000), as well as the most high-ranking Con-

Grappling with Loss

federate officials, were to be excluded from this unless they applied for and received an official pardon from the president.[22] Johnson would prove to be generous in the issuance of those pardons over the course of the next year; it was now in the Union's interest, Johnson believed, to reverse course when it came to Southern lands. Under his administration, the land would be stripped of its emancipatory meaning and put to work in the service of reintegrating white people into the Union.

And this spelled the end of the refugee camps. All of the camps, from the newly erected ones to the planned settlements and the leased and government farms, were to be shut down and physically erased from the landscape over the course of 1865. Officials in the new Freedmen's Bureau, however, immediately recognized that Johnson's amnesty plan undermined their agency's congressional mandate to reserve land for freed people and moved to blunt its effect. O. O. Howard, the commissioner of the bureau, issued an order to his subcommissioners in each state to go ahead and reserve and even distribute the land before it could be restored to its original owners. He believed—or hoped— that land already allotted to freed people would not be given back to white owners. The quartermaster general, Montgomery Meigs, who had overseen so much of the army's employment of refugees during the war, also argued strenuously for the president to make it a condition of the pardons to set aside five to ten acres of land for each black family already living on the property. But Johnson not only ignored such compromises, but he also forced Commissioner Howard to rescind his order and to issue a new one that aligned with his amnesty program. As Howard described it, Circular No. 15, issued on September 12, 1865, reduced the federal government's claim to abandoned and confiscated land and thus "effectually defeated the *intention* of all that legislation which used the abandoned estates . . . to give to loyal refugees and freedmen allotments of and titles to land."[23]

It would now be the Freedmen's Bureau's job to clear out the landscape of refugee camps—a direct reversal of its founding mission.[24] Over the course of the summer and fall of 1865, as bureau officials fanned out across the South to set up field offices, they brought news to the freed people of their imminent evictions. Thomas P. Jackson, a bureau commissioner working near Norfolk, addressed the residents of government farms in September by noting that the United States government "has led you out of the 'wilderness of Slavery' and Set your feet in 'the promised land of liberty.'" Now, he told them, within thirty days "you must prepare to leave this or any government farm in the district."[25]

Jackson was one of the more willing bureau agents to deliver the news. The commissioner himself, O. O. Howard, was more reluctant. Dispatched by

President Johnson in October to take the news to the estimated 40,000 residents of the lands secured by General Sherman, Howard found the task agonizing. After meeting with residents of Edisto Island, South Carolina, Howard implored Secretary of War Stanton: "My task is a hard one. . . . Something must be done to give these people and others the prospect of homesteads."[26] Howard also received pleading reports from his assistant commissioners seeking a reprieve, such as the letter from Col. Orlando Brown on the Virginia Peninsula pointing out that an estimated 20,000 people would be "forced to leave their homes" if he followed through with the orders. "I would respectfully ask your early attention to this matter," Brown wrote to Howard in October, "as the lands on the Peninsula are being rapidly restored to their former owners."[27] But Howard's hands were tied—and the evictions continued that fall. "All Contraband Camps Breaking Up," summed up the Louisville *Daily Union Press* in September.[28]

To a refugee who had resided in a camp or on a government farm for one, two, or even four years, the closing of the camps was more than the abstract loss of a promise of land or a dream extinguished, as the story of postwar land restoration is often told. It was a tangible loss of something concrete, something they believed they already possessed and even improved. The emptying of refugee camps meant the destruction of new homes, stores, and points of employment with an army that would now withdraw and eventually disappear. It meant the abandonment of gardens, despite a (largely ignored) order from Commissioner Howard to delay the restoration of land until the freedmen could harvest "the fruits of their industry." It meant the reversion of structures used for churches and schools to their previous uses. In Hampton, Virginia, for example, this began in July 1865, when the courthouse that had been turned into a school for refugees "quietly passed," as the *American Missionary* put it, to civil authorities. At eleven o'clock one morning, the former court's justices simply showed up and gaveled themselves back into session.[29]

Few refugees were ready to leave when ordered to go, or at least willing to leave quickly without making an attempt to maintain possession of the land. Some simply did not budge. "There seems to be no prospect of this village being abandoned and its people scattered out into the country unless it is done by force," wrote Horace James, a Freedmen's Bureau agent in the Trent River settlement of coastal North Carolina. "It seems to me not desirable to use such force." But other federal officials did. On a property known as the Celeys plantation, outside of Hampton, nearly 200 freed people resisted their removal

Grappling with Loss

and were subsequently greeted by a dozen armed soldiers sent there from Fort Monroe. The soldiers did not open fire on the people—but they did proceed with something else that was devastating. They "unroofed every hut," as one report put it, thus destroying the most fundamental claim each man, woman, and child had made to the land. Without a roof—without a shelter to anchor them there—the freed people finally evacuated the camp.[30]

While some of the settlers managed to stand their ground—at Trent River, they held off their eviction for nearly two more years—other freed people organized public meetings, airing their claims in newspapers and seeking some kind of compromise.[31] The refugees living on the Sinclair and Shields farms, the Whitehursts among them, did not immediately leave and tried to make a deal with the returning Confederates. Jefferson Sinclair had arrived back on the property that summer with his family and, according to the residents, was "seeking by every means in their power to take from us our homes." It appeared he would have little trouble. Crucially, Charles Wilder had never received legal title to that land following his auction bid, thanks to his transaction being stalled by the court martial proceedings. The residents of the farm then tried to buy the land directly: they pooled what savings they had, hired a local attorney to represent them, and offered "a liberal some of money" to Sinclair. The ex-Confederate quickly rejected the offer, telling the freed people that his family "will have all that they before possessed or nothing."[32]

The residents next held a public meeting in August at the First Baptist Church in Hampton, where they doubled down and pledged not to leave the land until forced out "by legal authority." "*Resolved,*" they continued, "that we will purchase or lease, at fair prices, of the United States Government its interests in these lots." That was their remaining hope: to persuade federal officials to hold on to the government's "interests" in the land and to stop its restoration to Confederate owners. That way the government could then turn around and sell it—or at least lease it—to the freed people. "We are anxious and willing," the meeting declared in a statement later published in sympathetic newspapers, "to build up a city upon our lands" that would be "as orderly, as prosperous, as religious, as patriotic, and as intelligent as could be done by any other people." But first they needed to "secure the fee to the lands."[33]

The future of the refugee camps—the ability of an encampment to become a village or town devoted to freedom—thus turned on the process of securing legal ownership of the land. And there were some hopeful signs of federal government willingness to intercede and secure title for freed people—two conspicuous signs. The property of Confederate president Jefferson Davis at Davis Bend, Mississippi, remained in government possession through 1865, even as four other plantations on Davis Bend had been restored to white owners. The people who remained on the property paid rent to Freedmen's Bureau officials, and the village endured for years to come, some of the land eventually purchased by freed people themselves.[34] At the same time, the property of Gen. Robert E. Lee in Arlington, Virginia, had become government owned, thanks to his wife, Mary, defaulting on her federal taxes in 1864 and the U.S. government buying it at auction (and putting much of it to use as a national cemetery). The settlement known as Freedman's Village would remain for years to come, with residents paying rent until the federal government finally required them to leave by 1900.[35] These proved to be exceptional cases involving exceptional former Confederates, however, individuals the United States was more inclined to punish in a conspicuous way by taking legal title of their land. Most places did not witness this kind of federal intervention.

The majority of refugees, instead, were on their own to secure legal title, or even to rent lands, and they found that prospect nearly impossible. White men returning to restored lands simply "will not sell or rent land to Freedmen," an official in Mississippi summed up the pervasive problem; or if they did, they charged inordinately steep prices that made it impossible for a newly freed person to acquire land.[36] White Southerners were playing the role of "land monopolist," protecting their "cursed monopolies," as other sympathetic white observers charged.[37] And according to a group of freed people from Edisto Island, South Carolina, who wrote to President Andrew Johnson in late October, "Land monopoly is injurious to the advancement of the course of freedom." "If government Does not make some provision by which we as Freedmen can obtain A Homestead," the Edisto Island letter continued, "we have Not bettered our condition." The federal government needed to break open that "monopoly" by holding on to the confiscated and abandoned land; only then would freed people have a chance to break in and purchase or rent it. "We are ready to pay for this land," they concluded the letter to Johnson. "Shall not we who Are freedman [sic] and have been always true to this Union have the same rights as are enjoyed by Others?"[38]

The freed people, by and large, believed they had "rights" to purchase or rent the land. And those rights deserved as much, if not more, protection from the federal government than the rights of returning white Confederates to re-take possession of the land. "Have we broken any Law of these United States? Have we forfieted [sic] our rights of property In Land?" the Edisto Island letter queried. "If not then! are not our rights as A free people and good citizens of these United States To be considered before the rights of those who were Found in rebellion against this good and just Goverment [sic]."[39] Their claim was at least equal to the white people's claim to resume ownership—if not greater. Freed people had improved the land during the war years, investing money in building new houses and cultivating the fields.[40] But even more important and valuable were the time, work, and lives they had invested to secure victory for the Union. It was thus a betrayal of that wartime service to see the property rights of rebellious white men protected to a greater extent than their own. "The most bitter ringleaders and fermenters of treason before, during, and since the war, are restored to all the rights of citizenship with all their property real or personal," Charles Wilder objected that fall, "while thousands of true loyal men are left out in the cold."[41]

Yet, with the passage of time that year, more and more federal officials got in line with the process of land restoration. Some even became convinced that the freed people were asking for too much. A white officer at a meeting in Norfolk in November 1865, for example, described as one of the "representatives of the Government," lectured the audience that "the Government could not give them everything." His statement channeled a fast-emerging narrative that took hold among federal officials and returning Confederates alike that fall: that freed people were sitting idly by, expecting free land to be given to them as some kind of gift. It was a self-serving view of the situation, allowing federal officials charged with the difficult task of restoring land to reframe the process as a principled fight against dependency and idleness. But it was also nonsense. William Roscoe Davis, the black minister who had traveled the Northern states back in early 1862 to publicize the ordeal of the Fort Monroe refugees, fired back at a Norfolk meeting that "the colored people did not expect any lands to be given to them." What they did expect was that "if the Government confiscated lands[,] that these lands would be rented or sold to them." For again, "they never expected to have the lands given them for nothing."[42]

Their claim to purchase or rent the land was even more than a "right," they argued. "This is our home," explained the freed people of Edisto Island.[43] It was a home established under the most trying conditions, amid violence and military campaigns, vulnerable to being lost to incoming soldiers or to floods, yet erected by their own hands. They now faced the prospect of being "driven off from their hard earned homes," as a missionary in Virginia put it, although the work and struggle involved was only part of what made these structures significant.[44] These were the spaces where children had been born, where families reunited after years apart, where the injured and sick recovered or where they departed this life. These were the spaces where they had picked up the pieces from slavery, and where they had begun to envision the future. These were "homes" in a similar way that white Americans venerated them in their sentimental fiction and advice literature—physical spaces that were the emotional centers of their worlds, the anchor in a tumultuous world of change. The Shields and Sinclair farm residents thus vowed that "we will not leave our happy homes," a sentiment that military or Freedmen's Bureau officials should have understood.[45]

But some government agents had always been uneasy about the proliferation of refugee camps during the war and were thus willing to overlook these arguments. They did not see "homes" in the camps so much as they saw unhealthy "jumbling" and "huddling" and "crowding," as officials had repeatedly complained about during the war. The end of the military conflict, and the rise of Andrew Johnson's policy of restoration, thus presented not so much an abrupt change of course but an extension of what some had desired all along. "The good of the community and the freedmen," one army official in Terrabonne Parish, Louisiana, summed up, "requires that such congregating should be prohibited & broken up."[46] But now there was an added urgency to the matter: returning white Confederates had begun fanning the flames of this uneasiness by charging that these spaces were about to erupt in violence. "It is reported, on what is believed to be reliable authority, that the negro freedmen on the Peninsula are preparing for insurrection," claimed the Richmond *Commercial Bulletin* in November, and as evidence, the paper pointed directly to the spatial concentration of freed people. "Between the village of Hampton and the town of Williamsburg, there are some twenty-five or thirty thousand negroes, who are huddled together in tents, huts, and shanties of every conceivable shape and build." The camps were like one great tinderbox, these reports of ex-rebels contended, ready to blow.[47]

This rumor quickly spread across the South and forced freed people to respond with steadfast reassurance. "The negroes had no idea of an insurrection," one newspaper paraphrased William Roscoe Davis in Virginia. "They did not rebel when they were in slavery and would not do it now."[48] "That we are contemplating and preparing for insurrection and riotous and disorderly proceedings," a mass meeting of freed people in Norfolk concurred, "are vile falsehoods designed to provoke acts of unlawful violence against us."[49] They spoke from recent experience: in the last month reports had surfaced in eastern Virginia of a minié ball piercing the wall of a school in Hampton and passing "within a few feet" of the teacher inside, and of an "assassination" attempt against Superintendent Charles Wilder that came in the form of a bullet shot from "a thicket of bushes."[50] White Southerners had begun targeting the buildings, the people, and the activities associated with refugee camps, resorting to violence in the name of stopping "insurrection," when what they really sought was to reclaim their lands and destroy the claim that freed people had made toward their futures. State authorities reorganized white militia forces; local groups of white men formed their own vigilante forces. And federal government officials, while condemning white violence, nonetheless worked toward the same end by ridding the landscape of the concentrations of black people.[51]

﹀

The process of closing the camps, including the Sinclair farm where the White-hursts rented, largely took place over an eight-month period through the end of 1865. Yet the determination of some freed people to stay, which only intensified as the question of where to go next grew more difficult to answer, extended the process in some places for a year or two more. Nowhere was this more evident than at Camp Nelson, Kentucky.[52]

Gabriel Burdett was still in Texas with his regiment that summer when orders came sending him back east to work for the Freedmen's Bureau at Camp Nelson. The bureau's commissioner for Tennessee and Kentucky, Brig. Gen. Clinton B. Fisk, had received a recommendation directly from John Fee, advising him that Burdett was "capable of doing more good than any white soldier whom I could use the detail of," Fisk later paraphrased [53] But as Burdett boarded the ship and the trains that would take him back to the region, under orders to "secure homes and employment for the families," he must have felt deeply conflicted about the effort to close down a place he would later call the "first free spot of ground in Kentucky."[54]

It was still, after all, one of the *only* free spots of ground in the state, for slavery was still technically legal in Kentucky after the war's end. Since the state was exempt from the Emancipation Proclamation, only enslaved people who enlisted, or who were wives or children of those who enlisted, were legally freed. As a result, "in the whole Christian world, there remain but three slave States," Union general Lovell Rousseau remarked that summer, "Cuba, Brazil and Kentucky." (Rousseau overlooked Delaware, which also still legalized slavery.) "The companionship cannot much flatter her self-esteem," added the *New York Times*.[55] And it also meant that refugee camps in places like Paducah, Columbus, Louisville, and Camp Nelson remained essential to freedom-seeking people, who, despite the formal end of military hostilities, still needed to get inside the Union army's sphere to have any claim to freedom recognized. Men enlisting in the army, as well as their wives and children, continued to flow into the camps in large numbers (although a reported 130,000 remained behind in slavery by early August, without a legal basis to claim freedom). An average of 100 new arrivals appeared at Camp Nelson each week that summer; the number of weekly food rations issued subsequently doubled between April and mid-July. They knew, as John Fee put it, that "all can have freedom who will come within a military post."[56]

Efforts to save Camp Nelson came quickly from various directions. One group of men identifying themselves as those "delegated by the Colored People of Kentuckey [sic]" took their case all the way to Washington, D.C., and in a petition urged President Johnson to keep military troops and protection in the state, arguing that without it white Kentuckians "like an uncaged wild beast will rage fiercely among us." A camp like Camp Nelson was, for them, an important sphere of physical protection.[57] Their ally John Fee, meanwhile, drew on his personal ties to the antislavery senator Charles Sumner to plead that Camp Nelson's land "be confiscated" by the federal government, so it could then be sold in smaller plots to the state's freed people.[58] Theron E. Hall, the superintendent of the Refugee Home, turned to Secretary of War Stanton and urged him to do whatever he could to keep the camp open. "I beg you to examine this subject carefully ere you decide to discontinue this 'Home,' this 'City of refuge,'" Hall wrote, enclosing in his letter affidavits from black soldiers describing the ordeals of their families during the previous year's expulsion. The camp, he reminded the secretary, was a place where "they can flee and be safe." The end of the war did not end that need.[59]

But the region's bureau commissioner, Clinton B. Fisk, was by midsummer already experienced at closing down camps, having focused on shuttering all refugee camps across Tennessee—a task he completed by October 1865.[60] "He has been very successful," the Louisville *Daily Union Press* observed, in his "constant effort to break up all contraband camps in his district."[61] To Fisk, a brigadier general who had served in Missouri and Arkansas during the war, it was a matter of military efficiency, of relieving the government "of the burthens these Camps are bringing upon it" (by which he meant the money "lavishly expended in the erection of buildings").[62] He expected to bring that same efficiency to Kentucky in July. "My positive instructions from Washington are 'to break up the Refugee Home at Camp Nelson at the earliest possible day consistent with humanity & c.,'" he wrote to John Fee, who had been sending the commissioner regular letters on the subject. Fisk acknowledged Fee's concerns about the humanitarian crisis that could follow the closing of camps, and the particularly acute form that crisis could take in Kentucky. "It is a difficult matter to conduct a Bureau for Freedmen in a Slave State," he conceded in a letter to O. O. Howard. But he still made clear where his priorities lay in a subsequent order to a subordinate in Lexington. Do "*everything* to break up the camp and not entail *suffering*," he ordered in mid-August, but still "get rid of the families there now."[63] It would be a tall order.

Gabriel Burdett now had to reverse the momentum of his wartime efforts, displacing the people he once encouraged to settle at Camp Nelson and scattering them across the central Kentucky countryside. The first step, as General Fisk outlined the process, was to cut off their food rations, for as the army well knew from its wartime use of rations to regulate the labor force, there was leverage in food.[64] The loss of food would force mobility, inducing the population to leave the camp and, driven by hunger, go anywhere else where nourishment could be found (although, as another official conceded, "I do fill their baskets when they leave and send none empty away"—his gesture to prevent "suffering").[65] The hope of General Fisk was that they would not simply regroup elsewhere and form a new camp or enter another camp that had not yet been shuttered. "I trust that your people will not lodge in the Cincinnati Freedmen's Camp," he wrote to the Camp Nelson agents, "look out for that." Instead, "*homes, homes, homes* is the word." That, to Fisk, was shorthand for resettling them in a more permanent situation, one that would not only keep individual families together but also situate them where they could earn wages and support themselves independently.[66]

The task before Burdett and other agents around him thus involved more than pushing people off the restored lands: they were to assist ex-slaves with negotiating new free labor arrangements with white landowners, drafting contracts and setting the terms of compensation. It was a fraught process almost everywhere and anywhere it was attempted.[67] The problems started with the basic assumption that the refugees should—and would—return to the old place of their enslavement. "You will ascertain from where they come and send them into the Counties from which they have been sent to us," General Fisk ordered a subcommissioner in August. And if any refugees proved too old or infirm to be hired as free laborers, agents should either "require their old Masters to provide for them" or "refer such cases to the Superintendents of the poor." ("What poor house in any county," exclaimed a frustrated AMA missionary, "will receive a Black pauper?")[68] And what former slave would want to work for the former owner from whom he or she had fled, often under violent circumstances? Plenty of enslaved people who never fled during the Civil War simply stayed on the property of their enslavement—but those in the refugee camps were precisely those who had chosen to leave. "None desire to return to their old homes," came a report from eastern Virginia in June. The freed people, noted another, are "saying they will starve before they will work for those who sold their children, and then fought and killed their husbands and sons to keep them slaves!"[69] But the bureau pressed ahead.

The resettlement process was all the more complex in Kentucky, where state laws protecting slavery not only remained in effect but were strengthened that fall. In one case that October, described by bureau agent R. E. Farwell, a group of refugees, mostly women and children and "many of whom were free," set off in a wagon for Danville, a town about fifteen miles southwest of Camp Nelson. At least one of the women, the "wife of a soldier," had been hired by a white man living in the area and was on her way to begin her work. Yet, as the wagon got close to Danville, it was stopped "by a man who told the driver that he could not go into town with his load and that the citizens had passed a law against it." The man then threatened the driver "with personal violence" and forced the government agent to turn around and head back to Camp Nelson, "leaving the refugees by the road side." The incident shook Farwell and forced him to throw up his hands in frustration. "Such acts are of every day occurrence," he reported to his superiors, contending that "under these circumstances I cannot execute Genl Fisks order" to shut down the Refugee Home.[70]

White Kentuckians, like the one who stopped the wagon that day, were desperate to strengthen their hold on the slave system. They feared that some of their fellow planters might bend under federal pressure, though, and begin hiring their slaves as free laborers. It was for that reason that the state assembly, controlled by conservative white Democrats, passed new state laws that fall to keep white Kentuckians solidified in their protection of slavery. One such law, enforced that day in Danville, prohibited the transportation of slaves without an owner's consent.[71] To restrict the mobility of a "slave," and the ability of a government wagon, railroad, or anyone else to help them move, would have the effect of restoring an owner's control over that individual—over where a man or woman worked and for whom. The law had a chilling effect, impeding not only the government wagons heading out of Camp Nelson, but also the private railroads that now, in response, refused passage to black people.[72]

Other state laws imposed a fine on any person who hired a slave belonging to another white man. The law "affixes a penalty of $5 per day upon every one doing so," reported the *Frankfort Commonwealth* newspaper, an amount so steep that it dissuaded anyone willing to hire black people as free laborers.[73] So, too, did lawsuits. "Men who are humane & kind dare not hire them for fear of litigation," R. E. Farwell noted in another report.[74] Slave owners had been turning to the state courts to sue men who hired their slaves—and, thanks to the sympathetic justices on the Kentucky Court of Appeals, sometimes succeeded.[75] All of this managed to tie the hands of Freedmen's Bureau agents trying to resettle the refugees outside Camp Nelson.

The bureau's task was made even more difficult by the timing of its efforts. It was fall by the time bureau agents like Farwell and Burdett sought employ-

Grappling with Loss

ment for the ex-slaves, which was too late for the planting season and therefore too late to expect a significant amount of white demand for black laborers.
"The fact is this camp ought to have been closed up when the people wanted
labor," Farwell explained. "I think if it had been they would have behaved a
little better." The timing was poor in another way too, for on October 12, in the
midst of the resettlement efforts, President Johnson repealed martial law. "The
work might have been pushed through and the Camp closed in the summer
months," Farwell reported, "when Martial law ruled the state."[76] But by October he had far less leverage and power to defend the freed people's claims to
freedom, and the people themselves were thus rendered far more vulnerable
to civil authorities — and thus to their enslavers. "*How can* I break up this camp
under such circumstances," Farwell asked rhetorically. To do so would effectively "drive *free women & children* into cruel bondage."[77]

Unless, bureau agents soon realized, they could induce the refugees to
leave the state altogether, in a revival of the wartime efforts to remove refugees
from the South. There had already been some ex-slaves who left the state on
their own, going north into Ohio, with the help of passes issued by the sympathetic Maj. Gen. John Palmer, now in command of the District of Kentucky.
This migration continued, in some cases with the additional assistance of the
Freedmen's Bureau, which provided food and funds to cover transportation
expenses to resettle refugees in towns like Urbana, Landau, and Xenia, Ohio.[78]
But leaving the state was out of the question for many, if not most, refugees,
especially those whose families remained separated, like the women who made
it to Camp Nelson without their children, or the wives still waiting for husbands to return from Texas. "They do not want to leave the State while the husband is away," R. E. Farwell explained, "and even if I did compel them to go to
Ohio, there are few left who could find homes with all their little children."[79]

Migration out of state threatened to scatter the families who had sought to
reunite and live together at places like Camp Nelson. That is why a subsequent
effort to resettle Kentucky refugees in Mississippi was also bound to fail. Gen.
Stephen Burbridge, formerly in command of the Department of Kentucky,
partnered with a Mississippian identified only as Harrow ("a very good speci-
men of the swell head, whiskey drinking Southern planter," noted R. E. Farwell) and secured permission from the bureau to transport as many as 100 refugees, many of them children, to be hired out to cotton planters. "The children
can be apprenticed at Vicksburgh [*sic*]," General Fisk enthused while ordering
Farwell to put the plan in motion. (And be sure to "close the camp as rapidly
as humanity will permit," Fisk once again reminded him.)[80] But the refugees
saw little that was humane in a plan that would separate them from family and

send them to a far-off and foreign place, to work on the cotton plantations they had only heard about. "The Freedmen are greatly prejudiced against going to the South," a camp official explained to Fisk when only seventy-five could be "induced" to go.[81] But Farwell soon saw an indirect gain from the plan. "The emigration idea works like a charm," he explained, "for I push and it creates a panic and ten go other ways while one goes to Miss." Most, it was suspected, headed west toward Louisville instead.[82]

And indeed, cities, which had already attracted large numbers of migrants during the war, now became even more sought-after destinations when the closing of camps shut off alternative points of refuge. In cities freed people could continue to live independently, although they faced the prospect of paying exorbitant rents, as well as a labor market that could not absorb them all. And often, life in a city meant living on the outskirts of town, in less desirable and sometimes less healthy low-lying areas.[83] This was a source of frustration for bureau agents trying to disperse them into the countryside. "I regret to say," a bureau official in Memphis wrote in August, that "many freed people prefer a life of precarious subsistence and comparative idleness in the suburbs of the city, to a more comfortable home and honest labor in the country." Convinced that returning to their old plantations was preferable, this official asked Fisk for permission to use military force to remove them. Fisk denied the request but sympathized with the problem. "Genl Fisk is discouraged about the success of the colored people," one AMA official observed in late 1865, and "advises that they be not aggregated in towns or cities."[84]

The prospect of cities filling up helped redouble efforts to find other means of scattering the population, involving even the most sympathetic white allies. Camp Nelson's John Fee, for example, hatched a plan to pool the money of white Northerners and purchase land in the mountains of eastern Kentucky. Where prime agricultural land elsewhere in the state was running at $50 to $100 per acre, he argued, it could be had for one to five dollars in the mountains and thus easily subdivided and sold again to freed people. "I would avoid aggregating in one county or part of the state," he assured his AMA colleagues.[85]

Others devised plans inspired by another federal program that involved resettling people on rural property: the Homestead Act. Enacted in 1862 as a means of settling the West, the act carved up federally owned land into 160-acre plots, distributing them to settlers willing to move and farm on the land for five years, after which they would receive legal title to the land. It seemed to some bureau agents a perfect fit for the current dilemma facing freed people. And if the ex-slaves did not want to move west, some reasoned, then perhaps public lands in the South could be made attractive for their settlement. A bu-

Grappling with Loss

reau agent in Florida even drew up plans in late 1865 for a colony of new settlers in that state, to be overseen by its own territorial government. Then, in June 1866, came the Southern Homestead Act, a variation on the original, which offered eighty-acre parcels in Alabama, Arkansas, Florida, Louisiana, and Mississippi to any individuals, black or white, who could prove their loyalty to the Union during the war. But relatively few former slaves were enticed by this program, given the costs, both financial and familial, involved in resettling so far away, and given that the land itself tended to be forested or swampy and thus unsuitable for agricultural use. Only about 4,000 African Americans took advantage of the Southern Homestead Act by 1869.[86]

~~~

Gabriel Burdett stayed at Camp Nelson — and by this point Lucinda and their children had joined him too. This fact is known because it made its way into the pages of the *New Haven Daily Palladium* in December 1865, courtesy of John Fee's correspondence with members of a Connecticut freedmen's aid society. "Gabriel Burdett, a colored soldier and preacher of rare ability and excellence," opened the report, "has a wife, two children of his own, and two orphan children in his family. All sleep and eat, cook and live, in one room sixteen feet square" at Camp Nelson. Burdett's modest circumstances at the Refugee Home prompted Fee's plea that the Connecticut residents continue to send aid to the South, just as they had during the war.[87] In another letter from around that same time, Fee detailed that Burdett was living with his "sister-in-law and nine children" too. This was likely Clarissa Burdett, whom Gabriel had helped reunite with her children following her owner's ongoing, violent attempts to keep them apart earlier that year. Clarissa's husband, Elijah, was still in the army at that moment but in a St. Louis hospital, suffering from chronic bronchitis.[88]

There was no question that most refugees wanted to stay put not just in Kentucky but on the Camp Nelson land specifically. By November 1, 1865, 1,620 of them still resided there (about half of the estimated 3,000 who were there the previous July).[89] "Many of them, I know, suffer for food," observed a Freedmen's Bureau agent, "yet so strong is thier [*sic*] attachment to Camp Nelson that they prefer to remain thier and suffer, rather than except employment at good wages elsewhere."[90] Neither threats of migration to Mississippi nor the cutting of the food supply forced them out. "I can constantly decrease the issue of rations," bureau agent R. E. Farwell explained, "but many will not leave till they see that the buildings are to be removed."[91] That was what ultimately mattered: the availability of shelter, the very thing that had first allowed them to claim a place in the Union army's orbit. As long as the shelter remained, they would find a way to stay and survive; and that was true across the South, where the physical destruction of cabins and huts often marked the final step in the closing of a camp. At Camp Nelson, though, those shelters remained in existence longer than the bureau expected or encouraged.

The owner of the 200 acres on which the camp's Refugee Home sat, it turned out, did not easily fit into the mold of the aggrieved white planter ready to wipe out any evidence of emancipation from his property. Joseph Moss was a loyal Unionist who had watched as the refugee homes and gardens grew up on his land, and as his hemp factory, grain stores, and fifteen acres of timber were damaged in various ways by the presence of Union troops. He had not been a slaveholder — though it is possible he had hired out slaves — and thus lost no enslaved property to the refugee camp on his land. But by the end of the war, when he could no longer envision a thriving future for his agricultural enterprise, he decided to sell rather than reclaim his farm. And among the buyers he was willing to deal with were the freed people.[92]

Gabriel Burdett seized the opportunity. He did not have the capital to purchase any of the land himself; with so many family members to support, his monthly government pay did not stretch that far, and he instead found himself continually appealing to AMA officials in New York for supplemental money. But he joined with his AMA allies in the region, John Fee and Abisha Scofield, as well as another black soldier named George Blakeman, to try and facilitate the sale of land to other freed people, and they approached bureau commissioner O. O. Howard with their plans for doing so. Black soldiers returning from Texas, the men explained in late October, "desire to buy the land, divide it into lots, attach one of the cottages to each lot (from 4 to 5 acres each)." That desire was growing by the day. "Martial law now repealed," they continued, the veterans "are unwilling to thrust their families into the country," making a clustered village like Camp Nelson necessary for physical safety. But there was one hitch to moving forward: they could purchase the land from Moss, but the federal government claimed ownership of the buildings erected on that land. And it had recently announced plans to sell those buildings at a public auction.[93]

"We, the undersigned," Burdett and others appealed to Howard, "request that the buildings of, and all the appurtenances to the Refugee Home in Camp Nelson Ky be conveyed to us." They pointed out that the auction was unlikely to yield significant revenue for the government anyway, so why not simply pass the buildings over to those who occupied them? They did not elaborate on the refugees' right to them, although they could have: the original lumber may have been paid for by the army, but the buildings themselves, now number-

Grappling with Loss

ing 125 total, were built by the refugees' own hands. To lose them would take away not only their physical stake in freedom but also the value of their labor to build them. For good measure, though, Burdett and his allies made sure to assuage a prevailing concern among white officials. "We also propose to intersperse white families, who are true friends," the letter continued, making sure to point out that a densely populated community of black people would not result from the sales. "The precedent will be good."[94]

But Howard did not approve the plan. He stayed the auction a few more months to help with the process of clearing out the camp, but his goal was only to facilitate the closing — not to encourage the formation of a permanent settlement. The refugees still needed to leave. And yet, in a testament to the ways in which private arrangements could at times be struck, and could forestall the work of authorities trying to empty out the camps, Joseph Moss began renting his land to the freed people in three-acre plots, while Burdett, Fee, and Scofield set to work trying to raise money in the North to purchase the buildings from the government.[95] The effort was pressing and time sensitive: Moss was falling under a great deal of pressure from white neighbors not to sell. "The rebs are using all their power with him to stop the trade," Scofield reported to AMA headquarters.[96]

Burdett thus prepared for the end. The potential closing of the camp represented more than the loss of homes or a lost opportunity to establish independent agricultural enterprises. It meant the loss of his mission too — the loss of all the work he had undertaken already to pursue religious freedom for himself, his family, and all the ex-slaves around him. The concentration of people in a place like Camp Nelson, in close physical proximity, had been crucial to the formation of new, independent churches, as well as schools. Now, to send them back to farms and plantations would break up schools and churches and make it far more difficult for ministers like him to reach the dispersed ex-slave population. "Shall *we try to teach them all over the state in their scattered condition* & teach society thus to reach *them*," John Fee wondered aloud, "or *shall we* arrange villages & *schools* for them."[97] That was the remaining choice: purchase land and maintain "villages" like Camp Nelson, or find other ways of dispersing their teachings across the state.

Gabriel Burdett increasingly turned his attention to the latter. While awaiting the fate of Camp Nelson, he embarked in late 1865 on what he would call the "church reconstruction of the South," an effort to make sure that new, independent black churches were established throughout central Kentucky. On horseback he "passed through the countryside 'gathering souls,'" as he described it, preaching to ex-slaves and organizing new churches in their rural communities. He even returned to Garrard County, where he found his former neighbors "anxious to have us visit them and help them." Together they established a new church that, like the Camp Nelson Church of Christ, was nonsectarian and thus free from white denominational governance.[98] A greater degree of religious freedom was thus coming to Garrard County, a reality that even the Forks Church acknowledged in 1869, when it formally "excluded" Gabriel Burdett for "nonattendance."[99]

The Thirteenth Amendment to the U.S. Constitution was finally ratified in December 1865, guaranteeing freedom for *all* enslaved people, everywhere, for the first time. Clinton Fisk issued a statement conveying the news on the day after Christmas—and included with it paternalistic guidance on how to act in the days and months ahead. "Let the past be forgotten," he urged the freed people. "Treat all with respect. Avoid disputes."[100] If only it were so simple. With nearly half of the 858,000 acres of confiscated and abandoned land in the South restored to antebellum white owners by the end of 1865, it was simply impossible to forget the past.[101] "Slavery is not dead; the African is not free," declared the *True Southerner* newspaper in January 1866. "The Government," it continued, "urged on by the rebel slave owners is trying to send these poor creatures from their hiding places back to the auction block and to the cruel mercies of the lash and passions of their masters." The past, in fact, only seemed to be coming closer into view.[102]

Eliza Bogan returned to Phillips County, Arkansas, in early 1866. After boarding a ship to New Orleans, and then another to take her up the Mississippi River again, Eliza reversed the route of the journey that had taken her from slavery into combat and war. The Forty-Sixth USCT mustered out in late January, after spending nearly nine months in Clarksville and Brownsville, Texas. Eliza arrived back in the region with Dennis Bogan, Silas Small's Forty-Sixth USCT comrade who had helped her nurse her sick husband. The two had "assumed marriage relations" about two to three months after Silas's death and had just had a child together—a daughter, Mary, born in Texas in December 1865.[103] The three were set to start over again as a family, a familiar position for Eliza, who had already coped with the loss of three other husbands in slavery and war. This time, though, things in Phillips County looked different. The state of Arkansas had reorganized itself nearly two years earlier and reentered the Union in April 1864, with a new state constitution that abolished slavery.[104] And with the Thirteenth Amendment ensuring that that would never be repealed, there was no question that slavery was legally over in the state. There

Grappling with Loss

was even a new newspaper in town published by white people, the Helena *Western Clarion*, that was outspoken in its embrace of "the reconstruction of the American Union without slavery."[105]

Yet the refugee camps that once occupied space in and around Helena had disappeared. And disappeared quickly. It started with a devastating flood during the spring of 1865, of which "among its many victims, the Freedmen stand foremost," according to a report in the *Freedmen's Bulletin*. "Living in camps located often on the very margin of the river," the newspaper explained, "their homes have been inundated; and in many instances their whole possessions swept away." But nature was not all that effectively closed the camp. A local ordinance passed by the newly reconvened city council in August 1865 decreed that "all buildings or other obstructions in the public streets and alleys must be removed." It was a vague provision that could easily be applied to freed people's shelters — and it came with a promise to be "rigidly enforced."[106] And then, as in so many other regions, the Freedmen's Bureau got to work breaking down the camps too, holding a public auction to sell government buildings and other property. By mid-September 1865, a bureau report from Helena noted that "the entire number of Refugees has been reduced to about 12 persons in all."[107] It was one of the fastest camp closings to occur anywhere in the occupied South.

There was no Charles Wilder in Helena, bidding on properties in an attempt to save and subdivide land for freed people. There was no Gabriel Burdett or John Fee with connections to philanthropic Northerners, seeking to do the same. That was the lesson of those other places: in the absence of a federal government commitment to keep camps open across the South, it fell to resourceful individuals to step forward and try to broker some private arrangement. In Helena, there was simply no one to take the lead. Wilder's counterpart in the region, the superintendent of freedmen Capt. A. L. Thayer, was no help at all: he had been arrested and court-martialed in 1865 on a series of embezzlement charges after defrauding the freed people in his district. Thayer was accused of, among other things, taking coats intended for freed people and selling them into Confederate lines, and taking the cotton harvested by freed people and selling it without giving them any of the return. Thayer also helped Confederate sympathizers in the region get their cotton to market through Federal lines, which added "aid and comfort to the enemy" to the list of charges against him.[108] Thayer was unusually greedy and treasonous in his conduct, but his underlying interest in promoting the region's cotton over the needs of freed people was not unusual.

In the Mississippi Valley, the federal government's long-standing interest in sustaining the cotton economy helped grease the wheels pushing freed people back to plantations and restoring those lands to their antebellum white owners. Local army officials and the returning planters thus came together swiftly.[109] This was evident in the words of Thayer's successor, Capt. Henry Sweeney, when he addressed the black population of Helena in a public forum that November. He first disabused the crowd of any hope that refugee camp lands would be preserved for them. "There is no such intention on the part of the Government," he declared. Such an initiative was not only impossible, as "those very lands and plantations are being restored to their owners every day," but also "injurious to your interests," since it would make ex-slaves "careless about seeking employment." Anyone who wanted land must "earn it yourself." Sweeney assumed that freed people had no desire to work, no desire to save money, no desire to purchase land—in short, no desire to embrace the principles and ethics of free labor. Work hard, he urged the crowd, "save your money," and, for good measure, "be more polite to white people." "Prove that you are worthy of being free," he closed, and "that the blood of so many good men has not been shed in vain."[110]

Eliza Bogan returned to Phillips County after having witnessed more than her share of that bloodshed. She had spent nearly three years surrounded by the "good men" of whom Sweeney spoke. She knew full well what the men had sacrificed, and what she had sacrificed herself as a "company woman." Silas Small and sixteen other men in his company had given their lives.[111] Their company had dodged guerrillas in Louisiana, been imprisoned in Mississippi before escaping, and seen combat at Mound Plantation and near the Yazoo River. Eliza herself had scrubbed and cleaned and nursed and cooked all along the way. There could have been no doubt in her mind that she had proven herself more than "worthy" of freedom. And yet, as she returned to Arkansas, having just served the United States alongside its soldiers, she now found her willingness to work hard and sacrifice questioned by men—by *Union* men—like Captain Sweeney.

Not all officials downplayed the meaning of black military service. That their service to the nation had demonstrated an entitlement to, and fitness for, citizenship was an argument that black veterans had been making forcefully during the war and its aftermath. The "citizen soldier" ideal was pervasive in American culture and effectively pressed black veterans' claims to citizenship rights in the war's aftermath, influencing, in particular, congressional deliberations over the extension of voting rights to black men.[112] But the course of political change was no mirror of what took place on the ground, in daily life. And in places like Phillips County, Arkansas, a black man's or woman's military service triggered far more complex everyday interactions with white people, from the willingness of a Union official like Captain Sweeney to essentially overlook or downplay it by omission, to more overt attempts by former Confederates to deny returning veterans their freedom. The political boost afforded by veteran status, they learned, could be accompanied by backlash and loss too.

Service in the Union army marked Eliza and Dennis Bogan, and so many others like them, in the eyes of angry and resentful ex-Confederates. Reeling from loss of both the war and slavery, and seeing in the service of armed black soldiers a demonstration of their long-held insurrectionist fears, white Southerners in communities throughout the South clamored for the removal of black troops. Black soldiers were disloyal—traitorous—in their eyes, and with guns in hand, what might they do next? Kill all white people in their midst? White Southern hysteria quickly fed a determination to distance themselves, as far as possible, from the presence of black soldiers and veterans. False reports of "outrages" committed by black military men presented to Freedmen's Bureau officials helped remove some men from their communities; other ex-Confederates simply refused to hire black veterans or anyone close to them.[113] "A great many I found who were very willing to work," a Quaker teacher in Vicksburg remarked of women seeking employment, "but unfortunately for them, they were *soldiers'* wives, and the citizens refuse to give employment to this class. They still seem to hate the 'niggers in blue' with a *perfect hatred*."[114]

Other setbacks emanating from military service compounded the problem. Many veterans came home injured or still suffering the lingering effects of illness, with disabilities that would render them less able to work as they once did. Among the other members of the Forty-Sixth USCT who returned home with Eliza and Dennis Bogan, for example, Frank McKeal brought home an injury to his right hip, sustained from a fall while building a bridge in Texas; Charles Bogan had a dislocated shoulder; Jerry Steele suffered from "paralysis"; and John McKeel suffered from chronic diarrhea and a gunshot wound to the right leg. Although disabled soldiers could apply for federal pensions, they initially had to meet a threshold of "total disability" to be successful, and none of these men would do that successfully for at least thirteen years. They would have to find a way to work with their injuries and disabilities.[115]

Mustering out from the army also brought a loss of income. As the Union army demobilized and contracted its reach across the South, employment opportunities contracted too, for soldiers and civilians alike. Eliza Bogan lost her job. Dennis Bogan lost his job. All refugees across the South lost their employment with the quartermaster's, engineer, and other military departments.[116] Thousands of carpenters, stevedores, teamsters, and other hard laborers, along with hospital stewards, laundresses, cooks, and anyone engaged in private service for an officer, all lost their employment with the army. In eastern Virginia alone, for example, an estimated 5,000 saw their jobs disappear with the army's demobilization in 1865.[117]

Many lost those positions without having been fully paid for their work in the first place, thanks to the army's chronic problem of not paying wages. "Not less than one hundred thousand dollars is due from the Government to the dead soldiers in this camp alone," observed the AMA's Abisha Scofield at Camp Nelson, for example. Scofield, like other agents elsewhere, tried to help veterans and their families file claims for back pay; in Hampton, Virginia, many of those denied wages back in 1861 now filed petitions, including Edward Whitehurst's brother, Immanuel Savage. It was a process steeped in corruption, however, as unscrupulous agents, ostensibly assisting with paperwork, charged steep fees to freed people and cheated them in other ways. The Northern lawyer assisting Savage, for example, was eventually banished from eastern Virginia for his deeds — and there is no evidence that Savage, or any of those owed wages for the first year at Fort Monroe, ever collected back pay.[118]

Eliza and Dennis Bogan thus returned with little capital to invest in land at the precise moment when any savings were crucial for establishing themselves independently. This was compounded in Eliza's case by competing demands on the money she did earn and receive. While Eliza was in Memphis with the Forty-Sixth USCT in early 1865, and before embarking to Texas, the aging mother of Silas Small, Indiana Kelly, appeared before her in a "hard up" condition. "I gave her five dollars," Eliza later recalled, in addition to another five dollars she loaned to Jerry Steele, Kelly's son-in-law, so he could help support Kelly too.[119] What little money Eliza had was spread too thin across her family network to be accumulated and used to buy land. She and Dennis faced little alternative than to search for white planters willing to hire them.

They did not return to their former owners' properties, however. Both white men had died — Monroe Bogan was killed in his confrontation with West Bogan, and Josiah McKiel succumbed to illness just after the war ended. The properties remained in the white descendants' possession, but having fallen significantly in value after the war, and with outstanding debts to be paid by the estate, both properties were sold to new owners by 1870.[120] Men from other places, especially Northern states, continued to arrive in the region, just as they had during the war, snapping up devalued properties like these and reestablishing plantation operations. One of them was a man named Samuel Brooks, a Philadelphian by birth who had served one year in the Union army before heading to Mississippi to lease a plantation and set himself up as a planter. His arrival in Phillips County in 1866 brought a man more willing to hire people who had worn Union blue, and it was to Brooks that Eliza and Dennis turned when they sought employment. No record survives, however, that describes the terms of their work—whether they rented property from Brooks or had a bureau-negotiated contract for wages.[121]

~~~

It was against significant odds, then, that some black soldiers in Helena managed to save one part of the refugee camp before it disappeared: the orphan asylum. Established in 1864, at the behest of the army and with the support of Indiana Quakers, the Helena asylum had become a refuge for children whose parents were off fighting in the war, or had died amid the city's repeated outbreaks of disease, or had otherwise become separated from them during slavery.[122] The asylum provided not just shelter, food, and clothing, but also schooling and religious instruction. And it was not a unique effort: orphan asylums had increased in number throughout the occupied South in the war's final two years, especially in places relatively insulated from active combat, such as Hampton, Nashville, Memphis, and Natchez.[123] The institutions performed the crucial role of absorbing the segment of the refugee population—children—that never fit very well in the military system.

The Helena asylum was located in a small, two-story frame house that was vulnerable to being reclaimed and its residents evicted when the Confederates returned. And indeed, by December 1865, federal officials took steps to close the asylum by announcing that they would begin cutting off the orphans' rations.[124] The announcement alarmed those who worked in the asylum alongside the Indiana Quakers, not the least of which were ex-slaves from the region like Mildred Williams, a cook; Betsy Dawson, the asylum's laundress; and Stephen Patton, a black minister who labored there as a teacher. The asylum's fate absorbed the attention of other freed people too: at the asylum's anniversary observance that spring, local black grocers lent support in the form of peaches, blackberries, and sugar cakes for the children to enjoy, while William H. Grey, who in two years would become one of the first black members of the Arkansas General Assembly, appeared as the featured speaker. All were determined to preserve the asylum. But it was the soldiers of the Fifty-Sixth USCT, who had spent the last year of the war on garrison duty in Helena, who were able to do something about it.[125]

The soldiers pooled what savings they had from their military pay—$60.60 collected by Company K, $470 from Company F—and also held a fundraising concert. By the summer they had collected a total of $2,166.75, enough to purchase thirty acres of land located eight miles outside of Helena. The regiment could not retain title to the land, so it immediately deeded the acreage to the Indiana Yearly Meeting of Friends, which turned around and purchased fifty adjoining acres. The soldiers, detailed by their sympathetic white commander, then cleared the land of mature oak and poplar trees and began building log structures to house the new asylum. Two 100-foot-long buildings soon arose along two sides of a square, while a school and superintendent's house filled out the space. In the center the soldiers erected a flagstaff, where they hoisted an American flag to the sounds of cheers at the asylum's dedication ceremony on July 4, 1866.[126]

The Fifty-Sixth USCT soldiers could not save the Helena refugee camp in its entirety. And individually, few to none of them could have purchased tracts of land for themselves. But they still recognized that they could collectively preserve at least *some* aspect of the refugee camp's infrastructure. Their chosen focus on the orphan asylum was not unusual, and it stemmed from a basic, stark reality: that children, especially those without family support, stood to lose the most from the closing of the refugee camps. They were now targets of new state and local "Black Codes" that forced orphans into work as apprentices on plantations — positions, effectively, of enslavement.[127] "Let us protect the unprotected and the fatherless," a Quaker observer wrote in the *Freedmen's Record* of the urgency before them, "that they shall not again be under the blighting curse of slavery."[128] And that the Fifty-Sixth USCT soldiers did.

The asylum they established eventually went further. It evolved first into something more like a community center for freed people, where the first black Quaker meeting in North America would be established, as well as the site of a new hospital established by the Freedmen's Bureau. By 1869 it had expanded into a normal school for training black teachers that would become known as Southland College at the dawn of the twentieth century.[129] Many of the Fifty-Sixth USCT soldiers, however, did not live to see the results of their work: while in the process of being mustered out later in 1866, nearly 200 of them succumbed to an outbreak of cholera.[130]

⤙⤚⤙⤚

Orphan asylums, schools, and churches were about all that outlived the refugee camps. The survival of these particular institutions depended entirely on local efforts; no policy decree from Washington pushed these institutions forward. It was more of an ad hoc effort, an alignment of available funds with available land, led by individuals able and willing to stick their necks out and risk backlash from Confederate sympathizers, which explains why some institutions

Grappling with Loss

survived and others folded. Another successful effort involved an AMA-led purchase of a 125-acre farm in eastern Virginia that remained in government hands and had housed a wartime school for refugees, the Butler Freedmen's School. The land and the school became the basis for the AMA's push to establish the Hampton Normal and Agricultural Institute in 1868. It survives to the present day as Hampton University.[131]

In Kentucky, saving the Camp Nelson church and school would require holding off an onslaught of violent resistance. Local white neighbors continued to pressure the landowner, Joseph Moss, not to sell the land beneath the Refugee Home — and to stop the freed people from buying it. Mobs of white people, self-styled "regulators," described variously as a roving "band of 20, or 30 men" and as "armed ruffians," descended on the shelters of the freed people on a near-nightly basis in the fall of 1866, targeting those, including Gabriel and Lucinda Burdett, who were renting plots of land from Joseph Moss. At times they pretended to be agents of the Freedmen's Bureau in order to get inside, whereupon they "plundered" and robbed the families of their possessions, especially arms and money. Appeals to the overtaxed Freedmen's Bureau to provide protection were met with only promises and with an order that the freed people should arm and defend themselves. A group of twelve to fifteen freedmen tried to do so, but they soon learned that after working long days it was enormously difficult to keep watch all night. That effort was quickly abandoned.[132]

Later that fall, though, on November 19, 1866, the freed people at Camp Nelson mobilized again to resist armed white men who had launched what one missionary would term an eight-day "siege" of their residences. One of the homes belonged to John Burnside, the Burdetts' former neighbor from Garrard County who had endured his family's expulsion from Camp Nelson two years before. Burnside refused to flee when the intruders broke in, and instead "stood for his family and fought like a tiger," as the AMA missionary Abisha Scofield put it. Burnside managed to shoot and kill at least one of the white men before being pulled out of his house, knocked down, and "left in his yard for dead." Burnside survived, and so would others, thanks in part to the actions of Gabriel Burdett, who "found the courage to mount the wagon with us and drive us safe to Nicholasville."[133]

The Freedmen's Bureau then made good on its promise and sent troops into the camp. It was only temporary, but it was enough to settle the situation so that the long-awaited land transaction could proceed. Joseph Moss did not sell to the freed people after all — that much the mobs had guaranteed — but he did sell to a white man, John Fee. The minister purchased 130 acres of the land after piecing together funds from his own family's resources. His wife, Matilda, sold "what land she had in a free State," and Fee himself borrowed $500 more. Just over 100 acres of the purchase was then set aside for the Camp Nelson school, which was rechristened Ariel Academy; the rest housed the Camp Nelson Church of Christ as well as some families, who purchased small lots from Fee.[134] Part of Camp Nelson, at least, would endure.

But the school and the church, like others that survived in the South, remained vulnerable in the years ahead. So much of what had grown up around these institutions disappeared—the employment in the army, the shipments of clothing from Northern benevolent organizations, the food rations and medical care, much of the housing, and many of the people. Now-dispersed schools and churches and asylums were the lone physical reminders of the vast landscape of refugee settlements that had once lined the region's waterways and taken root on plantations. These institutions now sat, relatively isolated, beyond the military sphere of protection, as the army increasingly withdrew from the South and sent its soldiers home.[135] The freed people who remained thus looked ahead to a very different future. Never had their lives inside the Civil War's refugee camps matched their dreams of the future, their visions of freedom. Never had they been entirely safe or secure. And their lives outside those camps in the years ahead would reveal that their time in the wilderness was not yet over. They would keep searching for the Promised Land well into the future too.

Epilogue

The rapid destruction of shelters and the closing of the camps embodied in a particularly stark way how freedom for formerly enslaved people was something to be continually constructed—built and rebuilt again—rather than a status instantly and permanently obtained. By 1866 it was clear that their journeys through the wilderness would continue well into the future. Edward and Emma Whitehurst, Eliza Bogan, and Gabriel Burdett headed in many separate directions from that point on, each continuing to search for their long-envisioned freedom over the next several decades, and into the next century. Yet their time inside military lines in the 1860s still left an imprint on all of them—and would continue to affect the course of their lives and movements ahead.

Five years after the war's end, Edward and Emma Whitehurst had worked and saved long enough to achieve the economic independence they had long sought. The federal population census in 1870 listed Edward as the owner of $800 in real estate, meaning that he had become a landowner for the first time in his life. This most basic aspiration for freed people, the one dashed for so many others with the restoration of lands to ex-Confederates, had been realized by the Whitehursts.[1] After losing their savings from slavery when they lost the store, after scraping by for the remainder of the hostilities by selling a horse and borrowing money for medical care, the Whitehursts had managed to grow and harvest and sell enough products from the lands they rented to build their savings back up again. And with that land came independence: independence from the control of a landlord or employer, and the independence to set the terms and conditions of their own labor.

Their ability to save money was only part of what made this purchase possible. What also fell into place was that the Whitehursts managed to find a white landowner willing to sell to them. Identified by Edward in a postwar document as Frank H. Dennis, this white Virginian had owned 150 acres near Hampton with his brother, Henry, before the war, as well as twenty-five enslaved people, but the men eventually abandoned the land once the Union army moved in. By mid-1863 the property had become a refugee settlement — a "government farm"—employing men and women to work the land in exchange for wages paid from the return on the harvests. Yet two years later it was back in the hands of the Dennis brothers, part of the Union's restoration of abandoned lands. Why Frank Dennis then began renting, and eventually selling, his land to freed people is impossible to answer from the records that remain. But he started doing so at least as early as 1866, when Charles Smith, one of the employees in the Whitehursts' old store, is recorded as a renter on the property.[2]

With the purchase of land, Edward Whitehurst's occupation in the census was identified as "Farmer," while Emma's was "Keeping House." Her designation could have meant any number of things. Perhaps she withdrew from field labor, like some freedwomen did, in a move that distanced her from the agricultural work associated with slavery; or perhaps this was merely a designation imposed on her by the census taker, while she engaged in work both in the household and in the fields. It is also possible that she was involved in caring for the other residents of their household: a fifty-six-year-old woman named Catherine Tucker and her two children, six-year-old Susan and four-year-old Jane; a thirteen-year-old named Maria Baker; and a fifteen-year-old named Charles Johnson. It is not clear whether this mother and two children, or the other two apparently parentless children, were somehow related to the Whitehursts or whether they were boarders, bringing in an additional source of income.[3]

Even as they purchased property and settled in, the Whitehursts did not look solely ahead to the future. Their past would always be with them, and at times they did look back on their time inside Union lines. Fifteen years after it happened, in 1877, Edward Whitehurst thought a lot about the Union soldiers' destruction of the store in August 1862. He never forgot that they had not been paid for everything stolen, and he never wavered in his belief that they should have been compensated. And when he got word of the United States' efforts to reimburse loyal Union citizens for property destroyed in the course of the war through the newly created Southern Claims Commission, Edward seized the chance to seek their long-awaited compensation. In late July of that year, along with his brother, Immanuel Savage, now working as an oysterman, as well as

Charles Smith, Whitehurst traveled across Hampton Roads to Norfolk, where a special federal commissioner waited to hear their stories. (There is no indication that Emma Whitehurst made the trip with them.) Each man took turns answering a series of questions and narrating the events of the day, recounting the exact amounts of ginger cakes and butter taken. Edward signed his name in full to a transcript of his testimony, indicating that he had learned to write in the intervening years, and requested payment for $722 in property damages. His claim then made its way to Washington for final determination.[4]

The commission acknowledged that "there is no doubt of his loyalty" to the Union, a prerequisite for a successful claim, but they reduced Edward's request and ultimately paid him just $115 for his losses. That amount would cover the corn and fodder "taken by the army for its use," according to the commissioners, while the pigs were "not to be regarded as an army supply," and the rest of the food "must be charged to pillage." In other words, the vast majority of the property taken that day, the commissioners determined over a decade later, had not been taken as a legitimate army need. And thus, Edward Whitehurst found himself, and his pursuit of freedom, once again entangled in subjective judgments of military necessity (although the commissioners did not explain how exactly they made those judgments). From here the journeys of Edward and Emma Whitehurst disappear from the historical record—it is not even clear how long they lived or when they died.[5]

In 1877, the same year that Edward Whitehurst filed his claim, Gabriel and Lucinda Burdett packed up their children and their belongings and left Kentucky for good. They headed to Kansas, which Gabriel was persuaded "is the place for me," and joined thousands more freed people from central Kentucky streaming into the prairie state in hopes of starting over yet again. Gabriel had worked nearly his entire life to make Kentucky a free place, from his days as a preacher at the Forks Church to his teaching and ministering at Camp Nelson. But now, twelve years after the end of the war, he lamented that he and his fellow black Kentuckians remained only "partially free" and that, in Kentucky, a "perfect reign of terror" awaited them and their children in the years ahead.[6]

It took some time to come to this realization. Back in April 1866, Gabriel had been appointed to the board of trustees of Berea College—the first African American to assume that position—which meant that he deeply involved himself in the governance of the South's first integrated institution of higher education. He and Lucinda made their home on the old Refugee Home land, now called the village of Ariel, having purchased a small plot of land, about three acres, from John Fee. Gabriel also assumed the pastorate of the Camp Nelson Church of Christ for the first time, in addition to becoming a trustee of Ariel Academy.[7] Meanwhile, Lucinda gave birth to three more children, including a son born in 1870, whom they named Charles W. Sumner.[8]

The naming of their son after a prominent abolitionist senator from Massachusetts revealed more than a tribute to antislavery leaders. By this point Gabriel Burdett was openly aligned with Sumner's Republican Party, because of what "the Republican party has done for the colorade man," he later explained.[9] Beyond emancipation itself, Radical Republicans like Sumner had secured voting rights for black men, with the ratification of the Fifteenth Amendment in 1870. Burdett's Republican loyalty also had everything to do with his desire to oppose his old enslaver, Hiram Burdett. At an abolitionist reunion in Chicago in 1874, Gabriel Burdett explained to attendees that since his owner had been a Whig before the war, he initially decided he "would belong to the other party," the Democrats. But then he eventually learned "that the Democrats were worse," encompassing the most conservative white Kentuckians who resisted emancipation. So Burdett "shook them both," he explained, and "became a thorough Radical."[10]

Like many other black ministers, Burdett never drew clear lines between religion and politics anyway and thus transitioned quickly into formal political roles. He attended the second statewide convention of black Kentuckians in 1867, an event called to openly advocate for full civil rights, and was elected one of five vice presidents there.[11] Then by 1872 the state organization of the Republican Party selected him to serve as an elector at its national convention, supporting the reelection of Ulysses S. Grant for president. Burdett began canvassing the central part of the state, retracing the routes he had traveled to establish black churches, this time urging black voters to head to the polls in support of Republican candidates. "Now clothed with all the rights of an American citizen," Burdett made his pitch, they could either "give the enemy an occasion to say the negro is not ready" or "fight the battle through." Burdett, a Union veteran campaigning on behalf of the former general, did not hesitate to view electoral politics in martial terms. "God being my helper," he declared, "I will meet the enemy on the battle ground."[12]

Four years later he served as one of twenty-four Kentucky delegates to the 1876 Republican National Convention in Cincinnati.[13] Yet it was this closely contested election that marked a turning point, sending him into disillusionment with the party. Although the Republican Rutherford B. Hayes assumed the presidency in its aftermath, he did so thanks to a deal struck with Democrats to resolve an Electoral College dispute, which gave Hayes the victory in exchange for the removal of the last Federal troops from the South. Republicans would now withdraw the last military protection for freed people and thus abandon Reconstruction altogether. Burdett had little choice but to stick with the Republicans in the months ahead but experienced firsthand what it meant to align with a weakened party in his state. In August 1877 he attended a Republican meeting in Lexington, where he was supposed to speak but was "prevented from proceeding by the throwing of rotten eggs, sticks, and stones."[14] Burdett was now in his opponents' crosshairs, and it seemed ever more likely that he and his family would remain targets of this kind of racial violence, which white Democrats were inflicting on African Americans all across the South in order to suppress black political participation and re store Democratic rule.

The next year Burdett thus resigned from the Berea College board of trustees and made plans to leave Kentucky. He and Lucinda joined what he called a "great uprising of the colorade people" in the state, as they departed "this land where the foot of the slave has marked the soil" and headed out west, where he believed "all men are regarded as a man." Others called it an "Exodus," and those who went to Kansas, "Exodusters," people searching for the Promised Land in a state that was established free in the 1850s after a long and bitter fight. The Burdetts joined 6,990 other Kentucky-born African Americans who migrated to Kansas by 1880. Some of them had been urged to go by Gabriel himself; he had been exhorting his fellow freed people that if they remained in Kentucky, they would be "crushed down under the heel of these tyrants who look down upon them with contempt and disdain."[15]

Burdett never abandoned politics after moving to Kansas but instead left the Republican Party in favor of the Prohibition Party and its temperance crusade. The party nominated him as its candidate for Kansas state auditor in 1888 and 1892; Burdett, in turn, campaigned on behalf of the party's nominee for president in 1888, Clinton B. Fisk, who, in a twist of fate, was the same Freedmen's Bureau commissioner who had overseen the closing of Camp Nelson and whom Burdett probably knew personally.[16] And in other ways, too, he had cause to look back on his time inside military lines—in particular, when he applied for a veteran's pension in July 1890, the first year in which he was eligible. (In 1895 he started receiving payments of eight dollars per month.)[17] Within the next two decades, he was also admitted to the National Home for Disabled Volunteer Soldiers in Leavenworth, Kansas, suffering from "Cardiac Hypertrophy," "Dermatitis," and a "right Inguinal Hernia." In what had to be especially trying for a minister and teacher, he was also struggling with "Senility." Gabriel Burdett died in November 1914 at the age of eighty-five.[18]

Lucinda lived for two more years, after moving into the home of their daughter, Gertrude, in Plattsburg, Missouri. It was not until the time of Lucinda's death, in May 1916, that for the first time she emerged, in her own right, in any surviving documents. "Mrs. Lucinda Burdett, wife of the late Rev. Gabriel Burdett, died, after an illness of several months," an obituary published in the African American newspaper the *Kansas City Sun* noted. A funeral had already been held in her honor, where "the floral tributes were many." "She was a good mother," as well as "a devoted and faithful Christian," it continued, before revealing something else: she had "professed a hope in Christ in 1868." Three to four years *after* Gabriel had already been ordained and started performing baptisms at Camp Nelson? This line of the obituary, so precise in identifying the year of her conversion, opens up all sorts of unanswerable questions about Lucinda in retrospect. We know she and her husband were together at Camp Nelson at least by 1865. Had she forged her own spiritual path even after that point? Separate from her minister husband's? And what might this say about their marriage, or why their daughter apparently wanted to make this clear in the obituary?[19] These questions, like so many others, remain unanswered.

∽↝

Three years after Lucinda Burdett's death, in Phillips County, Arkansas, Eliza Bogan was living amid one of the worst racial massacres to ever grip the postwar South. About twenty-five miles southeast of her residence was the town of Elaine, Arkansas, where black people were struggling to make a living as sharecroppers. One evening in September 1919, over 100 of them gathered inside a church for a meeting of the Progressive Farmers and Household Union of America. The union was planning to push for fairer, more equitable payment for their share of cotton and other cash crops; without this they would continue to fall deeper and deeper into the debt that was grinding them into poverty. The union took the precaution of stationing black men as guards outside the church during the proceedings, but this did not stop white opponents from showing up at the church anyway, armed and ready. At some point shots broke out, though who fired the first one is still unknown. Yet word quickly circulated among white people in Phillips County that an "insurrection" was under way, and hundreds of whites, some of them hastily deputized by the county's sheriff, descended on Elaine to put it down. They burned the church and then fanned out from Elaine, mobs of white people shooting, burning, and hanging any black people they could find. The governor soon called in federal troops to calm the situation—a first since Reconstruction—but the troops began shooting at black people too. The Elaine Massacre, as it is known, was nothing less than a mass lynching that resulted in the deaths of at least 200 black people. It would give Eliza Bogan's home of Phillips County the distinction of having the highest number of lynchings in the nation — ever.[20]

Eliza Bogan, by then around the age of ninety, may not have been in Elaine in those days, but perhaps someone else she knew was — a veteran of the Forty-Sixth USCT or one of his children; a former neighbor from slavery; or even her own children.[21] At the very least, she would have known what had happened there and might have felt it deeply, for one did not have to be directly connected to the events to feel the terror of mob violence. She could easily identify with the plight of the sharecroppers gathered at the church; the contours of her postwar life had, in many ways, matched the contours of those who organized for the union. After their return to Helena in 1866, she and Dennis had also become sharecroppers. As the system did for other freed people, sharecropping seemed to provide them, at least at first, with a degree of control over their labor they did not have before. The system varied in details, but generally sharecroppers took control of a portion of a landowner's property, paying him a "share" of the crop yield in return, working independently and without the surveillance of the landowner. But the system could entangle them in debt too.[22]

At some point Dennis entered into an arrangement with a landowner named John Reed to rent and work eighteen acres of cotton land and six acres of corn. But to get that operation up and running, Dennis had to acquire his own tools, seeds, fertilizer, and other supplies, which he did from a local merchant named C. R. Coolidge. Dennis did not have the capital to purchase these supplies, so he instead bought them on credit from Coolidge, agreeing to repay the merchant once the crops were harvested and he got his return. But this could only work if Dennis received good prices for his shares of cotton and corn — if the cotton prices themselves remained stable and if Coolidge did not charge an exorbitant interest rate for the supplies, like so many other Southern merchants, enabled by state laws, did. It did not work for Dennis, as it turned out, for by 1877 he fell into debt in the amount of $300 to Coolidge, a situation that brought him to court and into an agreement that signed his share of the land over to Coolidge until he could find a way of paying off the debt. And this is exactly how so many other sharecroppers, like those gathered in Elaine in 1919, found themselves spiraling into debt and poverty.[23]

The Bogans' economic hardship was compounded by personal setbacks too. Eliza and Dennis's first daughter, Mary, had died at the age of eight months, back in 1866. And then their marriage itself was strained. Although they had gotten legally married after the war, in 1869, it was a step that Eliza greeted with something less than enthusiasm. It was Samuel Brooks, the white man who hired them after their return to Helena, who "advised me to marry him by a ceremony," and who, as a justice of the peace, officiated at the ceremony. To a woman who had seen her marriages torn apart by planters in slavery, the intervention of a white man in her private, marital life could not have been entirely welcomed. It is likely she felt pressured as much as "advised," for although conceding that legal marriage seemed "right," it was not something she looked back upon with any fondness. Dennis, she later admitted, had proven himself to be a "bad fellow" by that time, with a habit of "running out after women." The ceremony did nothing to change that. "There was not any difference in our Relations before and after we had the ceremony," Eliza recalled. The state may have now recognized her marriage — and her right to marry — for the first time; but the marriage itself was hardly liberated from social pressures, like the meddling control of white men.[24]

Eliza and Dennis continued to live together with their surviving daughter, Fanny, until Dennis died in 1882. He was the fourth husband Eliza lost in her lifetime. Dennis's death turned Eliza into a soldier's widow again, though it was a particularly meaningful designation by the 1890s because it enabled her to apply for a federal pension based on Dennis's service. And in March 1892, encouraged by a man named Alfred Miller, whom she identified only as a "colored man" who "has been doing my writing," Eliza appeared before a special examiner from the U.S. Pension Bureau who had traveled to Helena to collect depositions from pension applicants. Like Edward Whitehurst did when he appeared before the Southern Claims Commission, or Gabriel Burdett did before the Pension Bureau, Eliza reflected on her life, telling her story of living and working and surviving inside Union lines with Dennis and the Forty-Sixth USCT. Never having learned to write, she signed her name on the application with an X; she was then awarded eight dollars per month by the federal government, an amount that increased to fifty dollars per month by 1926.[25] And thus, for the first time since mustering out from the Forty-Sixth USCT, Eliza drew compensation for military service — but only for Dennis's service, not for her own. Still, it offered an important financial lifeline at a crucial time when, as she noted in her application, she claimed to "have no income," "never owned any real estate," and had few possessions other than clothing, which was "very scant at that."[26]

Eliza lived the rest of her years with her daughter Fanny, in what turned out to be the most long-standing, unbroken relationship of her life. She kept on working well into her eighties too but had left fieldwork well behind. Eliza identified herself as a midwife in her pension application; in 1910, a census taker listed her as a "Doctor," suggesting that her work went beyond delivering children and into other aspects of healing too. Between this work, Fanny's labor in domestic service, and the monthly widow's pension, at some point the two women had climbed out of debt and saved enough to purchase a home by 1910. It would have been a meaningful transaction: for Eliza at least, it marked the first time that she would live on a property not claimed or owned by a white man.[27] She would thus live out her life having achieved the sort of financial independence that proved difficult for many former slaves mired in sharecropping, especially for women. And yet, just twenty-five miles away from that house, many others lost their lives in the Elaine Massacre in 1919, a reminder of how tenuous her journey to freedom remained. Eliza Bogan died in September 1928.[28]

～～

Eliza Bogan, the Burdetts, and the Whitehursts were no longer enslaved, and they had all found a way to live independently and to own their own property. But in the Jim Crow South, where segregated public facilities offered a daily reminder of their second class citizenship, and where voting rights were taken away by literacy tests and poll taxes and outright violence, no African American person had made it out of the wilderness just yet. Before leaving Kentucky for Kansas, Gabriel Burdett remained hopeful that he would get there—that the last leg of his journey would finally deliver him and his family to the Promised Land. "We still hope the day will come," he wrote to an AMA colleague in 1876, "when we as a people will come out from under the yoke of bondage and oppression."[29] His time—their time—in the Civil War's refugee camps, it turned out, had only been a beginning.

Their journeys through the war and the military sphere may have been relatively short, just four years in a much longer pursuit of freedom and equal citizenship in the United States. But in those years, as they built new lives for themselves in and around the Union army, the Civil War's refugees from slavery positioned themselves on the front lines of the nation's monumental battle against slavery. To hook their emancipation to a war effort to save the Union was to never know how things would turn out, to never be sure that freedom would come. Sometimes, the short-term calculus of military necessity aligned very well with their pursuit of freedom, as in the occupation of land that opened up places to live or in the demand for labor that created employment and made food rations forthcoming. And the Union's military victory in 1865 was the most crucial moment that secured the legal end of slavery altogether. But at other times along the way, the Union army's calculations of military necessity led to repeated losses for refugees—the loss of shelter, the loss of employment, the loss of family, and the loss of land that came at war's end. Never did their interests align completely; never did the pursuit of military victory fully advance former slaves to the freedom they had long envisioned.

Those who survived their time in the Civil War's refugee camps left behind stories too often overlooked in the nation's triumphant celebrations of emancipation. We revere the Emancipation Proclamation without knowing how tenuous the emancipation process really was. We admire battlefield triumphs without seeing the many thousands of men, women, and children who were there and who risked everything to ensure that the war ended with the "new birth of freedom" that President Lincoln envisioned.[30] The very act of enduring—of simply *living*—inside the war's slave refugee camps was an elemental part of the story of slavery's destruction in the United States. It was a struggle that Eliza Bogan, Gabriel Burdett, and the Whitehursts never left behind and never forgot as they moved forward in their lives. And it is one that we would do well to remember today, as the nation tries to move forward toward a more honest reckoning with its tangled history of slavery, race, and civil war.

notes

ABBREVIATIONS

AFIC   American Freedmen's Inquiry Commission

AMA-KY   American Missionary Association Archives
Microfilm, Kentucky, Amistad Research Center,
Tulane University, New Orleans, Louisiana

AMA-VA   American Missionary Association Archives
Microfilm, Virginia, Amistad Research Center,
Tulane University, New Orleans, Louisiana

BRFAL   Record Group 105: Records of the Bureau of Refugees,
Freedmen, and Abandoned Lands, 1861–1879, National
Archives and Records Administration, Washington, D.C.

CCF   Consolidated Correspondence File

CMSR   Compiled Military Service Records, National Archives
and Records Administration, Washington, D.C.

CWPF   Civil War Pension File, Case Files of Approved Pension
Applications of Veterans Who Served in the Army and Navy Mainly
in the Civil War and the War with Spain, 1861–1934, Record Group
15: Records of the Veterans Administration, 1773–1985, National
Archives and Records Administration, Washington, D.C.

DEA   District of Eastern Arkansas

DKY   Department of Kentucky

DVANC   Department of Virginia and North Carolina

FCCA   Friends Collection and College Archives,
Earlham College, Richmond, Indiana

FFAR   Friends Freedmen's Association Records, Record Group 4/024

FHL   Friends Historical Library, Swarthmore College,
Swarthmore, Pennsylvania

FSL   Family Search Library, Lexington, Kentucky

HL   Houghton Library, Harvard University, Cambridge, Massachusetts

IA   Invalid's Application

IC   Invalid's Certificate
LC   Manuscript Division, Library of Congress, Washington, D.C.
M999   M999: Records of the Assistant Commissioner
for the State of Tennessee
NARA   National Archives and Records Administration, Washington, D.C.
OR   United States War Department. *The War of the Rebellion:
A Compilation of the Official Records of the Union and Confederate
Armies.* Washington, D.C.: Government Printing Office, 1880–1901.
RG 92   Record Group 92: Records of the Quartermaster General, 1774–1985,
National Archives and Records Administration, Washington, D.C.
RG 94   Record Group 94: Records of the Adjutant
General's Office, 1780s–1917, National Archives and
Records Administration, Washington, D.C.
RG 153   Record Group 153: Records of the Judge Advocate
General, 1800–1967, National Archives and
Records Administration, Washington, D.C.
RG 393   Record Group 393: Records of U.S. Army Continental
Commands, 1821–1920, National Archives and
Records Administration, Washington, D.C.
SCC   Southern Claims Commission, Approved Claims, 1871–1880:
Virginia, Ser. 732, M2094, Record Group 217: Records of the
Accounting Officers of the Department of the Treasury, 1775–1927,
National Archives and Records Administration, Washington, D.C.
USCHA   United States Colored Heavy Artillery
USCT   United States Colored Troops
WA   Widow's Application
WC   Widow's Certificate

PROLOGUE

1. Edward Whitehurst Testimony, July 31, 1877, Approved Claim of Edward Whitehurst, SCC; on the burned-out condition of Hampton, Virginia, see Megan Kate Nelson, *Ruin Nation*, 19–29.

2. Maria Mann to Aunt Mary, [February?], April 7, May 18, 1863, and Maria Mann to Elisa, February 10, 1863, Mann Papers, LC; population and death toll estimates from Samuel Sawyer to Brig. Gen. Buford, September 25, 1863, ser. 4687, General and Special Orders Received and Other Records, DEA, RG 393, pt. 2; report of Samuel Shipley in Friends Association of Philadelphia, *Statistics of the Operations*, 12; Christ, *Civil War Arkansas*, 122.

3. John G. Fee to Bro. Jocelyn, July 18, 1864, and Gabriel Burdett to John G. Fee, January 20, 1865, AMA-KY; Inspection report of Major Murray Davis, April 17, 1865, in Sears, *Camp Nelson, Kentucky*, 199–205; "Camp Nelson, Kentucky. Its Location and Strength — Its Improvements — Its Government, Operations, &c," Louisville *Daily Union Press*, April 10, 1865.

4. "Slaves Interested," *Liberator*, May 3, 1861; "What of the Slaves?," *Liberator*, May 10, 1861; "We Don't Like It," *Liberator*, May 31, 1861.

5. For text of Abraham Lincoln's first inaugural address on March 4, 1861, see Lincoln, *First Inaugural Address, The Avalon Project.*

6. Benjamin Butler to Lt. Gen. Winfield Scott, May 24, 1861, Butler Papers, LC. It has become legendary in the historical literature that the individuals who first approached Benjamin Butler were three men. But my investigation suggests that this story has erased the women and children who fled to Fort Monroe in these initial days too; not only was their presence depicted in an artist's rendering of the slaves' first meeting with Butler, published two weeks later in *Frank Leslie's Illustrated Newspaper*, but Butler himself acknowledged their arrival in his subsequent correspondence with Gen. Winfield Scott. "Stampede among the Negroes in Virginia," *Frank Leslie's Illustrated Newspaper*, June 8, 1861; Benjamin Butler to Lt. Gen. Winfield Scott, May 27, 1861, Butler Papers, LC.

7. Benjamin Butler to Lt. Gen. Winfield Scott, May 24, 1861, Butler Papers, LC; on Butler's antebellum record on slavery, see Oakes, *Freedom National*, 91–92.

INTRODUCTION

1. An estimate of Civil War refugees from slavery, along with a discussion of the difficulties involved in making that estimate, can be found in Berlin et al., *Slaves No More*, 178–82. Estimates from previous wars are wide-ranging but agree that "tens of thousands" fled to British Army lines during the Revolution. Quarles, *Negro in the American Revolution*, 119; Frey, *Water from the Rock*, 211; Schama, *Rough Crossings*, 5–8. Alan Taylor estimates that 5,000 fled during the War of 1812; see Taylor, *Internal Enemy*, 441–42.

2. The total number of refugee settlements will likely grow as historical study of this subject continues. In this study, I have identified 299 settlements that, as described in subsequent chapters, ranged in size and function, from urban clusters to island settlements to plantations transformed into free labor enterprises. All of these settlements shared at least two qualities: each provided a place for refugees from slavery to settle, and each fell under Union army supervision and control.

3. The final report of the American Freedmen's Inquiry Commission in 1864 is the most well known of these reports because of its role in creating the Freedmen's Bureau, but it was neither the first nor the last study emanating from the federal government. "Final Report of the American Freedmen's Inquiry Commission to the Secretary of War," AFIC Records, Letters Received, ser. 12, M619, RG 94. Other reports include *Africans in Fort Monroe Military District*; *Report of Commissioners of Investigation of Colored Refugees in Kentucky, Tennessee, and Alabama*; and report of LeBaron Russell to Sec. Edwin Stanton, December 25, 1862, AFIC Papers, HL.

4. The more conventional scholarly view points to the Freedmen's Bureau as a watershed moment in the rise of the federal welfare state, or as a new "experiment in social policy," as Eric Foner has put it. See Foner, *Reconstruction*, 142; and Dauber, *Sympathetic State*, 37–43. But these views tend to overlook the way in which the bureau itself was built directly on the bureaucracy and policies put in place during wartime, and is thus better understood as a culmination of what began at Fort Monroe in 1861, rather than as a new beginning in 1865.

5. Scholarly work on the slave refugee camps is best described as being in its infancy, dominated by scattered examinations of particular places and particular moments. Synthetic studies that examine the overall, cumulative meaning and impact of this phenomenon are emerging only recently, beginning with Manning, *Troubled Refuge*, a study of how the camps worked to transform ideas about citizenship. The editors of the Freedmen and Southern Society Project, in their monumental six-volume series

Freedom: A Documentary History of Emancipation, have laid the groundwork for much more scholarly work on the subject. Previous studies that illuminate particular places where refugees settled include Rose, *Rehearsal for Reconstruction;* Hermann, *Pursuit of a Dream;* Greenwood, *First Fruits of Freedom;* Click, *Time Full of Trial;* Engs, *Freedom's First Generation;* Schwalm, *Emancipation's Diaspora;* Romeo, *Gender and the Jubilee;* Silkenat, *Driven from Home;* Reidy, "'Coming from the Shadow'"; Walker, "Corinth"; and Cimprich, *Slavery's End in Tennessee.* Other notable studies that illuminate particular themes in the slave refugee experience that transcend place include Du Bois, *Black Reconstruction in America;* Glymph, "'This Species of Property'"; Sternhell, *Routes of War;* Jim Downs, *Sick from Freedom;* Long, *Doctoring Freedom;* Schwalm, "Between Slavery and Freedom"; Heather Andrea Williams, *Self-Taught;* Hahn, *Nation under Our Feet;* Gerteis, *From Contraband to Freedman;* Litwack, *Been in the Storm;* and Tomblin, *Bluejackets and Contrabands.*

6. On gradual emancipation in the Northern states see Leslie M. Harris, *In the Shadow;* Shane White, *Somewhat More Independent;* and Melish, *Disowning Slavery.* On gradual emancipation and apprenticeship in the British West Indies, see, for example, Holt, *The Problem of Freedom;* Foner, *Nothing but Freedom,* esp. chap. 1; Rugemer, *Problem of Emancipation;* and Scully and Paton, *Gender and Slavery.*

7. [Untitled], *Friend,* November 21, 1863.

8. *Report of a Committee,* 3; H. S. Beals to Rev. Jocelyn, November [?], 1863, AMA-VA; *Report of Indiana Yearly Meeting's Executive Committee,* 41; [untitled], *Friend,* February 4, 1865.

9. J. & Sarah Smith to Samuel Shipley, April 28, 1864, in *Freedmen's Friend,* June 1864, FHL.

10. Estimate from Eltis, "A Brief Overview."

11. H. S. Beals to Rev. Jocelyn, October 27, 1863, AMA-VA.

12. "Colored Refugees," *American Missionary,* February 1862.

13. On the slaves' identification with the Exodus story in the antebellum period, see Raboteau, *Slave Religion,* 311–13; Rable, *God's Almost Chosen Peoples,* 288, 382–83; and Glaude, *Exodus!*

14. "The Freedmen's Aid Commission," *Freedmen's Bulletin,* March 1865. In *Been in the Storm* (133) the historian Leon Litwack makes the same analogy that was made between the refugee camp experience and the ordeal of the Israelites in the wilderness.

15. "'Colored Refugees,'" *Liberator,* February 14, 1862; "Colored Refugees," *American Missionary,* February 1862. See also the Reverend Henry Ward Beecher's critique of the term in "Mr. Beecher on Fremont and Contrabands," *Liberator,* November 1, 1861. For an in-depth exploration of the use of the term "contraband" in American culture, see Kate Masur, "'A Rare Phenomenon.'"

16. The U.N. definition of refugee can be found at "What is a Refugee?," USA for UNHCR. See also Bon Tempo, *Americans at the Gate,* 1; and Hyndman, *Managing Displacement,* xv, 8–14, 120.

17. On the evolution of early American refugee policy, see Everest, *Moses Hazen,* 113–41; Ashli White, *Encountering Revolution,* 70–86; Dauber, *Sympathetic State,* 19; Baseler, *Asylum for Mankind,* esp. 1–13; Zolberg, Suhrke, and Aguayo, *Escape from Violence,* 3–33; and Sharpe, "Humanity Begins at Home."

18. See Berlin, *Long Emancipation;* Rael, *Eight-Eight Years;* Sinha, *Slave's Cause;* and Hahn, *Political Worlds,* 1–54.

19. Representative quotes from Rothman, *Beyond Freedom's Reach*, 7.

20. This is not to deny that the revolutions in Haiti and Cuba were characterized by significant tensions between the causes of emancipation and political independence, or that the fusion of the two was in any way automatic or inevitable. See accounts of those struggles in, for example, Popkin, *You Are All Free*; and Ferrer, *Insurgent Cuba*, 1–42. See also Kerr-Ritchie, *Freedom's Seekers*. But in the United States the two causes seemed less organically joined. The Union to be saved was guided by a constitution that appeared to sanction black people's enslavement and, through the fugitive slave provision, put the federal government to work in stopping their attempts to liberate themselves. This put the enslaved in the awkward position of trying to pull some liberating logic out of a cause — the Union — that had long enslaved them.

21. Eaton, *Report of the General Superintendent*, 4.

22. See "Featured Document: The Emancipation Proclamation." Lincoln's reliance on "military necessity" as a legal and political justification for emancipation is well covered in Foner, *Fiery Trial*, 243; Louis P. Masur, *Lincoln's Hundred Days*; Witt, *Lincoln's Code*, 217–19, 234–37; and Guelzo, *Lincoln's Emancipation Proclamation*, 237–39.

23. Those who discuss "military emancipation" from the vantage point of policy makers in Washington, D.C., include, for example, Oakes, *Freedom National*; and Gregory P. Downs, *After Appomattox*. Edward L. Ayers and Scott Nesbit have addressed this issue of perspective by calling for the joining of all "scales" of action — national, military district, local — in order to better understand the course of emancipation. See Ayers and Nesbit, "Seeing Emancipation." Chandra Manning has begun to do this in *Troubled Refuge*, with an examination of the "mutually beneficial alliance" (14) forged between the army and the refugees. Other studies that take a more ground-level view of military emancipation have tended to focus the scope on particular subgroups of people — on laborers or soldiers or women. On laborers, see Brasher, *Peninsula Campaign*; on soldiers, see Emberton, *Beyond Redemption*; Reid, *Freedom for Themselves*; and Keith P. Wilson, *Campfires of Freedom*; and on women, see Romeo, *Gender and the Jubilee*.

24. This book moves along the lines of the "material turn" emerging in humanities scholarship in the twenty-first century, also referred to as the "new materialism," which foregrounds inquiry into human interactions with the physical world. This wave of scholarship has cut across the literatures of environmental history, cultural geography, and material culture studies, among other fields, and while influential works appear throughout the notes to this book, overviews include Coole and Frost, *New Materialisms*, 1–39; Miller, *Cultural Histories*; and Otter, "Locating Matter." Notable recent studies that have brought this perspective to bear on the history of the Civil War in particular include Megan Kate Nelson, *Ruin Nation*; Meier, *Nature's Civil War*; Brady, *War upon the Land*; Fiege, "Gettysburg"; and Thomas, Nash, and Shepard, "Places of Exchange." See also the June 2017 special issue of *Civil War History* devoted to the war's material culture, e.g., Luskey and Phillips, "Muster."

25. Thinking about the material history of the refugee camps makes it possible to ask new questions about emancipation, and to move away from the more commonly asked questions of "why" emancipation came (as in political and policy studies) or "who" freed the slaves (a preoccupation of social history). This book, instead, asks the question of "how": How exactly did emancipation work in everyday life? This line of inquiry gets at the basic "infrastructure" of emancipation, reflecting a related impulse in history and humanities studies to examine the role that material forms play in mediating everyday

social relations. See, for example, Burchardt and Höhne, "Infrastructure of Diversity." Such an orientation is already evident in studies of antebellum slavery that focus on enslavement as a material condition, such as Johnson, *River of Dark Dreams*, esp. 9, 210. See also Camp, *Closer to Freedom*; and Baptist, *Half Has Never Been Told*.

26. "Argument" quote from Brasher, *Peninsula Campaign*, 7.

27. This point, I hope, will help settle a rapidly emerging debate about the army's relationship to freedom-seeking people during the Civil War. Although some historians, such as Jim Downs in *Sick from Freedom*, have argued powerfully for the ways in which the army failed the freed people and left them to suffer, others, such as Gregory P. Downs (*After Appomattox*), Glenn David Brasher (*Peninsula Campaign*), and Chandra Manning (*Troubled Refuge*), view the army as the freed people's best ally in the pursuit of freedom and citizenship. The reality is that both characterizations are true—and my interest here is in understanding *how* the army could be both at once. Paying closer attention to the ever-shifting logic of military necessity helps answer that question.

The elasticity of military necessity itself is well summed up in the Union's laws of war, which after 1863 defined military necessity broadly as "those measures which are indispensable for securing the ends of war." Witt, *Lincoln's Code*, 235.

28. On the Lieber Code, see Witt, *Lincoln's Code*, 3–8, 197–219; and Dilbeck, *More Civil War*, 1–11, 69–96 (quote p. 160).

29. Du Bois, *Black Reconstruction*, esp. chap. 4; "Stampede of Contrabands to Kansas," *Pine and Palm*, September 14, 1861; "From Our Superintendent of Schools," *Freedmen's Bulletin*, July 1864; John Eaton, Supt. of Contrabands, Dept. of Tennessee, to Asst. Adjutant Genl. Jno. A. Rawlins, April 29, 1863, AFIC Records, Letters Received, ser. 12, reel 200, M619, RG 94.

30. Du Bois, *Black Reconstruction*, 65; Foner, *Fiery Trial*, 167; Bennett, *Union Jacks*, 159; Quarles, *Negro in the Civil War*, 46.

31. It should be noted that these metaphors conveying the size and force of the refugees' movement have assisted historians in arguing that flight from slavery during the war constituted a slave rebellion, perhaps the greatest one in American history. See, most notably, Du Bois, *Black Reconstruction*, esp. chap. 4; and Hahn, *Political Worlds*, 55–114. See also Roediger, *Seizing Freedom*, 25–66; and Lause, *Free Labor*, 55–67. Whether to characterize it as a "rebellion" (or a "strike") is not my concern here; rather, *Embattled Freedom* focuses less on the whole and more on the parts—on the individual people, places, and contingent moments that can help us better understand *how* emancipation unfolded in the ways that it did across the wartime South. The importance of asking questions about the individual—and, in particular, of viewing African American subjects as individualized people rather than as a "monolith" or as a "composite"—is well explored in Kidada E. Williams, "Maintaining a Radical Vision."

32. Like other scholars of emancipation, I am indebted to the Freedmen and Southern Society Project for seeing this documentary evidence and making a portion of it accessible to researchers. See the six-volume series, Berlin et al., *Freedom*.

33. My approach is informed by James C. Scott, *Domination*, 1–16; and by the example set by studies like Smallwood, *Saltwater Slavery*, esp. 4–6.

34. On gender, power, and the archive of slavery, see Fuentes, *Dispossessed Lives*, 1–12 (quote p. 2). Other important meditations on the archive of the Civil War, emancipation, and Reconstruction include Glymph, "Black Women and Children"; Jim Downs, "Emancipating the Evidence"; Sternhell, "Afterlives"; and Kidada E. Williams,

"Maintaining a Radical Vision." On archives and the production of knowledge more generally, see Blouin and Rosenberg, *Processing the Past*. Recent examples that illustrate the value of microhistorical approaches for understanding the process of emancipation include Nathans, *To Free a Family*; Cecelski, *Fire of Freedom*; Rothman, *Beyond Freedom's Reach*; and Blight, *Slave No More*.

35. Report of LeBaron Russell to Sec. Edwin Stanton, December 25, 1862, 6, AFIC Papers, HL. A similar point is made in Litwack, *Been in the Storm*, 6, 173.

36. The importance of understanding what came before emancipation—specifically, how the experience of enslavement shaped the ideas and strategies of those who became free—has been well made in the historiography. Representative examples include O'Donovan, *Becoming Free*; Glymph, *Out of the House*; and Hahn, *Nation under Our Feet*.

37. This point is also made in Long, *Doctoring Freedom*.

38. See Jim Downs, *Sick from Freedom*; Schwalm, "Surviving Wartime Emancipation"; and Long, *Doctoring Freedom*, 44–69.

39. Report of LeBaron Russell to Sec. Edwin Stanton, December 25, 1862, 7, AFIC Papers, HL.

EDWARD AND EMMA WHITEHURST IN SLAVERY

1. Whitehurst's 1877 claim file indicates his birth year was 1830. Edward Whitehurst Testimony, July 31, 1877, Approved Claim of Edward Whitehurst, SCC. On slaves who sought liberation by purchasing themselves from their owners, see Schweninger, *Black Property Owners*, 65–67; and Hunter, *Bound in Wedlock*, 93–94.

2. On the acquisition of property by enslaved people, see Penningroth, *Claims of Kinfolk*, 4–7, 45–55; see also Saville, *Work of Reconstruction*, 9–11.

3. On the transformation of the eastern Virginia economy and slavery, see Medford, "Transition from Slavery," 8–33; Engs, *Freedom's First Generation*, 8; Zaborney, *Slaves for Hire*, 10–12, 163; Schermerhorn, *Money over Mastery*, 4, 143; and Lynda J. Morgan, *Emancipation*, 18–27, 57–60.

4. Edward Whitehurst Testimony, July 31, 1877, Approved Claim of Edward Whitehurst, SCC. On self-hiring, see Martin, *Divided Mastery*, 161–83; Zaborney, *Slaves for Hire*, 23, 66–83, 132–34; Schermerhorn, *Money over Mastery*, 109–10, 137–38, 148–49; Medford, "Transition from Slavery," 37–38; and Penningroth, *Claims of Kinfolk*, 53–55.

5. On the daily conditions of overwork, see Penningroth, *Claims of Kinfolk*, 54.

6. On the unfree conditions of hired-out slavery, see Martin, *Divided Mastery*, 2–3, 161–65; and Zaborney, *Slaves for Hire*, 1–5.

7. On how hired-out slaves became "well versed" in market practices, see Penningroth, *Claims of Kinfolk*, 61–63.

8. Engs, *Freedom's First Generation*, 14; Medford, "Transition from Slavery," 35–38; Zaborney, *Slaves for Hire*, 12.

9. Stephanie Camp describes the "geography of containment" that kept enslaved women confined to plantations more so than men in *Closer to Freedom*. It was not uncommon for property accumulated by a married couple to remain in the hands of these less mobile women. See Penningroth, *Claims of Kinfolk*, 105–6.

10. See agricultural census record of Edward and Emma's owner, William Ivy, in Ancestry.com, *1850 United States Federal Census, Nonpopulation Schedules (Agriculture)*, Elizabeth City County, Virginia.

11. On the Ivy and Parrish families, see *Genealogies of Virginia Families*, 803–9, 821; Stauffer, "Old Farms," second installment, 333–34; Stauffer, "Old Farms," third installment, 136; Ancestry.com, *1850 United States Federal Census*, Elizabeth City County, Virginia; and Ancestry.com, *Virginia, Select Marriages*.

12. Engs, *Freedom's First Generation*, 7–10; Stauffer, "Old Farms," first installment, 203.

13. No antebellum or wartime records, nor the 1870 federal census (the first population census in which the Whitehursts would appear), mention any children specifically belonging to Edward or Emma. *Genealogies of Virginia Families*, 803–21; Ancestry.com, *1860 United States Federal Census*, Elizabeth City County, Virginia; Ancestry.com, *1860 United States Federal Census — Slave Schedules*, Elizabeth City County, Virginia; Death Records, Elizabeth City County, Virginia, reel 9, Hampton Public Library, Hampton, Virginia.

14. West, *When the Yankees Came*, 47.

15. See envelope notes on Mattie Parish to Major General Ord, January 13, 1865, Union Provost Marshals' File of Paper Relating to Individual Citizens, Mattie Parish Case File, M345, War Department Collection of Confederate Records, Record Group 109, NARA.

16. *Genealogies of Virginia Families*, 809; Stauffer, "Old Farms," second installment, 340. On the general phenomenon of elite white refugeeing, see Sternhell, *Routes of War*, 140–45; and Litwack, *Been in the Storm*, 111–13.

17. John Oliver to Mr. Jocelyn, July 28, 1862, AMA-VA; *Genealogies of Virginia Families*, 803–21; Stauffer, "Old Farms," second installment, 336.

18. William Ivy, Co. I, 3rd Virginia Cavalry, CMSR; *Genealogies of Virginia Families*, 821. Ivy's overseer, according to the census, was a man named John Barnes; Ancestry.com, *1860 United States Federal Census*, Elizabeth City County, Virginia; John Barnes, Co. B, 32nd Virginia Infantry, CMSR.

19. Genealogical notes, Mallory Family Papers, Virginia Historical Society, Richmond, Virginia.

20. Benjamin Butler to Lt. Gen. Winfield Scott, May 24, 1861, Butler Papers, LC.

21. *Tribune* correspondent quoted in "The Negroes," *Pine and Palm*, June 29, 1861.

22. Pierce, "Contrabands at Fortress Monroe," 628; on the general function of that communications "telegraph," see McCurry, *Confederate Reckoning*, 227–29.

23. Benjamin Butler to Lt. Gen. Winfield Scott, May 24, 1861, Butler Papers, LC; distance between properties described in Mattie Parish to Major General Ord, January 13, 1865, Union Provost Marshals' File of Paper Relating to Individual Citizens, Mattie Parish Case File, M345, War Department Collection of Confederate Records, Record Group 109, NARA.

24. Edward Whitehurst Testimony, July 31, 1877, Approved Claim of Edward Whitehurst, SCC.

CHAPTER 1

1. Information about the crops cultivated on the Parker West property from Ancestry .com, *1850 United States Federal Census, Nonpopulation Schedules (Agriculture)*, Elizabeth City County, Virginia.

2. Roswell Farnham Diary, June 4–6, 1861, Vermont Historical Society, Barre, Vermont. The nineteen men, women, and children remaining on the West property were among twenty-nine owned by Parker West in 1860. Ancestry.com, *1860 United States Federal Census — Slave Schedules*, Elizabeth City County, Virginia.

3. Roswell Farnham Diary, June 4–6, 1861, Vermont Historical Society, Barre, Vermont; West, *When the Yankees Came*, 4.

4. Messner, "General John Wolcott Phelps," 24–26; Benjamin F. Butler to Montgomery Blair, July 23, 1861, Butler Papers, LC; see also Brasher, *Peninsula Campaign*, 40–41.

5. Phelps would end up in New Orleans the next year, at Camp Parapet, where he began arming black men in preparation for military service—in defiance of both U.S. policy at the time and, ironically, his superior in the region, Gen. Benjamin Butler (who would follow Phelps to Louisiana after leaving Fort Monroe himself). Rothman, *Beyond Freedom's Reach*, 79–81.

6. Farnham's list may be the very first list of "contrabands" generated anywhere during the war that has survived into the present. Roswell Farnham Diary, June 6, 1861, Vermont Historical Society, Barre, Vermont; Benjamin F. Butler to Col. Phelps, May 28, 1861, Butler Papers, LC.

7. Benjamin Butler to Lt. Gen. Winfield Scott, May 24, 1861, Butler Papers, LC.

8. Although the Whitehursts' names do not appear in the portion of Farnham's record that has survived, there is good reason to believe, based on the timing of their movements, that they were met by Farnham and may have been listed on a portion of his record that has not survived. Roswell Farnham Diary, June 6, 1861, Vermont Historical Society, Barre, Vermont.

9. "The Services of the Contrabands," *Pine and Palm*, June 29, 1861; unnumbered order of Gen. Benjamin Butler, May 30, 1861, Butler Papers, LC

10. On the inspection of bodies in the slave trade, see Johnson, *Soul by Soul*, 135–62.

11. Edward Whitehurst Testimony, July 31, 1877, Approved Claim of Edward Whitehurst, SCC; on women's initial labor assignment in hospitals, see "The Escape of Slaves to the Fortress," *New York Tribune*, May 31, 1861.

12. "A Slave's Notion of a 'Kind Massa,'" *Pine and Palm*, June 22, 1861.

13. Pierce, "Contrabands at Fortress Monroe," 638.

14. Berlin et al., *Wartime Genesis: Upper South*, 20.

15. Pierce, "Contrabands at Fortress Monroe," 627; *Tribune* reporter quoted in "The Services of the Contrabands," *Pine and Palm*, June 29, 1861.

16. Benjamin F. Butler to Secretary Simon Cameron, printed in "Contraband Negroes," *Pine and Palm*, August 17, 1861; on the way statements like Butler's evoked popular beliefs about race and climate, see Valencius, *Health of the Country*, 236–37; Jordan, *White over Black*, 261; and Steinberg, *Down to Earth*, 71.

17. Discussion of various types of labor at Fort Monroe can be found in Report of Persons or Articles Hired by C. Wilder (1863, File 1205); G. Tallmadge (1861, File 456), C. G. Sawtelle (1862, File 780), E. C. Becker (1862, File 57), P. C. Pitkin (1862, File 701), A. Gage (1862, File 1259), C. Wilder (1862, File 1429), ser. 238, RG 92; quote from Special Order 112, May 3, 1862, by order of General John Wool, vol. 214/513 VaNc, ser. 5172, General & Special Orders Issued, Provost Marshal, DVANC, RG 393, pt. 1.

18. "The Contrabands in Camp," *Pine and Palm*, August 31, 1861; report of LeBaron Russell to Sec. Edwin Stanton, December 25, 1862, 1–2, AFIC Papers, HL.

19. "The Services of the Contrabands," *Pine and Palm*, June 29, 1861.

20. On the Union's reliance on "contraband intelligence," see Brasher, *Peninsula Campaign*, 82–86, 119–31.

21. Quarstein, "First Blood," 47–53; Norris, "Lexington," 48–55; Charles Smith Testimony, July 31, 1877, Approved Claim of Edward Whitehurst, SCC; on other African

American guides and scouts enlisted to help with the Bethel expedition, see Brasher, *Peninsula Campaign*, 42–44.

22. Charles Smith would later state, "I have known him all my life," in reference to Whitehurst. Charles Smith Testimony, July 31, 1877, Approved Claim of Edward Whitehurst, SCC.

23. Report of Gen. Benjamin F. Butler, June 10, 1861, *OR*, ser. 1, vol. 2, chap. 9, p. 78; Norris, "Lexington," 51–54.

24. Report of Col. John Bendix, June 12, 1861, *OR*, ser. 1, vol. 2, chap. 9, p. 88; Norris, "Lexington," 51–54.

25. *Raleigh Register* quoted in Norris, "Lexington," 55.

26. Benjamin F. Butler to Secretary Simon Cameron, July 30, 1861, in "Contraband Negroes," *Pine and Palm*, August 17, 1861; Quarstein, *Hampton and Newport News*, 56–57.

27. Quoted in Quarstein, *Hampton and Newport News*, 56; J. Bankhead Magruder to Col. Robert Johnston, July 22, 1861, *OR*, ser. 1, vol. 2, chap. 9, pp. 991–92.

28. Report of Brig. Gen. John B. Magruder, August [2?], 1861, *OR*, ser. 1, vol. 4, chap. 9, p. 570.

29. "Stealing Slaves to Sell South," *Pine and Palm*, August 24, 1861; Edward Whitehurst Testimony, July 31, 1877, Approved Claim of Edward Whitehurst, SCC.

30. "Stampede of Slaves from Hampton to Fortress Monroe," *Harper's Weekly*, August 17, 1861; "Two Thousand Contrabands at Fort Monroe," *Pine and Palm*, August 10, 1861.

31. Phelps played a role in the Union's capture of New Orleans the next year and in that region remained a crucial, outspoken leader in favor of admitting refugee slaves into Union lines. See McClaughry, "John Wolcott Phelps," 268–71; and Rothman, *Beyond Freedom's Reach*, 79–81.

32. In particular, Butler learned that Gen. Irvin McDowell had refused to admit refugee slaves into Union lines at the recent battle at Manassas. Benjamin Butler to Col. E. D. Baker, July 29, 1861, Butler Papers, LC; Benjamin Butler to Secretary Simon Cameron, July 30, 1861, in "Contraband Negroes," *Pine and Palm*, August 17, 1861.

33. On the First Confiscation Act, see Syrett, *Civil War Confiscation Acts*, 191. Butler's willingness to open the lines to all enslaved people is evident in the 350 children on his "List of Negroes Claiming Protection and Food at Fortress Monroe," July 29, 1861, in Butler Papers, LC. My view of the relatively conservative nature of the First Confiscation Act departs from James Oakes's contention that it was an act of emancipation (see Oakes, *Freedom National*, 122), and is closer to that of Leslie Schwalm in "Between Slavery and Freedom" (143). The *Liberator* newspaper similarly criticized the narrowness of the Confiscation Act in "The Grand Question," *Liberator*, August 9, 1861.

34. Simon Cameron was the first secretary of war but would be replaced by Edwin Stanton in January 1862. Benjamin Butler to Secretary Simon Cameron, July 30, 1861, in "Contraband Negroes," *Pine and Palm*, August 17, 1861. Butler had received fawning letters from Northern abolitionists all summer, praising his leadership with regard to refugees from slavery. Examples of these letters abound in Butler Papers, LC. This no doubt had something to do with the general's defensiveness regarding his slavery policies—and with his decision to make his letter to Cameron a public one.

35. Magruder's rank had changed by the time he spotted Butler's letter; he had been recently promoted from colonel to brigadier general in the Confederate army. Quarstein, *Hampton and Newport News*, 58; report of Brig. Gen. J. Bankhead Magruder, August 9, 1861, *OR*, ser. 1, vol. 4, chap. 13, p. 571.

36. Report of Benjamin Butler, August 8, 1861, *OR*, ser. 1, vol. 4, chap. 13, p. 567.

37. Edward Whitehurst Testimony, July 31, 1877, Approved Claim of Edward Whitehurst, SCC.

38. Some historians have confused the less visible position of women in army records with the army's belief in women's "uselessness." See, for example, McCurry, *Confederate Reckoning*, 266, 272–73. In contrast, I would argue that they were still considered militarily useful — even integral — but in different ways, such as in private service, that were less formally organized and thus difficult for a historian to see and track in retrospect.

39. Edward Whitehurst Testimony, July 31, 1877, Approved Claim of Edward Whitehurst, SCC.

40. Edward Whitehurst Testimony, July 31, 1877, Approved Claim of Edward Whitehurst, SCC.

41. Estimate from [untitled], *Liberator*, December 13, 1861.

42. Charles Smith Testimony, July 31, 1877, Approved Claim of Edward Whitehurst, SCC.

43. Evidence of employees hired in Charles Smith Testimony, July 31, 1877, Approved Claim of Edward Whitehurst, SCC; complaint of Edward Whitehouse and Thomas Ware, August 4, 1862, Letters Received, ser. 5063, DVANC, RG 393, pt. 1.

44. L. C. Lockwood to Messrs. Whipple, Jocelyn, and Tappan, September 3, 1861, in *American Missionary*, October 1861.

45. Brasher, *Peninsula Campaign*, 104; Cobb and Holt, *Images of America*, 38.

46. "Sunday Service in a Virginian Hospital," *Pine and Palm*, September 21, 1861; L. C. Lockwood to Messrs. Whipple, Jocelyn, and Tappan, September 3, 1861, in *American Missionary*, October 1861.

47. L. C. Lockwood to Messrs. Whipple, Jocelyn, and Tappan, September 16, 1861, in *American Missionary*, October 1861; Fen, "Lewis C. Lockwood," 38–39.

48. L. C. Lockwood to Messrs. Whipple, Jocelyn, and Tappan, September 16, 1861, in *American Missionary*, October 1861.

49. Hunter, *Bound in Wedlock*, 8, 16, 164, 302.

50. Lockwood spelled their last name "Whitehouse" in this and in subsequent documents, but I am retaining the spelling "Whitehurst" in the body of the text because that is the spelling Edward used when he signed his own name in 1877. Alternate spellings will be used in the relevant notes. Report of Lewis Lockwood from Fort Monroe, October 10, 1861, in Marriage Records of the Office of the Commissioner, Washington Headquarters, M1875, reel 5, BRFAL; report of Lewis Lockwood, September 16, 1861, in "Mission to the Freed 'Contrabands' at Fortress Monroe, Va.," *American Missionary*, October 1861; Edward Whitehurst Testimony, July 31, 1877, Approved Claim of Edward Whitehurst, SCC. On the widespread practice of marrying refugees inside Union lines, including a discussion of Lewis Lockwood's work, see Hunter, *Bound in Wedlock*, 121–64; and Berlin and Rowland, *Families and Freedom*, 155–91.

51. Whitehurst and Savage are referred to as half brothers in Emanuel Savage Testimony, July 31, 1877, Approved Claim of Edward Whitehurst, SCC. Savage's first name is spelled differently in each document in which he appears — Immanuel, Manual, Manuel, and Emanuel — and in all cases he signed his name only with an *X* and thus left behind no record of how he himself would have spelled his name. I am therefore using "Immanuel" because it is the spelling listed in his marriage record, the closest thing to a legal authentication of his name. Alternate versions will appear in the notes to reflect

the spelling used in each corresponding source. Report of Lewis Lockwood from Fort Monroe, October 10, 1861, in Marriage Records of the Office of the Commissioner, Washington Headquarters, M1875, reel 5, BRFAL.

52. Petition of Manual Savage, September 22, 1865, ser. 225, CCF: "Negroes," RG 92.

53. *Africans in Fort Monroe Military District*, 8; Pierce, "Contrabands at Fortress Monroe," 634–35.

54. Petition of Manual Savage, September 22, 1865, ser. 225, CCF: "Negroes," RG 92.

55. Lockwood's list of married couples is one of the earliest lists of refugees from slavery, listed individually by name, to have survived to the present. I tracked those sixty-four names through the federal records and found twenty-one of them in other government records that revealed something about their labor in Union lines (fourteen of them were documented in the first year). See, for other examples, petition of Richard Jones, September 2, 1865, and petition of Nancy Jones, September 12, 1865, ser. 225, CCF: "Negroes," RG 92; and report of Lewis Lockwood from Fort Monroe, October 10, 1861, in Marriage Records of the Office of the Commissioner, Washington Headquarters, M1875, reel 5, BRFAL.

56. See petitions of George Sheldon, William Holloway, Wilson Hope, Edwin Sheppard, Abraham Wells, John Ale, Jacob Wallace, Richard Jones, Henry Tabb, Robert Goulding, Cole Druit, David Bird, John Walker, Suthey Parker, Peter Blue, Samuel Giles, and William Giles, all in ser. 225, CCF: "Negroes," RG 92.

57. Capt. G. Tallmadge to T. J. Hainie, July 25, 1861, Letters Received, ser. 5063, box 1, DVANC, RG 393, pt. 1.

58. "The Contrabands," *Pine and Palm*, October 5, 1861; Capt. G. Tallmadge to General, November 26, 1861, ser. 225, CCF: "Fort Monroe," RG 92.

59. Petition of William Giles, September 2, 1865, ser. 225, CCF: "Negroes," RG 92.

60. Report of LeBaron Russell to Sec. Edwin Stanton, December 25, 1862, 11, AFIC Papers, HL.

61. Petitions of Nancy Jones, September 12, 1865, and Richard Jones, September 2, 1865, ser. 225, CCF: "Negroes," RG 92.

62. Lewis Lockwood to Brethren, January 4, 1862, AMA-VA.

63. Petitions of William Giles, September 2, 1865, and Manual Savage, September 22, 1865, ser. 225, CCF: "Negroes," RG 92.

64. Petition of Peter Herbert, September 2, 1865, ser. 225, CCF: "Negroes," RG 92.

65. Some historians have attributed these problems to faulty record keeping and to the strain on the national treasury that also impeded the payment of soldiers' wages. See Berlin et al., *Slaves No More*, 107; and Manning, "Working for Citizenship," 53. But this interpretation does not fully account for the unique problems surrounding the payment of refugee laborers' wages, which, as the first year in and around Fort Monroe would reveal, were fundamentally tied up with race and with the reluctance of some white officials to accept that ex-slaves were entitled to the full benefits of free labor. That is how the refugees themselves diagnosed the situation, as this chapter shows.

66. See Berlin et al., *Wartime Genesis: Upper South*, 22.

67. Simon Cameron to Benjamin Butler, May 30, 1861, Butler Papers, LC.

68. Simon Cameron to Benjamin Butler, August 11, 1861, in *Pine and Palm*, August 17, 1861.

69. Hauptman, "General John E. Wool," 5, 14.

70. General Order No. 34, November 1, 1861, by order of Major General Wool, vol. -/4,

ser. 5078, General Orders Issued, DVANC, RG 393, pt. 1; C. Staforth Stewart et al. to Maj. Gen. John Wool, October 31, 1861, Letters Received, ser. 5063, DVANC, RG 393, pt. 1.

71. "The Freedmen at Fortress Monroe," *American Missionary*, January 1862; General Order No. 22, March 18, 1862, Orders Received, ser. 1650, Fort Monroe, RG 393, pt. 4.

72. On the treatment of vagrants in the antebellum North, see Schmidt, *Free to Work*, chap. 2; on the general contempt for the poor and the emphasis on work relief, see Dorsey, *Reforming Men and Women*, 51–68.

73. General Order No. 34, November 1, 1861, by order of Major General Wool, vol. -/4, ser. 5078, General Orders Issued, DVANC, RG 393, pt. 1.

74. "Colored Refugees," *American Missionary*, February 1862.

75. Special Order No. 72, October 14, 1861, by order of Maj. Gen. Wool, vol. -/5, ser. 5084, Special Orders Issued, DVANC, RG 393, pt. 1.

76. Petition of Manual Savage, September 22, 1865, ser. 225, CCF: "Negroes," RG 92.

77. In postwar testimony, Immanuel Savage mentioned being inside the Whitehursts' store by August 1862. Emanuel Savage Testimony, July 31, 1877, Approved Claim of Edward Whitehurst, SCC.

78. Official's words recounted in Lewis Lockwood to Brethren, January 3, 1862, AMA-VA.

79. *Africans in Fort Monroe Military District*, 10.

80. Capt. G. Tallmadge to General, November 26, 1861, ser. 225, CCF: "Fort Monroe," RG 92; Lewis C. Lockwood to Brethren, January 3, 4, 1862, AMA-VA.

81. "Colored Refugees," *American Missionary*, February 1862.

82. Arthur P. Davis, "William Roscoe Davis," 75–77 (I am grateful to Thulani Davis for bringing this article to my attention); "Colored Refugees," *American Missionary*, February 1862; "Novel and Interesting Meeting," *Pine and Palm*, January 23, 1862.

83. Lockwood was concerned that overly positive newspaper accounts would divert any philanthropic money from the North to other regions, like the South Carolina coast, rather than to eastern Virginia. Lewis C. Lockwood to Brethren, January 3, 1862, AMA-VA.

84. Lewis C. Lockwood to Brethren, January 7, 1862, AMA-VA.

85. Arthur P. Davis, "William Roscoe Davis," 80; "Novel and Interesting Meeting," *Pine and Palm* (reprinted from *New York Independent*), January 23, 1862; "William Davis — The Ex-Slave," *American Missionary*, April 1862.

86. General Order No. 5, by order of General John Wool, January 30, 1862, vol. -/4, ser. 5078, General Orders Issued, DVANC, RG 393, pt. 1.

87. *Africans in Fort Monroe Military District*, 1; Lewis Lockwood to Brethren, February 5, 1862, AMA-VA.

88. Lewis Lockwood to Brethren, February 5, 1862, AMA-VA.

89. The handwritten report was submitted to General Wool on March 12, 1862; it was later published on March 25. The published version omitted one section of the original handwritten report detailing Sergeant Smith's physical abuse. See *Africans in Fort Monroe Military District*, 5, 10. For the original, handwritten commissioners' report, see Letters Received, ser. 12, M619, reel 149 (#222V-1862), RG 94. (Note: the report is misidentified on the microfilm as a report of the AFIC.)

90. Charles Wilder to *New York Tribune*, June 6, 1862, AMA-VA.

91. *Africans in Fort Monroe Military District*, 4, 11.

92. Cannon, *Personal Reminiscences*, 66–70.

93. Sec. Edwin Stanton to John E. Wool, March 12, 1862, box 19, John Ellis Wool Papers, New York State Library, Albany, New York.

94. *Africans in Fort Monroe Military District.* The report was sent to Congress after the House of Representatives passed a resolution earlier in the month requesting data on the refugees at Fort Monroe. Resolution of the U.S. House of Representatives, March 7, 1862, Letters Received, ser. 12, M619, reel 149 (#166R-1862), RG 94; General Order No. 22, by command of Major General Wool, March 18, 1862, vol. -/4, ser. 5078, General Orders Issued, DVANC, RG 393, pt. 1.

95. Charles Wilder to *New York Tribune,* May [n.d.], 1862, AMA-VA.

96. L. C. Lockwood to Brethren, April 11, 1862, AMA-VA; McPherson, *Battle Cry of Freedom,* 375–77.

97. The actual total was 1,508 (652 men, 341 women, and 515 children), from *Africans in Fort Monroe Military District,* 10; L. C. Lockwood to Brethren, April 11, 1862, AMA-VA. On the campaign more generally, see McPherson, *Battle Cry of Freedom,* 424–27; and Gallagher, *Richmond Campaign,* 1–22.

98. Marten, "'Feeling of Restless Anxiety'"; Brasher, *Peninsula Campaign,* 102–7, 135–38; Charles Wilder to Mr. Whiting, July 2, 1862, AMA-VA.

99. Dr. J. M. Cuyler to General, March 29, 1862, Letters Received, ser. 5063, DVANC, RG 393, pt. 1; Charles Wilder to [unnamed], March 31, 1862, AMA-VA.

100. Charles Wilder to [unnamed], March 31, 1862; L. C. Lockwood to Brethren, March 18, April 11, 1862, AMA-VA.

101. L. C. Lockwood to Brethren, March 18, 1862, AMA-VA.

102. On the Peninsula campaign, see Brasher, *Peninsula Campaign;* and Gallagher, *Richmond Campaign.*

103. Complaint of Edward Whitehouse and Thomas Ware, August 4, 1862, Letters Received, ser. 5063, DVANC, RG 393, pt. 1.

104. Complaint of Edward Whitehouse and Thomas Ware, August 4, 1862, Letters Received, ser. 5063, DVANC, RG 393, pt. 1. On the new possibilities for written expression and testimony opened up by the war, see Hager, *Word by Word,* 138–80; and Romeo, *Gender and the Jubilee.* Although women frequently offered testimony to military authorities too, in this particular case Emma Whitehurst did not file the petition alongside her husband. It is impossible to determine exactly why not, but Emma may have assumed that military officials were more likely to listen to a man's word over a woman's.

105. Reply of W. H. Baum, August 8, 1862, in Complaint of Edward Whitehouse and Thomas Ware, August 4, 1862, Letters Received, ser. 5063, DVANC, RG 393, pt. 1.

106. Maj. William P. Jones to Gen. John Dix, June 5, 1862, Letters Received, ser. 5063, DVANC, RG 393, pt. 1.

107. See Daily Reports of Events, ser. 5173, DVANC, RG 393, pt. 1.

108. Lt. W. H. Baum to Maj. Gen. Dix, August 8, 1862, Letters Received, ser. 5063, DVANC, RG 393, pt. 1.

109. Complaint of Edward Whitehouse and Thomas Ware, August 4, 1862, Letters Received, ser. 5063, DVANC, RG 393, pt. 1.

110. Lt. W. H. Baum to Maj. Gen. Dix, August 8, 1862, Letters Received, ser. 5063, DVANC, RG 393, pt. 1.

111. Daily Reports of Events, March 15, 24, 1862, ser. 5173, DVANC, RG 393, pt. 1.

112. The Second Confiscation Act, Freedmen and Southern Society Project; see also Ash, *When the Yankees Came,* 30–31, 53–56.

113. The Second Confiscation Act, Freedmen and Southern Society Project.

114. Lucy Chase to Sarah Cope, November 28, 1863, minute book 2, box 12, ser. 13: Women's Aid Committee, FFAR, FHL.

115. Col. John Eaton Testimony, April 29, 1863, AFIC Records, Letters Received, ser. 12, M619, reel 200, RG 94; Special Orders No. 319, by order of Brig. Gen. Buford, November 27, 1864, ser. 4686, Special Orders, DEA, RG 393, pt. 2; Edward Whitehurst Testimony, July 31, 1877, Approved Claim of Edward Whitehurst, SCC.

116. Penningroth, *Claims of Kinfolk*, 3, 6–7, 45.

117. Col. John Eaton Testimony, April 29, 1863, AFIC Records, Letters Received, ser. 12, M619, reel 200, RG 94.

118. Lorenzo Thomas to Brig. Gen. S. C. Hawkins, October 11, 1863, ser. 159, Generals' Papers: Lorenzo Thomas, box 2, RG 94.

119. Eaton, *Report of the General Superintendent*, 18; see also James O. Pierce to Chaplain Jonathan E. Thomas, May 4, 1863, Letters Sent, ser. 4664, DEA, RG 393, pt. 2.

120. *Revised United States Army Regulations*, 493–512.

121. Eaton, *Report of the General Superintendent*, 18.

122. John Oliver to Mr. S. S. Jocelyn, September [?], 1862, AMA-VA. On the widespread phenomenon of Union soldiers plundering the spaces of slaves or refugees in the South, see Megan Kate Nelson, *Ruin Nation*, 92–93; Litwack, *Been in the Storm*, 124–25; and Wiley, *Life of Billy Yank*, 114.

123. See Daily Reports of Events, ser. 5173, DVANC, RG 393, pt. 1; for more on the problems surrounding former slaves' property claims in wartime, see Penningroth, *Claims of Kinfolk*, 131–41.

124. Charles Wilder to Maj. Gen. Dix, June 27, 1862, Letters Received, ser. 5063, DVANC, RG 393, pt. 1.

125. Edward Whitehurst Testimony, July 31, 1877, Approved Claim of Edward Whitehurst, SCC.

126. Testimony of Edward Whitehurst, Emanuel Savage, and Cyrus Johnson, July 31, 1877, in Approved Claim of Edward Whitehurst, SCC. For another similar case, see Penningroth, *Claims of Kinfolk*, 1–5.

127. Charles P. Day to Bro. Whiting, August [22?], 1862, AMA-VA.

128. John Oliver to Mr. S. S. Jocelyn, September [?], 1862, AMA-VA.

129. Maj. Gen. Dix to Capt. Edwin Ludlow, July 18, 1862, Letters Sent, ser. 5046, DVANC, RG 393, pt. 1; Ludlow replied two days later, on July 20, that he had rounded up 455 men. Capt. Edwin Ludlow to Maj. Gen. Dix, July 20, 1862, Letters Received, ser. 5063, DVANC, RG 393, pt. 1; Special Order 213, July 24, 1862, Letters Received, ser. 5063, DVANC, RG 393, pt. 1. On McClellan's demand for soldiers, see Gallagher, "Civil War Watershed," 16; and Waugh, *Lincoln and McClellan*, 122–23. Descriptions of the impressments in Charles Wilder to Rev. Whipple, August 31, 1862, AMA-VA (quote); and Charles P. Day to S. S. Jocelyn, August 11, 1862, and John Oliver to Mr. S. S. Jocelyn, September [?], 1862, AMA-VA. On Dix's views on slavery and emancipation, see Voegeli, "Rejected Alternative," 768–69.

130. [Unsigned letter], August 8, 1862, in "Persecution at Fortress Monroe," *Liberator*, August 22, 1862. See also George Whipple to Rev. Jocelyn, August 7, 1862, AMA-VA.

131. "Persecution at Fortress Monroe," *Liberator*, August 22, 1862.

132. Charles Wilder to George Whipple, August 31, 1862, and George Whipple to Rev. Jocelyn, August 7, 1862, AMA-VA.

133. Three hundred sixty of the 1,582 men impressed by the end of August deserted at Harrison's Landing. P. C. Pitkin Report, August 1862, Report of Persons and Articles Hired, ser. 238, file no. 701, RG 92.

134. Charles Wilder to George Whipple, September 6, 1862, AMA-VA.

135. The conventional wisdom on the Peninsula campaign's significance for emancipation holds true when it comes to policy making in Washington, D.C. Works that represent this view include Foner, *Fiery Trial*, 216–20; Blair, "Seven Days," 153–77; and Brasher, *Peninsula Campaign*, 161.

136. C. P. Day to W. E. Whiting, September 30, 1862, AMA-VA; on unpaid wages, see report of LeBaron Russell to Sec. Edwin Stanton, December 25, 1862, 10–11, AFIC Papers, HL.

137. Untitled resolutions, "Meeting of the colored people of Hampton," November 23, 1862, AMA-VA.

138. See correspondence between Dix and President Lincoln in A. Lincoln to Maj. Gen. Dix, October 26, 1862, Letters Received, ser. 12, M619, reel 130 (#1327PV-1862), RG 94. On Segar, see Foner, *Fiery Trial*, 239. Dix reported that the Unionist men sought the exemption in order to spare themselves "the stain upon their character" that came from being classified as a rebellious district, as well as the additional tax burden the Union had recently levied on "insurrectionary districts" in the Direct Tax Act of 1862.

139. Charles Wilder to Rev. Jocelyn, December 28, 1862, AMA-VA; Charles Day to Rev. Whipple, December 11, 1862, AMA-VA.

140. John Oliver to Rev. Jocelyn, January 14, 1863, AMA-VA.

141. Report of LeBaron Russell to Sec. Edwin Stanton, December 25, 1862, 8, AFIC Papers, HL.

CHAPTER 2

1. "Featured Document: The Emancipation Proclamation."

2. The Second Confiscation Act did not protect or liberate people owned by slaveholders who claimed to be "loyal" to the Union. And since those claims of loyalty were most common in the regions exempted by the Emancipation Proclamation, the Second Confiscation Act turned out to be a limited tool for liberating people in those places.

3. Article of War, March 13, 1862, in H. R. 299, 37th Cong., 2d Sess. Many historians give the March 1862 article of war only a passing reference, if they mention it at all. See, for example, Oakes, *Freedom National*, 189; and Gerteis, *From Contraband to Freedman*, 22. An exception is Eric Foner, in *Fiery Trial*, 195–96, 215–17, who argues that it "publicly made the eventual end of slavery a national goal, and claimed a new national authority to promote it" (196).

4. My thinking about cultural landscapes is informed by Lefebvre, *Production of Space*, 26; Schein, *Landscape and Race*, esp. chap. 1; Crang, *Cultural Geography*; Megan Kate Nelson, *Ruin Nation*; and Isaac, *Transformation of Virginia*, 13; and about the specific cultural landscapes of slavery and freedom, by Lipsitz, "Racialization of Space," 10–23; LaRoche, *Free Black Communities*; Camp, *Closer to Freedom*, esp. chaps. 1, 4; Vlach, *Back of the Big House*, esp. chaps. 1, 11; and Ellis and Ginsburg, *Cabin, Quarter, Plantation*.

5. Special Order No. 2, by order of General Lorenzo Thomas, February 4, 1864, Generals' Papers: Lorenzo Thomas, ser. 159, Special Orders and Appointments, RG 94.

6. General John A. Dix to [?] Corcoran, November 26, 1862, Letters Sent, vol. -/3, ser. 5046, DVANC, RG 393, pt. 1.

7. This qualifies the findings of Michele Landis Dauber, who has argued that the Freedmen's Bureau's establishment in 1865 marked this precedent-setting moment. Still, as Dauber rightly points out, there was something exceptional about the outpouring of relief during a moment of national crisis in the 1860s, for African Americans still had a far more difficult time being seen as "blameless" by federal authorities in the decades that followed. On the early origins of federal humanitarian relief, see Dauber, *Sympathetic State*, esp. 1–43, 275n64. See also Shire, "Turning Sufferers into Settlers," 490.

8. Col. John Eaton Testimony, April 29, 1863, AFIC Records, Letters Received, ser. 12, reel 200, RG 94.

9. Witt, *Lincoln's Code*, 3–8, 197–219; see also Dilbeck, *More Civil War*. All of this should caution historians away from assuming that the military reflexively disregarded the welfare of refugees and "did not provide ex-slaves with the necessities to survive." Jim Downs, *Sick from Freedom*, 4, 37–38.

10. Mark R. Wilson, "Extensive Side," 297–337.

11. *Second Annual Report of the Western Freedmen's Aid Commission*, 6; "Appeal for the Contrabands at Helena, Ark.," October 11, 1862, HL; Col. John Eaton Testimony, April 29, 1863, AFIC Records, Letters Received, ser. 12, M619, reel 200, RG 94.

12. Testimony of Captain Wills, June 1864, *Report of Commissioners of Investigation of Colored Refugees in Kentucky, Tennessee, and Alabama*, 5.

13. Col. John Eaton Testimony, April 29, 1863, AFIC Records, Letters Received, ser. 12, M619, reel 200, RG 94.

14. John Oliver to Rev. Jocelyn, November 3, 1862, AMA-VA; see also *Africans in Fort Monroe Military District*, 6.

15. *Second Annual Report of the New England Freedmen's Aid Society*, 38; *Report of a Committee*, 5.

16. *Report of Indiana Yearly Meeting's Executive Committee*, 57.

17. Testimony of Captain Wills, June 1864, *Report of Commissioners of Investigation of Colored Refugees in Kentucky, Tennessee, and Alabama*, 5.

18. C. P. Day to Rev. Jocelyn, September 30, 1862, AMA-VA.

19. Megan Kate Nelson, *Ruin Nation*, 122–23; Dean E. Nelson, "'Right Nice Little House[s],'" 178–79.

20. "The Freed People in Virginia," *Friends Review*, October 4, 1862.

21. *Revised United States Army Regulations*, 74–77; see also Geier, Orr, and Reeves, *Huts and History*, 11.

22. *Report of a Committee*, 5.

23. Report of Samuel Shipley in Friends Association of Philadelphia, *Statistics of the Operations*, 12; Brig. Gen. Buford to Capt. D. P. Allen, October 12, 1863, Letters Sent, vol. 37/96, ser. 4664, DEA, RG 393, pt. 2.

24. Maria Mann to Aunt Mary, [February?], April 7, 1863, and Maria Mann to Elisa, February 10, 1863, Mann Papers, LC.

25. On the more widespread correlation between land elevation and race in the South, particularly in and around its urban centers, see John Kellogg's study of Atlanta and Richmond in "Negro Urban Clusters," 310–21.

26. On the soldiers' pursuit of higher ground, see Whitehorne, "Blueprint for Nineteenth-Century Camps," 30; and Balicki, "'Masterly Inactivity,'" 114.

27. On the ways in which the natural world has been exploited in the process of "naturalizing" racial difference, see Brahinsky, Sasser, and Minkoff-Zern, "Race, Space, and Nature."

28. Report extracts, December 24, 1863, minute book 1, ser. 13: Women's Aid Committee, FFAR, FHL.

29. Special Order No. 2, by order of General Lorenzo Thomas, February 4, 1864, Special Orders and Appointments, ser. 159, Generals' Papers: Lorenzo Thomas, RG 94.

30. General John A. Dix to Capt. G. Tallmadge, July 7, 1862, Letters Sent, vol. -/3, ser. 5046, DVANC, RG 393, pt. 1.

31. Megan Kate Nelson, *Ruin Nation*, 104; Dean E. Nelson, "'Right Nice Little House[s],'" 180.

32. Friends Association of Philadelphia, *Statistics of the Operations*, 15.

33. *Extracts from Reports of the Superintendents of Freedmen*, 11.

34. William P. Moffatt to Rev. Whipple, February 22, 1864, AMA-VA.

35. A. D. Olds to AFIC, August 20, 1863, box 2, AFIC Papers, HL; Friends Association of Philadelphia, *Statistics of the Operations*, 20; Berlin et al., *Wartime Genesis: Upper South*, 476.

36. Lorenzo Thomas to E. D. Townsend, July 30, 1864, Orders and Letters Sent, July 1864–April 1865, ser. 159, Generals' Papers: Lorenzo Thomas, RG 94; Maria Mann to Aunt Mary, April 7, 1863, Mann Papers, LC. See also "Appeal for the Contrabands at Helena, Ark.," October 11, 1862, HL.

37. Vlach, *Back of the Big House*, 21.

38. Lewis C. Lockwood to Brethren, April 15, 1862, AMA-VA; *Second Annual Report of the Western Freedmen's Aid Commission*, 42; "Coloured Freedmen," *Friend*, October 3, 1863.

39. *Report of Commissioners of Investigation of Colored Refugees in Kentucky, Tennessee, and Alabama*, 10.

40. Kerber, *Women of the Republic*, 8–12; Gunderson, "Independence, Citizenship"; Fraser and Gordon, "Genealogy of Dependency," 315.

41. *Report of Commissioners of Investigation of Colored Refugees in Kentucky, Tennessee, and Alabama*, 20.

42. *Freedmen's Bulletin*, July 1864, 4.

43. William D. Whipple, Assistant Adjutant General, to Capt. G. Tallmadge, April 1, 1862, Letters Sent, ser. 5046, DVANC, RG 393, pt. 1.

44. Lewis C. Lockwood to Brethren, April 15, 1862, AMA-VA.

45. Yeatman, *Report on the Condition*, 15; see also "The Coloured Freedmen of Yorktown, Norfolk, and Hampton," *Friend*, December 26, 1863.

46. Vlach, *Back of the Big House*, 165.

47. "The Coloured Freedmen of Yorktown, Norfolk, and Hampton," *Friend*, December 26, 1863; Friends Association of Philadelphia, *Statistics of the Operations*, 7.

48. "The Coloured Freedmen of Yorktown, Norfolk, and Hampton," *Friend*, December 26, 1863.

49. Examples of "town" and "village" throughout this chapter; "colony" discussed in Eaton, *Report of the General Superintendent*, 41.

50. "Uniontown Near Suffolk, Corporal Sykes," May 11, 1863, AFIC Records, Letters Received, ser. 12, M619, reel 199, RG 94. W. O. King to Rev. Jocelyn, April 11, 1863, AMA-VA. See also John T. Farnham Diary, Wichita State University, Wichita, Kansas. Thank you to Bill Andrews for sharing a transcription of this diary with me.

51. Reidy, "'Coming from the Shadow,'" 403–28 (quote p. 411); "The Freedman's Settlement at Arlington," *Liberator*, January 1, 1863; "A Freedmen's Village," *Liberator*, August 5, 1864.

52. On Mitchelville, see "Gen. Mitchel on the 'Freedmen,'" *American Missionary*, December 1862; Byrd with DeAngelis, "Tracing Transformations"; and Tetzlaff, "Mitchelville."

53. "Whitall" was John M. Whitall, and "Shipley" was Samuel Shipley, both Quakers from Philadelphia who were heavily involved in refugee affairs during the war. "Abstract of the Report of the Sub-Committee Which Visited the Freedman's Settlements in South Eastern Virginia," *Freedmen's Friend*, December 1864, FHL; "Abstract of the Census Taken Lately at Acreville and Neighborhood by Our Teachers There," *Freedmen's Friend*, April 1865, FHL.

54. John T. Farnham Diary, March 11, 1863, Wichita State University, Wichita, Kansas. The AMA attributed the camp to Sikes's vision in W. O. King to Rev. Jocelyn, April 11, 1862, AMA-VA. Note: Sikes's name is spelled alternatively "Sykes" and "Sikes" in the records. Freetown discussed in Thomas Jackson to Rev. Jocelyn, Rolleston, August 27, 1863, and Newtown in Ellen Benton to Rev. S. S. Jocelyn, Tyler House, December [?], 1863, both in AMA-VA.

55. On the more general association made by Northerners, especially Northern Republican politicians, between reworking the Southern social order and reworking its physical order and infrastructure, see Foner, *Free Soil*, 38–39.

56. *Africans in Fort Monroe Military District*, 6.

57. Major Thomas J. Newsham Report, May 31, 1863, vol. 26/46AC, ser. 245, inspection reports, 16th Army Corps, RG 393, pt. 4; Provost Marshal Daily Reports of Events, Fort Monroe, vol. 223/542, 543, 544 VaNc, ser. 5173, DVANC, RG 393, pt. 1.

58. Economic historian Gerald David Jaynes has detected a similar impulse in the eventual creation of the Freedmen's Bureau. Jaynes argues that bureau officials were influenced by the English philosopher Jeremy Bentham, who envisioned the "panopticon": an architectural form that could enable reformers to watch over students, prisoners, or residents of workhouses and ensure that their teachings were being followed. See Jaynes, *Branches without Roots*, 20–23; see also Otter, *Victorian Eye*, 109–15.

59. On the visual inspections performed by planters and overseers, and how the design of a plantation could facilitate them, see Walter Johnson's discussion of "visual mastery" in *River of Dark Dreams*, 166–68.

60. For a different, but useful, exploration of the tension between inspection and the liberal social order in Victorian Britain, see Otter, *Victorian Eye*, chap. 3.

61. See, for many other examples, Heather Andrea Williams, *Help Me to Find My People*; and Berlin and Rowland, *Families and Freedom*.

62. Col. William A. Pile Testimony, [n.d.], AFIC Records, Letters Received, ser. 12, M619, reel 201, RG 94; Eaton, *Report of the General Superintendent*, 73.

63. Dr. J. M. Cuyler to General John A. Dix, July 16, 1862, Letters Received, ser. 5063, DVANC, RG 393, pt. 1.

64. Report of LeBaron Russell to Sec. Edwin Stanton, December 25, 1862, 8, AFIC Papers, HL.

65. Humphreys, *Marrow of Tragedy*, 78–84; Jim Downs, *Sick from Freedom*, 55.

66. Yeatman, *Report on the Condition*, 3, 15.

67. For an overview of colonization, see David Brion Davis, *Problem of Slavery*, 83–125;

see Witt, *Lincoln's Code*, chap. 7, for a discussion of long-standing fears of insurrection and the ways this mitigated support for emancipation during the Civil War.

68. "Featured Document: The Emancipation Proclamation."

69. Eaton, *Report of the General Superintendent*, 73.

70. Rosen, *Terror*, 7; Hunter, *Bound in Wedlock*, 135–44; Kerber, "Republican Mother"; Jan Lewis, "Republican Wife."

71. Col. William A. Pile Testimony, [n.d.], AFIC Records, Letters Received, ser. 12, reel 201, RG 94; see also report of LeBaron Russell to Sec. Edwin Stanton, December 25, 1862, AFIC Papers, HL.

72. Col. William A. Pile Testimony, [n.d.], AFIC Records, Letters Received, ser. 12, M619, reel 201, RG 94.

73. Lipsitz, "Racialization of Space"; Hannah Rosen also refers to the home as a "key signifier of freedom" in *Terror*, 190.

74. Lucy Chase report from Norfolk, December 24, 1863, minute book 1, ser. 13: Women's Aid Committee, FFAR, FHL.

75. Vlach, *Back of the Big House*, 5–14, 228 (quote p. 14); see also Lipsitz, "Racialization of Space," 14; Isaac, *Transformation of Virginia*, 32–42; Camp, *Closer to Freedom*, 7; and Fett, *Working Cures*, 56, 85, 197.

76. C. P. Day to Rev. S. S. Jocelyn, August 11, 1862, AMA-VA.

77. On the reconstruction of families during emancipation, see Heather Andrea Williams, *Help Me to Find My People*; Saville, *Work of Reconstruction*, 107–10; and Berlin and Rowland, *Families and Freedom*.

78. Figures determined by taking the 1860 population total for slave and free black people in each city and subtracting it from army estimates of the total black population in those cities in 1864. Ancestry.com, *1860 United States Federal Census*, Population and Slave Schedules; "Some Figures," *Freedmen's Bulletin*, September 1864; *Third Report of a Committee*, 9.

79. Reidy, "'Coming from the Shadow,'" 414.

80. Eaton, *Report of the General Superintendent*, 17; Yeatman, *Report on the Condition*, 4.

81. See Megan Kate Nelson, *Ruin Nation*, chap. 1.

82. "Report of a Committee on Freedmen to Friends' Board of Control, Representing the Associated Yearly Meetings of the West, for the Relief of Freedmen," January 10, 1865, in *Friends Review*, April 29, 1865; on housing in Nashville, see Cimprich, *Slavery's End in Tennessee*, 46–47.

83. Prof. Woodbury to Friend Whipple, December 2, 1863, AMA-VA.

84. See the discussion of "garrisoned towns" in Ash, *When the Yankees Came*, 76–107; on physical security as a reason to migrate into cities in the postwar period, see Emberton, *Beyond Redemption*, 76–81.

85. Rosen, *Terror*, 35; Hahn, *Nation under Our Feet*, 119–20.

86. Susan Drummond to Mr. Jocelyn, January 1, 1864, AMA-VA.

87. H. L. Beals to Rev. Whipple, March 3, 1864, AMA-VA.

CHAPTER 3

1. Andrew Johnson Testimony, November 23, 1863, AFIC Records, Letters Received, ser. 12, M619, reel 201, RG 94.

2. The result was a distinctly militarized chapter in the larger history of how race

relations assumed spatial forms in the United States, ranging from plantation landscapes to Jim Crow segregation and redlining in the twentieth century. My thinking about race and space has been influenced by Kobayashi, "Critical 'Race' Approaches"; Schein, *Landscape and Race*, esp. chap. 1; Lipsitz, "The Racialization of Space"; Schwalm, *Emancipation's Diaspora*, 82–85; LaRoche, *Free Black Communities*; Camp, *Closer to Freedom*, esp. chaps. 1, 4; and Vlach, *Back of the Big House*, esp. chaps. 1, 11.

3. It is worth noting that the army officer charged with overseeing the removal of the Cherokee in the 1830s was John E. Wool, the commander at Fort Monroe in 1862 during the controversy over nonpayment of black laborers' wages; see Hauptman, "General John E. Wool." I point out these resonances between the Native and refugee removals to highlight yet another interconnection between the Civil War in the East and the contestations over labor, citizenship, and federal authority in the West in the nineteenth century. Overviews of this rapidly expanding literature include Stacey L. Smith, "Beyond North and South"; and Arenson and Graybill, *Civil War Wests*.

4. Brahinsky, Sasser, and Minkoff-Zern, "Race, Space, and Nature."

5. T. A. Walker Report, *Extracts from Reports of the Superintendents of Freedmen*, 24.

6. Yeatman, *Report on the Condition*, 14.

7. John T. Farnham Diary, March 25, April 7, 1863, Wichita State University, Wichita, Kansas; Compiled Census Data, *1860 United States Federal Census*, Monroe County, New York.

8. This extended the objectification of women's bodies that was endemic to slavery. See, for example, Camp, "Pleasures of Resistance"; and Jennifer Morgan, "'Some Could Suckle.'"

9. George Whipple to Rev. S. S. Jocelyn, August 7, 1862, AMA-VA.

10. Charles E. Brown Report, January 14, 1863, Letters Received, ser. 5063, DVANC, RG 393, pt. 1.

11. R. W. Smith to Rev. Jocelyn, September 28, 1863, AMA-VA; C. P. Day to Rev. Jocelyn, August 11, 1863, AFIC Papers, HL; Colonel John Eaton Testimony April 29, 1863, AFIC Records, Letters Received, ser. 12, M619, reel 200, RG 94.

12. Cannon, *Personal Reminiscences*, 54; on race and rape in the Civil War, see Barber and Ritter, "'Physical Abuse'"; and Feimster, "Rape and Justice." On the particularly acute threat of rape faced by black women in particular, see Fellman, *Inside War*, 210–14; and Litwack, *Been in the Storm*, 129–30.

13. T. P. Jackson to Rev. Whipple, March 28, 1863, AMA-VA; Charles E. Brown Report, January 14, 1863, Letters Received, ser. 5063, DVANC, RG 393, pt. 1. Related discussion of the violation of domestic spaces of freedom-seeking people in Rosen, *Terror*, 190–91.

14. Rosen, *Terror*, 190–91.

15. On black women's sexuality in the white imagination, see Deborah Gray White, *Ar'n't I a Woman*; and Jennifer Morgan, *Laboring Women*.

16. *Minutes of the First Annual Meeting of the Northwestern Freedmen's Aid Commission*, 10.

17. On race and sex in the postemancipation period, see, for example, Feimster, *Southern Horrors*; Hodes, *White Women*; Rosen, *Terror*; and Sommerville, *Rape and Race*.

18. General John A. Dix Testimony, May 5, 1863, AFIC Records, Letters Received, ser. 12, M619, reel 200, RG 94.

19. Colonel John Eaton Testimony, April 29, 1863, AFIC Records, Letters Received, ser. 12, M619, reel 200, RG 94.

20. Maj. Gen. John A. Dix to Hon. Edwin Stanton, December 13, 1862, Letters Sent, vol. -/3, ser. 5046, DVANC, RG 393, pt. 1.

21. Brig. Gen. Michael Corcoran to Maj. Gen. John Dix, November 26, 1862, Letters Received, ser. 5063, DVANC, RG 393, pt. 1.

22. Dix acknowledged that troops "turned them out of their houses which they have built themselves," in Maj. Gen. John Dix to Brig. Gen. Michael Corcoran, November 26, 1862, Letters Sent, vol. -/3, ser. 5046, DVANC, RG 393, pt. 1; report of LeBaron Russell to Sec. Edwin Stanton, December 25, 1862, AFIC Papers, HL.

23. Twenty-eight thousand is a conservative estimate, since population figures were not available for all of the islands. This estimate is based on the totals for the Sea Islands of South Carolina compiled by the Freedmen and Southern Society Project (16,000), along with my own compilation of the largest known population totals for every other island, as noted in military and missionary records (12,761). Berlin et al., *Wartime Genesis: Lower South*, 99.

24. Dix quoted in *Report of a Committee*, 11.

25. Col. Samuel Thomas quoted in Eaton, *Report of the General Superintendent*, 11.

26. Brig. Gen. Buford to Capt. T. H. Harris, November 19, 1863, Letters Sent, vol. 37/96, ser. 4664, DEA, RG 393, pt. 2.

27. Yeatman, *Report on the Condition*, 2.

28. Brig. Gen. Buford to Captain Holebaugh, December 30, 1863, Letters Sent, vol. 37/96, ser. 4664, DEA, RG 393, pt. 2.

29. Special Orders No. 33, by order of Brig. Gen. Buford, October 26, 1863, Special Orders, vol. 42/109 DArk, ser. 4686, DEA, RG 393, pt. 2.

30. Special Orders No. 262, by order of Brig. Gen. Buford, October 3, 1864, Special Orders, vol. 42/109 DArk, ser. 4686, DEA, RG 393, pt. 2.

31. "Brutal Treatment of Slaves by Gen. Corcoran," *Liberator*, December 26, 1862.

32. John Oliver to Rev. Jocelyn, November 25, 1862, AMA-VA.

33. Report of LeBaron Russell to Sec. Edwin Stanton, December 25, 1862, AFIC Papers, HL.

34. Brig. Gen. Michael Corcoran to Maj. Gen. John A. Dix, November 26, 1862, Letters Received, ser. 5063, DVANC, RG 393, pt. 1.

35. *Report of a Committee*, 15.

36. Maj. Gen. John A. Dix to Hon. Edwin Stanton, December 13, 1862, Letters Sent, vol. -/3, ser. 5046, DVANC, RG 393, pt. 1.

37. See Rediker, *Outlaws of the Atlantic*, 13–14; and Klebaner, "Public Poor Relief."

38. "Report of the Women's Aid Association of Friends for the Relief of Coloured Refugees," *Friend*, October 24, 1863.

39. "Brutal Treatment of Slaves by Gen. Corcoran," republished in *Liberator*, December 26, 1862.

40. Russell worked with the Boston Educational Commission for Freedmen, later the New England Freedmen's Aid Society. Report of LeBaron Russell to Sec. Edwin Stanton, December 25, 1862, AFIC Papers, HL.

41. W. O. King to Rev. Jocelyn, April 11, 1863, AMA-VA.

42. Brig. Gen. Buford to Captain Holebaugh, December 30, 1863, Letters Sent, vol. 37/96, ser. 4664, DEA, RG 393, pt. 2.

43. Brig. Gen. [Buford?] to Capt. Kincaid, November 25, 1863, Letters Sent, vol. 37/96, ser. 4664, DEA, RG 393, pt. 2; Special Orders No. 109, by order of Brig. Gen. Buford, April 24, 1864, Special Orders, vol. 42/109 DArk, ser. 4686, DEA, RG 393, pt. 2.

44. Brig. Gen. Buford to Captain Holebaugh, December 30, 1863, Letters Sent, vol. 37/96, ser. 4664, DEA, RG 393, pt. 2.

45. Eaton, *Report of the General Superintendent*, 24–25.

46. *Freedmen's Bulletin*, July 1864, 5.

47. Lorenzo Thomas to Edwin Stanton, September 14, 1864, Orders and Letters Sent, ser. 159, Generals' Papers: Lorenzo Thomas, RG 94.

48. "Letter from Samuel R. Shipley," *Friends Review*, January 30, 1864.

49. *Second Annual Report of the Western Freedmen's Aid Commission*, 42.

50. Report of Henry Sweeney, *Freedmen's Bulletin*, April 1, 1865; Megan Kate Nelson observes a similar outcome following tree removal in *Ruin Nation*, 113.

51. John Eaton to Gen. S. D. Webster, [May ?, 1863], Mississippi Pre-Bureau Records, M1914, reel 1, BRFAL; D. O. McCord, Medical Director, to Col. John Eaton Jr., Memphis, July [?], 1865, Mississippi Pre-Bureau Records, M1914, reel 1, BRFAL.

52. "From our Superintendent of Schools," *Freedmen's Bulletin*, July 1864.

53. C. B. Wilder to [?], March 31, 1862, AMA-VA.

54. J. & Sarah Smith to Samuel Shipley, April 28, 1864, in *Freedmen's Friend*, June 1864, FIIL.

55. C. P. Day Testimony, August 11, 1863, AFIC Papers, HL.

56. Ancestry.com, *1860 United States Federal Census*, Giles County, Tennessee; "From Nashville," *Freedmen's Bulletin*, March 1865; Lt. James B. Nesbitt to Brvt. Maj. Genl. Fisk, December 16, 1865, in Berlin et al., *Wartime Genesis: Upper South*, 475–76.

57. See *Extracts from Reports of the Superintendents of Freedmen*, 46; Berlin et al., *Wartime Genesis: Upper South*, 199–200; and *Second Annual Report of the Western Freedmen's Aid Commission*, 29.

58. John Eaton to George Whipple, February 26, 1863, quoted in Walker, "Corinth," 8; Rev. Carruthers Report to Brethren, December 1863, quoted in Walker, "Corinth," 19; see also D. O. McCord Report, *Extracts from Reports of the Superintendents of Freedmen*, 41.

59. George N. Greene to Bro. Jocelyn, June 24, 1863, AMA-VA; "Uniontown Near Suffolk, Corporal Sykes," [n.d.], AFIC Records, Letters Received, ser. 12, M619, reel 199, RG 94.

60. Schwalm, *Emancipation's Diaspora*, esp. 74–80 (estimate pp. 2, 46); Romeo, *Gender and the Jubilee*, 32–38; descriptions of Northern removals from the Mississippi Valley include Brig. Gen. Buford to Lt. Col. H. Binmore, October 10, 1863, Letters Sent, ser. 4664, DEA, RG 393, pt. 2; and Special Orders No. 19, by order of Brig. Gen. Prentiss, March 3, 1863, and Special Orders No. 27, by order of Brig. Gen. Prentiss, March 11, 1863, both in Special Orders, ser. 4686, DEA, RG 393, pt. 2.

61. Brig. Gen. Buford to Lt. Col. H. Binmore, October 10, 1863, Letters Sent, ser. 4664, DEA, RG 393, pt. 2; Voegeli, "Rejected Alternative," 772.

62. Gen. John Dix to Secretary of War Stanton, September 12, 1862, and Gen. John Dix to Gov. Morgan, September 23, 1862, Letters Sent, ser. 5046, DVANC, RG 393, pt. 1; Asst. Secretary of War Watson to Gen. John Dix, September 19, 1862, ser. 159, Generals' Papers: John A. Dix, RG 94; see also Voegeli, "Rejected Alternative," 766–68.

63. Governor Andrew to Maj. John A. Bolles, A. D. C., October 16, 1862, Letters Received, ser. 5063, DVANC, RG 393, pt. 1; Voegeli, "Rejected Alternative," 770–71.

64. Rev. W. S. Bell to Rev. S. S. Jocelyn, September 5, 1863, AMA-VA.

65. Appeal of the Contraband Relief Commission, December 9, 1862, enclosed in

W. H. Ladd to Sec. Stanton, December 29, 1862, Letters Received, ser. 12, M619, reel 114, RG 94.

66. Jefferson, "Notes on the State of Virginia," 49–50.

67. See Valencius, *Health of the Country*, 236–37; Jordan, *White over Black*, 261; and Fredrickson, *Black Image*, 71.

68. "Henry Ward Beecher on the War and Negro Catching," *Liberator*, July 19, 1861. See also Schwalm, *Emancipation's Diaspora*, 82–106; see discussion of "isothermalism" in Neely, "Colonization and the Myth," 64–65.

69. Voegeli, "Rejected Alternative," 769–70, 777–78.

70. Schwalm, *Emancipation's Diaspora*, 76; [unsigned, likely Brig. Gen. Buford] to Maj. Gen. Steele, November 18, 1863, Letters Sent, ser. 4664, DEA, RG 393, pt. 2; Maj. General Hurlbut to Brig. Gen. Buford, October 14, 1863, General and Special Orders Received, ser. 4687, DEA, RG 393, pt. 2. See also Manning, *Troubled Refuge*, 113–14.

71. Voegeli, "Rejected Alternative," 773; "The Rights of Colored Citizens," *Friends Review*, March 7, 1863; Schwalm, *Emancipation's Diaspora*, 102–4.

72. Voegeli, "Rejected Alternative," 789.

73. Historians acknowledge that white Northerners supported colonization for varying reasons during the war, although most see it as an attempt to make emancipation palatable politically. However, from the vantage point of the refugee camps, it becomes evident that colonization was valued for its military purpose too: for separating refugees and white soldiers and depopulating the overpopulated places. Mark Neely similarly disputes the notion that colonization was primarily a tactic utilized by Northern Republicans to make emancipation acceptable politically. See Neely, "Colonization and the Myth," 45–74. On wartime colonization efforts generally, see Magness and Page, *Colonization after Emancipation*; Oakes, *Freedom National*, 277–82; and Louis P. Masur, *Lincoln's Hundred Days*, 88–91. Various colonization schemes are discussed in "The Freed-People of the South," *Friends Review*, April 5, 1862, 488–89; and Charles Wilder to Brethren, October 24, 1862, AMA-VA.

74. "The Vexed Question of Living Contraband Articles of War," *Pine and Palm*, June 8, 1861; see also "The Regeneration of Virginia," *Pine and Palm*, July 27, 1861; [untitled], *Liberator*, June 14, 1861; Montgomery Blair to Benjamin Butler, June 7, 1861, Butler Papers, LC; on the colonization-loving Blair family, see Neely, "Colonization and the Myth," 57.

75. Oakes, *Freedom National*, 280; Neely, "Colonization and the Myth," 62–65.

76. Neely, "Colonization and the Myth," 48–53 (quote p. 53); "Postmaster General Blair and Frederick Douglass," *Douglass Monthly*, October 1862, 724–25.

77. Lewis Lockwood to Brethren, April 11, 15, 17, 1862, AMA-VA.

78. Petition of Île à Vache Settlers, January 28, 1864, Records Related to the Suppression of the African Slave Trade and Negro Colonization, M160, Records of the Office of the Secretary of the Interior, Record Group 48, NARA. Thank you to Joan Charles for sharing a transcription of this petition with me. Charles Wilder to Mr. Whiting, March 26, 1863, Thomas Peake to Bro., March 26, 1863, and Palmer Letts to Mr. Whiting, March 24, 1863, AMA-VA; Oakes, *Freedom National*, 279–81.

79. Petition of Île à Vache Settlers, January 28, 1864, Records Related to the Suppression of the African Slave Trade and Negro Colonization, M160, Records of the Office of the Secretary of the Interior, Record Group 48, NARA; report of William Evans Jr. and J. Wistar Evans, *Freedmen's Friend*, June 1864, FHL; Abraham Lincoln to Edwin Stanton, February 3, 1864, ser. 225, CCF: "Vache Island," RG 92.

80. Benjamin Butler to Lewis Tappan, August 10, 1861, AMA-VA.

81. Lewis Lockwood to Brethren, April 17, 1862, AMA-VA; "The Slaves in Virginia," *Friends Review*, July 12, 1862; "The Rights of Colored Citizens," *Friends Review*, March 7, 1863.

82. Horace James to AFIC, November 13, 1863, AFIC Papers, HL.

83. "The Slaves in Virginia," *Friends Review*, July 12, 1862.

84. See Carole Emberton's discussion of the meaning of the "home place" to the enslaved and ex-slaves in "Household and Home Place." Thank you to Carole Emberton for providing me with a copy of this chapter.

ELIZA BOGAN IN SLAVERY

1. Deposition of Eliza Bogan, March 9, 1892, in Dennis Bogan File, Co. E, 46th USCT, WA 549935, WC 458509, CWPF. Eliza first appears in the historical record as "Eliza Bogan," a last name she acquired by marriage after the war. Since no conclusive evidence exists of the last name(s) she used before and during the war, I will use "Bogan" throughout this book to refer to her.

2. Ancestry.com, *1820 United States Federal Census*, Chowan County, North Carolina. A note about spelling: The name "McKiel" or "McKeal" is spelled variously in the records. For the enslaved on the property who had that last name, it is generally spelled "McKeal" (or in one case, "McKeel"), while Josiah McKiel's name is usually spelled "McKiel." It is not clear if these spellings reflect the intentions of those named, but I have taken the records as my guide and will continue to spell their names in these different ways throughout this book.

3. See Heather Andrea Williams's discussion of the family separations wrought by planter migrations and the slave trade in *Help Me to Find My People*, chaps. 1–2, including a case of another Chowan County migration to the cotton South, 70–77. Eliza Bogan's listing in the 1920 census lists "Africa" as the birthplace of both her parents. Ancestry.com, *1920 United States Federal Census*, Phillips County, Arkansas.

4. Howerton, *Legislative Manual*, 197.

5. Records related to *State v. Josiah McKiel* in Chowan County Slave Records, 1829, Chowan County Minute Docket, Superior Court Records, 1828–1838, North Carolina State Archives, Raleigh, North Carolina. Thank you to Rose Buchanan for her assistance in obtaining these records.

6. Jacobs, *Incidents*, was originally published in 1861.

7. That same year, McKiel also sat on the local jury that heard *State v. Mann*. In that notorious case, which drew national attention, the North Carolina Supreme Court eventually sanctioned slave owner brutality. "The power of the master must be absolute," concluded Judge Thomas Ruffin, "to render the submission of the slave perfect." See Greene, "Thomas Ruffin."

8. McKiel left for Arkansas sometime between 1830, when he was last listed in the census records for North Carolina, and 1833, when he first appeared in deed records from Phillips County, Arkansas. See Ancestry.com, *1830 United States Federal Census — Slave Schedules*, Chowan County, North Carolina; property deed, February 22, 1837, book D, p. 446, Property Deed Records, Phillips County Circuit Court Clerk's Office, Helena, Arkansas; "Great Bargains for Planters," *Southern Shield*, January 5, 1850. On the booming cotton economy in the early to mid-1830s, see Baptist, *Half Has Never Been Told*, 215–59.

9. Description of the landscape in Joseph R. Edwards to Sister Mary, July 31, 1863, in Sarna, "Civil War and Reconstruction," 3–4; Pope, "Helena, Arkansas."

10. On McKiel's financial tribulations—and rebound—in the 1830s, see "McKiel et al. vs. the Real Estate Bank," 92–595; Real Estate Tax Assessment Record Book, 1860, 63, Phillips County Circuit Court Clerk's Office, Helena, Arkansas.

11. Descriptions of Helena from "Planters Hotel," *Southern Shield*, March 2, 1850; "Negroes for Sale," *Southern Shield*, February 8, 1851; Ancestry.com, *1850 United States Federal Census*, and *1860 United States Federal Census—Slave Schedules*, Phillips County, Arkansas.

12. McKiel would later be described as a "pioneer" in the region in an 1890 history. He was appointed postmaster in 1833, and he also became a member of a railroad convention held to advocate for the extension of the Fulton & Cairo Railroad in 1853. *Biographical and Historical Memoirs of Eastern Arkansas*, 744–45; Petition to the Postmaster General by Citizens of Phillips County, February 25, 1833, in *Territory of Arkansas Territory*, 691–93; "Proceedings of the Railroad Convention," *Southern Shield*, July 30, 1853.

13. Baptist, *Half Has Never Been Told*, 111–44; see also Johnson, *River of Dark Dreams*, 244.

14. A discussion of McKiel's decision not to have an overseer in Deposition of Nancy Washington, October 4, 1900, in Silas Small File, Co. E, 46th USCT, WC 393571, WC 509810, Mother's Application No. 546042, CWPF.

15. Kolchin, *Unfree Labor*, 137.

16. Deposition of Eliza Bogan, May 3, 1900, in Dennis Bogan File, Co. E, 46th USCT, WA 549935, WC 458509, CWPF.

17. Estimates range from 1857 to 1861 for the departure date of Isom Patterson. On Eliza's first two marriages, see Deposition of Eliza Bogan, May 3, 1900, in Dennis Bogan File, Co. E, 46th USCT, WA 549935, WC 458509, CWPF; and Deposition of Frank McKeal, October 4, 1900, and Deposition of Nancy Washington, October 4, 1900, in Silas Small File, Co. E, 46th USCT, WC 393571, WC 509810, Mother's Application No. 546042, CWPF.

18. Deposition of Eliza Bogan, May 3, 1900, in Dennis Bogan File, Co. E, 46th USCT, WA 549935, WC 458509, CWPF.

19. Eliza Bogan's succession of marriages was not an uncommon pattern in the family lives of enslaved people, who repeatedly confronted separation and death. Hunter, *Bound in Wedlock*, 33.

20. On the Eliza-Hester-Nancy connection, see Deposition of Hester McKeal, October 4, 1900, and Deposition of Nancy Washington, October 4, 1900, in Silas Small File, Co. E, 46th USCT, WC 393571, WC 509810, Mother's Application No. 546042, CWPF.

21. Steele and Bogan listed in Ancestry.com, *1860 United States Federal Census—Slave Schedules*, Phillips County, Arkansas; Sullivan listed in Real Estate Tax Assessment Record Book, 1860, 65, Phillips County Circuit Court Clerk's Office, Helena, Arkansas.

22. Ancestry.com, *1860 United States Federal Census—Slave Schedules*, Phillips County, Arkansas.

23. Deposition of Anna Banks, March 9, 1892, in Silas Small File, Co. E, 46th USCT, WC 393571, WC 509810, Mother's Application No. 546042, CWPF.

24. Deposition of Indiana Kelly, May 4, 1900, in Silas Small File, Co. E, 46th USCT, WC 393571, WC 509810, Mother's Application No. 546042, CWPF.

25. Silas Small, Co. E, 46th USCT, CMSR, lists his birth in Green County, Alabama, in 1843; Deposition of Indiana Kelly, May 4, 1900, in Silas Small File, Co. E, 46th USCT, WC 393571, WC 509810, Mother's Application No. 546042, CWPF; Jerry Steele, Co. E, 46th

USCT, CMSR; Deposition of Guilford Sullivan, May 19, 1902, in Jerry Steele File, Co. E, 46th USCT, IA 495951, IC 1045368, WA 627839, WC 536377, CWPF.

26. On the function and meaning of slave neighborhoods, see Kaye, *Joining Places*.

27. Deposition of Jere [Jerry] Steele, March 10, 1892, in Dennis Bogan File, Co. E, 46th USCT, WA 549935, WC 458509, CWPF.

28. Deposition of Frank McKeal, October 4, 1900, in Silas Small File, Co. E, 46th USCT, WC 393571, WC 509810, Mother's Application No. 546042, CWPF.

29. "When ever any of Judge McKeal's house servants got married he always said the marriage ceremony for them," Eliza's niece, Nancy Washington, later explained of the slave owner's marriage practices, but Eliza "was not a house servant she was a regular cotton field hand." Deposition of Nancy Washington, October 4, 1900, and Deposition of Eliza Bogan, February 27, 1901, in Silas Small File, Co. E, 46th USCT, WC 393571, WC 509810, Mother's Application No. 546042, CWPF; Deposition of Eliza Bogan, May 3, 1900, in Dennis Bogan File, Co. E, 46th USCT, WA 549935, WC 458509, CWPF.

30. Deposition of Eliza Bogan, March 9, 1892, in Dennis Bogan File, Co. E, 46th USCT, WA 549935, WC 458509, CWPF.

31. Deposition of Eliza Bogan, March 9, 1892, in Dennis Bogan File, Co. E, 46th USCT, WA 549935, WC 458509, CWPF.

32. On the legalities of enslaved marriage — or the lack thereof — see Heather Andrea Williams, *Help Me to Find My People*, 49–52; and Hunter, *Bound in Wedlock*, 61–85 (discussion of the term "slave marriage," 8).

CHAPTER 4

1. Brent and Brent, *Civil War Helena*, 12–14; on the labor of the three men, see Deposition of Guilford Sullivan, May 19, 1902, in Jerry Steele File, Co. E, 46th USCT, IA 495951, IC 1045368, WA 627839, WC 536377, CWPF; Deposition of Frank McKeal, October 4, 1900, in Silas Small File, Co. E, 46th USCT, WC 393571, WC 509810, Mother's Application No. 546042, CWPF. On the arrival of the Union army in Helena, see Moneyhon, "Civil War in Phillips County," 23–25.

2. Orders to "emancipate" at least 313 people appear in Curtis's records from March to July 1862. This number does not capture everyone, as many of the orders are listed with a man's name followed by "and family," making a precise count difficult. See orders in Special Orders, vol. 164/345 DMo, ser. 4685, District of Southwest Missouri, RG 393, pt. 2; see also Schwalm, *Emancipation's Diaspora*, 58–59.

3. Boulden, "Frederick Steele"; General Order No. 48, quoted in "Appeal for the Contrabands at Helena, Ark.," October 11, 1862, HL.

4. C. C. Washburn to Secretary of War, September 6, 1862, in Berlin et al., *Wartime Genesis: Lower South*, 665.

5. "The Slave-Catching General," *Commonwealth*, January 10, 1863.

6. Steele declared that all wages earned by laborers would be withheld, pending a determination of their former owners' loyalty. If the owner was found to be "loyal," then the wages would go to him — not to the laborer. This is exactly what Gen. John E. Wool at Fort Monroe had stopped doing one year before. Berlin et al., *Wartime Genesis: Lower South*, 629; see also "General Thomas at Helena," *Commonwealth*, April 24, 1863.

7. "Appeal for the Contrabands at Helena, Ark.," October 11, 1862, HL; "The Contrabands at Helena, Ark. AN APPEAL FOR AID," *New York Times*, November 8, 1863.

On the general deficiencies in army medical care for refugees, see Jim Downs, *Sick from Freedom*; and Schwalm, "Surviving Wartime Emancipation."

8. Deposition of Eliza Bogan, May 3, 1900, in Dennis Bogan File, Co. E, 46th USCT, WA 549935, WC 458509, CWPF; Deposition of Anna Banks, March 9, 1892, in Silas Small File, Co. E, 46th USCT, WC 393571, WC 509810, Mother's Application No. 546042, CWPF.

9. Deposition of Eliza Bogan, May 3, 1900, in Dennis Bogan File, Co. E, 46th USCT, WA 549935, WC 458509, CWPF.

10. On the complex long-term implications of military combat as the means for achieving freedom, see Emberton, *Beyond Redemption*, 102–35.

11. Steele was promoted to the rank of major general and would go on to command one of the Union divisions at Vicksburg later that year; he was replaced at Helena by Brig. Gen. Benjamin F. Prentiss. Brig. Gen. William A. Gorman to Major General Curtis, February 13, 1863, *OR*, ser. 1, vol. 2, chap. 34, p. 110; Samuel Sawyer to Brig. Gen. Buford, September 25, 1863, General and Special Orders Received and Other Records, ser. 4687, DEA, RG 393, pt. 2.

12. Maria Mann to Elisa, February 10, 1863, and Maria Mann to Aunt Mary, [n.d., likely February 1863], Mann Papers, LC.

13. Quoted in Gerteis, *From Contraband to Freedman*, 120.

14. Corinth and Grand Junction: John Eaton, Supt. of Contrabands, Dept. of Tennessee, to Asst. Adjutant Genl. Jno. A. Rawlins, April 29, 1863, AFIC Records, Letters Received, ser. 12, M619, reel 200, RG 94; Lake Providence: L. S. Livermore, Superintendent of Contrabands at Lake Providence, to Secretary of War, February 19, 1863, in Berlin et al., *Wartime Genesis: Lower South*, 680.

15. Cyrus Boyd quoted in Hess, *Civil War in the West*, 143.

16. Secretary Edwin M. Stanton to General Lorenzo Thomas, March 25, 1863, Letters Received, ser. 363, box 3, RG 94.

17. Lorenzo Thomas telegram to Secretary of War Edwin Stanton, April 6, 1863, Orders and Letters Sent, ser. 159, Generals' Papers: Lorenzo Thomas, RG 94.

18. William F. Allen diary, October 6, 1864, William F. Allen Papers, Wisconsin Historical Society, Madison, Wisconsin. Thank you to Joe Brent for sharing a copy of this diary with me.

19. Secretary Edwin M. Stanton to General Lorenzo Thomas, March 25, 1863, Letters Received, ser. 363, box 3, RG 94.

20. Lorenzo Thomas telegram to Secretary of War Edwin Stanton, April 6, 1863, Orders and Letters Sent, ser. 159, Generals' Papers: Lorenzo Thomas, RG 94.

21. George Flanders to My Dear Mother, April 10 1863, in Fry, *Following*, 171–72; Underhill, *Helena to Vicksburg*, 65; Minos Miller to Mother, April 10, 1863, Miller Papers, University of Arkansas Libraries, Fayetteville, Arkansas. Thanks to Joe Brent for sharing copies of these letters with me.

22. Allen diary, October 6, 1864; Lorenzo Thomas telegram to Secretary of War Edwin Stanton, April 12, 1863, Orders and Letters Sent, ser. 159, Generals' Papers: Lorenzo Thomas, RG 94.

23. See Hess, *Civil War in the West*, 143–44.

24. My emphasis on continuity qualifies some of the prevailing interpretations of military service as a transformative moment in the life of a formerly enslaved man. For discussions of the way military service established men as "community leaders," see Foner, *Forever Free*, 54; or became a "political crucible" for black men, see Hahn, *Nation under Our Feet*, 90–110 (quote p. 90); or forged a new "martial manhood" that could

simultaneously limit men's (and especially women's) progress toward full citizenship, see Emberton, *Beyond Redemption*, 104–8. I am similarly concerned with what combat meant to these men—but in this case, how it could also represent a new form of the same long-standing struggle they had always waged against their enslavers.

25. Berlin, Reidy, and Rowland, *Black Military Experience*, 117.

26. Silas Small, Co. E, 46th USCT, CMSR.

27. Deposition of Indiana Kelly, May 4, 1900, in Silas Small File, Co. E, 46th USCT, WC 393571, WC 509810, Mother's Application No. 546042, CWPF.

28. Frank McKeal (enlisted April 17), John McKeel (April 17), Jerry Steele (April 16), Dennis Bogan (April 10), and Charles Bogan (April 10), all Co. E, 46th USCT, CMSR; Lewis Bogan (April 15), Co. G, 46th USCT, CMSR.

29. Special Orders No. 58, April 13, 1863, by the order of Maj. Gen. Prentiss, vol. 42/109 DArk, Special Orders Issued, ser. 4686, DEA, RG 393, pt. 2.

30. For 1860 cotton production figures, see Baptist, *Half Has Never Been Told*, 113–16.

31. Lorenzo Thomas to Secretary of War Edwin Stanton, April 1, 1863, Orders and Letters Sent, ser. 159, Generals' Papers: Lorenzo Thomas, RG 94.

32. Gerteis, *From Contraband to Freedman*, 124.

33. Lorenzo Thomas to Secretary Stanton, April 12, 1863, Letters Received, ser. 12, M619, reel 160, RG 94.

34. In a notable departure from the "contraband fund" system utilized in the first year of the war at Fort Monroe, it was not the workers who were taxed to support nonworkers like the aged and infirm; instead, the lessees incurred a 1 percent tax on their cotton cultivation in order to subsidize these "Home Farms" and "Infirmary Farms." Gerteis, *From Contraband to Freedman*, 123–24, 141; Eaton, *Report of the General Superintendent*, 69; Yeatman, *Report on the Condition*, 7.

35. "The Labor of the Contrabands," *Friend*, February 28, 1863.

36. Quoted in Guelzo, *Lincoln's Emancipation Proclamation*, 79.

37. Lorenzo Thomas to Secretary Stanton, April 12, 1863, Letters Received, ser. 12, M619, reel 160, RG 94.

38. Louis Gerteis also makes the point that this plantation labor plan strengthened the Union militarily in *From Contraband to Freedman*, 116–23.

39. Jensen, *Patriots, Settlers*, 181–84.

40. This was evident in the French Army's actions in Algeria in the 1950s, as well as in the "strategic hamlet" program of the United States and South Vietnam during the Vietnam War. See, for example, Sutton, "Population Resettlement"; and Catton, "Counter-insurgency."

41. General Lorenzo Thomas quoted in Gerteis, *From Contraband to Freedman*, 123.

42. *Extracts from Reports of the Superintendents*, 58.

43. Though it cannot be denied that only men could enlist as soldiers and thus faced a wider and more official "martial" road to freedom, what happened in the Mississippi Valley also reveals that women, too, encountered their own "martial" paths to liberation. Leslie Schwalm likewise argues that Thomas's plan was a turning point, carving out a specific role for women in the Union war effort, in "Between Slavery and Freedom." A similar point is made forcefully in Manning, *Troubled Refuge*, 15–16, and in Hunter, *Bound in Wedlock*, 147–49. For works that argue for the distinctly masculine character of military emancipation, see Emberton, *Beyond Redemption*, esp. chap. 4; McCurry, *Confederate Reckoning*, esp. chap. 7; and Jim Downs, *Sick from Freedom*, 26.

44. Quoted in Lucy Chase Testimony, May 10, 1863, AFIC Records, Letters Received, ser. 12, M619, reel 200, RG 94.

45. Union army regulations outlawed the use of a whip, or "flogging," in August 1861, and though it continued to exist in practice, the official ban was extended to refugee policy too. See *Revised United States Army Regulations*, 499; and Adj. Gen. Lorenzo Thomas to Hon. Edwin M. Stanton, April 12, 1863, in Berlin et al., *Wartime Genesis: Lower South*, 700.

46. Eaton, *Report of the General Superintendent*, 63.

47. Of the estimated 400,000 acres, according to a March 1864 report, 166,729 acres were in the hands of lessees; the rest of the acreage remained in the control of original owners now pledging loyalty to the Union. William P. Mellen to Samuel P. Chase, March 29, 1864, in Berlin et al., *Wartime Genesis: Lower South*, 798–802.

48. Deposition of Hester McKeal, October 4, 1900, in Silas Small File, Co. E, 46th USCT, WC 393571, WC 509810, Mother's Application No. 546042, CWPF.

49. Clarksville: Thomas Nichols to James Harlan, May 9, 1863, Records of the Tennessee Assistant Commissioner, M999, reel 7, BRFAL; Corinth and Grand Junction: John Eaton to Asst. Adjutant Genl. Jno. A. Rawlins, April 29, 1863, AFIC Records, Letters Received, ser. 12, M619, reel 200, RG 94.

50. See Camp, *Closer to Freedom*, 36–38; Franklin and Schweninger, *Runaway Slaves*, 212.

51. For more on the violence inflicted on enslaved people who remained behind on plantations, see chapter 7, "Keeping Faith." On McKiel's loyalty, see "The Situation in Arkansas," *North American and United States Gazette*, August 11, 1863; Betty M. Faust, "Diary of Sue Cook," January 3, 1864, 33–34.

52. Berlin et al., *Wartime Genesis: Lower South*, 638.

53. Deposition of Inda [Indiana] Kelly, May 19, 1902, in Jerry Steele File, Co. E, 46th USCT, IA 495951, IC 1045368, WA 627839, WC 536377, CWPF; Deposition of Matilda Yount, February 27, 1901, and Deposition of Hester McKeal, October 4, 1900, in Silas Small File, Co. E, 46th USCT, WC 393571, WC 509810, Mother's Application No. 546042, CWPF.

54. Deposition of Hester McKeal, October 4, 1900, in Silas Small File, Co. E, 46th USCT, WC 393571, WC 509810, Mother's Application No. 546042, CWPF.

55. Moneyhon, "Civil War in Phillips County," 27; Gerteis, *From Contraband to Freedman*, 125.

56. Hess, *Civil War in the West*, 145–48.

57. On the movements of the First Arkansas AD, see Civil War Soldiers and Sailors System, National Park Service, Washington, D.C.; on the aims of the Confederates, see Bailey, *Between the Enemy and Texas*, 138.

58. Deposition of Eliza Bogan, March 9, 1892, in Dennis Bogan File, Co. E, 46th USCT, WA 549935, WC 458509, CWPF.

59. Maria Mann to Aunt Mary, May 18, 1863, Mann Papers, LC.

60. Christ, *Civil War Arkansas*, 122.

61. Christ, 117–21; Brent and Brent, *Civil War Helena*, 25–29.

62. General Orders No. 36, July 7, 1863, by order of Major General B. M. Prentiss, vol. 44/113 DArk, ser. 4680, General Orders Issued, DEA, RG 393, pt. 2.

63. Christ, *Civil War Arkansas*, 142–43.

64. Christ, 116.

65. Samuel Sawyer to Brig. Gen. Buford, September 25, 1863, ser. 4687, General and Special Orders Received and Other Records, DEA, RG 393, pt. 2.

66. Maria Mann to [?], [undated, sometime before July 23, 1863], Mann Papers, LC.

67. Maria Mann to [?], [undated, sometime before July 23, 1863], Mann Papers, LC.

68. Special Order No. 128, by order of Brig. Gen. L. F. Ross, July 12, 1863, vol. 42/109 DArk, ser. 4684, Special Orders, DEA, RG 393, pt. 2; Schwalm, *Emancipation's Diaspora*, 77–79; Romeo, *Gender and the Jubilee*, 32–38.

69. Maria Mann to [?], [undated, sometime before July 23, 1863], Mann Papers, LC.

70. General John P. Hawkins, quoted in Berlin et al., *Wartime Genesis: Lower South*, 635; similar sentiment in report of Samuel Shipley, in Friends Association of Philadelphia, *Statistics of the Operations*, 23.

71. Yeatman, *Report on the Condition*, 7; Berlin et al., *Wartime Genesis: Lower South*, 632; see also Bercaw, *Gendered Freedoms*, 33–40; and Gerteis, *From Contraband to Freedman*, 164–66.

72. Eaton, *Report of the General Superintendent*, 53, 55, 63.

73. Deposition of Eliza Bogan, March 9, 1892, in Dennis Bogan File, Co. E, 46th USCT, WA 549935, WC 458509, CWPF.

74. Deposition of Inda [Indiana] Kelly, May 19, 1902, in Jerry Steele File, Co. E, 46th USCT, IA 495951, IC 1045368, WA 627839, WC 536377, CWPF; Deposition of Matilda Yount, February 27, 1901, in Silas Small File, Co. E, 46th USCT, WC 393571, WC 509810, Mother's Application No. 546042, CWPF.

75. Bailey, *Between the Enemy and Texas*, 138–39; on the plantations and their acreage, see Major Julian Bryant to Captain, October 10, 1863, in Berlin et al., *Wartime Genesis: Lower South*, 735; and Barnickel, *Milliken's Bend*, 38–39.

76. Bailey, *Between the Enemy and Texas*, 139–40; Barnickel, *Milliken's Bend*, 122–24.

77. O. D. Greene, Assistant Adjutant General, to Sir, August 27, 1884, in Jerry Steele File, Co. E, 46th USCT, IA 495951, IC 1045368, WA 627839, WC 536377, CWPF.

78. Barnickel, *Milliken's Bend*.

79. Bailey, *Between the Enemy and Texas*, 139–41; Major Julian Bryant to Captain, October 10, 1863, in Berlin et al., *Wartime Genesis: Lower South*, 733; an example of the "missing in action" designation is in Charles Bogan, Co. E, 46th USCT, CMSR.

80. Berlin, Reidy, and Rowland, *Black Military Experience*, 567–68.

81. Deposition of Charles Bogan, September 20, 1881, in Charles Bogan File, Co. E, 46th USCT, IA 332003, IC 665401, CWPF.

82. Silas Small's service record is incomplete on the question of his movements, so I have relied on those of others in his company to offer a guide. Silas Small, Co. E, 46th USCT, CMSR; Deposition of John McKeel, June 10, 1891, in John McKeel File, Co. E, 46th USCT, IA 855201, CWPF; Dennis Bogan and Charles Bogan, both in Co. E, 46th USCT, CMSR; Lewis Bogan, Co. G, 46th USCT, CMSR.

83. Dennis Bogan, Co. E, 46th USCT, CMSR.

84. John McKeel, Co. E, 46th USCT, CMSR; Frank McKeal, Co. E., 46th USCT, CMSR.

85. Charles Bogan, Co. E, 46th USCT, CMSR.

86. See also Lewis Bogan, Co. G, 46th USCT, CMSR; and Jerry Steele, Co. E, 46th USCT, CMSR.

87. Inadequate Confederate security forces, both state and national, undoubtedly played a role in enabling their escape. See Lorien Foote's discussion of white Federal soldiers' escapes in South Carolina in "'They Cover the Land.'"

88. Deposition of Eliza Bogan, February 27, 1901, in Silas Small File, Co. E, 46th USCT, WC 393571, WC 509810, Mother's Application No. 546042, CWPF.

89. Deposition of Eliza Bogan, March 9, 1892, in Dennis Bogan File, Co. E, 46th USCT, WA 549935, WC 458509, CWPF.

90. Leslie Schwalm makes a similar point in *Emancipation's Diaspora*, 130–31; see Thavolia Glymph's discussion of a woman who chose the "road of war" in "Rose's War."

91. *Revised United States Army Regulations*, 24.

92. *Revised United States Army Regulations*, 38, 246; one government report referred to laundresses as "mustered"; see A. L. Mitchell Report, May 31, 1864, in *Extracts from Reports of the Superintendents*, 22.

93. Deposition of Eliza Bogan, February 27, 1901, in Silas Small File, Co. E, 46th USCT, WC 393571, WC 509810, Mother's Application No. 546042, CWPF. See another description of her work in Deposition of Matilda Yount, February 27, 1901, in Silas Small File, Co. E, 46th USCT, WC 393571, WC 509810, Mother's Application No. 546042, CWPF.

94. Schultz, *Women at the Front*, 22, 187.

95. Schultz, 56–57; on the experience of another African American laundress in a Civil War regiment, see Taylor, *Reminiscences*.

96. Regimental Books and Papers, Co. E, 46th USCT, RG 94.

97. On the rape of black women by Union and Confederate soldiers alike, see Barber and Ritter, "'Physical Abuse'"; and Fellman, *Inside War*, 210–14.

98. Circular, February 25, 1864, by order of Brig. Gen. I. F. Shepard, regimental books and papers, Co. E, 46th USCT, RG 94.

99. Deposition of Eliza Bogan, March 9, 1892, in Dennis Bogan File, Co. E, 46th USCT, WA 549935, WC 458509, CWPF.

100. The order did allow that wives of soldiers could also visit their husbands in camp with approval from the regimental commander. Circular, February 25, 1864, by order of Brig. Gen. I. F. Shepard, regimental books and papers, Co. E, 46th USCT, RG 94.

101. Sutherland, *Savage Conflict*, 265.

102. John Eaton to Levi Coffin, July 5, 1864, in *Extracts from Reports of the Superintendents*, 56.

103. E. & I. S. Beard to Samuel Shipley, April 30, 1864, in *Freedmen's Friend*, June 1864, FHL.

104. Samuel Thomas to John Eaton, June 15, 1864, in *Extracts from Reports of the Superintendents*, 26; on the conditions of captivity, see *Appeal of the Western Freedmen's Aid Commission*, 5.

105. E. & I. S. Beard to Samuel Shipley, April 30, 1864, in *Freedmen's Friend*, June 1864, FHL; report of James and Sarah Smith, April 25, 1864, in *Report of Indiana Yearly Meeting's Executive Committee*, 43.

106. *Appeal of the Western Freedmen's Aid Commission*, 5; *Report of Indiana Yearly Meeting's Executive Committee*, 26, 29.

107. Samuel Thomas to John Eaton, June 15, 1864, in *Extracts from Reports of the Superintendents*, 30.

108. *Report of Indiana Yearly Meeting's Executive Committee*, 29; "From Mrs. Newcomb," *Freedmen's Bulletin*, September 1864.

109. Friends Association of Philadelphia, *Statistics of the Operations*, 13; description of attacks in Special Order No. 91, April 2, 1864, by order of Brig. Gen. Buford, vol. 42/109

DArk, ser. 4686, Special Orders, DEA, RG 393, pt. 2; Brig. Gen. Buford to Lorenzo Thomas, April 8, 1864, Letters Received, ser. 363, RG 94.

110. Eaton, *Report of the General Superintendent*, 53.

111. John Eaton to Levi Coffin, July 5, 1864, in *Extracts from Reports of the Superintendents*, 56.

112. Brig. Gen. Buford to Major W. D. Green, March 5, 1864, Letters Sent, ser. 4664, DEA, RG 393, pt. 2.

113. Major George Yount, 63rd USCT, to Col. Eaton, May 18, 1864, in *Extracts from Reports of the Superintendents*, 7; Berlin et al., *Wartime Genesis: Lower South*, 644; on the worsening of the guerrilla situation in 1864, see Hess, *Civil War in the West*, 244.

114. Berlin et al., *Wartime Genesis: Lower South*, 644.

115. John Eaton to Levi Coffin, July 5, 1864, in *Extracts from Reports of Superintendents*, 61; see also Brig. Gen. Buford to Brig. Gen. L. Thomas, April 1, 1864, Letters Received, ser. 363, RG 94.

116. Eaton, *Report of the General Superintendent*, 57.

117. Berlin et al., *Wartime Genesis: Lower South*, 646. Black lessees occupied an estimated 7,000 of the 100,000 acres of leased land, in increments of 5 to 150 acres each. "Limit and Census of the Department," *Freedmen's Bulletin*, supplement, September 1864; Eaton, *Report of the General Superintendent*, 50–51 (quote p. 56).

118. Berlin et al., *Wartime Genesis: Lower South*, 642; Hess, *Civil War in the West*, 233.

119. Eaton, *Report of the General Superintendent*, 15; Hess, *Civil War in the West*, 212.

120. Hess, *Civil War in the West*, 236 (quote p. 244).

121. Berlin, Reidy, and Rowland, *Black Military Experience*, 519.

122. Hess, *Civil War in the West*, 234–35; Litwack, *Been in the Storm*, 90–91.

123. Brig. Gen. Buford to Major W. D. Green, March 5, 1864, Letters Sent, ser. 4664, DEA, RG 393, pt. 2.

124. *Report of Indiana Yearly Meeting's Executive Committee*, 29; A. L. Mitchell to John Eaton, May 31, 1864, in *Extracts from Reports of the Superintendents*, 21.

125. Berlin et al., *Wartime Genesis: Lower South*, 648. Population totals taken from the following: Vicksburg — *Second Annual Report of the New England Freedmen's Aid Society*, 38; Col. S. Thomas, Tri-Monthly Report of Freedmen and Employees in Freedmen Department to Draw Rations, September 1864, Mississippi Pre-Bureau Records, M1914, reel 1, BRFAL; and "Report of a Committee on Freedmen," *Friends Review*, May 6, 1865, 564; Memphis — *Second Annual Report of the New England Freedmen's Aid Society*, April 21, 1864, 37; and "Report of a Committee on Freedmen," *Friends Review*, May 6, 1865, 564; Helena — D. O. McCord Report, in *Extracts from Reports of the Superintendents*, 41; and A. R. [Gillurn?], Judge Advocate, to Col. Eaton, July 1, 1864, Letters Received, ser. 269, Department of Arkansas, RG 393, pt. 1; see also Bercaw, *Gendered Freedoms*, 40.

126. Eaton, *Report of the General Superintendent*, 24–25, 53.

127. Col. Samuel Thomas report, in Eaton, *Report of the General Superintendent*, 35.

128. Major George Young, 63rd USCT, to Col. Eaton, May 18, 1864, in *Extracts from Reports of Superintendents*, 7–8.

129. Special Order No. 75, by order of Brig. Gen. Buford, December 8, 1863, Special Orders, ser. 4686, Department of Arkansas, RG 393, pt. 2.

130. Lt. Geo. A Hanaford, Post Adjutant, to Lt. Jno. McQueen, June 10, 1864, vol. 107/254, ser. 902, Letters Sent, Camp Nelson, RG 393, pt. 4; Capt. E. F. Covell, 10th MI

Cav, to Capt. T. E. Hall, January 17, 1864, vol. 237/577, Register of Letters Received and Endorsements Sent, ser. 1661, Provost Marshal, Camp Nelson, RG 393, pt. 4. On the proliferation of gun ownership among freed people and its association with freedom and citizenship rights, see Emberton, *Beyond Redemption*, 146–53.

131. See Berlin et al., *Wartime Genesis: Lower South*, 644, on how laborers often turned down employment in places they deemed too dangerous.

132. Deposition of Eliza Bogan, February 27, 1901, in Silas Small File, Co. E, 46th USCT, WC 393571, WC 509810, Mother's Application No. 546042, CWPF.

133. A. L. Mitchell to John Eaton, May 31, 1864, in *Extracts from Reports of the Superintendents*, 21.

134. Deposition of Eliza Bogan, March 9, 1892, in Dennis Bogan File, Co. E, 46th USCT, WA 549935, WC 458509, CWPF.

135. *Appeal of the Western Freedmen's Aid Commission*, 4–5.

136. Deposition of Eliza Bogan, March 9, 1892, in Dennis Bogan File, Co. E, 46th USCT, WA 549935, WC 458509, CWPF.

137. See Schultz, *Women at the Front*, 199, 207, 209; Susie King Taylor, *Reminiscences*.

138. On African American healing practices in slavery, see Fett, *Working Cures*; and Long, *Doctoring Freedom*.

139. D. O. McCord to Col. Eaton, June 28, 1864, in *Extracts from Reports of the Superintendents*, 39–48; "Departments of Supervision," *Freedmen's Bulletin*, September 1864.

140. Deposition of Anna Banks, March 9, 1892, in Silas Small File, Co. E, 46th USCT, WC 393571, WC 509810, Mother's Application No. 546042, CWPF; Deposition of Inda [Indiana] Kelly, May 19, 1902, in Jerry Steele File, Co. E, 46th USCT, IA 495951, IC 1045368, WA 627839, WC 536377, CWPF.

141. Regimental Books and Papers, 46th USCT, RG 94; this point is also made persuasively in Jim Downs, *Sick from Freedom*.

142. Deposition of Eliza Bogan, February 27, 1901, in Silas Small File, Co. E, 46th USCT, WC 393571, WC 509810, Mother's Application No. 546042, CWPF.

143. Deposition of Matilda Yount, February 27, 1901, in Silas Small File, Co. E, 46th USCT, WC 393571, WC 509810, Mother's Application No. 546042, CWPF.

144. Deposition of Eliza Bogan, February 27, 1901, in Silas Small File, Co. E, 46th USCT, WC 393571, WC 509810, Mother's Application No. 546042, CWPF.

145. "The Situation in Arkansas," *North American and United States Gazette*, August 11, 1863.

146. "Document 40: Restoration of Arkansas, Proceedings of a Public Meeting in Helena, January 2, 1864," in Moore, *Rebellion Record*, 324–26; on the convention, see Moneyhon, *Impact of the Civil War*, 160–64.

147. Monroe Bogan first appeared in the local Phillips County, Arkansas, records on July 2, 1859, when he purchased land for $1,000. Property deed, July 2, 1859, book Q, p. 461, Property Deed Records, Phillips County Circuit Court Clerk's Office, Helena, Arkansas; see also Court Martial Case File of West Bogan, Case No. NN1823, RG 153; Ancestry.com, *1860 United States Federal Census*, Population and Slave Schedules, Phillips County, Arkansas; Ancestry.com, *1850 United States Federal Census*, Population and Slave Schedules, Union County, South Carolina; Dennis Bogan, Co. E., 46th USCT, CMSR.

148. Joseph Holt to the President, May 30, 1864, Court Martial Case File of West Bogan, Case No. NN1823, RG 153; Brig. Gen. Buford to Major General F. Steele, February 8, 1864,

vol. 37/97, Letters Sent, ser. 4664, DEA, RG 393, pt. 2. Bogan once testified in a court case related to brutality against a slave that an assault involving 200–300 stripes was a "light whipping." *The State v. William Harlan* in *Reports of Cases at Law*, 470–73.

149. Lewis Bogan, Co. G, 46th USCT, CMSR; Dennis Bogan and Charles Bogan, both in Co. E, 46th USCT, CMSR.

150. Testimony of Anderson Bulter, February 2, 1864, Court Martial Case File of West Bogan, Case No. NN1823, RG 153; West Bogan statement to Brig. Gen. Buford, summarized in Brig. Gen. Buford to Major General F. Steele, February 8, 1864, vol. 37/97, Letters Sent, ser. 4664, DEA, RG 393, pt. 2.

151. Court Martial Case File of West Bogan, Case No. NN1823, RG 153.

152. Brig. Gen. Buford to Captain F. H. Harris, December 26, 1863, vol. 37/96, and Brig. Gen. Buford to Major General F. Steele, February 8, 1864, vol. 37/97, both in Letters Sent, ser. 4664, DEA, RG 393, pt. 2; John J. Herrick Statement, Court Martial Case File of West Bogan, Case No. NN1823, RG 153.

153. General Court Martial Order No. 211, July 25, 1864, RG 94; Court Martial Case File of West Bogan, Case No. NN1823, RG 153.

154. "Marriage Among the Freedmen," *Friends Review*, April 15, 1864.

155. As a result of not getting legally married, Eliza did not receive Silas's soldier's bounty when he died; that went to his mother, Indiana Kelly. Deposition of Eliza Bogan, March 9, 1892, in Dennis Bogan File, Co. E, 46th USCT, WA 549935, WC 458509, CWPF.

156. Deposition of Eliza Bogan, March 9, 1892, in Dennis Bogan File, Co. E, 46th USCT, WA 549935, WC 458509, CWPF.

157. Court Martial Case File of West Bogan, Case No. NN1823, RG 153; Brig. Gen. Buford to Major General F. Steele, February 8, 1864, vol. 37/97, Letters Sent, ser. 4664, DEA, RG 393, pt. 2; John Fabian Witt notes that Joseph Holt was a defender of the self-defense rights of former slaves in *Lincoln's Code*, 265, 270–71. Frederick Steele, a brigadier general when he was in command at Helena, had been promoted to the rank of major general by this time.

158. Court Martial Case File of West Bogan, Case No. NN1823, RG 153.

159. Leonard, *Lincoln's Forgotten Ally*, chap. 5; Court Martial Case File of West Bogan, Case No. NN1823, RG 153; on the way that fear of slave insurrection shaped Union policy on emancipation, see Witt, *Lincoln's Code*, 201; "Featured Document: The Emancipation Proclamation."

CHAPTER 5

1. Story retold in report of A. N. S[cofield], April 14, 1864, box 12, ser. 13: Women's Aid Committee, FFAR, FHL; see also *Third Report of a Committee*, 4.

2. "From Mrs. Newcomb," *Freedmen's Bulletin*, September 1864; *Appeal of the Western Freedmen's Aid Commission*, 4.

3. On the "body politics" of liberation, see, for example, Camp, "Pleasures of Resistance," 533–72; and Long, *Doctoring Freedom*.

4. Representative examples of Civil War scholarship that has explored the centrality of food, and especially the contestation over it, include Cashin, "Hungry People," 160–75; Mark M. Smith, *Smell of Battle*, 92–106; McCurry, *Confederate Reckoning*, 178–217; and Andrew F. Smith, *Starving the South*.

5. Mark M. Smith, *Smell of Battle*, 92–106; Clampitt, *Occupied Vicksburg*, 98–100. On

the way in which the Union's laws of war permitted the starving of civilians to encourage enemy surrender, see Witt, *Lincoln's Code*, 233. Other studies that take up the relationship between food resources and Union military strategy include Brady, *War upon the Land*, 22–23, 123–26; Cashin, "Hungry People," 162–63; Grimsley, *Hard Hand of War*, 101–6; Andrew F. Smith, *Starving the South*; and Fiege, "Gettysburg," 93–109.

6. Benjamin F. Butler to Lt. Gen. Scott, May 27, 1861, Butler Papers, LC.

7. *Report of Commissioners of Investigation of Colored Refugees in Kentucky, Tennessee, and Alabama*, 20; "Freedmen's Aid Commission," *Freedmen's Bulletin*, March 1865. The ration system, like the provision of shelter discussed in chapter 2, was one area where humanitarianism asserted itself in the army's actions, most obviously in the fact that the people who were the least necessary to the military — children — were provided with food relief too. This qualifies other accounts of the ration system as one that only served the military's interests. See Jim Downs, *Sick from Freedom*, 68.

8. *Revised United States Army Regulations*, 244.

9. Examples of orders include General Order No. 5, by order of Maj. Gen. John Dix, January 26, 1863, vol. -/4, ser. 5078, General Orders Issued, DVANC, RG 393, pt. 1; and General Order No. 27, by order of Brig. Gen. Canby, January 16, 1864, Letters Received, ser. 12, M619, RG 94.

10. Wiley, *Life of Billy Yank*, 224–40; Meier, *Nature's Civil War*, 6, 112; Humphreys, *Intensely Human*, 55–56, 128–29.

11. Maria Mann to Aunt Mary, [February 1863?], Mann Papers, LC.

12. *Second Annual Report of the Western Freedmen's Aid Commission*, 10.

13. The forms are described in *Revised United States Army Regulations*, 252–60; Deaver's account in *Report of Commissioners of Investigation of Colored Refugees in Kentucky, Tennessee, and Alabama*, 6–9.

14. Testimony of Major Wentz Supt. of Norfolk and Petersburgh RR, [n.d., probably May 1863], AFIC Records, Letters Received, ser. 12, M619, reel 200, RG 94.

15. On the corruption surrounding soldiers' rations, see Wiley, *Life of Billy Yank*, 229–30.

16. *Africans in Fort Monroe Military District*, 5–6.

17. Ned Baxter, Samuel Owens, "and forty three other contrabands from Roanoke Island" to Gen. Benjamin Butler, September [n.d.], 1864, Misc. Letters & Reports Received, ser. 5076, Department of Virginia, RG 393, pt. 1.

18. *Second Annual Report of the Western Freedmen's Aid Commission*, 29; *Appeal of the Western Freedmen's Aid Commission*, 4.

19. On the regulations surrounding the rations of hospitalized soldiers, see *Revised United States Army Regulations*, 247–48.

20. Special Circular, March 10, 1864, ser. 225, CCF: "Freedmen's Aid Commission, Northwestern (1864)," RG 92.

21. See, for example, Charles Wilder to George Whipple, July 25, 1862, and T. P. Jackson to George Whipple, March 28, 1863, AMA-VA.

22. On "blamelessness" as a measure — and standard — for relief from the federal government in the nineteenth century, see Dauber, *Sympathetic State*. The fleeting nature of "blamelessness" in the Civil War reflects a broader and more long-standing aspect of humanitarianism noted by anthropologist and sociologist Didier Fassin: that moments of emergencies, which create temporary periods of solidarity among a people (and thus quickly enable the flow of humanitarian relief to the "blameless"), soon give way to situations in which "the preexisting inequalities of conditions are exposed and the

complacent indifference of the privileged classes toward the victims is revealed." Fassin, *Humanitarian Reason*, 181–99 (quote p. 199).

23. Charles Wilder to Major General Ord, January 23, 1865, Letters Received, ser. 12, M619, reel 429, RG 94.

24. On antebellum social welfare policies, see, for example, Katz, *In the Shadow*, 17–19; Dorsey, *Reforming Men and Women*, 56–58; and Lebsock, *Free Women of Petersburg*, 212–15.

25. Examples of ration books in Mississippi Pre-Bureau Records, M1914, reel 4, and Virginia Pre-Bureau Records, M1913, reels 115, 127, BRFAL. This wartime process of determining need—and guarding against ex-slaves' dependency on the federal government—anticipated similar actions undertaken by the Freedmen's Bureau just after the war. See Schwalm, *Hard Fight for We*, 249–60; Jim Downs, *Sick from Freedom*, chap. 5; Farmer-Kaiser, *Freedwomen*, esp. 37–63; and Faulkner, *Women's Radical Reconstruction*, 83–99.

26. Charles Wilder to Major General Ord, January 23, 1865, Letters Received, ser. 12, M619, reel 429, RG 94.

27. Testimony of Thomas Peake, April 1865, Court Martial Case File of Charles Wilder, Case No. MM2065, RG 153. Biographical information on the Peakes from Engs, *Freedom's First Generation*, 12–14.

28. Testimony of Thomas Peake, April 1865, Court Martial Case File of Charles Wilder, Case No. MM2065, RG 153.

29. Charles Wilder to Major General Ord, January 23, 1865, Letters Received, ser. 12, M619, reel 429, RG 94; Testimony of Thomas Peake, April 1865, Court Martial Case File of Charles Wilder, Case No. MM2065, RG 153.

30. Orders governing the amount of rations issued varied from place to place but generally followed the same pattern described above in areas distant from active campaigns. See Testimony of William Wakefield, [May 1863?], AFIC Records, Letters Received, ser. 12, M619, reel 200, RG 94; General Order No. 27, by order of Brig. Gen. Canby, January 16, 1864, Letters Received ser. 12, M619, reel 315, RG 94; Circular No. 1, by command of Major General Palmer, March 28, 1865 [mistakenly written "1864" in the original], vol. 10/11, ser. 2177, General Orders, DKY, RG 393, pt. 1.

31. Charles Wilder to Major General Ord, January 23, 1865, Letters Received, ser. 12, M619, reel 429, RG 94; see also Testimony of Selwyn E. Bickford, pp. 125–28, and Testimony of Mr. C. E. Hewins, April 1865, pp. 155–58, in Court Martial Case File of Charles Wilder, Case No. MM2065, RG 153.

32. Records Related to Issuance of Rations, 1863–64, vol. 3, pp. 1, 2, 4, 8, Virginia Pre-Bureau Records, M1913, reel 115, BRFAL.

33. A local population census taken in December 1864 noted there were 5,032 children (38 percent), 3,622 men (27 percent), and 4,651 women (35 percent). Both census and ration data in Charles Wilder, Report of Operations in Dept. Negro Affairs, First District, DVANC, December 30, 1864, Letters Received, ser. 12, M619, reel 429, RG 94.

34. Ben K. Johnston to Col. Eaton, June 27, 1864, *Extracts from Reports of the Superintendents*, 37.

35. This same impulse could be seen in antebellum poor relief, as most people who received such aid were, according to Michael Katz, "widows, children, old people, or the sick." Katz, *In the Shadow*, 42.

36. Records Related to Issuance of Rations, 1864, vol. 2, Virginia Pre-Bureau Records, M1913, reel 115, BRFAL.

37. Other historians have seen a similar effort by the federal government to shift women's dependency onto their husbands in the postwar work of the Freedmen's Bureau. See, for example, Schwalm, *Hard Fight for We*, 249–60; and Farmer-Kaiser, *Freedwomen*, 50–52.

38. Tera Hunter makes this point in *Bound in Wedlock*, 135–43.

39. Charles Wilder to Major General Ord, January 23, 1865, Letters Received, ser. 12, M619, reel 429, RG 94.

40. Testimony of Mr. C. E. Hewins, April 1865, p. 156, Court Martial Case File of Charles Wilder, Case No. MM2065, RG 153.

41. Charles Wilder, Report of Operations in Dept. Negro Affairs, First District, DVANC, December 30, 1864, and Lt. Col. Horace Porter to Bvt. Maj. Gen. John Turner, March 24, 1865, both in Letters Received, ser. 12, M619, reel 429, RG 94. Porter noted that the total expenditure on behalf of refugee slaves that year was $454,901.42, which means that the ration expenditure (at $412,534.52) made up the vast majority of the army's spending on behalf of refugees in his district—and likely elsewhere too.

42. Patricia Cline Cohen, *Calculating People*, 155–72 (quote p. 205).

43. Thomas T. S. Tucker to Rev. Jocelyn, December 24, 1862, AMA-VA; "Statistics, prepared from the Census of Blacks, taken in April 1863 at Newbern, N. Carolina," in Horace James to AFIC, November 13, 1863, AFIC Papers, HL; Brig. Gen. Buford to Lt. Col. Henry Binmore, November 14, 1863, vol. 37/96, pp. 207–8, Letters Sent, ser. 4664, DEA, RG 393, pt. 2; "Consolidated Census of Unemployed Contrabands within the Post of Murfreesboro, Tennessee, February 1, 1864," ser. 363, Letters Received, RG 94.

44. Charles Wilder, Report of Operations in Dept. Negro Affairs, First District, DVANC, p. 32, December 30, 1864, Letters Received, ser. 12, M619, reel 429, RG 94.

45. See, for example, Brig. Gen. Buford to Capt. F. H. Harris, December 14, 1863, Letters Sent, ser. 4664, DEA, RG 393, pt. 2.

46. Katz-Hyman and Rice, *World of a Slave*, 229–31; Genovese, *Roll, Jordan, Roll*, 63, 604.

47. On the way that the enslaved developed "knowledge of the environment" and used it to supplement their rations in slavery, see Stewart, *"What Nature Suffers,"* 128–36.

48. On Union foraging, see Wiley, *Life of Billy Yank*, 233–34; Meier, *Nature's Civil War*, 112; and Humphreys, *Intensely Human*, 129.

49. Maria Mann to Aunt Mary, [February 1863?], Mann Papers, LC.

50. *Appeal of the Western Freedmen's Aid Commission*, 3; "Friends Freedmen's Relief Association," *Friend*, February 27, 1864.

51. Report of Henry Rowntree, May 2, 1863, in *Friends Review*, May 16, 1863; "Report of the General Superintendent of Negro Affairs," *Freedmen's Friend*, October 1864, FHL.

52. George W. Young to Col. Eaton, May 18, 1864, *Extracts from Reports of the Superintendents*, 5–6.

53. Eaton, *Report of the General Superintendent*, 51.

54. George W. Young to Col. Eaton, May 18, 1864, *Extracts from Reports of the Superintendents*, 5–6, 28; see also Bercaw, *Gendered Freedoms*, 39.

55. "Abstract of the Report of the Sub-Committee Which Visited the Freedman's Settlements in Southeastern Virginia," *Freedmen's Friend*, December 1864, FHL.

56. *Report of Commissioners of Investigation of Colored Refugees in Kentucky, Tennessee, and Alabama*, 12.

57. Anne Gibbon to Lt. Col. Coughlin, April 25, 1864, M1913, reel 115, BRFAL.

58. Yeatman, *Report on the Condition*, 3.

59. "Departments of Supervision," *Freedmen's Bulletin*, September 1864; see also Col. John Eaton Testimony, April 29, 1863, AFIC Records, Letters Received, ser. 12, M619, reel 200, RG 94.

60. George W. Young to Col. Eaton, May 18, 1864, *Extracts from Reports of the Superintendents*, 5–6.

61. Testimony of William Badger, April 1865, p. 84, Court Martial Case File of Charles Wilder, Case No. MM2065, RG 153.

62. Berlin et al., *Wartime Genesis: Lower South*, 632–33. This same impulse was evident in the Mississippi Valley before the war too, as cotton planters grew insufficient produce and required the importation of food into the region. Johnson, *River of Dark Dreams*, 176–80.

63. General Order No. 14, by order of Maj. John L. Murphy, Helena, August 13, 1864, vol. 123 DArk, ser. 4702, Letters Sent, Orders Issued, and Other Records of the Provost Marshal, DEA, RG 393, pt. 2.

64. Court Martial Case File of William Phillips, Case No. LL0189, RG 153.

65. Court Martial Case File of the Men of the 13th USCHA, Case No. MM3377, RG 153.

66. On individual soldiers' foraging, see Cashin, "Hungry People," 163–65. On the Union's authorization of foraging raids on a broader, collective scale, see Brady, *War upon the Land*, 22–23, 123–26; Grimsley, *Hard Hand of War*, 101–4; and Meier, *Nature's Civil War*, 112–13.

67. Testimony of William Wakefield, [n.d., probably May 1863], AFIC Records, Letters Received, ser. 12, M619, reel 200, RG 94; Testimony of Dr. Brown, Superintendent of Contrabands at Norfolk, [n.d., probably May 1863], in Berlin et al., *Wartime Genesis: Lower South*, 149.

68. Cashin, "Hungry People," 160–69; Andrew F. Smith, *Starving the South*.

CHAPTER 6

1. Quotes from, respectively, T. E. Hall to Rev. Strieby, May 8, 1865, AMA-KY; C. P. Day to Rev. Jocelyn, May 20, 1863, AMA-VA; Lucy Chase Report, November 14, 1863, minute book 2, box 12, ser. 13: Women's Aid Committee, FFAR, FHL; *Report of a Committee of the Representatives of New York*, 16; William F. Mitchell to Sarah Cope, November 6, 1864, box 12, ser. 13: Women's Aid Committee, FFAR, FHL; and "Report of the Women's Aid Association of Friends for the Relief of Colored Refugees," *Friend*, October 24, 1863.

2. *Third Report of a Committee*, 2.

3. On the clothing allotments of the enslaved, see Katz-Hyman and Rice, *World of a Slave*, 125; Genovese, *Roll, Jordan, Roll*, 551; and Berry, "'We Sho Was Dressed Up,'" 74.

4. *Third Report of a Committee*, 3, 16.

5. Elkanah Beard Report, January 8, 1864, in *Friends Review*, February 6, 1864.

6. [Untitled], *Friend*, December 26, 1863.

7. On the issuance of uniforms to men, see Extracts of Report of Samuel Shipley, December 24, 1863, minute book 1, box 12, ser. 13: Women's Aid Committee, FFAR, FHL; Eaton, *Report of the General Superintendent*, 12.

8. *Minutes of the First Annual Meeting of the Northwestern Freedmen's Aid Commission*, 9; one army chaplain working with refugees in the Mississippi Valley wrote about having been "directed by Gen. Grant" to appeal to the "public" for clothing. Eaton, *Report of the General Superintendent*, 12.

9. On free transportation provided by the federal government, see *Minutes of the First*

Annual Meeting of the Northwestern Freedmen's Aid Commission, 6; Appeal of the Western Freedmen's Aid Commission, 9; and Order of Maj. Gen. John Dix, November 19, 1862, AMA-VA.

10. Other scholarly examinations of clothing in the Civil War that likewise see significant meaning in — and contestation over — this most basic object of everyday life include Beilein, "Guerrilla Shirt"; Cashin, "Trophies of War"; Cashin, "Torn Bonnets"; and Weicksel, "Dress of the Enemy."

11. September 19, 1862, minute book 1, box 12, ser. 13: Women's Aid Committee, FFAR, FHL.

12. *Third Report of a Committee*, 17.

13. "Relief for the Freedmen," *Friend*, December 5, 1863.

14. *Appeal of the Western Freedmen's Aid Commission*, 3; *Minutes of the First Annual Meeting of the Northwestern Freedmen's Aid Commission*, 9.

15. "Final Report of the 'Contraband Relief Commission of Cincinnati,'" *Friends Review*, January 7, 1865; *Second Annual Report of the Western Freedmen's Aid Commission*, 3–4, 11–12; *Second Report of the Executive Board of the Friends Association of Philadelphia*, 11.

16. These were just three of the donations collected by the Northwestern Freedmen's Aid Commission that month, which totaled $2,568.83 and filled up 139 packages. "Collections and Receipts of the Commission for the Month of June," *Freedmen's Bulletin*, July 1864.

17. "California for the Freedmen," *Freedmen's Bulletin*, July 1864.

18. Charles Wilder to Brethren, December 16, 1862, AMA-VA.

19. *Second Annual Report of the Western Freedmen's Aid Commission*, 3–4, 11–12.

20. "Epistle to Friends in America," *Friends Review*, July 15, 1865.

21. "Circular: Birmingham and Midland Association for the Help of the Refugees from Slavery in America," *Freedmen's Friend*, October 1864, FHL.

22. "Circular: Birmingham and Midland Association for the Help of the Refugees from Slavery in America," *Freedmen's Friend*, October 1864, FHL; "Aid to the Distressed Freedmen in the United States," *Friend*, July 23, 1864; *Second Report of the Executive Board of the Friends Association of Philadelphia*, 6.

23. Forty-five percent of the money (or $2,876.27) raised by the Women's Aid Committee of the Friends Freedmen's Association of Philadelphia during the first ten months of 1863, and then 53 percent raised during the following six months, through April 1864, came from British donors. "Report of the Women's Aid Association of Friends for the Relief of Coloured Refugees," *Friend*, October 24, 1863; "Report of the Women's Aid Association," *Friend*, May 21, 1864.

24. Minute book 1, March 12 (pp. 1–2), April 2 (p. 10), 16 (p. 14), 1862, box 12, ser. 13: Women's Aid Committee, FFAR, FHL.

25. Minute book 1, April 16, 1862, box 12, ser. 13: Women's Aid Committee, FFAR, FHL.

26. This "quick feeling of sympathy" reflected what anthropologist and sociologist Didier Fassin has observed as a "unanimous wave of solidarity" that often accompanies moments of humanitarian emergency, crossing latent class, ethnic, and racial lines — but only temporarily. Fassin, *Humanitarian Reason*, 199; "Second Report of the Executive Board of the Friends Association of Philadelphia," *Friends Review*, July 1, 1865.

27. "The Freedpeople in Virginia," *Friend*, May 30, 1863.

28. Hyndman, *Managing Displacement*, 29–60 (quote pp. 58–59).

29. Rev. W. S. Bell to Rev. Jocelyn, November 19, 1863, September [?], 1864, AMA-VA.

30. Edson, *Biographical and Portrait Cyclopedia*, 31; Sears, *Camp Nelson, Kentucky*, 121.

31. A. Scofield to Brethren, February 4, 1865, AMA-KY.

32. "Friends Freedmen's Relief Association," *Friend*, December 19, 1863; *Minutes of Indiana Yearly Meeting of Friends* (1863), 27; *Freedmen and Union Refugees' Department*; Minutes of Western Yearly Meeting of Friends (1865), 41, FCCA; Jim Downs makes a similar observation in *Sick from Freedom*, 52–53.

33. "Friends Freedmen's Association," *Friend*, January 16, 1864; Maria Mann to Elisa, February 10, 1863, Mann Papers, LC.

34. W. S. Bell to Rev. Jocelyn, February [?], 1864, AMA-VA.

35. Lucy Chase to Sarah Cope, November 28, 1863, box 12, ser. 13: Women's Aid Committee, FFAR, FHL.

36. W. S. Bell to Rev. Jocelyn, February [?], 1864, AMA-VA.

37. *Second Annual Report of the Western Freedmen's Aid Commission*, 17; see also C. P. Day to Rev. Jocelyn, May 20, 1863, AMA-VA.

38. *Report of Indiana Yearly Meeting's Executive Committee*, 12.

39. "More Blessed to Give than to Receive," *Freedmen's Bulletin*, July 1864; see also Report of Lt. Col. Horace Porter, February 5, 1865, Letters Received, ser. 12, M619, reel 429, RG 94.

40. Executive Board Minutes, February 15, May 3, 1864, ser. 2, FFAR, FHL.

41. Executive Board Minutes, May 17, 1864, ser. 2, FFAR, FHL.

42. Executive Board Minutes, October 4, 1864, January 16, 1865, ser. 2, FFAR, FHL; *Second Report of the Executive Board of the Friends Association of Philadelphia*, 15.

43. "The Store Movement," *Friend*, November 12, 1864.

44. "Freedmen's Stores in Virginia," *Freedmen's Friend*, June 1864, FHL; see also Report of Lt. Col. Horace Porter, February 5, 1865, p. 10, Letters Received, ser. 12, M619, reel 429, RG 94.

45. Executive Board Minutes, February 15, 1864, ser. 2, FFAR, FHL.

46. On the myriad intersections of consumerism and citizenship in the American political imagination over time, see, for example, Breen, *Marketplace of Revolution*; Lizabeth Cohen, *Consumer's Republic*.

47. Executive Board Minutes, December 6, 1864, ser. 2, FFAR, FHL; "Convention of Freedmen's Commissions," *Friends Review*, September 17, 1864.

48. "Freedmen's Stores in Virginia," *Freedmen's Friend*, June 1864, FHL.

49. "Freedmen's Stores," *Friend*, November 19, 1864.

50. [Untitled], *Friend*, June 25, 1864.

51. *Second Report of a Committee of the Representatives of New York*, 12.

52. "Second Annual Report of the Executive Committee on Freedmen," *Minutes of Indiana Yearly Meeting of Friends* (1865), 43–44; Ann Schofield to Sarah Cope, May 6, 1864, box 12, ser. 13: Women's Aid Committee, FFAR, FHL.

53. "Second Annual Report of the Executive Committee on Freedmen," *Minutes of Indiana Yearly Meeting of Friends* (1865), 43–44.

54. "Friends Freedmen's Relief Association," *Friend*, December 19, 1863.

55. Katz-Hyman and Rice, *World of a Slave*, 123–24.

56. "About Piece-Goods," *Freedmen's Bulletin*, September 1864.

57. Minute book 2, July 9, 1864, box 12, ser. 13: Women's Aid Committee, FFAR, FHL.

58. See discussion of cutting and clothing manufacture in Richmond, *Clothing the Poor*, 110–11.

59. Minute book 2, July 9, 1864, box 12, ser. 13: Women's Aid Committee, FFAR, FHL; on the sending of pieces to the South, see *Second Report of a Committee of the Representatives of New York*, 5; and "Friends Freedmen's Relief Association," *Friend*, December 19, 1863.

60. C. P. Day to Rev. Jocelyn, September 30, 1862, AMA-VA.

61. "The Freedpeople in Virginia," *Friend*, May 30, 1863. On the way that photographs conveyed to Northern audiences the visual transformation offered by clothing, see Willis and Krauthamer, *Envisioning Emancipation*, 18–19; and Emberton, *Beyond Redemption*, 102–4.

62. Crane, *Fashion*, 1–3, 63–67; see also Halttunen, *Confidence Men*, 62–67.

63. Maria Mann to Miss Peabody, April 19, 1863, Mann Papers, LC.

64. See Halttunen, *Confidence Men*, 62–67.

65. Maria Mann to Aunt Mary, April 7, 1863, Mann Papers, LC; minute book 2, June 13, 1863, box 12, ser. 13: Women's Aid Committee, FFAR, FHL; similar commentary described in Glymph, *House of Bondage*, 209–10.

66. Camp, *Closer to Freedom*, 78–79; Katz-Hyman and Rice, *World of a Slave*, 120.

67. Yeatman, *Report on the Condition*, 3; see also Rhoda Smith to Mrs. Cope, March 9, 1863, box 12, ser. 13: Women's Aid Committee, FFAR, FHL.

68. Maria Mann to Aunt Mary, April 19, May 18, August 14, 1863, Mann Papers, LC.

69. Maria Mann to Aunt Mary, May 18, 1863, Mann Papers, LC.

70. See discussion of the meaning of black men's uniforms in Emberton, *Beyond Redemption*, 102–4; and "The Western Freedmen," *Commonwealth*, March 20, 1863.

71. Maria Mann to Miss Peabody, April 19, 1863, Mann Papers, LC.

72. Maria Mann to Miss Peabody, April 19, 1863, Mann Papers, LC.

73. Glymph, *House of Bondage*, 205–18 (quotes pp. 205, 210).

74. See Camp, *Closer to Freedom*, 79–87 (quote p. 83); see also Katz-Hyman and Rice, *World of a Slave*, 123–24; and Berry, "'We Sho Was Dressed Up,'" 73–83.

75. This point is also made in Glymph, *House of Bondage*, 206.

76. Camp, *Closer to Freedom*, 82.

77. Helen James Report to Samuel Shipley, January 19, 1864, Friends Association of Philadelphia, *Statistics of the Operations*, 32–33.

78. Maria Mann to Aunt Mary, April 7, 1863, Mann Papers, LC.

79. Camp, "Pleasures of Resistance," 109; see also Foster, *New Raiments of Self*, 272–313.

80. Maria Mann to Aunt Mary, May 15, 1863, Mann Papers, LC.

81. Maria Mann to Miss Peabody, April 19, 1863, Mann Papers, LC.

82. Rhoda Smith to My Dear Cousin Sibbilla, May 12, 1863, AMA-VA.

83. John Oliver to Rev. S. S. Jocelyn, December 17, 1862, AMA-VA; "Freedmen," *American Missionary*, May 1863.

84. Report from Virginia, Minutes & Misc. Papers, box 12, ser. 13: Women's Aid Committee, FFAR, FHL.

85. C. P. Day letter, *Friend*, October 11, 1862.

GABRIEL BURDETT IN SLAVERY

1. "'The Old Liners.' Second Day's Proceedings in the Abolitionists Reunion," Chicago *Inter-Ocean*, June 11, 1874.

2. Gabriel Burdett was born in 1829, making him twenty-one years of age by 1850.

Declaration for Pension, May 11, 1912, in Gabriel Burdett File, Co. I, 114th USCT, IA 794724, WA 1037482, IC 740230, WC 786792, CWPF. On Hiram Burdett's land and slave holdings, see 1861 Tax Books, Garrard County, Kentucky Historical Society, Frankfort, Kentucky. For an overview of the "invisible church," see Raboteau, *Slave Religion*, esp. chap. 5; and Creel, *"Peculiar People,"* 298.

3. No records indicate where Lucinda was enslaved or who was her owner. Marriage described in Declaration for Widow's Pension, November 25, 1914, in Gabriel Burdett File, Co. I, 114th USCT, IA 794724, WA 1037482, IC 740230, WC 786792, CWPF.

4. *Churches of Lancaster and Garrard County*, 43–44; Calico, *History of Garrard County*, 320–37; Forks of Dix River Baptist Church Day Book, 36–41, FSL. Elijah Burdett's enslavement on the Hiram Burdett property is confirmed in Elijah Burdett, Co. H, 12th USCHA, CMSR; his family relationship to Gabriel Burdett is documented in Affidavit of Hannah Gill, April 7, 1896, in Elijah Burdett File, Co. H, 12th USCHA, IA 486409, IC 793272, CWPF; and his likely attendance at the church service is indicated by his 1857 marriage to Clarissa Alford by Willis Kemper, who was another black preacher at the Forks Church. See Declaration for Pension, June 12, 1883, in Elijah Burdett File, Co. H, 12th USCHA, Approved Pensions, Record Group 15, NARA.

5. Raboteau, *Slave Religion*, 152–71; Irons, *Origins of Proslavery Christianity*, 103–67; Harlow, "Long Life," 132–39; Fountain, *Slavery, Civil War*, 57–59; Creel, *"Peculiar People"*; Harding, "Religion and Resistance," 117–19.

6. Forks of Dix River Baptist Church Day Book, April 1859, 109, FSL.

7. See Raboteau, *Slave Religion*, 137; Lucas, *History of Blacks*, 140; Irons, *Origins of Proslavery Christianity*, 170–209.

8. Raboteau, *Slave Religion*, 135–38, 178, 201, 231–39; Lucas, *History of Blacks*, 121–30.

9. Raboteau, *Slave Religion*, 212–19 (quote p. 212); Creel, *"Peculiar People."*

10. Forks of Dix River Baptist Church Day Book, June 1862, 131–32, FSL.

11. Raboteau, *Slave Religion*, 293–300; Irons, *Origins of Proslavery Christianity*, 207–9.

12. "Colored Refugees," *American Missionary*, February 1862.

13. Forks of Dix River Baptist Church Day Book, October 8, 1861, 128, FSL.

14. Forks of Dix River Baptist Church Day Book, December 1861, 129, FSL.

15. On religion and space, see Carroll, "Religion in Space"; Stump, *Geography of Religion*, 221–349; Chidester and Linenthal, *American Sacred Space*, ix–42; and Tweed, "Space," 116–23.

16. Forks of Dix River Baptist Church Day Book, July 1862, 132, FSL.

CHAPTER 7

1. Ancestry.com, *1860 United States Federal Census*, Population and Slave Schedules, Garrard County, Kentucky; *Journal of the Senate of the Commonwealth of Kentucky*, 471.

2. See postwar claim by George Denny for compensation related to corn acquired, but not paid for, by the Union army. *Reports of Committees of the House of Representatives*, report no. 522.

3. "Names of Agents Employed in the Impressment of Negroes in the Several Counties," 107, and "List of Agents Employed in the Impressment of Negroes, Time of Service, and Amount Due," 116–17, in Letters Sent, Provost Marshal, ser. 1043, vol. 90/205, District of Kentucky, RG 393, pt. 2.

4. Special Order No. 18, June 3, 1863, by order of Col. J. K. Sigfried, vol. 128/310, General

Orders and Special Orders, ser. 693, Lexington, RG 393, pt. 4; General Order No. 37, July 25, 1863, and General Order No. 41, August 10, 1863, by order of Brig. Gen. Boyle, vol. 14/113, General Orders, ser. 2177, DKY, RG 393, pt. 1; Stephen McBride, "More Than a Depot."

5. "Unidentified List of Names," 11–12, July–September 1863, ser. 1039, District of Kentucky, RG 393, pt. 2. Although the finding aid for this collection lists this document as "unidentified," I have determined that it is the list of impressed workers, based on the date, the information taken, and its location in the District of Kentucky records.

6. Report of Persons or Articles Hired, T. E. Hall, File 59, March 1864, ser. 238, RG 92; General Order No. 41, August 10, 1863, by order of Brig. Gen. Boyle, vol. 14/113, General Orders, ser. 2177, DKY, RG 393, pt. 1.

7. Gabriel Burdett first appeared in the ledger book on July 1, 1863, suggesting that this was the beginning of his impressment period. "Unidentified List of Names," 11–12, July–September 1863, ser. 1039, District of Kentucky, RG 393, pt. 2.

8. General Order No. 2, November 27, 1862, by order of Brig. Gen. Boyle, vol. 12/112, General Orders, ser. 2177, DKY, RG 393, pt. 1. On the same actions taken by Union officials in other parts of Kentucky, see Berlin et al., *Destruction of Slavery*, 496–97; and Berlin et al., *Wartime Genesis: Upper South*, 627–29.

9. Berlin et al., *Wartime Genesis: Upper South*, 630.

10. Exceptions were camps at Paducah and Columbus, Kentucky, which were located in western Kentucky, close to the Mississippi River. These sites were opened for people fleeing slavery in states other than Kentucky—they were not open to "Kentucky" slaves (although that distinction was sometimes difficult for officials to enforce).

11. On proslavery Unionism in Kentucky, see Patrick A. Lewis, *For Slavery and Union*; Astor, *Rebels on the Border*; and Phillips, *Rivers Ran Backwards*. On Lincoln and Kentucky, see William C. Harris, *Lincoln*, 223–67; Freehling, *South vs. the South*, 52–53, 82–89 (quote p. 82); and Oakes, *Freedom National*, 145–91. On the way that Kentucky's white Unionists saw betrayal in Lincoln's actions, despite their exemption from the Emancipation Proclamation, see Harlow, *Religion, Race*, 155–70; and Marshall, *Creating a Confederate Kentucky*, 24–29.

12. Ancestry.com, *1860 United States Federal Census—Slave Schedules*, Boyle County, Kentucky.

13. Berlin et al., *Wartime Genesis: Upper South*, 626.

14. Union officials in Kentucky circumvented the March 1862 article of war by trying to prevent enslaved people from coming into Union camps in the first place. That way no soldier would be put in the position of turning them out again, and thus would not violate the article of war. See General Order No. 2, November 27, 1862, by order of Brig. Gen. Boyle, vol. 12/112, General Orders, ser. 2177, DKY, RG 393, pt. 1; see also Oakes, *Freedom National*, 177.

15. Brig. Gen. J. T. Boyle to Col. Dent, June 13, 1862, in Berlin et al., *Destruction of Slavery*, 497–98.

16. Descriptions of Camp Nelson in John G. Fee to Bro. Jocelyn, July 18, 1864, AMA-KY; inspection report of Major Murray Davis, April 17, 1865, in Sears, *Camp Nelson, Kentucky*, 199–205; "Camp Nelson, Kentucky. Its Location and Strength—Its Improvements—Its Government, Operations, &c.," Louisville *Daily Union Press*, April 10, 1865; and Stephen McBride, "More Than a Depot."

17. Rable, *God's Almost Chosen Peoples*, 110–26 (quote p. 119); Wiley, "'Holy Joes,'" 290–93.

18. On the process of making space sacred, see Stump, *Geography of Religion*, 301–49; Carroll, "Religion in Space," 1–8; and Chidester and Linenthal, *American Sacred Space*.

19. George P. Riley to Bro. John Fee, June 23, 1863, AMA-KY.

20. "The Contrabands in Camp," *Pine and Palm*, August 31, 1861; see also John T. Farnham Diary, July 9, 1863, Wichita State University, Wichita, Kansas. On the war's disruption of the slaveholding soundscape, see Mark M. Smith, *Smell of Battle*, 9–38.

21. Lewis C. Lockwood of the AMA arranged for the publication through Horace Waters of New York. "New Music," *American Missionary*, January 1862. See also Bercovitch and Patell, *Cambridge History*, 202; and Kate Masur, "'Rare Phenomenon,'" 1070.

22. "The Freedmen at Fortress Monroe," *American Missionary*, January 1862.

23. See, for example, Rable, *God's Almost Chosen Peoples*, chaps. 10, 12; Drew Gilpin Faust, *This Republic of Suffering*, chap. 6; Fredrickson, *Inner Civil War*, chap. 6; and Sean A. Scott, *Visitation of God*, 4, 36–46, 62–63.

24. Quoted in "Colored Refugees," *American Missionary*, February 1862.

25. Lewis Lockwood to Brethren, November 27, 1861, in "The Freedmen at Fortress Monroe," *American Missionary*, January 1862.

26. Quoted in "Colored Refugees," *American Missionary*, February 1862. On the general importance of Exodus to freedom-seeking people, see Raboteau, *Slave Religion*, 311–12; Rable, *God's Almost Chosen Peoples*, 19–20, 288–89; Glaude, *Exodus!*; and Harper, *End of Days*, 65–69. On Thornton, see Engs, *Freedom's First Generation*, 16.

27. Daniel L. Fountain refers to wartime refugee camps as "conversion camps" in *Slavery, Civil War*, 99–105; on the interrelationship between spiritual and physical freedom in the preaching of enslaved ministers, see Raboteau, *Slave Religion*, 304–6.

28. These scholarly estimates vary widely and tend to measure the proportion of Christians differently. Steven Hahn, for example, measures adult slaves who were "affiliated with Christian churches" (10–25 percent), while Daniel L. Fountain measures actual conversions to Christianity (38 percent). See Hahn, *Nation under Our Feet*, 45; and Fountain, *Slavery, Civil War*, 3, 16. Other discussions of the proportion of Christians among the enslaved population include Raboteau, *Slave Religion*, 212, 271, 313; and Rable, *God's Almost Chosen Peoples*, 125.

29. This qualifies an assumption running through the secondary literature that African Americans viewed Lincoln as Moses and the Union army as God's army. See Rable, *God's Almost Chosen Peoples*, 288; Litwack, *Been in the Storm*, 122; and Keith P. Wilson, *Campfires of Freedom*, 156.

30. Accounts from a white missionary a year later would imply that Burdett had been preaching for quite some time. John G. Fee to Rev. S. S. Jocelyn, August 8, 1864, AMA-KY.

31. Berlin et al., *Destruction of Slavery*, 508–9; "Unidentified List of Names," 11–12, July–September 1863, ser. 1039, District of Kentucky, RG 393, pt. 2. Though General Boyle ordered 6,000 men impressed, he only obtained a total of 2,300 men over time. See Schecter, "'First Free Spot,'" 23.

32. Since impressment only brought men into Union lines, it is most likely that Lucinda was still on her plantation. The children first appear by name in the 1870 federal census, and the ages listed here were calculated based on their census listings. Ancestry.com, *1870 United States Federal Census*, Jessamine County, Kentucky.

33. Robert Burdett was owned by Smith Alford of Garrard County but had been hired out to work for Hiram Burdett; he was on the Burdett property when he was impressed alongside Gabriel Burdett. Capt. Edw. G. Park to Brig. Gen. S. S. Fry, December 29, 1863, vol. 128/309, Letters Sent, ser. 690, Lexington, RG 393, pt. 4. An estimated 1,000 enslaved people had already been sold to the Deep South from Kentucky in 1863, a fact that President Lincoln found so shocking that he ordered Gen. Ambrose Burnside to put a stop to it. That explains why the Union came to Robert Burdett's rescue in this instance. On Lincoln's actions, see Berlin et al., *Destruction of Slavery*, 504–7.

34. On the roles of women in the religious communities of the enslaved, see Fett, *Working Cures*, 36–59, 111–41; and Stevenson, "'Marsa Never Sot.'"

35. General Orders No. 27, by order of Brig. Gen. Burbridge, March 4, 1864, vol. 14/114, p. 396, General Orders, ser. 2177, DKY, RG 393, pt. 1; Berlin et al., *Destruction of Slavery*, 510.

36. William C. Harris, *Lincoln*, 223–28, 239–41; Berlin et al., *Destruction of Slavery*, 510–11; John David Smith, "Recruitment."

37. T. E. Hall to Senator Henry Wilson, May 26, 1864, Letters Received, ser. 12, M619, RG 94.

38. Excerpts of Report of Mr. Butler, June 1864, in Sears, *Camp Nelson, Kentucky*, 84.

39. See Witt, *Lincoln's Code*, 7–8.

40. Orders No. 20, June 13, 1864, vol. 2, Special Orders and Appointments, Generals' Papers: Lorenzo Thomas, ser. 159, RG 94.

41. Bvt. Brig. Gen. to Miss Eliza G. McCoughlin, February 18, 1865, Letters Sent, Organization of the USCT, ser. 2246, DKY, RG 393, pt. 1.

42. Gabriel Burdett, Co. I, 114th USCT, CMSR; "'The Old Liners.' Second Day's Proceedings in the Abolitionists Reunion," Chicago *Inter-Ocean*, July 11, 1874.

43. Robert Burdett enlisted on August 18, and Gabriel's brother, Elijah Burdett, enlisted on September 6. Robert Burdett, Co. G, 12th USCHA, CMSR; Elijah Burdett, Co. H, 12th USCHA, CMSR. At least two other men from the Hiram Burdett property also enlisted that summer. See Hiram Burdett, Co. F, 114th USCT, CMSR; and Charles Burdett, Co. F, 114th USCT, CMSR. On the enlistment totals, see Berlin et al., *Destruction of Slavery*, 512.

44. John G. Fee to Bro. Jocelyn, August 8, 1864, in Sears, *Camp Nelson, Kentucky*, 109.

45. Affidavit of Clarissa Burdett, March 27, 1865, enclosed in T. E. Hall to O. O. Howard, June 22, 1865, M999, BRFAL.

46. The orders to expel the women and children included Brig. Gen. Speed Smith Fry to Lt. Geo. H. Hanaford, July 6, 1864, 24, Telegrams Sent and Received, ser. 904, Camp Nelson, RG 393, pt. 4; General Order No. 14, by command of Speed Smith Fry, August 9, 1864, ser. 905, General Orders, Camp Nelson, RG 393, pt. 4; Brig. Gen. Speed Smith Fry to Lt. Latham, August 29, 1864, 716, Register of Letters Received & Endorsements Sent, ser. 1661, Camp Nelson Provost Marshal, RG 393, pt. 4; General Order No. 23, by command of Thos. D. Sedgewick, September 16, 1864, 87, General Orders, ser. 905, Camp Nelson, RG 393, pt. 4; and Col. T. D. Sedgewick to Major A. J. Hogan, October 29, 1864, in Sears, *Camp Nelson, Kentucky*, 130.

47. Lester Williams to Rev. Strieby, July 3, 1865, AMA-KY.

48. Fee, *Non-Fellowship*; Harlow, *Religion, Race*, 99; Howard, *Evangelical War*, 19–36; Sears, *"Practical Recognition,"* 1.

49. Berea College Board of Trustees Minutes, July 15, 1859, Berea College, Berea, Kentucky; S. S. Jocelyn to John G. Fee, June 6, July 15, 1864, John G. Fee Papers, Berea

College, Berea, Kentucky; Howard, *Evangelical War*, 72, 101, 131–32; Sears, "John G. Fee," 29.

50. John G. Fee to Rev. S. S. Jocelyn, August 8, 1864, AMA-KY.

51. J. P. Green to Brother Jocelyn, September 22, 1862, AMA-VA.

52. John G. Fee to Rev. S. S. Jocelyn, August 8, 1864, AMA-KY.

53. W. O. King to Brother Jocelyn, August 4, 1863, AMA-VA. On white Northerners' views of black religious services in the camps, see Hahn, *Nation under Our Feet*, 230; Rable, *God's Almost Chosen Peoples*, 286; and Rose, *Rehearsal for Reconstruction*, 73–75.

54. Abisha Scofield to M. E. Strieby, November 1, 1864, in Sears, *Camp Nelson, Kentucky*, 131. On Scofield, who was once drummed out of his Congregational church for his radicalism on slavery, see Edson, *Biographical and Portrait Cyclopedia*, 31.

55. Abisha Scofield to M. E. Strieby, November 1, 1864, AMA-KY.

56. John Fee to Brother Whipple, October 2, 1865, in Sears, *Camp Nelson, Kentucky*, 267. I am grateful to Charles Irons for helping me puzzle out the circumstances of Burdett's ordination.

57. W. S. Bell to Rev. S. S. Jocelyn, August 8, 1863, AMA-VA; W. H. Woodbury to Brethren, November 7, 1863, AMA-VA; W. S. Bell to Rev. S. S. Jocelyn, February 1863, AMA-VA.

58. Mrs. Woodbury to Rev. Jocelyn, September 7, 1863, AMA-VA.

59. Gabriel Burdett to E. M. Cravath, November 2, 1870, AMA-KY.

60. At Fort Monroe, for example, Charles Wilder, one of the first AMA officials in the region, was installed as superintendent of contrabands in March 1862 and then nine months later assumed the military position of assistant quartermaster too, at the rank of captain. General Order No. 21, by command of Maj. Gen. Wool, March 15, 1862, vol. -/4, General Orders Issued, ser. 5078, DVANC, RG 393, pt. 1; Lt. Col. [S?]. A. Sikes to Capt. C. B. Wilder, January 28, 1863, Regimental Order Book, John Augustus Wilder Series, Loomis-Wilder Family Papers, Yale University Library, New Haven, Connecticut. See other examples in W. L. Coan to Bro. Whiting, December 11, 1863, and Prof. Woodbury to Rev. Whipple, December 12, 1863, both in AMA-VA; Special Order No. 7, by order of Brig. Gen. Gorman, January 8, 1863, vol. 42/108 DArk, Special Orders, ser. 4686, DEA, RG 393, pt. 2.

61. John G. Fee to Bro. Jocelyn, July 12, 1864, in Sears, *Camp Nelson, Kentucky*, 97–98.

62. Rev. S. S. Jocelyn to John G. Fee, July 15, 1864, John G. Fee Papers, Berea College, Berea, Kentucky; see also Fee, *Autobiography*, 175.

63. John G. Fee to Rev. S. S. Jocelyn, August 8, 1864, AMA-KY.

64. The 114th USCT arrived via steamer at Fort Monroe in January 1865. Regimental Books and Papers, 114th USCT, RG 94.

65. John G. Fee to Rev. S. S. Jocelyn, July 12, 1864, in Sears, *Camp Nelson, Kentucky*, 97.

66. Rev. J. B. Lowrey, "Monthly Report," August 29, 1864, AMA-KY.

67. John G. Fee to Bro. Strieby, August 16, 1864, in Sears, *Camp Nelson, Kentucky*, 113.

68. Heather Andrea Williams similarly observes that soldiers "taught as they learned," taking schooling with them as their regiments moved, in *Self-Taught*, 51.

69. John G. Fee to Rev. S. S. Jocelyn, July 18, 1864, in Sears, *Camp Nelson, Kentucky*, 101; Rev. J. B. Lowrey, "Monthly Report," August 29, 1864, AMA-KY.

70. Report of Capt. Charles B. Wilder to Major Geo. J. Carney, December 30, 1864, in Berlin et al., *Wartime Genesis: Upper South*, 212–19.

71. "Report of the Number of Freedpeople in the Eastern Dist. of Arkansas on the 1st Day of June 1865," General and Special Orders Received, ser. 4687, DEA, RG 393, pt. 2.

72. John Eaton to Levi Coffin, July 5, 1864, in *Extracts from Reports of the Superintendents*, 51.

73. *Report of the Board of Education for Freedmen*, 7.

74. Butchart, *Schooling the Freed People*, 4. Butchart notes that the percentage of African Americans in schools settled out at 10 percent in 1870, suggesting that the rate of wartime enrollment in the camps represented an unusually high spike.

75. "Indiana Freedmen's Aid Commission," *Friends Review*, June 25, 1864; Report from Virginia, March 18, 1865, box 12, ser. 13: Women's Aid Committee, FFAR, FHL; "Report of the Women's Aid Association of Friends for the Relief of Colored Refugees," *Friends Review*, October 31, 1863.

76. John G. Fee to Bro. Jocelyn, July 18, 1864, AMA-KY.

77. Report of Rev. A. L. Payson to Western Department, U.S. Sanitary Commission, August 1, 1864, in *Sanitary Reporter*, September 1, 1864.

78. "The Freedmen in Virginia," *Friends Review*, November 7, 1863.

79. Palmer Litts to Brother Jocelyn, Fortress Monroe, July 29, 1863, AMA-VA.

80. John G. Fee, "Monthly Report," August 1864, AMA-KY.

81. John G. Fee to Rev. S. S. Jocelyn, July 18, 1864, in Sears, *Camp Nelson, Kentucky*, 101.

82. John G. Fee to Bro. Jocelyn, July 18, 1864, AMA-KY.

83. Ann Scofield to Sarah Cope, May 6, 1864, minute book 2, box 12, ser. 13: Women's Aid Committee, FFAR, FHL. On spirituals, see Levine, "Slave Songs," 71–80; on the acquisition of reading skills, see Schweiger, "Literate South."

84. On the clandestine pursuit of learning among the enslaved, see Heather Andrea Williams, *Self-Taught*, 7–24; and Butchart, *Schooling the Freed People*, 9–15. On the meaning of reading more generally in the antebellum South, see Schweiger, "Literate South."

85. John G. Fee to Bro. Whipple, February 2, 1865, AMA-KY.

86. This point is made in Butchart, *Schooling the Freed People*, 5; and Heather Andrea Williams, *Self-Taught*, 30.

87. John G. Fee to Rev. S. S. Jocelyn, July 18, 1864, in Sears, *Camp Nelson, Kentucky*, 101.

88. On this point, see Hager, *Word by Word*, 7; and Heather Andrea Williams, *Self-Taught*, 30.

89. Minute book 1, May 2, 1863, box 12, ser. 13: Women's Aid Committee, FFAR, FHL; Mitchell, *First Lessons*, 17, 64.

90. Minute book 1, May 2, 1863, box 12, ser. 13: Women's Aid Committee, FFAR, FHL.

91. "The Virginia Refugees," *Friends Review*, January 31, 1863.

92. E. Congdon to Sarah Cope, July 9, 1864, box 12, ser. 13: Women's Aid Committee, FFAR, FHL.

93. "The Freedmen in Virginia," *Friends Review*, November 7, 1863; R. Nicholson to the Committee of the Freedmen's Association in Phila., January 17, 1865, and R. Nicholson to Sarah Cope, February 22, 1865, box 12, ser. 13: Women's Aid Committee, FFAR, FHL.

94. Jane Slocum letter, January 21, 1865, in *Freedmen's Friend*, March 1865, FHL.

95. "The Freedmen in Virginia," *Friends Review*, November 7, 1863.

96. Lewis Lockwood letter, September 14, 1861, in "Mission to the Freed 'Contrabands' at Fortress Monroe, Va.," *American Missionary*, October 1, 1861.

97. Testimony of Lucy Chase, May 10, 1863, AFIC Records, Letters Received, ser. 12, M619, reel 200, RG 94.

98. Lewis Lockwood letter, September 14, 1861, in "New Field of Usefulness," *American Missionary*, October 1861; *Third Report of a Committee*, 17; on the flow of Bibles to the South during the war, see "Refugee Home," *American Missionary*, November 1865.

99. Lewis Lockwood letter, September 10, 1861, in "New Field of Usefulness," *American Missionary*, October 1861.

100. In the aftermath of Nat Turner's rebellion in 1831, for example, the Kentucky Bible Society ceased distributing Bibles to the enslaved. Howard, *Evangelical War*, 40–42.

101. McDannell, *Material Christianity*, 68–91.

102. Lewis Lockwood to AMA Officials, November 27, 1861, in "The Freedmen at Fortress Monroe," *American Missionary*, January 1862.

103. John G. Fee to Bro. Jocelyn, August 1, 1864, in Sears, *Camp Nelson, Kentucky*, 107; Fee, *Autobiography*, 175.

104. Lewis C. Lockwood to AMA, September 16, 1861, in "New Field of Usefulness," *American Missionary*, October 1861.

105. "School-Houses," *American Missionary*, June 1866.

106. Hannah Cranston to Ellen L. Smith, November 29, 1864, box 12, ser. 13: Women's Aid Committee, FFAR, FHL; Lewis Lockwood to Brethren, January 4, 1862, AMA-VA.

107. "Department of Tennessee," *American Missionary*, May 1863; Schecter, "'First Free Spot,'" 40.

108. Eaton, *Report of the General Superintendent*, 48, 61, 82–83; see also R. W. Smith to Rev. Jocelyn, May 25, 1863, AMA-VA.

109. "School-Houses," *American Missionary*, June 1866.

110. "Report of the Women's Aid Association of Friends for the Relief of Coloured Refugees," *Friend*, October 24, 1863; Lucy Chase to Eliza Collins, May 15, 1863, box 12, ser. 13: Women's Aid Committee, FFAR, FHL; Nancy Battey to Friend, January 21, 1863, in *Freedmen's Friend*, March 1865, FHL.

111. Yeatman, *Report on the Condition*, 11.

112. Abisha Scofield to Bro. Strieby, December 1, 1864, AMA-KY.

113. Broadside: Hiram Burdett, November 9, 1864, University of Kentucky Libraries, Lexington, Kentucky; Hiram Burdett Settlement Papers, April 4, 1865, vol. Q, Wills, Garrard County, Kentucky Historical Society, Frankfort, Kentucky.

114. For an overview of the expulsion, see Amy Murrell Taylor, "How a Cold Snap"; Affidavit of John Vetter, December 16, 1864, ser. 225, CCF: "Camp Nelson, Kentucky," RG 92.

115. John Burnside Affidavit, December 15, 1864, ser. 225, CCF: "Camp Nelson, Kentucky," RG 92.

116. John Burnside Affidavit, December 15, 1864, ser. 225, CCF: "Camp Nelson, Kentucky," RG 92.

117. Affidavit of John Higgins, November 28, 1864, and Affidavit of John Vetter, December 16, 1864, ser. 225, CCF: "Camp Nelson, Kentucky," RG 92; and Affidavit of Joseph Miller, November 26, 1864, in Berlin, Reidy, and Rowland, *Black Military Experience*, 269–71.

118. John Fee letter, February 21, 1865, in *American Missionary*, April 1865.

119. Restieaux's work overseeing black laborers at the camp is documented in Report of Persons or Articles Hired, T. E. Hall, file 59, January, February 1864, ser. 238, RG 92.

120. Capt. T. E. Hall to Capt. J. Bates Dickson (Burbridge's assistant), November 26, 1864, Telegrams Received, ser. 2174, DKY, RG 393, pt. 1. Hall described his efforts to

circulate his letter and an affidavit from a soldier named Joseph Miller in T. E. Hall to "My Dear Friend Davis," December 14, 1864, AMA-KY; Affidavit of Joseph Miller, November 26, 1864, in Berlin, Reidy, and Rowland, *Black Military Experience*, 269–71; "Letter from Camp Nelson," *Cincinnati Commercial*, December 1, 1864; "Cruel Treatment of the Wives and Children of U.S. Colored Soldiers," *New York Tribune*, November 28, 1864, reprinted in *Liberator*, December 9, 1864.

121. Brig. Gen. S. S. Fry to Capt. E. B. W. Restieaux, December 15, 1864, in Sears, *Camp Nelson, Kentucky*, 150–51. Fry believed he was upholding Adj. Gen. Lorenzo Thomas's orders to keep women and children from entering Camp Nelson. But Thomas only tried to prevent women and children from *entering* the camp; those who still made it in had to be "provided for" and, according to the terms of the March 13, 1862, article of war, were not to be expelled. On Thomas's original orders see J. Bates Dickson to Col. Sedgewick, June 30, 1864, Telegrams Sent, ser. 2168, DKY, RG 393, pt. 1.

122. "Cruel Treatment of the Wives and Children of U.S. Colored Soldiers," *New York Tribune*, November 28, 1864, reprinted in *Liberator*, December 9, 1864; Lieber quoted in Witt, *Lincoln's Code*, 183.

123. Brig. Maj. Genl. Burbridge to Brig. Gen. S. S. Fry, [November 27?], 1864, in Sears, *Camp Nelson, Kentucky*, 137.

124. Col. Geo. V. Rutherford, by order of Quartermaster General Montgomery Meigs, to Capt. E. B. W. Restieaux, December 7, 1864, Letters Sent, ser. 9, M745, reel 48, RG 92.

125. E. D. Townsend to [T. E. Hall?], December 2, 1864, ser. 225, CCF: "Camp Nelson, Kentucky," RG 92.

126. Senator Wilson had introduced similar legislation unsuccessfully before, in May 1864. After receiving reports of what happened at Camp Nelson, however, he seemed to believe the time was right to get this legislation passed. See S. R. 55 and S. R. 82, 38th Cong., in *Century of Lawmaking*.

127. John G. Fee to Bro. Tappan, February 21, 1865, John G. Fee to Bro. Whipple, February 8, 1865, and Abisha Scofield to brethren, February 4, 1865, AMA-KY.

128. Report of Rev. H. W. Guthrie, January 9, 1865, *Second Annual Report of the Western Freedmen's Aid Commission*, 30.

129. John G. Fee to Bro. Tappan, February 21, 1865, AMA-KY.

130. John G. Fee to Bro. Whipple, February 8, 1865, AMA-KY.

131. *Second Annual Report of the Western Freedmen's Aid Commission*, 30, 32; E. Davis to Bro. Strieby, April 12, 1865, AMA-KY. A list of laborers hired to build the Refugee Home appears in Report of Persons and Articles Hired, E. B. W. Restieaux, file 122, March 1865, ser. 238, RG 92; John G. Fee to Bro. Tappan, February 21, 1865, and John G. Fee to Bro. Strieby, March 2, 1865, AMA-KY; and T. E. Hall to Capt. E. Harlan, June 4, 1865, Letters Received, ser. 2173, DKY, RG 393, pt. 1. For more on the housing and its architecture, see McBride and McBride, "Civil War Housing Insights."

132. John G. Fee to Bro. Whipple, February 8, 1865, AMA-KY; Special Order No. 14, March 13, 1865, in Gabriel Burdett, Co. I, 114th USCT, CMSR.

133. T. E. Hall to Rev. George Whipple, January 9, 186[5], in Sears, *Camp Nelson, Kentucky*, 164; T. E. Hall to M. E. Strieby, December 28, 1864, AMA-KY.

134. J. G. Fee to Bro. Whipple, January 10, 1865, in Sears, *Camp Nelson, Kentucky*, 164–65; John G. Fee to Bro. Whipple, February 8, 1865, AMA-KY.

135. Burdett may have become *the* highest-ranking black official; I have found

no evidence of another refugee reaching or surpassing the position of assistant superintendent in the refugee camps.

136. Gabriel Burdett to John G. Fee, January 20, 1865, AMA-KY.

137. Capt. Chas. M. Keyser to J. Bates Dickson, November 17, 1864, and Maj. Gen. S. G. Burbridge to Capt. J. Bates Dickson, November 29, 1864, Telegrams Received, ser. 2174, DKY, RG 393, pt. 1; Capt. J. Bates Dickson to Brig. Gen. S. S. Fry, December 1, 1864, Telegrams Sent, ser. 2168, DKY, RG 393, pt. 1; Brig. Gen. S. S. Fry to Capt. J. Bates Dickson, December 2, 1864, Telegrams Received, ser. 2174, DKY, RG 393, pt. 1.

138. Abisha Scofield to brethren, February 7, 1865, AMA-KY.

139. John G. Fee to Bro. Whipple, February 8, 25, 1865, AMA-KY.

140. T. E. Hall to Capt. E. Harlan, June 4, 1865, Letters Received, ser. 2173, DKY, RG 393, pt. 1; Gabriel Burdett to John G. Fee, January 20, 1865, AMA-KY.

141. Estimate from Lt. Philip Hayes in Louisville, who computed that as of the end of July 1865, 28,818 black men had enlisted in Kentucky. If an estimated two and a half family members were associated with each soldier, then the total freed equaled 72,045. Lt. Philip Hayes to Brig. Gen. Jas. Brisbin, July 27, 1865, Letters Received, ser. 2173, DKY, RG 393, pt. 1. This estimate was later publicized in Louisville *Daily Union Press*, August 1, 1865. On the legislative work to pass the March 3 bill, see Stanley, "Instead of Waiting."

142. Report dated April 20, 1865, in "Freedmen," *American Missionary*, June 1865.

143. Affidavit of Clarissa Burdett, March 27, 1865, enclosed in T. E. Hall to O. O. Howard, June 22, 1865, M999, BRFAL.

144. See, for example, Affidavit of Frances Johnson, March 25, 1865, enclosed in T. E. Hall to O. O. Howard, June 22, 1865, M999, BRFAL; "Freedmen," *American Missionary*, June 1865.

145. Capt. E. B. Harlan to Post Commandant, April 5, 1865, in Sears, *Camp Nelson, Kentucky*, 193.

146. News of this case appeared in a report of the Freedmen's Bureau shared with the U.S. House of Representatives the following year. *Inspector's Report of Affairs in Kentucky.*

147. John G. Fee to Brother Whipple, March 24, 1865, AMA-KY.

148. Regimental Books and Papers, Co. I, 114th USCT, RG 94.

149. Special Orders No. 50, April 27, 1865, by order of Lt. Col. George A. Hanaford, and Special Orders No. 70, by order of Col. F. H. Bierbower, May 22, 1865, both in Gabriel Burdett, Co. I, 114th USCT, CMSR.

150. Gabriel Burdett, Co. I, 114th USCT, CMSR.

CHAPTER 8

1. Regimental Books and Papers, Co. I, 114th USCT, RG 94.

2. On the sale of the horse, see deposition of Edward Whitehurst in an unrelated case that describes selling a horse to Albert Jones on October 26, 1863. Letters Sent and Proceedings of the Freedmen's Court, Williamsburg, M1913, reel 180, Records of the Field Offices for the State of Virginia, BRFAL; on the borrowing of money, see postwar claim made against Whitehurst for the amount of $23.25 by Robert Smith, also a freedman. Capt. J. W. Barnes to Capt. W. P. Austin, October 25, 1866, Letters Received, Fort Monroe, M1913, roll 128, Records of the Field Offices for the State of Virginia, BRFAL.

3. The leasing of plantations to Northern men did not take hold in eastern Virginia to

the same extent as it did in the Mississippi Valley, largely because there was no cotton there to entice Northern investors. Most plantations in Virginia were either divided up and leased out in smaller parcels to refugees, like the Whitehursts, or were simply converted into new government-sponsored refugee camps. Edward Whitehurst Testimony, July 31, 1877, Approved Claim of Edward Whitehurst, SCC; Major General Ord to E. M. Stanton, March 4, 1865, Staff Papers: Charles Wilder, ser. 158, RG 94.

4. A new Department of Negro Affairs had been created in the region, with a superintendent of Negro affairs replacing the original superintendent of contrabands position. Berlin et al., *Wartime Genesis: Upper South*, 106; [untitled], *Friends Review*, December 10, 1864; "What Gen. Butler is Doing," *Liberator*, January 6, 1865.

5. Morning Reports, Regimental Books and Papers, Co. I, 114th USCT, RG 94.

6. Morning Reports, Regimental Books and Papers, Co. E, 46th USCT, RG 94. On Brazos Santiago, see Reid, *Freedom for Themselves*, 267–68; and Bryant, *The 36th Infantry*, 123.

7. My depiction of contraction and loss complements Gregory P. Downs's recent account of the expansion of the Union army's presence into many new parts of the rural South over the course of 1865. The closing of the refugee camps shows that, even as the army expanded into new areas, it also contracted in the places where it had been. The simultaneous processes of expansion and contraction were really two sides of the same coin—both demonstrating how necessary the military's physical presence was to protect the interests and rights of freed people. Gregory P. Downs, *After Appomattox*, 24–35, 89–90. See also R. E. Farwell to General Fisk, December 22, 1865, M999, BRFAL.

8. The estimate of 200 remaining camps is taken from the data I collected while tracking all 299 camps identified in this study. Horace James to Sir, September 20, 1865, in Hahn et al., *Land and Labor*; "The Freedman," *Friends Review*, October 29, 1864.

9. W. S. Bell to Rev. Whipple, February 29, 1864, and H. L. Beals to Rev. Whipple, March 3, 1864, AMA-VA; "New England Friends and the Freedpeople," *Friends Review*, December 24, 1864. The Taylor farm was likely the property of William E. Taylor of Norfolk, who is listed as the owner of eleven enslaved people in Ancestry.com, *1860 United States Federal Census—Slave Schedules*, Norfolk County, Virginia. Army records identify individual plantations by the last name of the white landowner, and without any other descriptive information available, I have followed that naming convention.

10. Ancestry.com, *1860 United States Federal Census—Slave Schedules*, Issaquena County, Mississippi; A. McFarland to Wm. P. Mellen, March 11, 1864, in Berlin et al., *Wartime Genesis: Lower South*, 797–98; Oubre, *Forty Acres*, 17.

11. On "confiscated" and "abandoned" land, see Syrett, *Civil War Confiscation Acts*, 126–27; Oubre, *Forty Acres*, 3, 32; and Hahn et al., *Land and Labor*, 17–19, 395.

12. Hahn et al., *Land and Labor*, 19, 396 (quote p. 398); Litwack, *Been in the Storm*, 400–401; Cimbala, "Freedmen's Bureau," 599–600; Saville, *Work of Reconstruction*, chap. 3; Oubre, *Forty Acres*, 46–71; Cox, "Promise of Land."

13. Testimony of James Millward, 13–14, and Testimony of Judge Underwood, 101–2, in Court Martial Case File of Charles Wilder, Case No. MM2065, RG 153; Charles Wilder to the AFIC, August 26, 1863, box 4, AFIC Papers, HL. This land was likely available for auction thanks to the Direct Tax Act of 1862, which authorized the seizure and sale of land belonging to those who had failed to pay a federal land tax imposed in 1861, including lands owned by Confederate sympathizers. It was only sporadically implemented in the wartime South, however. Berlin et al., *Wartime Genesis: Upper South*, 35–36.

14. Testimony of Charles Wilder, 4–5, 10–13, and Testimony of James Millward, 13–14, in Court Martial Case File of Charles Wilder, Case No. MM2065, RG 153; "Report of the Committee of Stores," *Freedmen's Friend*, March 1865, FHL.

15. Edward Whitehurst Testimony, July 31, 1877, Approved Claim of Edward Whitehurst, SCC; "Can the Freedmen Take Care of Themselves?," *True Southerner*, November 24, 1865.

16. "Can the Freedmen Take Care of Themselves?," *True Southerner*, November 24, 1865; "List of Govt Buildings at Hampton, Va," May 18, 1866, ser. 225, CCF: "Hampton," RG 92.

17. Simpson, "Quandaries of Command," 135.

18. General Orders No. 26, February 22, 1865, Order Book, Loomis-Wilder Family Papers, Yale University, New Haven, Connecticut; Major General Ord to Hon. E. M. Stanton, March 4, 1865, and E. O. W. Smith to Brig. Gen. George H. Gordon, April 25, 1865, in Staff Papers· Charles Wilder, ser. 158, RG 94; "The Freedmen of General Butler's Late Department," *Liberator*, March 17, 1865.

19. Court Martial Case File of Charles Wilder, Case No. MM2065, RG 153; Bvt. Lt. Col. S. S. Seward to General Ord, May 16, 1865, Staff Papers: Charles Wilder, ser. 158, RG 94.

20. Hahn et al., *Land and Labor*, 18; Testimony of John C. Underwood, 105, Court Martial Case File of Charles Wilder, Case No. MM2065, RG 153.

21. Hodes, *Mourning Lincoln*, 56–57.

22. On Johnson's policies, see Hahn et al., *Land and Labor*, 399–400; and Foner, *Reconstruction*, 183–84.

23. Hahn et al., *Land and Labor*, 400–403, 417–18, 429–33 (quote p. 432). Circular No. 15, as John Syrett has described it, narrowed "the definition of both abandoned and confiscable property, thereby reducing the land the Freedmen's Bureau could retain and increasing the amount it had to restore to pardoned rebels." Syrett, *Civil War Confiscation Acts*, 148; Foner, *Reconstruction*, 158–61; Oubre, *Forty Acres*, 38.

24. On the Freedmen's Bureau's role, see Cimbala, "Freedmen's Bureau," 597–632; and Foner, *Reconstruction*, 160–64.

25. Thos. P. Jackson to the Freedmen living on Govt Farms, September 19, 1865, in Hahn et al., *Land and Labor*, 640.

26. Hahn et al., *Land and Labor*, 404–5 (quote p. 405); Oubre, *Forty Acres*, 47; estimate from Cimbala, "Freedmen's Bureau," 600.

27. O. Brown to Maj. Gen. O. O. Howard, October 4, 1865, in Hahn et al., *Land and Labor*, 435. See also Foner, *Reconstruction*, 162; and Oubre, *Forty Acres*, 80.

28. "All Contraband Camps Breaking Up," Louisville *Daily Union Press*, September 4, 1865.

29. Circular No. 3, May 22, 1865, in Hahn et al., *Land and Labor*, 414; "Reorganization in Eastern Virginia," *American Missionary*, November 1865. Jim Downs also notes that with the military's contraction in 1865 came the loss of any medical care refugees had been receiving from the Union army in *Sick from Freedom*, 68–69.

30. Capt. Horace James to Lieut. Fred. H. Beecher, September 20, 1865, in Hahn et al., *Land and Labor*, 714; Stauffer, "Old Farms," fourth installment, 265; Engs, *Freedom's First Generation*, 104–5.

31. [Untitled], *True Southerner*, December 7, 1865; Hahn et al., *Land and Labor*, 409; Litwack, *Been in the Storm*, 406–7; Cimbala, "Freedmen's Bureau," 609–24; Saville, *Work of Reconstruction*, 86–101.

32. "Can the Freedmen Take Care of Themselves?," *True Southerner*, November 24, 1865.

33. The meeting reportedly took place on August 21, 1865, but was not reported in the press until three months later. "Can the Freedmen Take Care of Themselves?,"

True Southerner, November 24, 1865; "Will the Freedmen Work," *American Missionary*, November 25, 1865.

34. Col. Samuel Thomas to O. O. Howard, January 10, 1866, in Hahn et al., *Land and Labor*, 744–46; Foner, *Reconstruction*, 162. For an in-depth account of the Davis land, which ended up back in Davis's hands in the 1880s, see Hermann, *Pursuit of a Dream*.

35. The Lee property was taxed and seized under the Direct Tax Act of 1862. Reidy, "'Coming from the Shadow.'"

36. Col. Samuel Thomas to O. O. Howard, September 19, 1865, in Hahn et al., *Land and Labor*, 433–34.

37. W. H. Hunt to O. O. Howard, December 2, 1865, in Hahn et al., *Land and Labor*, 459–61; John G. Fee to Clinton Fisk, November 2, 1865, M999, BRFAL.

38. Henry Bram et al. to the President of the United States, October 28, 1865, in Hahn et al., *Land and Labor*, 442–44. See also Jaynes, *Branches without Roots*, 7–10; and Cox, "Promise of Land," 431.

39. Henry Bram et al. to the President of the United States, October 28, 1865, in Hahn et al., *Land and Labor*, 442–44.

40. This point is made in Hahn et al., *Land and Labor*, 686; see also Col. Samuel Thomas to O. O. Howard, September 19, 1865, in Hahn et al., *Land and Labor*, 433–34.

41. Charles Wilder to Mrs. Dulley, October 18, 1865, published in [untitled], *True Southerner*, December 7, 1865. Similar sentiments expressed in Hahn et al., *Land and Labor*, 397; and "Can the Freedmen Take Care of Themselves?," *True Southerner*, November 24, 1865.

42. [Untitled], *True Southerner*, December 7, 1865. Sentiments like Davis's also evident in Horace James to Lieut. Fred. H. Beecher, September 20, 1865, in Hahn et al., *Land and Labor*, 714.

43. Henry Bram et al. to the President of the United States, October 28, 1865, in Hahn et al., *Land and Labor*, 443.

44. Report of Rev. W. D. Harris, December 1, 1865, in *American Missionary*, January 1866.

45. "Can the Freedmen Take Care of Themselves?," *True Southerner*, November 24, 1865. This sentiment about "home," and attachments to it, is ubiquitous in documents of this period. See also "The Overflow," *Freedmen's Bulletin*, June 1865; Orlando Brown to Maj. Gen. Howard, October 4, 1865, and Peter Johnson to Andrew Johnson, enclosed in Elizabeth James to Andrew Johnson, November 23, 1865, both in Hahn et al., *Land and Labor*, 435–36, 610–11, 724–25. On the general meaning of "home" to ex-slaves, see Emberton, "Household and Home Place."

46. Capt. Thos. Kanady to Lt. Z. K. Wood, December 28, 1865, in Hahn et al., *Land and Labor*, 878.

47. "Reported Insurrectionary Movement of Negroes," Richmond *Commercial Bulletin*, November 8, 1865, in Hahn et al., *Land and Labor*, 845–47. Other historians similarly contend that this insurrection hysteria was rooted in the process of land restoration during the fall of 1865 — but have missed the way in which the existence of refugee camps fed that hysteria by offering visible evidence of black people already congregated together in large numbers. See Hahn et al., *Land and Labor*, 796–808; and Hahn, *Nation under Our Feet*, 146–59.

48. [Untitled], *True Southerner*, December 7, 1865.

49. Resolutions of a meeting of "Colored Citizens" at First Baptist Church in Norfolk, December 6, 1865, in Hahn et al., *Land and Labor*, 456.

50. [Untitled], *True Southerner*, November 30, 1865; "Attempted Assassination," *True Southerner*, November 30, 1865.

51. Hahn et al., *Land and Labor*, 805–8; Hahn, *Nation under Our Feet*, 150–59.

52. For another example of how the process could become protracted, see Paul A. Cimbala's discussion of the Sherman reserve in Georgia in "Freedmen's Bureau," 631.

53. Clinton B. Fisk to Maj. Gen. O. O. Howard, July 21,1865, in Sears, *Camp Nelson, Kentucky*, 234. Special Order No. 407, by order of the Secretary of War, July 29, 1865, in Gabriel Burdett, Co. I, 114th USCT, CMSR. Burdett was officially assigned to the Nashville office of the bureau, which served as Fisk's headquarters, but it is evident that he spent most, if not all, of his time working in central Kentucky. See John G. Fee to Bro. Whipple, December 16, 1865, AMA-KY.

54. Maj. Gen. Clinton B. Fisk to Col. D. C. Jaquess, August 15, 1865, in Sears, *Camp Nelson, Kentucky*, 239–40; Gabriel Burdett to E. P. Smith, May 24, 1867, AMA-KY.

55. "From Louisville," *New York Times*, July 26, 1865.

56. Clinton B. Fisk Report to O. O. Howard, July 21, 1865, quoted in Schecter, "'First Free Spot,'" 89; Col. James F. Jaquess to Clinton B. Fisk, August 29, 1865, in Sears, *Camp Nelson, Kentucky*, 245; rations report, July 31, 1865, in Sears, *Camp Nelson, Kentucky*, 228. The military counted 129,137 people still in slavery in Kentucky by early August (out of the 230,000 enslaved before the war). "Actual Condition of Slavery in Kentucky—Letter from Gen. Palmer to the President," Louisville *Daily Union Press*, August 1, 1865; John G. Fee to Bro. Whipple, July 18, 1865, AMA-KY.

57. Chas. Roxborough et al. to Mr. President, late June 1865, in Berlin et al., *Destruction of Slavery*, 626–28.

58. John Fee to Hon. Chas. Sumner, June 6, 1865, in Sears, *Camp Nelson, Kentucky*, 209–10; see also John Fee to Bro. Whipple, June 9, 1865, and John Fee to Bro. Strieby, August 22, 1865, in Sears, *Camp Nelson, Kentucky*, 211, 243.

59. T. E. Hall to Secretary Stanton, June 22, 1865, M999, BRFAL.

60. Sears, *Camp Nelson, Kentucky*, lviii; Hahn et al., *Land and Labor*, 612; see also Notation of Clinton B. Fisk on J. P. Drouillard to General, July 16, 1865, in Hahn et al., *Land and Labor*, 621.

61. "All Contraband Camps Breaking Up," Louisville *Daily Union Press*, September 4, 1865.

62. Maj. Gen. Clinton B. Fisk to Col. D. C. Jaquess, August 15, 1865, and Clinton B. Fisk to O. O. Howard, July 20, 1865, both in Sears, *Camp Nelson, Kentucky*, 239, 232.

63. Clinton B. Fisk to John G. Fee, August 4, 1865, AMA-KY. See also letters of John G. Fee to Fisk, July 17–29, 1865, in M999, BRFAL; and Clinton B. Fisk to O. O. Howard, September 3, 1865, and Maj. Gen. Clinton B. Fisk to Col. D. C. Jacquess, August 15, 1865, in Sears, *Camp Nelson, Kentucky*, 239–40, 249.

64. Schecter, "'First Free Spot,'" 97; on a similar process in Virginia, see Engs, *Freedom's First Generation*, 116.

65. R. E. Farwell to Clinton B. Fisk, October 25, 1865, in Sears, *Camp Nelson, Kentucky*, 289.

66. Maj. Gen. Clinton B. Fisk to Capt. R. E. Farwell, October 23, 1865, and Maj. Gen. Clinton B. Fisk to Col. D. C. Jaquess, August 15, 1865, both in Sears, *Camp Nelson, Kentucky*, 239–40, 287.

67. See Cimbala, *Under the Guardianship*, 131–65; Foner, *Reconstruction*, 164–70; and Schwalm, *Hard Fight for We*, 187–233.

68. Maj. Gen. Clinton Fisk to Col. D. C. Jaquess, August 15, 1865, Clinton Fisk to R. E.

Farwell, October 18, 1865, and Abisha Scofield to Clinton B. Fisk, April 21, 1866, in Sears, *Camp Nelson, Kentucky*, 332–33. On the bureau's efforts to keep freed people on their old plantations, see Cimbala, *Under the Guardianship*, 134–35.

69. Report of N. Battey to P. C. Garret, June 29, 1865, in *Freedmen's Friend*, August 1865, FHL; Report of J. H. Vining, April 5, 1866, in *Freedmen's Friend*, April 5, 1866, FHL.

70. R. E. Farwell to Maj. General Palmer, October 21, 1865, ser. 2174, DKY, RG 393, pt. 1.

71. Hahn et al., *Land and Labor*, 653.

72. R. E. Farwell to Maj. General Palmer, October 21, 1865, ser. 2174, DKY, RG 393, pt. 1.

73. "The Work of Slavery," *Frankfort Commonwealth*, June 16, 1865.

74. R. E. Farwell to Clinton B. Fisk, October 16, 1865, M999, BRFAL.

75. See, for example, the case of *Corbin v. Marsh* (2 Duvall 193), in *Reports of Civil and Criminal Cases*.

76. R. E. Farwell to Clinton B. Fisk, October 25, 1865, M999, BRFAL. On the repeal of martial law in Kentucky, see "Martial Law in Kentucky," Louisville *Daily Union Press*, October 11, 1865; "Proclamation by the President — Martial Law Revoked in Kentucky," Louisville *Daily Union Press*, October 13, 1865; Hahn et al., *Land and Labor*, 653; and R. E. Farwell to Clinton Fisk, November 1, 1865, in Sears, *Camp Nelson, Kentucky*, 295.

77. R. E. Farwell to Clinton B. Fisk, October 16, 1865, M999, BRFAL.

78. Sears, *Camp Nelson, Kentucky*, lxiii–lix.

79. R. E. Farwell to Clinton Fisk, November 1, 1865, in Sears, *Camp Nelson, Kentucky*, 295; on similar failed efforts to drive refugees out of Virginia, see Engs, *Freedom's First Generation*, 117.

80. R. E. Farwell to Clinton Fisk, December 22, 1865, and Clinton B. Fisk to R. E. Farwell, December 25, 1865, in Sears, *Camp Nelson, Kentucky*, 306–8.

81. F. H. Bierbower to Clinton B. Fisk, January 3, 1866, in Sears, *Camp Nelson, Kentucky*, 312.

82. R. E. Farwell to Clinton B. Fisk, January 3, 1866, and F. H. Bierbower to Clinton B. Fisk, January 3, 1866, in Sears, *Camp Nelson, Kentucky*, 311–12.

83. On postwar migration into cities in the South, see Litwack, *Been in the Storm*, 177; Foner, *Reconstruction*, 154–55; and Emberton, *Beyond Redemption*, 76–81. On the settlement in low-lying areas around cities, see Kellogg, "Negro Urban Clusters," 313.

84. Brig. Gen. Davis Tillson to Capt. W. T. Clarke, August 18, 1865, in Hahn et al., *Land and Labor*, 266; John G. Fee to Bro. Whipple, December 16, 1865, AMA-KY.

85. *American Missionary*, January 1866; John G. Fee to Bro. Strieby, November 30, 1866, in Sears, *Camp Nelson, Kentucky*, 352.

86. Foner, *Reconstruction*, 246; Hahn et al., *Land and Labor*, 410, 435, 459–66; "Homesteads for Freedmen," *Freedmen's Bulletin*, July 1866; [untitled], *True Southerner*, March 22, 1866.

87. "Freedmen's Aid," *New Haven (Conn.) Daily Palladium*, December 16, 1865; see also Maria S. Kinney to Rev. John Fee, November 15, 1865, John G. Fee Papers, Berea College, Berea, Kentucky.

88. John G. Fee to Bro. Whipple, December 16, 1865, AMA-KY; Elijah Burdett, Co. H., 12th USCHA, CMSR. Elijah Burdett would be mustered out of service the next month, in January 1866.

89. John G. Fee to General Fisk, July 17, 1865, M999, BRFAL; R. E. Farwell to Clinton B. Fisk, November 1, 1865, in Sears, *Camp Nelson, Kentucky*, 293–95.

90. William H. Merrell to Lt. Levi F. Burnett, May 4, 1866, in Sears, *Camp Nelson, Kentucky*, 335.

91. R. E. Farwell to Clinton Fisk, January 26, 1866, in Sears, *Camp Nelson, Kentucky*, 317.

92. Joseph Moss does not appear in the 1850 or 1860 slave schedules of the U.S. federal census for Jessamine County, although given the size of his property and its agricultural operation, it is likely he hired laborers. On Moss's losses, see John G. Fee, Gabriel Burdett, Geo. Blakeman, A. Scofield to O. O. Howard, October 31, 1865, M999, BRFAL.

93. John G. Fee, Gabriel Burdett, Geo. Blakeman, A. Scofield to O. O. Howard, October 31, 1865, M999, BRFAL; on Blakeman, see Schecter, "'First Free Spot,'" 150.

94. John G. Fee, Gabriel Burdett, Geo. Blakeman, A. Scofield to O. O. Howard, October 31, 1865, M999, BRFAL. On the angry complaints from white Kentuckians about "colonies" of black people being established and how this affected the thinking of white officials, see Abisha Scofield to Bros. Strieby and Whipple, December 14, 1866, and John G. Fee to Bro. Whipple, January 16, 1866, AMA-KY; and Schecter, "'First Free Spot,'" 171.

95. Schecter, "'First Free Spot,'" 170–72; William H. Merrell to Lt. Levi F. Burnett, May 4, 1866, in Sears, *Camp Nelson, Kentucky*, 336; John Lawrence to Capt. H. S. Brown, June 8, 1866, in Sears, *Camp Nelson, Kentucky*, 343.

96. Abisha Scofield to Brother Smith, September 29, 1866, in Sears, *Camp Nelson, Kentucky*, 347.

97. John Fee to Bro. Whipple, June 9, 1865, in Sears, *Camp Nelson, Kentucky*, 212.

98. John Fee to George Whipple, January 25, 1867, in Sears, *Camp Nelson, Kentucky*, 363; Gabriel Burdett to E. M. Cravath, November 2, 1870, Gabriel Burdett to Bro. Cravath, February 1, 1872, and Gabriel Burdett to Bro. Cravath, December 5, 1873, all in AMA-KY; Lucas, *History of Blacks*, 227.

99. Forks of Dix River Baptist Church Day Book, 39, FSL.

100. "Freedmen's Bureau in Kentucky," Louisville *Daily Union Press*, December 29, 1865.

101. By January 31, 1866, the Freedmen's Bureau possessed only 464,000 of the original 858,000 acres. Oubre, *Forty Acres*, 37.

102. "Slavery in the South," *True Southerner*, January 18, 1866.

103. Deposition of Eliza Bogan, February 18, 1895, February 27, 1901, in Silas Small File, Co. E, 46th USCT, WC 393571, WC 509810, Mother's Application No. 546042, CWPF.

104. Moneyhon, *Impact of the Civil War*, 159–64.

105. "Salutary," Helena *Western Clarion*, April 1, 1865.

106. "The Overflow," *Freedmen's Bulletin*, June 1865; "Notice," Helena *Western Clarion*, August 19, 1865.

107. Col. Charles Bentzoni to Sir, February 2, 1866, ser. 2, Letters Received, Department of Arkansas, RG 393, pt. 1; Lt. Col. D. H. Williams to General, September 18, 1865, in Hahn et al., *Land and Labor*, 710.

108. Court Martial Case File of Capt. A. L. Thayer, Case No. OO895, RG 153; Special Orders No. 7, January 24, 1865, Orders and Letters Sent, ser. 159, Generals' Papers: Lorenzo Thomas, RG 94; Order No. 65, by order of John Eaton Jr., August 15, 1864, ser. 4688, Special Orders Received, RG 393, pt. 2.

109. "Letter from John Henry Douglas," November 9, 1865, in *Freedmen's Record*, December 1865, FCCA.

110. "Captain Sweeney's Speech," Helena *Western Clarion*, December 9, 1865.

111. Register of Deaths, Regimental Books and Papers, Company E, 46th USCT, RG 94.

112. Hahn, *Nation under Our Feet*, 102–11; Emberton, *Beyond Redemption*, 136–67; Shaffer, *After the Glory*.

113. On white Southern hostility to returning black veterans, see Litwack, *Been in the Storm*, 267–74; Berlin et al., *Slaves No More*, 233; Emberton, *Beyond Redemption*, 48–52; Rosen, *Terror*, 44–49; and Shaffer, *After the Glory*, 173–74.

114. "Letter from Lucinda B. Jenkins," *Freedmen's Record*, March 1866, FCCA; similar account in R. E. Farwell to Clinton B. Fisk, October 16, 1865, M999, BRFAL.

115. On the earliest phase of the pension program that required "total disability," see Prechtel-Kluskens, "'Reasonable Degree.'" Charles Bogan was the first to successfully apply for a pension, in 1879. See Charles Bogan File, Co. E, 46th USCT, IA 332003, IC 665401, CWPF; Jerry Steele File, Co. E, 46th USCT, IA 495951, IC 1045368, WA 627839, WC 536377, CWPF; Frank McKeal File, Co. E, 46th USCT, IA 922332, IC 1074490, WA 889749, WC 682143, CWPF. The Pension Bureau rejected John McKeel's claim on the grounds that his disability was not adequately proven. John McKeel File, Co. E, 46th USCT, IA 855201, CWPF.

116. The loss of employment has been an underappreciated aspect of the army's demobilization. See Hahn et al., *Land and Labor*, 686.

117. Engs, *Freedom's First Generation*, 85.

118. Abisha Scofield to Rev. Strieby, December 1, 1865, AMA-KY; Petition of Manual Savage, September 22, 1865, ser. 225, CCF: "Negroes," RG 92 (forty-seven other former Fort Monroe refugees filed petitions to the quartermaster at the same time); Engs, *Freedom's First Generation*, 94–95; Hahn et al., *Land and Labor*, 455–57.

119. Deposition of Eliza Bogan, March 9, 1892, in Dennis Bogan File, Co. E, 46th USCT, WA 549935, WC 458509, CWPF.

120. According to county tax records, the Monroe Bogan–owned acreage fell in value from $10,300 in 1860 to $3,808 in 1866; the Josiah McKiel–owned property fell from $41,400 to $14,686 during the same period. See Real Estate Tax Assessment Record Book, 1860, 63, 67, Phillips County Circuit Court Clerk's Office, Helena, Arkansas; and Phillips County Real Estate Tax Assessment Record Book, 1866, 5, 28, Arkansas State Archives, Little Rock, Arkansas. On the debts related to the two men's estates, see Phillips County Probate Court Records, roll 43 (pp. 208, 332, 352), 44 (p. 151), Arkansas State Archives, Little Rock, Arkansas.

121. On Brooks, see *Biographical and Historical Memoirs*, 753–54; Ancestry.com, *1870 United States Federal Census*, Phillips County, Arkansas. On employment with Brooks, see Deposition of Eliza Bogan, February 27, 1901, in Silas Small File, Co. E, 46th USCT, WC 393571, WC 509810, Mother's Application No. 546042, CWPF.

122. On the establishment of the asylum, see *Minutes of Indiana Yearly Meeting of Friends* (1864), 19; and Heather Andrea Williams, *Self-Taught*, 61.

123. "Report of the Women's Aid Association of Friends," *Friends Review*, May 28, 1864; "Letter from Wm. F. Mitchell to Sibilla Embree, March 20, 1865," *Freedmen's Friend*, April 1865, FHL; *Second Annual Report of the Western Freedmen's Aid Commission*, 13; "Memphis Colored Orphan Asylum," *Freedmen's Bulletin*, June 1865; *Second Annual Report of the Board of Directors of the Northwestern Freedmen's Aid Commission*, 13.

124. "Report of a Committee on Freedmen to Friends' Board of Control, Representing the Associated Yearly Meetings of the West, for the Relief of Freedmen," *Friends Review*, April 29, 1865; "Letter from John Henry Douglas," *Freedmen's Record*, December 1865, FCCA; "Helena Asylum," *Freedmen's Record*, December 1865, FCCA.

125. "The Anniversary," *Freedmen's Record*, June 1866, FCCA; see also Heather Andrea Williams, *Self-Taught*, 62. On William H. Grey and postwar Arkansas politics, see Rosen, *Terror*, 87–175.

126. [Illegible title], *Freedmen's Record*, September 1866, FCCA; "Dedication at Helena," *Freedmen's Record*, August 1866, FCCA; see also "History of Southland College," unsigned and undated, 12–13, Southland College Collection, FCCA. On the Fifty-Sixth USCT's efforts, see Heather Andrea Williams, *Self-Taught*, 57–64.

127. Jones, *Intimate Reconstructions*, 118–32; Zipf, "Reconstructing 'Free Woman.'"

128. "Re-Enslavement in Mississippi," *Freedmen's Record*, April 1866, FCCA.

129. Kennedy, *History of Southland College*, 39–42.

130. [Untitled], *Freedmen's Record*, September 1866, FCCA.

131. Engs, *Freedom's First Generation*, 145–48.

132. Abisha Scofield to Col. Johnson, September 10, 1866, and Abisha Scofield to Revd Strieby and Whipple, December 14, 1866, both in Sears, *Camp Nelson, Kentucky*, 344, 354–58; Lucas, *History of Blacks*, 193–94.

133. Abisha Scofield to Revd Strieby and Whipple, December 14, 1866, in Sears, *Camp Nelson, Kentucky*, 354–58.

134. Fee, *Autobiography*, 183; Abisha Scofield to Brother Whipple, October 4, 1866, and John G. Fee to Brother Whipple, June 18, 1867, AMA-KY; "Kentucky," *American Missionary*, November 1866; E. M. Cravath to John G. Fee, October 24, 1866, John G. Fee Papers, Berea College, Berea, Kentucky.

135. Gregory P. Downs notes that the number of military outposts increased again in 1867 with the rise of Military Reconstruction, but the number of soldiers continued to decline. Gregory P. Downs, *After Appomattox*, 188–92.

EPILOGUE

1. One hundred twenty other black households owned property in Elizabeth City County, according to the 1870 census, and owned on average four acres of land. Engs, *Freedom's First Generation*, 177; Ancestry.com, *1870 United States Federal Census*, Elizabeth City County, Virginia.

2. "I live on my own land that I bought from Frank H. Dennis," noted Whitehurst in Edward Whitehurst Testimony, July 31, 1877, Approved Claim of Edward Whitehurst, SCC. Frank Dennis's brother, Henry, is listed as the owner of the property in the 1860 census, while Frank (Francis) is a member of his household. The census may have failed to reflect Frank's stake in the property, or perhaps it changed hands and became Frank's legal property after 1860. Ancestry.com, *1860 United States Federal Census*, Elizabeth City County, Virginia; [unnamed], Provost Judge, to Capt. C. B. Wilder, April 13, 1863, Letters Sent, ser. 5046, DVANC, RG 393, pt. 1. As a tenant, Charles Smith got into a dispute with Frank Dennis over the clearing of timber in 1866. Case of Frank H. Dennis vs. Charles Smith, November 21, 1866, Freedmen's Court Records, M1913, roll 130, BRFAL.

3. The Whitehursts, the Tuckers, Baker, and Johnson are all listed in the census under the same "Family" number, which could indicate a family relationship among them. But it also appears that the census taker consistently classified all members of any households around them as members of one family. Ancestry.com, *1870 United States Federal Census*, Elizabeth City County, Virginia. On the reorganization of black women's labor in the postwar period, which involved innumerable combinations of domestic and field labor, see

Schwalm, *Hard Fight for We*; Hunter, *Bound in Wedlock*, 251–52; and Berlin and Rowland, *Families and Freedom*.

4. Edward Whitehurst Testimony, July 31, 1877, Approved Claim of Edward Whitehurst, SCC; occupation of Manuel Savage from Ancestry.com, *1870 United States Federal Census*, Elizabeth City County, Virginia. On the claims made by former slaves before the Southern Claims Commission, see Lee, *Claiming the Union*, 90–112.

5. On the rejection of claims based on "unofficial" army activity, such as pillage, see Mills, *Southern Loyalists*, x; Summary Report, December 6, 1877, Approved Claim of Edward Whitehurst, SCC. An Edward Whitehurst does appear in county death records for 1896, having died of consumption. But that Edward Whitehurst is listed as being thirty years of age — too young to be the same Edward Whitehurst considered here. It is possible that this age listing was a mistake, and that this was the same man — but no other corroborating evidence has surfaced to confirm that. Death Records, Elizabeth City County, Virginia, reel 9, Hampton Public Library, Hampton, Virginia.

6. Gabriel Burdett to Bro. Strieby, [n.d., likely 1876], and Gabriel Burdett to M. E. Strieby, August 25, 1876, AMA-KY.

7. Berea College Board of Trustees Minutes, April 12, 1866, Berea College, Berea, Kentucky; Gabriel Burdett to E. M. Cravath, November 2, 1870, AMA-KY; Lucas, *History of Blacks*, 227. Although John Fee once referred to the desire of the previous landowner, Joseph Moss, to "give" Gabriel Burdett three acres of land, there is no clear evidence that this gift ever happened; it is more likely that Burdett later purchased the land after it passed to John Fee. John G. Fee to Bro. Whipple, February 11, 1867, in Sears, *Camp Nelson, Kentucky*, 364; Sears, *"Practical Recognition,"* 78.

8. Charles W. Sumner Burdett was born May 10, 1870. This was three years after another son was born, John G. Burdett, whom they named after John G. Fee. They also had a daughter, Gertrude, in 1871. Pension Questionnaire, April 3, 1898, located in Gabriel Burdette [Burdett] Biographical File, Berea College, Berea, Kentucky.

9. Gabriel Burdett to E. M. Cravath, June 1, 1872, AMA-KY.

10. "'The Old Liners.' Second Day's Proceedings in the Abolitionists Reunion," Chicago *Inter-Ocean*, June 11, 1874.

11. Lucas, *History of Blacks*, 299.

12. Gabriel Burdett to E. M. Cravath, June 8, 1872, AMA-KY; Lucas, *History of Blacks*, 308.

13. "The Convention," Chicago *Inter-Ocean*, June 8, 1876.

14. "Disturbing a Republican Meeting in Lexington," San Francisco *Daily Evening Bulletin*, August 13, 1877.

15. Gabriel Burdett to M. E. Strieby, May 12, 1877, AMA-KY. The migration of black Kentuckians to Kansas was accompanied in the late 1870s by similar migrations from Tennessee, Mississippi, Louisiana, and Texas. See Painter, *Exodusters*, 146–51.

16. "Work of Kansas Prohibitionists," *Chicago Tribune*, July 20, 1888; "Prohibitionists in Kansas," *Chicago Tribune*, July 14, 1892; "Kansas Prohibitionists," *Daily Picayune*, July 14, 1892.

17. The Civil War pension system was started in 1862 for the limited purpose of supporting Union soldiers disabled by their wartime service as well as the dependents of men who were killed in the war. By 1890, however, Congress greatly expanded eligibility by abandoning the requirement of a war-related disability. Any veteran with a health-related impairment — which was increasingly common among this aging population — or any dependent of a veteran who had died since the war could now apply for a

pension, including Gabriel Burdett. See Regosin and Shaffer, *Voices of Emancipation*, 2–3; application, July 12, 1890, in Gabriel Burdett File, Co. I, 114th USCT, IA 794724, IC 740230, WA 1037482, WC 786792, CWPF.

18. Application, July 12, 1890, in Gabriel Burdett File, Co. I, 114th USCT, IA 794724, IC 740230, WA 1037482, WC 786792, CWPF; on soldiers' homes, see Marten, *Sing Not War*, 159–98.

19. *Kansas City Sun*, June 24, 1916, 4.

20. Estimates on the number killed in the Elaine Massacre range from 200 to 856. See Woodruff, *American Congo*, 85–109; *Lynching in America*; and "History of Lynchings in the South Documents Nearly 4,000 Names," *New York Times*, February 10, 2015.

21. Eliza Bogan's age is difficult to pinpoint—and the census only contributes to this difficulty by recording her age in an inconsistent fashion. In 1910 she is listed as eighty-one years old, but ten years later, in 1920, she is listed as 105 years old. No other records provide a more precise determination of her age, but if she was an infant at the time that her owner brought her to Arkansas back in the early 1830s, as she testified before the Pension Bureau, then it is likely she was born around 1830 and would have been close to ninety years old in 1919. Ancestry.com, *1910 United States Federal Census*, *1920 United States Federal Census*, Phillips County, Arkansas; Deposition of Eliza Bogan, March 9, 1892, in Dennis Bogan File, Co. E, 46th USCT, WA 549935, WC 458509, CWPF.

22. On sharecropping, see Litwack, *Been in the Storm*, 446–48; and Ayers, *Promise*, 195–202.

23. Even as Dennis Bogan entered into this agreement with Reed and Coolidge, he and Eliza still lived on the property of Samuel Brooks (where the terms of their labor, whether wage-based or a form of sharecropping, remain unclear). Property deed, March 24, 1877, book 151, p. 358, Property Deed Records, Phillips County Circuit Court Clerk's Office, Helena, Arkansas. The "C. R. Coolidge" identified in the deed was most likely Charles R. Coolidge, who appears three years later in the 1880 census with the occupation "Merchant." Ancestry.com, *1880 United States Federal Census*, Phillips County, Arkansas.

24. Deposition of Eliza Bogan, February 27, 1901, in Silas Small File, Co. E, 46th USCT, WC 393571, WC 509810, Mother's Application No. 546042, CWPF. On the continued intervention of white landowners in the intimate lives and marriages of ex-slaves after emancipation, see Hunter, *Bound in Wedlock*, 246–47.

25. Ancestry.com, *1880 United States Federal Census*, Phillips County, Arkansas; Deposition of Eliza Bogan, March 9, 1892, in Dennis Bogan File, Co. E, 46th USCT, WA 549935, WC 458509, CWPF.

26. Eliza Bogan did not apply for a widow's pension based on the service of her previous husband, Silas Small. Instead, his mother, Indiana Kelly, with whom she was in a dispute, filed for a mother's pension based on his service. Deposition of Eliza Bogan, February 18, 1895, in Silas Small File, Co. E, 46th USCT, WC 393571, WC 509810, Mother's Application No. 546042, CWPF.

27. Eliza Bogan and her daughter Fanny were listed as living together in the 1900, 1910, and 1920 censuses. In 1900, they lived with Fanny's husband, Austin Smith, and their six children, all as renters on farmland. In 1910, Fanny (spelled "Fannie" in the census) was by then a "widow" and is listed as the head of household and the owner of a home. In 1920 the census taker flipped this, listing Eliza as the head of household and the homeowner. It's not clear why this would have changed or whether it was meaningful. Fanny's occupations are listed as "laundress" in 1910 and "Chambermaid" in a private home in 1920; one

of Fanny's children, who was still living with them in 1920, was working as a "presser." Ancestry.com, *1900 United States Federal Census, 1910 United States Federal Census, 1920 United States Federal Census*, Phillips County, Arkansas.

28. Widow's pension application of Eliza Bogan, in Dennis Bogan File, Co. E, 46th USCT, WA 549935, WC 458509, CWPF.

29. Gabriel Burdett to Bro. Strieby, [n.d., likely 1876], AMA-KY.

30. On the Gettysburg Address and the meaning of Lincoln's words, see Foner, *Fiery Trial*, 268.

bibliography

PRIMARY SOURCES

Manuscript Collections

Albany, New York
    Manuscripts and Special Collections, New York State Library
        John Ellis Wool Papers
Barre, Vermont
    Vermont Historical Society
        Roswell Farnham Diary
Berea, Kentucky
    Special Collections and Archives, Berea College
        Berea College Board of Trustees Annual Reports
        Berea College Board of Trustees Minutes
        Gabriel Burdett Biographical File
        John G. Fee Papers
Cambridge, Massachusetts
    Houghton Library, Harvard University
        American Freedmen's Inquiry Commission Papers
        "Appeal for the Contrabands at Helena, Ark."
Fayetteville, Arkansas
    Special Collections, University of Arkansas Libraries
        Minos Miller Papers
Frankfort, Kentucky
    Kentucky Historical Society
        Family Files: Alford, Burdett
        Property Deeds, Garrard County
        Tax Books, Garrard County
        Wills, Garrard County
Hampton, Virginia
    Casemate Museum of Fort Monroe

Loose Illustrations
Hampton History Museum
 Chester Bradley Collection
 Evans Family Collection
Hampton Public Library
 Birth Records, Elizabeth City County, Virginia, 1853–1896
 Death Records, Elizabeth City County, Virginia, 1853–1896
 Hampton City Directory
Hampton University Archives
 Fort Monroe Collection
 Titustaua/Slabtown/Goose Alley Photographic Collection

Helena, Arkansas
Phillips County Circuit Court Clerk's Office
 Property Deed Records
 Real Estate Tax Assessment Record Book

Lexington, Kentucky
Family Search Library
 Forks of Dix River Baptist Church Day Book
Special Collections Research Center, University of Kentucky Libraries
 Broadside: Hiram Burdett
 Clay Family Papers
 John W. Jones Papers

Little Rock, Arkansas
Arkansas State Archives
 Mary Edmondson Diary
 Hudson and Reeve Family Papers
 "Map of Helena, Ark. and Vicinity, Showing the Location of Forts and Batteries"
 Phillips County Probate Court Records
 Phillips County Real Estate Tax Assessment Record Books
 Jefferson Robinson Diary

Louisville, Kentucky
Filson Historical Society
 Bibb Family Letters
 Bodley Family Letters
 Stephen Burbridge Letters
 James Hughes Papers
 Patriotic Covers & Misc. Materials
 Davy Walker Emancipation Certificate
 Winn-Cook Family Papers

Madison, Wisconsin
Wisconsin Historical Society
 William F. Allen Papers

New Haven, Connecticut
Manuscripts and Archives, Yale University Library
 Loomis-Wilder Family Papers

New Orleans, Louisiana
Amistad Research Center, Tulane University

American Missionary Association Archives Microfilm

Raleigh, North Carolina

North Carolina State Archives

Chowan County Minute Docket, Superior Court Records, 1828–1838

Richmond, Indiana

Friends Collection and College Archives, Earlham College

American Friend

Ruth Edwards Diary

Freedman

Freedmen's Record

Job Hadley Reminiscences

Martha Newlin Lindley Reminiscences

Minutes of the Indiana Yearly Meeting

Minutes of the Indiana Yearly Meeting, Committee on Freedmen's Relief

Minutes of the Rush Creek Monthly Meeting

Minutes of Western Yearly Meeting of Friends, 1858–1869

Southland College Collection

Richmond, Virginia

Virginia Historical Society

Cary Family Papers

Mallory Family Papers

Arthur E. O'Connor Papers

Swarthmore, Pennsylvania

Friends Historical Library, Swarthmore College

Freedmen's Friend

Friends Freedmen's Association Records, Record Group 4/024

Pennsylvania Yearly Meeting, Women's Meeting Minutes

Anne Sheppard Papers

Anna Wharton Papers

Women's Association of Philadelphia for the Relief of the Freedman

Washington, D.C.

Manuscript Division, Library of Congress

Benjamin F. Butler Papers

Mary Tyler Peabody Mann Papers

National Archives and Records Administration

Compiled Military Service Records

Record Group 15: Records of the Veterans Administration, 1773–1985

Record Group 48: Records of the Office of the Secretary of the Interior, 1826–1985

Record Group 92: Records of the Quartermaster General, 1774–1985

Record Group 94: Records of the Adjutant General's Office, 1780s–1917

Record Group 105: Records of the Bureau of Refugees,
Freedmen, and Abandoned Lands, 1861–1879

Record Group 109: War Department Collection
of Confederate Records, 1825–1900

Record Group 153: Records of the Judge Advocate General, 1800–1967

Record Group 217: Records of the Accounting Officers
of the Department of the Treasury, 1775–1927

Record Group 393: Records of U.S. Army Continental Commands, 1821–1920
National Park Service
The Civil War Soldiers and Sailors System. Accessed October 8, 2017.
https://www.nps.gov/civilwar/soldiers-and-sailors-database.htm
Wichita, Kansas
Special Collections, Wichita State University
John T. Farnham Diary

Newspapers and Periodicals

American Missionary
Atlantic Monthly
Christian Recorder
Chronicling America: Historic American Newspapers Database, Library of Congress
    Daily Picayune (New Orleans, La.)
    Kansas City Sun
Cincinnati Commercial
Colored Tennessean
Commonwealth (Boston)
Daily Union Press (Louisville, Ky.)
Douglass Monthly
Fold3.com Database
    Chicago Tribune
Frankfort (Ky.) Commonwealth
Frank Leslie's Illustrated Newspaper
Freedmen's Bulletin
Friend
Friends Review
Harper's Weekly
Liberator
National Freedman
New York Times
New York Tribune
Nineteenth-Century U.S. Newspapers Database, Gale Cengage
    Daily Evening Bulletin (San Francisco)
    Inter-Ocean (Chicago)
    New Haven (Conn.) Daily Palladium
North American and United States Gazette
Pine and Palm
Sanitary Reporter
Southern Shield
True Southerner
Western Clarion (Helena, Ark.)

Census Data

1820 United States Federal Census [database online]. Provo, Utah: Ancestry.com
    Operations, Inc., 2010.

1830 United States Federal Census [database online]. Provo, Utah: Ancestry.com
   Operations, Inc., 2010.
1830 United States Federal Census — Slave Schedules [database online]. Provo, Utah:
   Ancestry.com Operations, Inc., 2010.
1850 United States Federal Census [database online]. Provo, Utah: Ancestry.com
   Operations, Inc., 2009.
1850 United States Federal Census, Nonpopulation Schedules (Agriculture) [database online].
   Provo, Utah: Ancestry.com Operations, Inc., 2010.
1850 United States Federal Census — Slave Schedules [database online]. Provo, Utah:
   Ancestry.com Operations, Inc., 2004.
1860 United States Federal Census [database online]. Provo, Utah: Ancestry.com
   Operations, Inc., 2009.
1860 United States Federal Census — Slave Schedules [database online]. Provo, Utah:
   Ancestry.com Operations, Inc., 2010.
1870 United States Federal Census [database online]. Provo, Utah: Ancestry.com
   Operations, Inc., 2009.
1880 United States Federal Census [database online]. Provo, Utah: Ancestry.com
   Operations, Inc., 2010.
1900 United States Federal Census [database online]. Provo, Utah: Ancestry.com
   Operations, Inc., 2004.
1910 United States Federal Census [database online]. Lehi, Utah: Ancestry.com Operations,
   Inc., 2006.
1920 United States Federal Census [database online]. Provo, Utah: Ancestry.com
   Operations, Inc., 2010.
Compiled Census Data. *1860 United States Federal Census.* Monroe County, New York.
   Historical Census Browser, University of Virginia. Accessed March 24, 2015. http://
   mapserver.lib.virginia.edu/.

Published Federal Government Documents

Africans in Fort Monroe Military District. March 25, 1862. 37th Congress, 2nd Session,
   House Ex. Doc. 85.
Ancestry.com. *Virginia, Select Marriages, 1785–1940* [database online]. Provo, Utah:
   Ancestry.com Operations, Inc., 2014.
Article of War. March 13, 1862. H. R. 299, 37th Congress, 2nd Session.
A Century of Lawmaking for the New Nation: U.S. Congressional Documents and Debates,
   Library of Congress. Accessed May 24, 2011. http://memory.loc.gov/ammem/amlaw/.
"Civil War Service Records, Union Records." Digital Images. Fold3.com, 2015. Accessed
   July 2, 2015. http://www.fold3.com.
"Featured Document: The Emancipation Proclamation." National Archives and Records
   Administration. Accessed April 27, 2015. http://www.archives.gov/exhibits/featured
   _documents/emancipation_proclamation/.
Inspector's Report of Affairs in Kentucky. March 5, 1866. 39th Congress, 1st Session, House
   Ex. Doc. 70.
Lincoln, Abraham. First Inaugural Address, March 4, 1861. *The Avalon Project: Documents in
   Law, History, and Diplomacy,* Lillian Goldman Law Library, Yale University Law School.
   Accessed September 9, 2016. http://avalon.law.yale.edu/19th_century/lincoln1.asp.

Report of Commissioners of Investigation of Colored Refugees in Kentucky, Tennessee, and Alabama. December 28, 1864. 38th Congress, 2nd Session, Exec. Doc. No. 28. Washington, D.C.: Government Printing Office, 1865.

Reports of Committees of the House of Representatives. Vol. 2, 52nd Congress, 1st Session. Washington, D.C.: Government Printing Office, 1892.

Revised United States Army Regulations of 1861. Washington, D.C.: Government Printing Office, 1863. *Making of America* Digital Library, University of Michigan. Accessed May 23, 2015. http://quod.lib.umich.edu/m/moa/AGY4285.0001.001?rgn=main;view=fulltext.

The Second Confiscation Act. Freedmen and Southern Society Project, University of Maryland. Accessed April 17, 2017. http://www.freedmen.umd.edu/conact2.htm.

The Territory of Arkansas Territory, 1829–1836. Vol. 21 of *The Territorial Papers of the United States.* Washington, D.C.: Government Printing Office, 1954.

United States War Department. *The War of the Rebellion: A Compilation of the Official Records of the Union and Confederate Armies.* Washington, D.C.: Government Printing Office, 1880–1901.

Other Published Primary Sources

Appeal of the Western Freedmen's Aid Commission in Behalf of the National Freedmen. Cincinnati, Ohio: Methodist Book Concern, 1864.

Berlin, Ira, Barbara J. Fields, Thavolia Glymph, Joseph P. Reidy, and Leslie S. Rowland, eds. *The Destruction of Slavery.* Ser. 1, vol. 1, of *Freedom: A Documentary History of Emancipation, 1861–1867.* Cambridge: Cambridge University Press, 1985.

———. *Freedom: A Documentary History of Emancipation, 1861–1867.* 6 vols. Cambridge: Cambridge University Press, 1983–93.

Berlin, Ira, Thavolia Glymph, Steven F. Miller, Joseph P. Reidy, Leslie S. Rowland, and Julie Saville, eds. *The Wartime Genesis of Free Labor: The Lower South.* Ser. 1, vol. 3, of *Freedom: A Documentary History of Emancipation, 1861–1867.* Cambridge: Cambridge University Press, 1990.

Berlin, Ira, Steven F. Miller, Joseph P. Reidy, and Leslie S. Rowland, eds. *The Wartime Genesis of Free Labor: The Upper South.* Ser. 1, vol. 2, of *Freedom: A Documentary History of Emancipation, 1861–1867.* Cambridge: Cambridge University Press, 1993.

Berlin, Ira, Joseph P. Reidy, and Leslie S. Rowland, eds. *The Black Military Experience.* Ser. 2 of *Freedom: A Documentary History of Emancipation, 1861–1867.* Cambridge: Cambridge University Press, 1983.

Berlin, Ira, and Leslie S. Rowland, eds. *Families and Freedom: A Documentary History of African-American Kinship in the Civil War Era.* New York: New Press, 1997.

Biographical and Historical Memoirs of Eastern Arkansas. Chicago: Goodspead Publishing Company, 1890.

Cannon, Le Grand B. *Personal Reminiscences of the Rebellion, 1861–1866.* New York: Burr Printing House, 1895.

Eaton, Col. John. *Report of the General Superintendent of Freedmen, Department of the Tennessee and State of Arkansas, for 1864.* Memphis, 1865.

Extracts from Reports of the Superintendents of Freedmen, Compiled by Rev. Joseph Warren D. D., from Records in the Office of Col. John Eaton Jr., General Superintendent of Freedmen, Department of the Tennessee and State of Arkansas. Vicksburg, Miss.: Freedmen Press Prints, 1864.

Faust, Betty M., ed. "Diary of Sue Cook, 1864–1865." *Phillips County Historical Quarterly* 4 (December 1965): 29–42.

Fee, John G. *Autobiography of John G. Fee, Berea, Kentucky*. Chicago: National Christian Association, 1891.

―――. *Non-Fellowship with Slaveholders the Duty of Christians*. New York: John A. Cray, 1855.

Freedmen and Union Refugees' Department of the Mississippi Valley Sanitary Fair. St. Louis: 1864.

Friends Association of Philadelphia. *Statistics of the Operations of the Executive Board of Friends' Association of Philadelphia, and Its Vicinity, for the Relief of Colored Freedmen*. Philadelphia: Inquirer Printing Office, 1864.

Fry, Alice L., ed. *Following the Fifth Kansas Cavalry: The Letters*. Independence, Mo.: Two Trails Publishing, 1998.

Hahn, Steven, Steven F. Miller, Susan E. O'Donovan, John C. Rodrigue, and Leslie S. Rowland, eds. *Land and Labor, 1865*. Ser. 3, vol. 1, of *Freedom: A Documentary History of Emancipation, 1861–1867*. Chapel Hill: University of North Carolina Press, 2008.

Historical Register of the Officers and Students of Berea College: From the Beginning to June, 1915. Berea, Ky.: Berea College, 1916.

Howerton, W. H. *The Legislative Manual and Political Register of the State of North Carolina*. Raleigh, N.C.: Josiah Turner, Jr, State Printer and Binder, 1874.

Jacobs, Harriet Ann. *Incidents in the Life of a Slave Girl*. Edited by Nellie Y. McKay and Frances Smith Foster. New York: W. W. Norton, 2001.

Jefferson, Thomas. "Notes on the State of Virginia (1787)." In *Defending Slavery: Proslavery Thought in the Old South*, edited by Paul Finkelman, 47–54. Boston: Bedford St. Martin's, 2003.

Journal of the Senate of the Commonwealth of Kentucky. Frankfort, Ky.: Jno. B. Major, State Printer, 1861.

"McKiel et al. vs. the Real Estate Bank." In vol. 4 of *Report of Cases Argued and Determined in the Supreme Court of Law and Equity of the State of Arkansas*, edited by Albert Pike, 592. Little Rock, Ark.: B. J. Bordon, 1843.

Minutes of Indiana Yearly Meeting of Friends, Held at Richmond, Indiana. Cincinnati, Ohio: E. Morgan & Sons, 1865.

Minutes of Indiana Yearly Meeting of Friends; Held at Whitewater Meeting House, Richmond, Indiana. Cincinnati, Ohio: E. Morgan & Sons, 1863.

Minutes of Indiana Yearly Meeting of Friends; Held at Whitewater Meeting House, Richmond, Indiana. Cincinnati, Ohio: E. Morgan & Sons, 1864.

Minutes of the First Annual Meeting of the Northwestern Freedmen's Aid Commission, Held in the Second Presbyterian Church in Chicago, on Thursday Evening, April 14th, and on Friday Morning, April 15th, 1864. Chicago: James Barnet, 1864.

Mitchell, S. Augustus. *First Lessons in Geography for Young Children*. Philadelphia: E. H. Butler & Co, 1860. Baldwin Library of Historical Children's Literature, University of Florida. Accessed September 24, 2015. http://ufdc.ufl.edu/UF00003334/00001.

Moore, Frank, ed. *The Rebellion Record: A Diary of American Events*. Vol. 8. New York: D. Van Nostrand, 1865.

Pierce, Edward L. "The Contrabands at Fortress Monroe." *Atlantic Monthly* 8 (November 1861): 626–40.

Rawick, George P., ed. *The American Slave: A Composite Autobiography.* Westport, Conn.: Greenwood Press, 1972–79.

Report of a Committee of the Representatives of the New York Yearly Meeting of Friends upon the Condition and Wants of the Colored Refugees. New York, 1862.

Report of Indiana Yearly Meeting's Executive Committee, for the Relief of Colored Freedmen. Richmond, Ind.: Holloway & Davis, 1864.

Report of the Board of Education for Freedmen, Department of the Gulf, for the Year 1864. New Orleans: Printed at the Office of the True Delta, 1865.

Reports of Cases at Law, Argued and Determined in the Court of Appeals and Court of Errors of South Carolina. Vol. 5, *November 1851–May 1862, J. S. G. Richardson, Court Reporter.* Columbia, S.C.: A. S. Johnston, 1852.

Reports of Civil and Criminal Cases Decided by the Court of Appeals of Kentucky, 1785–1951. Vol. 2. Frankfort: Kentucky Yeoman Office, 1867.

Sears, Richard D., ed. *Camp Nelson, Kentucky: A Civil War History.* Lexington: University Press of Kentucky, 2002.

Second Annual Report of the Board of Directors of the Northwestern Freedmen's Aid Commission. Chicago: James Barnet, 1865.

Second Annual Report of the New England Freedmen's Aid Society. Boston: Published at the Office of the Society, 1864.

Second Annual Report of the Western Freedmen's Aid Commission. Cincinnati, Ohio: R. P. Thompson, 1865.

Second Report of a Committee of the Representatives of New York Yearly Meeting of Friends upon the Condition and Wants of the Colored Refugees. New York, 1863.

Second Report of the Executive Board of the Friends Association of Philadelphia and Its Vicinity, for the Relief of Colored Freedmen. Philadelphia: Ringwalt & Brown, 1865.

Taylor, Susie King. *Reminiscences of My Life in Camp: An African American Woman's Civil War Memoir.* Edited by Catherine Clinton. Athens: University of Georgia Press, 2006.

Third Report of a Committee of the Representatives of New York Yearly Meeting of Friends upon the Condition and Wants of the Colored Refugees. New York, 1864.

Underhill, Joshua Whittington. *Helena to Vicksburg, A Civil War Odyssey: The Personal Diary of Joshua Whittington Underhill, Surgeon, 46th Regiment, Indiana Volunteer Infantry.* Lincoln Center, Mass.: Heritage House, 2000.

Vockery, Bill, and Kathy Vockery, eds. *Vital Statistics of Garrard County, Kentucky: Births-Marriages-Deaths, 1852–1859, 1874–1878.* Lancaster, Ky.: Garrard Co. Historical Society, 1988.

West, George Benjamin. *When the Yankees Came: Civil War and Reconstruction on the Virginia Peninsula.* Edited by Parke Rouse Jr. Richmond, Va.: Dietz Press, 1977.

Yeatman, James E. *A Report on the Condition of the Freedmen of the Mississippi, Presented to the Western Sanitary Commission, December 17th, 1863.* St. Louis: Western Sanitary Commission Rooms, 1864.

SECONDARY SOURCES

Arenson, Adam, and Andrew R. Graybill, eds. *Civil War Wests: Testing the Limits of the United States.* Berkeley: University of California Press, 2015.

Ash, Stephen V. *When the Yankees Came: Conflict and Chaos in the Occupied South, 1861–1865.* Chapel Hill: University of North Carolina Press, 1995.

Astor, Aaron. *Rebels on the Border: Civil War, Emancipation, and the Reconstruction of Kentucky and Missouri*. Baton Rouge: Louisiana State University Press, 2012.

Ayers, Edward L. *Promise of the New South: Life After Reconstruction*. 15th anniversary ed. New York: Oxford University Press, 2007.

Ayers, Edward L., and Scott Nesbit. "Seeing Emancipation: Scale and Freedom in the American South." *Journal of the Civil War Era* 1 (March 2011): 3–24.

Bailey, Anne J. *Between the Enemy and Texas: Parsons's Texas Cavalry in the Civil War*. Fort Worth: Texas Christian University Press, 1989.

Balicki, Joseph F. "'Masterly Inactivity': The Confederate Cantonment Supporting the 1861–1862 Blockade of the Potomac River, Evansport, Virginia." In *Huts and History: The Historical Archaeology of Military Encampment during the American Civil War*, edited by Clarence R. Geier, David G. Orr, and Matthew B. Reeves, 125–47. Gainesville: University Press of Florida, 2006.

Baptist, Edward. *The Half Has Never Been Told: Slavery and the Making of American Capitalism*. New York: Basic Books, 2014.

Barber, E. Susan, and Charles F. Ritter. "'Physical Abuse . . . and Rough Handling': Race, Gender, and Sexual Justice in the Occupied South." In *Occupied Women: Gender, Military Occupation, and the American Civil War*, edited by LeeAnn Whites and Alecia P. Long, 49–66. Baton Rouge: Louisiana State University Press, 2009.

Barnickel, Linda. *Milliken's Bend: A Civil War Battle in History and Memory*. Baton Rouge: Louisiana State University Press, 2013.

Baseler, Marilyn C. *Asylum for Mankind: America, 1607–1800*. Ithaca, N.Y.: Cornell University Press, 1998.

Beilein, Joseph M., Jr. "The Guerrilla Shirt: A Labor of Love and the Style of Rebellion in Civil War Missouri." *Civil War History* 58 (June 2012): 151–79.

Bennett, Michael J. *Union Jacks: Yankee Sailors in the Civil War*. Chapel Hill: University of North Carolina Press, 2004.

Bercaw, Nancy. *Gendered Freedoms: Race, Rights, and the Politics of Household in the Delta, 1861–1875*. Gainesville: University Press of Florida, 2003.

Bercovitch, Sacvan, and Cyrus R. Patell, eds. *The Cambridge History of American Literature*. Vol. 4. Cambridge: Cambridge University Press, 1994.

Berlin, Ira. *The Long Emancipation: The Demise of Slavery in the United States*. Cambridge, Mass.: Harvard University Press, 2015.

Berlin, Ira, Barbara J. Fields, Steven F. Miller, Joseph P. Reidy, and Leslie S. Rowland. *Slaves No More: Three Essays on Emancipation and the Civil War*. Cambridge: Cambridge University Press, 1992.

Berry, Daina Ramey. "'We Sho Was Dressed Up': Slave Women, Material Culture, and the Decorative Arts in Wilkes County, Georgia." In *The Savannah River Valley to 1865: Fine Arts, Architecture, and Decorative Arts*, edited by Ashley Callahan, 73–83. Athens: Georgia Museum of Art, 2003.

Blair, William A. "The Seven Days and the Radical Persuasion: Convincing Moderates in the North of the Need for a Hard War." In *The Richmond Campaign of 1862: The Peninsula and the Seven Days*, edited by Gary Gallagher, 153–77. Chapel Hill: University of North Carolina Press, 2000.

Blight, David. *A Slave No More: Two Men Who Escaped to Freedom*. New York: Harcourt, 2007.

Blouin, Francis X., Jr., and William G. Rosenberg. *Processing the Past: Contesting Authority in History and the Archives*. New York: Oxford University Press, 2011.

Bon Tempo, Carl. *Americans at the Gate: The United States and Refugees during the Cold War*. Princeton, N.J.: Princeton University Press, 2008.

Boulden, Ben. "Frederick Steele." Encyclopedia of Arkansas History & Culture. Accessed July 23, 2014. http://www.encyclopediaofarkansas.net/encyclopedia/entry-detail.aspx ?entryID=1914.

Brady, Lisa M. *War upon the Land: Military Strategy and the Transformation of Southern Landscapes during the American Civil War*. Athens: University of Georgia Press, 2012.

Brahinsky, Rachel, Jade Sasser, and Laura-Anne Minkoff-Zern. "Race, Space, and Nature: An Introduction and Critique." *Antipode* 46 (November 2014): 1135–52.

Brasher, Glenn David. *The Peninsula Campaign and the Necessity of Emancipation: African Americans and Their Fight for Freedom*. Chapel Hill: University of North Carolina Press, 2012.

Breen, Timothy. *Marketplace of Revolution: How Consumer Politics Shaped American Independence*. New York: Oxford University Press, 2004.

Brent, Joseph E., and Maria Campbell Brent. *Civil War Helena: A Research Project and Interpretive Plan*. Part 2, *Helena and Phillips County, Arkansas*. Versailles, Ky.: Mudpuppy and Waterdog, 2009.

Bryant, James K., II. *The 36th Infantry United States Colored Troops in the Civil War: A History and Roster*. Jefferson, N.C.: McFarland, 2012.

Burchardt, Marian, and Stefan Höhne. "The Infrastructure of Diversity: Materiality and Culture in Urban Space—An Introduction." *New Diversities* 17, no. 2 (2015): 1–13.

Butchart, Ronald E. *Schooling the Freed People: Teaching, Learning, and the Struggle for Black Freedom, 1861–1876*. Chapel Hill: University of North Carolina Press, 2010.

Byrd, Dana E., with Tyler DeAngelis. "Tracing Transformations: Hilton Head Island's Journey to Freedom, 1860–1865." *Nineteenth-Century Art Worldwide* 14 (Autumn 2015). http://www.19thc-artworldwide.org/autumn15/byrd-hilton-head-island-journey-to -freedom-1860–1865.

Calico, Forrest. *History of Garrard County Kentucky and Its Churches*. New York: Hobson Book Press, 1947.

Camp, Stephanie M. H. *Closer to Freedom: Enslaved Women and Everyday Resistance in the Plantation South*. Chapel Hill: University of North Carolina Press, 2004.

———. "The Pleasures of Resistance: Enslaved Women and Body Politics in the Plantation South, 1830–1861." In *New Studies in the History of American Slavery*, edited by Stephanie M. H. Camp and Edward E. Baptist, 87–126. Athens: University of Georgia Press, 2006.

Carroll, Bret. "Religion in Space: Spatial Approaches to American Religious Studies." Oxford Research Encyclopedia of Religion. Published August 2015. http://religion .oxfordre.com.

Cashin, Joan. "Hungry People in the Wartime South: Civilians, Armies, and the Food Supply." In *Weirding the War: Tales from the Civil War's Ragged Edges*, edited by Stephen Berry, 160–75. Athens: University of Georgia Press, 2011.

———. "Torn Bonnets and Stolen Silks: Fashion, Gender, Race, and Danger in the Wartime South." *Civil War History* 61 (December 2015): 338–61.

———. "Trophies of War: Material Culture in the Civil War Era." *Journal of the Civil War Era* 1 (September 2011): 339–67.

Catton, Philip. "Counter-insurgency and Nation Building: The Strategic Hamlet Programme in South Vietnam, 1961–1963." *International History Review* 21 (1999): 918–40.

Cecelski, David S. *The Fire of Freedom: Abraham Galloway and the Slaves' Civil War*. Chapel Hill: University of North Carolina Press, 2012.

Chidester, David, and Edward T. Linenthal, eds. *American Sacred Space*. Bloomington: Indiana University Press, 1995.

Christ, Mark K. *Civil War Arkansas, 1863: The Battle for a State*. Norman: University of Oklahoma Press, 2010.

Churches of Lancaster and Garrard County. Lancaster, Ky.: Central Record, 1960.

Cimbala, Paul A. "The Freedmen's Bureau, the Freedmen, and Sherman's Grant in Reconstruction Georgia, 1865–1867." *Journal of Southern History* 53 (November 1989): 597–632.

———. *Under the Guardianship of the Nation: The Freedmen's Bureau and the Reconstruction of Georgia, 1865–1870*. Athens: University of Georgia Press, 1997.

Cimprich, John. *Slavery's End in Tennessee, 1861–1865*. Tuscaloosa: University of Alabama Press, 1985.

Clampitt, Bradley R. *Occupied Vicksburg*. Baton Rouge: Louisiana State University Press, 2016.

Click, Patricia C. *Time Full of Trial: The Roanoke Island Freedmen's Colony, 1862–1867*. Chapel Hill: University of North Carolina Press, 2001.

Clinton, Catherine, and Nina Silber, eds. *Battle Scars: Gender and Sexuality in the American Civil War*. New York: Oxford University Press, 2006.

Cobb, J. Michael, and Whythe Holt. *Images of America: Hampton*. Charleston, S.C.: Arcadia, 2008.

Cohen, Lizabeth. *A Consumer's Republic: The Politics of Mass Consumption in Postwar America*. New York: Vintage, 2003.

Cohen, Patricia Cline. *A Calculating People: The Spread of Numeracy in Early America*. Chicago: University of Chicago Press, 1982.

Coole, Diana, and Samantha Frost, eds. *New Materialisms: Ontology, Agency, and Politics*. Durham, N.C.: Duke University Press, 2010.

Cooper, Frederick, Thomas C. Holt, and Rebecca J. Scott. *Beyond Slavery: Explorations of Race, Labor, and Citizenship in Postemancipation Societies*. Chapel Hill: University of North Carolina Press, 2005.

Cox, LaWanda. "The Promise of Land for the Freedmen." *Mississippi Valley Historical Review* 45 (December 1958): 413–40.

Crane, Diana. *Fashion and Its Social Agendas: Class, Gender, and Identity in Clothing*. Chicago: University of Chicago Press, 2000.

Crang, Mike. *Cultural Geography*. London: Routledge, 1998.

Creel, Margaret Washington. *"A Peculiar People": Slave Religion and Community Culture among the Gullahs*. New York: New York University Press, 1988.

Dauber, Michele Landis. *The Sympathetic State: Disaster Relief and the Origins of the American Welfare State*. Chicago: University of Chicago Press, 2013.

Davis, Arthur P. "William Roscoe Davis and His Descendants." *Negro History Bulletin* 13 (January 1950): 75–95.

Davis, David Brion. *The Problem of Slavery in the Age of Emancipation*. New York: Vintage, 2014.

Dilbeck, D. H. *A More Civil War: How the Union Waged a Just War*. Chapel Hill: University of North Carolina Press, 2016.

Dorsey, Bruce. *Reforming Men and Women: Gender in the Antebellum City*. Ithaca, N.Y.: Cornell University Press, 2002.

Downs, Gregory P. *After Appomattox: Military Occupation and the Ends of War*. Cambridge, Mass.: Harvard University Press, 2015.

Downs, Jim. "Emancipating the Evidence: The Ontology of the Freedmen's Bureau Records." In *Beyond Freedom: Disrupting the History of Emancipation*, edited by David W. Blight and Jim Downs, 160–180. Athens: University of Georgia Press, 2017.

———. *Sick from Freedom: African-American Illness and Suffering during the Civil War and Reconstruction*. New York: Oxford University Press, 2012.

Du Bois, W. E. B. *Black Reconstruction in America, 1860–1880*. New York: Atheneum, 1992. First published in 1935 by Harcourt, Brace, and Company.

Edson, Obed. *Biographical and Portrait Cyclopedia of Chautauqua County, New York*. Philadelphia: John M. Gresham, 1891.

Ellis, Clifton, and Rebecca Ginsburg, eds. *Cabin, Quarter, Plantation: Architecture and Landscapes of North American Slavery*. New Haven, Conn.: Yale University Press, 2010.

Eltis, David. "A Brief Overview of the Trans-Atlantic Slave Trade." Voyages: The Trans-Atlantic Slave Trade Database. Accessed April 16, 2017. http://www.slavevoyages.org/assessment/essays.

Emberton, Carole. *Beyond Redemption: Race, Violence, and the American South after the Civil War*. Chicago: University of Chicago Press, 2013.

———. "Household and Home Place: The Emotional Community of the Plantation in Slavery and Freedom." In *From Home Front to Battlefield: The Civil War as a Household War*, edited by LeeAnn Whites and Lisa Tendrich Frank. Athens: University of Georgia Press, forthcoming.

Engs, Robert Francis. *Freedom's First Generation: Black Hampton, Virginia, 1861–1890*. Philadelphia: University of Pennsylvania Press, 1979.

Everest, Allen S. *Moses Hazen and the Canadian Refugees in the American Revolution*. Syracuse, N.Y.: Syracuse University Press, 1976.

Farmer-Kaiser, Mary. *Freedwomen and the Freedmen's Bureau: Race, Gender, and Public Policy in the Age of Emancipation*. New York: Fordham University Press, 2010.

Fassin, Didier. *Humanitarian Reason: A Moral History of the Present*. Berkeley: University of California Press, 2012.

Faulkner, Carol. *Women's Radical Reconstruction: The Freedmen's Aid Movement*. Philadelphia: University of Pennsylvania Press, 2004.

Faust, Drew Gilpin. *This Republic of Suffering: Death and the American Civil War*. New York: Alfred A. Knopf, 2008.

Feimster, Crystal N. "Rape and Justice in the Civil War." *New York Times*, April 25, 2013. http://opinionator.blogs.nytimes.com.

———. *Southern Horrors: Women and the Politics of Rape and Lynching*. Cambridge, Mass.: Harvard University Press, 2011.

Fellman, Michael. *Inside War: The Guerrilla Conflict in Missouri during the American Civil War*. New York: Oxford University Press, 1989.

Fen, Sing-nan. "Lewis C. Lockwood." *History of Education Quarterly* 3 (March 1963): 38–42.

Ferrer, Ada. *Insurgent Cuba: Race, Nation, and Revolution, 1868–1898*. Chapel Hill: University of North Carolina Press, 1999.

Fett, Sharla. *Working Cures: Healing, Health, and Power on Southern Slave Plantations.* Chapel Hill: University of North Carolina Press, 2000.

Fiege, Mark. "Gettysburg and the Organic Nature of the American Civil War." In *Natural Enemy, Natural Ally: Toward an Environmental History of Warfare*, edited by Richard P. Tucker, 93–109. Corvallis: Oregon State University Press, 2004.

Fields, Barbara J. *Slavery and Freedom on the Middle Ground: Maryland during the Nineteenth Century*. New Haven, Conn.: Yale University Press, 1985.

Foner, Eric. *The Fiery Trial: Abraham Lincoln and American Slavery*. New York: W. W. Norton, 2010.

———. *Forever Free: The Story of Emancipation and Reconstruction*. New York: Alfred A. Knopf, 2005.

———. *Free Soil, Free Labor, Free Men: The Ideology of the Republican Party before the Civil War*. New York: Oxford University Press, 1970.

———. *Nothing but Freedom: Emancipation and Its Legacy*. Baton Rouge: Louisiana State University Press, 1983.

———. *Reconstruction: America's Unfinished Revolution, 1863–1877*. Updated ed. New York: HarperCollins, 2014.

Foote, Lorien. "'They Cover the Land Like the Locusts of Egypt': Fugitive Federal Prisoners of War and the Collapse of the Confederacy." *Journal of the Civil War Era* 6 (March 2016): 30–55.

Forbes, Ella. *African American Women During the Civil War*. New York: Routledge, 1998.

Foster, Helen Bradley. *New Raiments of Self: African American Clothing in the Antebellum South*. Oxford: Berg, 1997.

Fountain, Daniel L. *Slavery, Civil War, and Salvation: African American Slaves and Christianity, 1830–1870*. Baton Rouge: Louisiana State University Press, 2010.

Frankel, Noralee. *Freedom's Women: Black Women and Families in Civil War Era Mississippi*. Bloomington: Indiana University Press, 1999.

Franklin, John Hope, and Loren Schweninger. *Runaway Slaves: Rebels on the Plantation*. New York: Oxford University Press, 2000.

Fraser, Nancy, and Linda Gordon. "A Genealogy of Dependency: Tracing a Keyword of the U.S. Welfare State." *Signs* 19 (Winter 1994): 309–36.

Fredrickson, George M. *The Black Image in the White Mind: The Debate on Afro-American Character and Destiny, 1817–1914*. New York: Harper & Row, 1971.

———. *The Inner Civil War: Northern Intellectuals and the Crisis of the Union*. New York: Harper & Row, 1965.

Freehling, William W. *The South vs. the South: How Anti-Confederate Southerners Shaped the Course of the Civil War*. New York: Oxford University Press, 2002.

Frey, Sylvia R. *Water from the Rock: Black Resistance in a Revolutionary Age*. Princeton, N.J.: Princeton University Press, 1991.

Fuentes, Marisa J. *Dispossessed Lives: Enslaved Women, Violence, and the Archive*. Philadelphia: University of Pennsylvania Press, 2016.

Gallagher, Gary. "A Civil War Watershed: The 1862 Richmond Campaign in Perspective." In *The Richmond Campaign of 1862: The Peninsula and the Seven Days*, edited by Gary Gallagher, 3–27. Chapel Hill: University of North Carolina Press, 2000.

————, ed. *The Richmond Campaign of 1862: The Peninsula and the Seven Days*. Chapel Hill: University of North Carolina Press, 2000.

Geier, Clarence R., David G. Orr, and Matthew B. Reeves, eds. *Huts and History: The Historical Archaeology of Military Encampment during the American Civil War*. Gainesville: University Press of Florida, 2006.

Genealogies of Virginia Families from the William and Mary Quarterly. Vol. 5. Baltimore: Genealogical Publishing Company, 1982.

Genovese, Eugene D. *Roll, Jordan, Roll: The World the Slaves Made*. New York: Vintage, 1976.

Gerteis, Louis S. *From Contraband to Freedman: Federal Policy toward Southern Blacks, 1861–1865*. Westport, Conn.: Greenwood, 1973.

Glatthaar, Joseph T. *Forged in Battle: The Civil War Alliance of Black Soldiers and White Officers*. New York: Free Press, 1990.

Glaude, Eddie S., Jr. *Exodus! Religion, Race, and Nation in Early Nineteenth-Century Black America*. Chicago: University of Chicago Press, 2000.

Glymph, Thavolia. "Black Women and Children in the Civil War: Archive Notes." In *Beyond Freedom: Disrupting the History of Emancipation*, edited by David W. Blight and Jim Downs, 121–35. Athens: University of Georgia Press, 2017.

————. *Out of the House of Bondage: The Transformation of the Plantation Household*. New York: Cambridge University Press, 2008.

————. "Rose's War and the Gendered Politics of a Slave Insurgency in the Civil War." *Journal of the Civil War Era* 3 (December 2013): 501–32.

————. "'This Species of Property': Female Slave Contrabands in the Civil War." In *A Woman's War: Southern Women, Civil War, and the Confederate Legacy*, edited by Edward D. C. Campbell Jr. and Kym S. Rice, 55–71. Charlottesville: University of Virginia Press, 1996.

Greene, Sally. "Thomas Ruffin and the Perils of Public Homage." *North Carolina Law Review* 87 (March 2009): 702–55.

Greenwood, Janette Thomas. *First Fruits of Freedom: The Migration of Former Slaves and Their Search for Racial Equality in Worcester, Massachusetts, 1862–1900*. Chapel Hill: University of North Carolina Press, 2010.

Grimsley, Mark. *The Hard Hand of War: Union Military Policy toward Southern Civilians, 1861–1865*. Cambridge: Cambridge University Press, 1997.

Guelzo, Allen C. *Lincoln's Emancipation Proclamation: The End of Slavery in America*. New York: Simon & Schuster, 2004.

Gunderson, Joan. "Independence, Citizenship, and the American Revolution." *Signs* 13 (Autumn 1987): 59–77.

Hager, Christopher. *Word by Word: Emancipation and the Act of Writing*. Cambridge, Mass.: Harvard University Press, 2013.

Hahn, Steven. *A Nation under Our Feet: Black Political Struggles in the Rural South from Slavery to the Great Migration*. Cambridge, Mass.: Belknap Press of Harvard University Press, 2003.

————. *The Political Worlds of Slavery and Freedom*. Cambridge, Mass.: Harvard University Press, 2009.

Halttunen, Karen. *Confidence Men and Painted Women: A Study of Middle-Class Culture in America, 1830–1870*. New Haven, Conn.: Yale University Press, 1982.

Harding, Vincent. "Religion and Resistance among Antebellum Slaves, 1800–1860."

In *African-American Religion: Interpretive Essays in History and Culture*, edited by
Timothy E. Fulop and Albert J. Raboteau, 107–32. New York: Routledge, 1997.

Harlow, Luke E. "The Long Life of Proslavery Religion." In *The World the Civil War Made*,
edited by Gregory P. Downs and Kate Masur, 132–58. Chapel Hill: University of North
Carolina Press, 2015.

———. *Religion, Race, and the Making of Confederate Kentucky, 1830–1880*. New York:
Cambridge University Press, 2014.

Harper, Matthew. *The End of Days: African American Religion and Politics in the Age of
Emancipation*. Chapel Hill: University of North Carolina Press, 2016.

Harris, Leslie M. *In the Shadow of Slavery: African Americans in New York City, 1626–1863*.
Chicago: University of Chicago Press, 2004.

Harris, William C. *Lincoln and the Border States: Preserving the Union*. Lawrence:
University Press of Kansas, 2011.

Hauptman, Laurence. "General John E. Wool in Cherokee County, 1836–1837:
A Reinterpretation." *The Georgia Historical Quarterly* 85 (Spring 2001): 1–26.

Hermann, Janet Sharp. *The Pursuit of a Dream*. New York: Oxford University Press, 1981.

Hess, Earl J. *The Civil War in the West: Victory and Defeat from the Appalachians to the
Mississippi*. Chapel Hill: University of North Carolina Press, 2012.

Hodes, Martha. *Mourning Lincoln*. New Haven, Conn.: Yale University Press, 2015.

———. *White Women, Black Men: Illicit Sex in the Nineteenth-Century South*. New Haven,
Conn.: Yale University Press, 1997.

Holt, Thomas C. *The Problem of Freedom: Race, Labor, and Politics in Jamaica and Britain,
1832–1938*. Baltimore: Johns Hopkins University Press, 1992.

Howard, Victor B. *The Evangelical War against Slavery and Caste: The Life and Times of
John G. Fee*. Selinsgrove, Pa.: Susquehanna University Press, 1996.

Humphreys, Margaret. *Intensely Human: The Health of the Black Soldier in the American
Civil War*. Baltimore: Johns Hopkins University Press, 2008.

———. *Marrow of Tragedy: The Health Crisis of the American Civil War*. Baltimore: Johns
Hopkins University Press, 2013.

Hunter, Tera. *Bound in Wedlock: Slave and Free Black Marriage in the Nineteenth Century*.
Cambridge, Mass.: Harvard University Press, 2017.

Hyndman, Jennifer. *Managing Displacement: Refugees and the Politics of Humanitarianism*.
Minneapolis: University of Minnesota Press, 2000.

Irons, Charles. *Origins of Proslavery Christianity: White and Black Evangelicals in Colonial
and Antebellum Virginia*. Chapel Hill: University of North Carolina Press, 2008.

Isaac, Rhys. *Transformation of Virginia, 1740–1790*. Chapel Hill: University of North
Carolina Press, 1982.

Jaynes, Gerald David. *Branches without Roots: Genesis of the Black Working Class in the
American South, 1862–1882*. New York: Oxford University Press, 1989.

Jensen, Laura. *Patriots, Settlers, and the Origins of American Social Policy*. Cambridge:
Cambridge University Press, 2003.

Johnson, Walter. *River of Dark Dreams: Slavery and Empire in the Cotton Kingdom*.
Cambridge, Mass.: Harvard University Press, 2013.

———. *Soul by Soul: Life Inside the Antebellum Slave Market*. Cambridge, Mass.: Harvard
University Press, 1999.

Jones, Catherine A. *Intimate Reconstructions: Children in Postemancipation Virginia*.
Charlottesville: University Press of Virginia, 2015.

Jordan, Winthrop D. *White over Black: American Attitudes toward the Negro, 1550–1812.* Chapel Hill: University of North Carolina Press, 1968.

Katz, Michael B. *In the Shadow of the Poorhouse: A Social History of Welfare in America.* New York: Basic Books, 1986.

Katz-Hyman, Martha B., and Kym S. Rice, eds. *World of a Slave: Encyclopedia of the Material Life of the Slaves in the United States.* Vol. 1. Santa Barbara: Greenwood, 2011.

Kaye, Anthony. *Joining Places: Slave Neighborhoods in the Old South.* Chapel Hill: University of North Carolina Press, 2007.

Kellogg, John. "Negro Urban Clusters in the Postbellum South." *Geographical Review* 67 (July 1977): 310–21.

Kennedy, Thomas C. *A History of Southland College: The Society of Friends and Black Education in Arkansas.* Fayetteville: University of Arkansas Press, 2009.

Kerber, Linda K. "The Republican Mother: Women and the Enlightenment—an American Perspective." *American Quarterly* 28 (Summer 1976): 187–205.

————. *Women of the Republic: Intellect and Ideology in Revolutionary America.* New York: W. W. Norton, 1980.

Kerr-Ritchie, Jeffrey R. *Freedom's Seekers: Essays on Comparative Emancipation.* Baton Rouge: Louisiana State University Press, 2013.

Klebaner, Benjamin Joseph. "Public Poor Relief in Charleston, 1800–1860." *South Carolina Historical Magazine* 55 (October 1954): 210–20.

Kobayashi, Audrey. "Critical 'Race' Approaches." In *Wiley-Blackwell Companion to Cultural Geography,* edited by Nuala Johnson, Richard H. Schein, and Jamie Winders, 57–71. Somerset, N.J.: John Wiley & Sons, 2013.

Kolchin, Peter. *Unfree Labor: American Slavery and Russian Serfdom.* Cambridge, Mass.: Harvard University Press, 1987.

LaRoche, Cheryl Janifer. *Free Black Communities and the Underground Railroad: The Geography of Resistance.* Urbana: University of Illinois Press, 2014.

Lause, Mark A. *Free Labor: The Civil War and the Making of an American Working Class.* Urbana: University of Illinois Press, 2015.

Lebsock, Suzanne. *The Free Women of Petersburg: Status and Culture in a Southern Town, 1784–1860.* New York: W. W. Norton, 1984.

Lee, Susanna Michele. *Claiming the Union: Citizenship in the Post–Civil War South.* Cambridge: Cambridge University Press, 2014.

Lefebvre, Henri. *The Production of Space.* Translated by Donald Nicholson-Smith. Oxford: Blackwell, 1991.

Leonard, Elizabeth D. *Lincoln's Forgotten Ally: Judge Advocate General Joseph Holt of Kentucky.* Chapel Hill: University of North Carolina Press, 2011.

Levine, Lawrence W. "Slave Songs and Slave Consciousness: An Exploration in Neglected Sources." In *African-American Religion: Interpretive Essays in History and Culture,* edited by Timothy E. Fulop and Albert J. Raboteau, 57–88. New York: Routledge, 1997.

Lewis, Jan. "The Republican Wife: Virtue and Seduction in the Early Republic." *William and Mary Quarterly* 44 (October 1987): 689–721.

Lewis, Patrick A. *For Slavery and Union: Benjamin Buckner and Kentucky Loyalties in the Civil War.* Lexington: University Press of Kentucky, 2015.

Lipsitz, George. "The Racialization of Space and the Spatialization of Race: Theorizing the Hidden Architecture of Landscape." *Landscape Journal* 26 (January 2007): 10–23.

Lischer, Sarah Kenyon. *Dangerous Sanctuaries: Refugee Camps, Civil War, and the Dilemmas of Humanitarian Aid*. Ithaca, N.Y.: Cornell University Press, 2005.

Litwack, Leon. *Been in the Storm So Long: The Aftermath of Slavery*. New York: Alfred A. Knopf, 1979.

Long, Gretchen. *Doctoring Freedom: The Politics of African American Medical Care in Slavery and Emancipation*. Chapel Hill: University of North Carolina Press, 2012.

Lucas, Marion. *A History of Blacks in Kentucky: From Slavery to Segregation, 1760–1891*. 2nd ed. Lexington: University Press of Kentucky, 2003.

Luskey, Brian, and Jason Phillips. "Muster: Inspecting Material Cultures of the Civil War." *Civil War History* 63 (June 2017): 103–12.

Lynching in America: Confronting the Legacy of Racial Terror. Montgomery, Ala.: Equal Justice Initiative, 2015. http://eji.org/reports/lynching-in-america.

Magness, Phillip W., and Sebastian N. Page. *Colonization after Emancipation: Lincoln and the Movement for Black Resettlement*. Columbia: University of Missouri Press, 2011.

Manning, Chandra. *Troubled Refuge: Struggling for Freedom in the Civil War*. New York: Vintage, 2017.

———. "Working for Citizenship in the Civil War's Contraband Camps." *Journal of the Civil War Era* 4 (June 2014): 172–204.

Marshall, Anne E. *Creating a Confederate Kentucky: The Lost Cause and Civil War Memory in a Border State*. Chapel Hill: University of North Carolina Press, 2010.

Marten, James. "'A Feeling of Restless Anxiety'. Loyalty and Race in the Peninsula Campaign and Beyond." In *The Richmond Campaign of 1862: The Peninsula and the Seven Days*, edited by Gary Gallagher, 121–52. Chapel Hill: University of North Carolina Press, 2000.

———. *Sing Not War: The Lives of Union and Confederate Veterans in Gilded Age America*. Chapel Hill: University of North Carolina Press, 2011.

Martin, Jonathan D. *Divided Mastery: Slave Hiring in the American South*. Cambridge, Mass.: Harvard University Press, 2004.

Masur, Kate. *An Example for All the Land: Emancipation and the Struggle for Equality in Washington*. Chapel Hill: University of North Carolina Press, 2010.

———. "'A Rare Phenomenon of Philological Vegetation': The Word 'Contraband' and the Meanings of Emancipation in the United States." *Journal of American History* 93 (March 2007): 1050–84.

Masur, Louis P. *Lincoln's Hundred Days: The Emancipation Proclamation and the War for the Union*. Cambridge, Mass.: Belknap Press of Harvard University Press, 2012.

McBride, Stephen. "Civil War Material Culture and Camp Life in Central Kentucky: Archeological Investigations at Camp Nelson." In *Look to the Earth: Historical Archeology and the American Civil War*, edited by Clarence R. Geier Jr. and Susan E. Winter, 130–57. Knoxville: University of Tennessee Press, 1994.

———. "More Than a Depot." History of Camp Nelson. Accessed August 26, 2015. http://www.campnelson.org/history/.

McBride, Stephen, and Kim A. McBride. "Civil War Housing Insights from Camp Nelson, Kentucky." In *Huts and History: The Historical Archaeology of Military Encampment during the American Civil War*, edited by Clarence R. Geier, David G. Orr, and Matthew B. Reeves, 136–71. Gainesville: University Press of Florida, 2006.

McClaughry, John. "John Wolcott Phelps: The Civil War General Who Became a Forgotten Presidential Candidate in 1880." *Vermont History* 38 (Autumn 1970): 263–90.

McCurry, Stephanie. *Confederate Reckoning: Power and Politics in the Civil War South.* Cambridge, Mass.: Harvard University Press, 2012.

McDannell, Colleen. *Material Christianity: Religion and Popular Culture in America.* New Haven, Conn.: Yale University Press, 1995.

McPherson, James M. *Battle Cry of Freedom: The Civil War Era.* New York: Ballantine Books, 1989.

Medford, Edna Greene. "The Transition from Slavery to Freedom in a Diversified Economy: Virginia's Lower Peninsula, 1860–1900." PhD diss., University of Maryland, College Park, 1987.

Meier, Kathryn Shively. *Nature's Civil War: Common Soldiers and the Environment in 1862 Virginia.* Chapel Hill: University of North Carolina Press, 2013.

Melish, Joanne Pope. *Disowning Slavery: Gradual Emancipation and "Race" in New England, 1780–1860.* Ithaca, N.Y.: Cornell University Press, 1998.

Merchant, Carolyn. "Shades of Darkness: Race and Environmental History." *Environmental History* 8 (July 2003): 380–94.

Messner, William F. "General John Wolcott Phelps and Conservative Reform in Nineteenth Century America." *Vermont History* 53 (Winter 1985): 17–35.

Miller, Peter N., ed. *Cultural Histories of the Material World.* Ann Arbor: University of Michigan Press, 2013.

Mills, Gary B. *Southern Loyalists in the Civil War: The Southern Claims Commission.* Baltimore: Clearfield, 1994.

Moneyhon, Carl H. "The Civil War in Phillips County, Arkansas." *Phillips County Historical Quarterly* 19 (June and August 1981): 18–36.

———. *The Impact of the Civil War and Reconstruction on Arkansas: Persistence in the Midst of Ruin.* Fayetteville: University of Arkansas Press, 2002.

Morgan, Jennifer. *Laboring Women: Reproduction and Gender in New World Slavery.* Philadelphia: University of Pennsylvania Press, 2004.

———. "'Some Could Suckle over Their Shoulder': Male Travelers, Female Bodies, and the Gendering of Racial Ideology, 1500–1770." *William and Mary Quarterly,* 3rd ser., 54 (January 1997): 167–92.

Morgan, Lynda J. *Emancipation in Virginia's Tobacco Belt, 1850–1870.* Athens: University of Georgia Press, 1992.

Morris, Christopher. *The Big Muddy: An Environmental History of the Mississippi and Its Peoples from Hernando de Soto to Hurricane Katrina.* New York: Oxford University Press, 2012.

Nathans, Sydney. *To Free a Family: The Journey of Mary Walker.* Cambridge, Mass.: Harvard University Press, 2012.

Neely, Mark E., Jr. "Colonization and the Myth That Lincoln Prepared the People for Emancipation." In *Lincoln's Proclamation: Emancipation Reconsidered,* edited by William A. Blair and Karen Fisher Younger, 45–74. Chapel Hill: University of North Carolina Press, 2009.

Nelson, Dean E. "'Right Nice Little House[s]': Winter Camp Architecture of the American Civil War." In *Huts and History: The Historical Archaeology of Military Encampment during the American Civil War,* edited by Clarence R. Geier, David G. Orr, and Matthew B. Reeves, 177–93. Gainesville: University Press of Florida, 2006.

Nelson, Megan Kate. *Ruin Nation: Destruction and the American Civil War.* Athens: University of Georgia Press, 2012.

Norris, David A. "The Lexington of the Civil War." *American History* 36 (October 2001): 48–55.

Oakes, James. *Freedom National: The Destruction of Slavery in the United States, 1861–1865.* New York: W. W. Norton, 2013.

O'Donovan, Susan Eva. *Becoming Free in the Cotton South.* Cambridge, Mass.: Harvard University Press, 2010.

Otter, Chris. "Locating Matter: The Place of Materiality in Urban History." In *Material Powers: Cultural Studies, History, and the Material Turn,* edited by Tony Bennett and Patrick Joyce, 38–59. London: Routledge, 2010.

———. *The Victorian Eye: A Political History of Light and Vision in Britain, 1800–1910.* Chicago: University of Chicago Press, 2008.

Oubre, Claude F. *Forty Acres and a Mule: The Freedmen's Bureau and Land Ownership.* Baton Rouge: Louisiana State University Press, 1978.

Painter, Nell Irvin. *Exodusters: Black Migration to Kansas after Reconstruction.* New York: Alfred A. Knopf, 1977.

Penningroth, Dylan C. *The Claims of Kinfolk: African American Property and Community in the Nineteenth-Century South.* Chapel Hill: University of North Carolina Press, 2003.

Phillips, Christopher. *The Rivers Ran Backwards: The Civil War and the Remaking of the American Middle Border.* New York: Oxford University Press, 2016.

Pope, Anne Connaway. "Helena, Arkansas: At the Intersection of the Hills, the River, and the Delta." Pamphlet. Helena: Helena Museum of Phillips County, Arkansas, 2003.

Popkin, Jeremy. *You Are All Free: The Haitian Revolution and the Abolition of Slavery.* Cambridge: Cambridge University Press, 2010.

Prechtel-Kluskens, Claire. "'A Reasonable Degree of Promptitude': Civil War Pension Application Processing, 1861–1885." *Prologue* 42 (Spring 2010): 26–35. https://www.archives.gov/publications/prologue/2010/spring/civilwarpension.html.

Quarles, Benjamin. *The Negro in the American Revolution.* Chapel Hill: University of North Carolina Press, 1961.

———. *The Negro in the Civil War.* Boston: Little, Brown, 1953.

Quarstein, John V. "First Blood at Big Bethel." *Civil War Times* 50 (April 2011): 47–53.

———. *Hampton and Newport News in the Civil War: War Comes to the Peninsula.* Lynchburg, Va.: H. E. Howard, 1998.

Rable, George C. *God's Almost Chosen Peoples: A Religious History of the American Civil War.* Chapel Hill: University of North Carolina Press, 2010.

Raboteau, Albert J. *Slave Religion: The "Invisible Institution" in the Antebellum South.* New York: Oxford University Press, 1978.

Rael, Patrick. *Eight-Eight Years: The Long Demise of Slavery in the United States, 1777–1865.* Athens: University of Georgia Press, 2015.

Rediker, Marcus. *Outlaws of the Atlantic: Sailors, Pirates, and Motley Crews in the Age of Sail.* New York: Beacon, 2014.

Regosin, Elizabeth R., and Donald R. Shaffer. *Voices of Emancipation: Understanding Slavery, the Civil War, and Reconstruction through the U.S. Pension Bureau Files.* New York: New York University Press, 2008.

Reid, Richard. *Freedom for Themselves: North Carolina's Black Soldiers in the Civil War Era.* Chapel Hill: University of North Carolina Press, 2012.

Reidy, Joseph P. "'Coming from the Shadow of the Past': The Transition from Slavery to Freedom at Freedmen's Village, 1863–1900." *The Virginia Magazine of History and Biography* 95 (October 1987): 403–28.

———. *From Slavery to Agrarian Capitalism in the Cotton Plantation South: Central Georgia, 1800–1880.* Chapel Hill: University of North Carolina Press, 1992.

Richardson, Joe M. *Christian Reconstruction: The American Missionary Association and Southern Blacks, 1861–1890.* Athens: University of Georgia Press, 1986.

Richmond, Vivienne. *Clothing the Poor in Nineteenth-Century England.* Cambridge: Cambridge University Press, 2013.

Robinson, Armstead L. *Bitter Fruits of Bondage: The Demise of Slavery and the Collapse of the Confederacy, 1861–1865.* Charlottesville: University of Virginia Press, 2005.

Roediger, David. *Seizing Freedom: Slave Emancipation and Liberty for All.* New York: Verso, 2014.

Romeo, Sharon. *Gender and the Jubilee: Black Freedom and the Reconstruction of Citizenship in Civil War Missouri.* Athens: University of Georgia Press, 2016.

Rose, Willie Lee. *Rehearsal for Reconstruction: The Port Royal Experiment.* New York: Oxford University Press, 1964.

Rosen, Hannah. *Terror in the Heart of Freedom: Citizenship, Sexual Violence, and the Meaning of Race in the Postemancipation South.* Chapel Hill: University of North Carolina Press, 2009.

Rothman, Adam. *Beyond Freedom's Reach: A Kidnapping in the Twilight of Slavery.* Cambridge, Mass.: Harvard University Press, 2015.

Rugemer, Edward Bartlett. *The Problem of Emancipation: The Caribbean Roots of the American Civil War.* Baton Rouge: Louisiana State University Press, 2008.

Sarna, Jan, ed. "Civil War and Reconstruction." *Phillips County Historical Quarterly* 16 (June 1978): 3–6.

Saville, Julie. *The Work of Reconstruction: From Slave to Wage Laborer in South Carolina, 1860–1870.* Cambridge: Cambridge University Press, 1994.

Schama, Simon. *Rough Crossings: The Slaves, the British, and the American Revolution.* New York: HarperCollins, 2005.

Schecter, Patricia. "'The First Free Spot of Ground in Kentucky': The Story of Camp Nelson." Undergraduate thesis, Mount Holyoke College, 1986.

Schein, Richard, ed. *Landscape and Race in the United States.* New York: Taylor & Francis, 2006.

Schermerhorn, Calvin. *Money over Mastery, Family over Freedom: Slavery in the Antebellum Upper South.* Baltimore: Johns Hopkins University Press, 2011.

Schmidt, James D. *Free to Work: Labor Law, Emancipation, and Reconstruction, 1815–1880.* Athens: University of Georgia Press, 1998.

Schultz, Jane E. *Women at the Front: Hospital Workers in Civil War America.* Chapel Hill: University of North Carolina Press, 2007.

Schwalm, Leslie. "Between Slavery and Freedom: African American Women and Occupation in the Slave South." In *Occupied Women: Gender, Military Occupation, and the American Civil War,* edited by LeeAnn Whites and Alecia P. Long, 137–54. Baton Rouge: Louisiana State University Press, 2009.

———. *Emancipation's Diaspora: Race and Reconstruction in the Upper Midwest.* Chapel Hill: University of North Carolina Press, 2009.

———. *A Hard Fight for We: Women's Transition from Slavery to Freedom in South Carolina.* Champaign: University of Illinois Press, 1997.

————. "Surviving Wartime Emancipation: African Americans and the Cost of Civil War." *Journal of Law, Medicine, and Ethics* 39 (Spring 2011): 21–27.

Schweiger, Beth Barton. "The Literate South: Reading before Emancipation." *Journal of the Civil War Era* 3 (September 2013): 331–59.

Schweninger, Loren. *Black Property Owners in the South, 1790–1915*. Urbana: University of Illinois Press, 1990.

Scott, James C. *Domination and the Arts of Resistance: Hidden Transcripts*. New Haven, Conn.: Yale University Press, 1990.

Scott, Sean A. *A Visitation of God: Northern Civilians Interpret the Civil War*. New York: Oxford University Press, 2011.

Scully, Pamela, and Diana Paton, eds. *Gender and Slavery in the Atlantic World*. Durham, N.C.: Duke University Press, 2005.

Sears, Richard D. "John G. Fee, Camp Nelson, and Kentucky Blacks, 1864–1865." *Register of the Kentucky Historical Society* 85 (Winter 1987): 29–45.

————. *"A Practical Recognition of the Brotherhood of Man": John G. Fee and the Camp Nelson Experience*. Berea, Ky.: Berea College Press, 1986.

Shaffer, Donald. *After the Glory: The Struggles of Black Civil War Veterans*. Lawrence: University Press of Kansas, 2004.

Sharpe, Bethany. "Humanity Begins at Home: America's First Refugees and the Roots of Humanitarianism." Unpublished paper, University of Kentucky, 2012.

Shire, Laurel Clark. "Turning Sufferers into Settlers: Gender, Welfare, and National Expansion in Frontier Florida." *Journal of the Early Republic* 33 (Fall 2013): 489–521.

Silkenat, David. *Driven from Home: North Carolina's Civil War Refugee Crisis*. Athens: University of Georgia Press, 2016.

Simpson, Brooks D. "Quandaries of Command: Ulysses S. Grant and Black Soldiers." In *Union and Emancipation: Essays on Politics and Race in the Civil War Era*, edited by David W. Blight and Brooks D. Simpson, 123–50. Kent, Ohio: Kent State University Press, 1997.

Sinha, Manisha. *The Slave's Cause: A History of Abolition*. New Haven, Conn.: Yale University Press, 2016.

Smallwood, Stephanie. *Saltwater Slavery: A Middle Passage from Africa to American Diaspora*. Cambridge, Mass.: Harvard University Press, 2009.

Smith, Andrew F. *Starving the South: How the North Won the Civil War*. New York: St. Martin's Press, 2011.

Smith, John David. "The Recruitment of Negro Soldiers in Kentucky, 1863–1865." *Register of the Kentucky Historical Society* 72 (October 1974): 364–90.

————, ed. *Black Soldiers in Blue: African American Troops in the Civil War Era*. Chapel Hill: University of North Carolina Press, 2002.

Smith, Mark M. *The Smell of Battle, the Taste of Siege: A Sensory History of the Civil War*. New York: Oxford University Press, 2014.

Smith, Stacey L. "Beyond North and South: Putting the West in the Civil War and Reconstruction." *Journal of the Civil War Era* 6 (December 2016): 566–91.

Sommerville, Diane Miller. *Rape and Race in the Nineteenth-Century South*. Chapel Hill: University of North Carolina Press, 2004.

Stanley, Amy Dru. "Instead of Waiting for the Thirteenth Amendment: The War Power, Slave Marriage, and Inviolate Human Rights." *American Historical Review* 115 (June 2010): 732–65.

Stauffer, W. T. "The Old Farms out of Which the City of Newport News Was Erected, with Some Account of the Families Which Dwelt Thereon." First installment. *William and Mary Quarterly* 14 (July 1934): 203–15.

———. "The Old Farms out of Which the City of Newport News Was Erected, with Some Account of the Families Which Dwelt Thereon." Second installment. *William and Mary Quarterly* 14 (October 1934): 333–41.

———. "The Old Farms out of Which the City of Newport News Was Erected, with Some Account of the Families Which Dwelt Thereon." Third installment. *William and Mary Quarterly* 15 (April 1935): 126–37.

———. "The Old Farms out of Which the City of Newport News Was Erected, with Some Account of the Families Which Dwelt Thereon." Fourth installment. *William and Mary Quarterly* 15 (July 1935): 250–66.

Steinberg, Ted. *Down to Earth: Nature's Role in American History*. New York: Oxford University Press, 2002.

Sternhell, Yael. "The Afterlives of a Confederate Archive: Civil War Documents and the Making of Sectional Reconciliation." *Journal of American History* 102 (March 2016): 1025–50.

———. *Routes of War: The World of Movement in the Confederate South*. Cambridge, Mass.: Harvard University Press, 2012.

Stevenson, Brenda E. "'Marsa Never Sot Aunt Rebecca Down': Enslaved Women, Religion, and Social Power in the Antebellum South." *Journal of African American History* 90 (Autumn 2005): 345–67.

Stewart, Mart A. *"What Nature Suffers to Groe": Life, Labor, and Landscape on the Georgia Coast, 1680–1920*. Athens: University of Georgia Press, 1996.

Stump, Roger W. *The Geography of Religion: Faith, Place, and Space*. Lanham, Md.: Rowman & Littlefield, 2008.

Sutherland, Daniel E. *A Savage Conflict: The Decisive Role of Guerrillas in the American Civil War*. Chapel Hill: University of North Carolina Press, 2010.

Sutton, Keith. "Population Resettlement: Traumatic Upheavals and the Algerian Experience." *Journal of Modern African Studies* 15 (June 1977): 279–300.

Syrett, John. *The Civil War Confiscation Acts: Failing to Reconstruct the South*. New York: Fordham University Press, 2005.

Taylor, Alan. *The Internal Enemy: Slavery and War in Virginia, 1772–1832*. New York: W. W. Norton, 2013.

Taylor, Amy Murrell. "How a Cold Snap in Kentucky Led to Freedom for Thousands: An Environmental Story of Emancipation." In *Weirding the War: Stories from the Civil War's Ragged Edges*, edited by Stephen Berry, 191–214. Athens: University of Georgia Press, 2011.

Tetzlaff, Monica. "Mitchelville: An Early Experiment in Self-Governance." In *The Forgotten History: Civil War Hilton Head Island*, edited by Charles C. McCracken and Faith M. McCracken, 81–90. Hilton Head, S.C.: Time and Again Publication, 1993.

Thomas, William G., III, Kaci Nash, and Robert Shepard. "Places of Exchange: An Analysis of Human and Matériel Flows in Civil War Alexandria, Virginia." *Civil War History* 62 (December 2016): 359–98.

Tomblin, Barbara Brooks. *Bluejackets and Contrabands: African Americans and the Union Navy*. Lexington: University Press of Kentucky, 2009.

Tweed, Thomas. "Space." *Material Religion* 7 (March 2011): 116–23.

Valencius, Conevery Boton. *The Health of the Country: How American Settlers Understood Themselves and Their Land*. New York: Basic Books, 2002.

Vlach, John Michael. *Back of the Big House: The Architecture of Plantation Slavery*. Chapel Hill: University of North Carolina Press, 1993.

Voegeli, Jacque. "A Rejected Alternative: Union Policy and the Relocation of Southern 'Contrabands' at the Dawn of Emancipation." *Journal of Southern History* 69 (November 2003): 765–90.

Walker, Cam. "Corinth: The Story of a Contraband Camp." *Civil War History* 20 (March 1974): 5–22.

Waugh, John C. *Lincoln and McClellan: The Troubled Partnership between a President and His General*. New York: Palgrave, 2010.

Weicksel, Sarah Jones. "The Dress of the Enemy: Clothing and Disease in the Civil War Era." *Civil War History* 63 (June 2017): 133–50.

"What is a Refugee?" USA for UNHCR: The UN Refugee Agency. Accessed October 21, 2016. http://www.unrefugees.org/what-is-a-refugee/.

White, Ashli. *Encountering Revolution: Haiti and the Making of the Early Republic*. Baltimore: Johns Hopkins University Press, 2010.

White, Deborah Gray. *Ar'n't I a Woman: Female Slaves in the Plantation South*. New York: W. W. Norton, 1985.

White, Shane. *Somewhat More Independent: The End of Slavery in New York City, 1770–1810*. Athens: University of Georgia Press, 2004.

Whitehorne, Joseph W. A. "Blueprint for Nineteenth-Century Camps." In *Huts and History: The Historical Archaeology of Military Encampment during the American Civil War*, edited by Clarence R. Geier, David G. Orr, and Matthew B. Reeves, 28–50. Gainesville: University Press of Florida, 2006.

Wiley, Bell. "'Holy Joes' of the Sixties: A Study of Civil War Chaplains." *Huntington Library Quarterly* 16 (May 1953): 290–93.

———. *The Life of Billy Yank: The Common Soldier of the Union*. Indianapolis: Charter Books, 1952.

Williams, Heather Andrea. *Help Me to Find My People: The African American Search for Family Lost in Slavery*. Chapel Hill: University of North Carolina Press, 2012.

———. *Self-Taught: African American Education in Slavery and Freedom*. Chapel Hill: University of North Carolina Press, 2005.

Williams, Kidada E. "Maintaining a Radical Vision of African Americans in the Age of Freedom." *Journal of the Civil War Era* 7 (March 2017). https://journalofthecivilwarera.org/forum-the-future-of-reconstruction-studies/.

Willis, Deborah, and Barbara Krauthamer. *Envisioning Emancipation: Black Americans and the End of Slavery*. Philadelphia: Temple University Press, 2013.

Wilson, Keith P. *Campfires of Freedom: The Camp Life of Black Soldiers during the Civil War*. Kent, Ohio: Kent State University Press, 2002.

Wilson, Mark R. "The Extensive Side of Nineteenth-Century Military Economy: The Tent Industry in the Northern United States during the Civil War." *Enterprise and Society* 2 (June 2001): 297–337.

Witt, John Fabian. *Lincoln's Code: The Laws of War in American History*. New York: Free Press, 2013.

Woodruff, Nan Elizabeth. *American Congo: The African American Freedom Struggle in the Delta*. Cambridge, Mass.: Harvard University Press, 2003.

Zaborney, John J. *Slaves for Hire: Renting Enslaved Laborers in Antebellum Virginia*. Baton Rouge: Louisiana State University Press, 2012.

Zipf, Karin L. "Reconstructing 'Free Woman': African American Women, Apprenticeship, and Custody Rights during Reconstruction." *Journal of Women's History* 12 (Spring 2000): 8–31.

Zolberg, Aristide R., Astri Suhrke, and Sergio Aguayo. *Escape from Violence: Conflict and the Refugee Crisis in the Developing World*. New York: Oxford University Press, 1989.

index

bodies: subjected to inspection and control, 26–27, 85, 127–28, 156, 157–58, 163–64, 167–72; Union confiscation of, 53–54; and theories of illness, 77; injuries to, 130, 141; quest for self-determination of, 140–41, 156, 157–58, 170–73. *See also* clothing; illness and disease; rape

Bogan, Charles, 112, 125, 126, 233

Bogan, Dennis, 112, 135–37, 230, 232–35, 245–46, 309n23

Bogan, Eliza, 1–2, 4, 16, 17, 180, 273n1, 309n21; family of, 101, 103–5, 106, 108, 116–18, 119, 123–24, 126, 134–36, 137, 210, 230, 234, 245–47, 274n19, 283n155; in slavery, 101–5, 108, 116–17; decision to flee, 116–18; as laundress, 126–37; as nurse and midwife, 135–36, 246–47; in Texas, 210; postwar return to Phillips County, 230, 232–35, 239; postemancipation labor of, 245–47, 309n23; pension application of, 246, 309n26; living with daughter, 246–47, 309n27

Bogan, Fanny, 246–47, 309n27

Bogan, Lewis, 112

Bogan, Maria, 137

Bogan, Mary, 230, 245

Bogan, Monroe, 103, 136–39, 234, 282n147, 282n148, 306n120

Bogan, West, 137–39, 234

Boston, Mass., 43, 168

Boycan, Charles, 25

Boycan, Dick, 25

Boycan, Lewis, 25

Boycan, Mary, 25

Boycan, Sylvia, 25

Boycan, Tiny, 25

Boyd, Cyrus, 110

Boyle, Gen. Jeremiah T., 180

Bracken County, Ky., 189

Bramlette, Thomas, 186

Brasher, Glenn David, 254n27

Brazil, 221

Brazos Santiago, Tex., 210

Breckinridge, John C., 3

Bright, Phillip, 147

Brooks, Mary, 147

Brooks, Samuel, 234–35, 246, 309n23

Brown, Charles E., 85

Brown, John, 189

Brown, Orlando, 216

Brown, Thomas J., 93

British West Indies, 8, 38

Brownsville, Tex., 210, 230

Buford, Gen. N. B., 96, 132, 134

Burbridge, Gen. Stephen, 202–3, 205, 225

Burdett, Charles W. Sumner, 242, 308n8

Burdett, Clarissa, 175, 188, 206–7, 227, 291n4

Burdett, Elijah, 175, 187–88, 206–7, 227, 291n4, 294n43, 304n88

Burdett, Gabriel, 2, 4, 16, 17, 239, 246, 248, 291n2, 291n4, 292n7, 294n33; family of, 174, 175, 185–86, 188, 205, 227, 241–42, 244; in slavery, 174–78; as minister, 175–78, 183–85, 189–96, 197–98, 204–6, 207, 229–30, 241–43; impressment of, 179–82; enlistment of, 187; as army recruiting agent, 187–88, 192; ordination of, 190–91; as teacher, 192–200; literacy of, 195–96, 204–5; as assistant superintendent of Camp Nelson Refugee Home, 204–8, 298n135; and baptisms, 207; as soldier, 208, 209–10; as Freedmen's Bureau agent, 221–30, 231, 237, 303n53; establishment of black churches, 229–30; exclusion from Forks Church, 230; as member of Berea College Board of Trustees, 241, 243; migration to Kansas, 241, 243, 247; purchase of land, postwar, 241–42, 308n7; and party politics, 242–43; death of, 243–44

Burdett, Gertrude, 244, 308n8

Burdett, Hiram, 175, 180, 187–88, 242, 294n33

Burdett, John G., 308n8

Burdett, Lucinda, 175, 185, 188, 201, 205, 237, 241, 243–44, 291n3, 293n32

Burdett, Mary, 185

Burdett, Robert, 185–86, 187–88, 206, 294n33

Burdett, Smith, 185

Bureau of Refugees, Freedmen, and Abandoned Lands. *See* Freedmen's Bureau

Burnside, Gen. Ambrose, 179, 294n33; army of, 53
Burnside, John, 175, 201–2, 237
Burnside, Mary Ellen, 201–2
Butchart, Ronald E., 296n74
Butler, Gen. Benjamin, 24, 28, 29–30, 99, 144, 258n33, 258n34; "contraband" order of, 3–4, 9, 25–26, 30, 32, 38, 97, 115, 141–42, 251n6; departure from Fort Monroe, 32, 257n5; return to Fort Monroe, 210, 214. *See also* contraband order
Butler Freedmen's School, 237

Cairo, Ill., 94, 96
Cameron, Simon, 32, 38, 45, 258n34
Camp, Stephanie, 170–71, 255n9
Camp Butler, 25, 29, 30, 35
Camp Dick Robinson, 177–78
Camp Hamilton, 67, 79
Camp Nelson, Ky., 2, 7, 162, 179–87, 206–7, 234, 244; religious life and teaching at, 185–86, 188–200 passim, 204–5, 208; November 1864 expulsion from, 200–203; efforts to close, 221–30 passim, 243; efforts to save, 227–30, 237–38
Camp Nelson Church of Christ, 191–92, 230, 238, 242
Camp Nelson School for Colored Soldiers, 193–200
Canada, 5, 10, 96
Cannon, Maj. Le Grand B., 43, 45
Carey, Mr., 183
Castleton, Vt., 159
Celeys plantation, 216
Chase, Lucy, 78, 163, 197
Cherokee, removal of, 39, 269n3
Chesapeake Female Seminary, 34
Chicago, 94, 159, 196, 242
Chickasaw Bluffs, 66
Children, 8–9, 16, 25, 39–40, 45, 47, 53, 60, 67, 76, 86, 98, 109, 219, 258n33; in slavery, 21–22, 103, 137, 200, 223; reunited with parents, 79, 207, 227; separation from parents, 81, 116–18, 122, 188, 205, 206–7, 225; numbers of, in camps, 84, 116–17, 262n97, 285n33; forced movement of, 87, 93, 108; deaths of, 93, 130, 203; exclusion

from camps, 108, 185–86, 201–3, 298n121; labor of, 113–15, 225; flight to Union lines of, 116–18; and food, 142, 144, 147, 149–50, 284n7; clothing of, 158–59, 167, 172; in schools, 193, 197; emancipated as children of soldiers, 203, 206, 227; orphans, 235–36
cholera, 236
Chowan County, N.C., 101–4
church. *See* religious life
Cincinnati, 159, 189, 196, 203, 208, 223, 242. *See also* Contraband Relief Commission of Cincinnati
Circular No. 15, 215
Clarksville, Tenn., 70, 116
Clarksville, Tex., 230
Clinton, La., 125
clothing: lack of, 122, 157–58; difficulty obtaining in war, 158; military uniforms, 158, 169; desire to purchase, 165–66; and race, 167–72. *See also* negro cloth; stores
clothing relief: federal government transport of, 158; private efforts to provide, 158–73, 203, 288n23; volume of, 159, 288n16; geographic reach of, 159–60; manufacture of, in northern states, 160–61; reasons for donating, 161–62; distribution of, 162–64; manufacture of, in refugee camps, 166–67. *See also* stores
Coffin, Levi, 160
Cohen, Patricia Cline, 151
Collins, Mary Forster, 157
colonization, 77, 97–99, 189, 272n73
Columbus, Ky., 110, 221, 292n10
combat roles, refugee, 109. *See also* military labor, of refugees; United States Colored Troops
communication networks: among the enslaved, 24; in urban areas, 81–82
Company E. *See* Forty-Sixth United States Colored Troops
Confederate Congress, 125
Confiscation Acts, 51; First, 32, 258n33; Second, 50, 58, 106–7, 264n2
Constitution, U.S., 117
consumerism, 164–65. *See also* stores

of, 110–12; and sanction of self-defense, 138–39

Emberton, Carole, 276n24

emetic, 135

environment: flooding, 1, 62, 66, 92, 212, 219, 231; metaphors of, 14–15, 31; land elevation, effect of, 65–66, 106, 226; climate and race, beliefs about, 95–97, 99; swamps and bayous, 131; and food acquisition, 152–53, 210; and clothing, 158; and military defenses, 182; weather, 201–4. *See also* army worm; food; gardens; illness and disease; islands; Mississippi River

exclusion laws, state, 96

Exodus, analogy to, 9, 167, 183, 184–85, 187, 215, 243

Exodusters. *See* Kansas: exodus to

families: reunification of, 6, 79–81, 108, 123, 126, 134, 203, 206–7; separations of, by Union, 54, 89–90, 108, 134, 150, 185–86, 188, 200–203; separations of, because of military service, 119, 225; separations of, by slave owners, 207; financial support within, 234; postwar, 240, 307n3. *See also* children; marriage; slavery: family life in

Farnham, John T., 84–85, 257n6

Farnham, Lt. Roswell, 26, 27

Farwell, R. E., 224–25, 227

Fassin, Didier, 288n26

federal government: and new bureaucracy for refugee affairs, 6–7, 14, 44, 109, 192, 203–4; commissioners studying refugees, 7, 17, 43–46, 56, 71, 73, 90, 142, 143, 261n89, 262n94. *See also* Freedmen's Bureau; superintendents; Union army; United States Colored Troops

Fee, John G., 189–95, 198, 200, 203–5, 207, 221, 226–29, 231, 237–38, 308n7

Fee, Matilda, 238

Fifteenth Amendment, 242

Fifteenth Iowa Regiment, 110

Fifth Kansas Cavalry, 111

Fifty-Fourth Massachusetts Regiment, 95

Fifty-Sixth United States Colored Troops, 235–36

First Arkansas African Descent. *See* Forty-Sixth United States Colored Troops

First Baptist Church, of Hampton, Va., 217

First New York Mounted Rifles, 74

First Rhode Island Regiment, 3

First Vermont Regiment, 25, 29–30, 31

Fisk, Gen. Clinton B., 221–22, 223, 225–26, 230, 243

Flanders, George, 111

Flora, 206

Florida, 226–27

Foner, Eric, 55, 264n3, 276n24

food, 140–56 passim, 210; relationship to liberation, 141; and military strategy, 141, 142–43, 156; and social control, 149–50; efforts to control supply of, by refugees, 152–56; violent conflict surrounding, 155–56. *See also* foraging; gardens; hunger; slavery: food supply of enslaved

food rations, army, 41, 127, 141–56, 202, 221; of soldiers and refugees, compared, 142–43; dishonest and neglectful distribution of, 143–44; illegal sale of, 144; inadequate nutrition of, 144; process of determining need for, 146–51; tickets to obtain, 147–48; duration of, 147–50; gender differentiation in, 147–50; expense of, 151, 286n41; reductions in, 154–55; refugee preference for purchasing, 156; and camp closures, 223, 227

Foote, Lorien, 279n87

foraging, 70, 140, 152; Union regulation of, 155–56

Forks of Dix River Baptist Church, 175–78, 185, 189, 191, 195, 230, 241

Forrest, Gen. Nathan Bedford, 93, 132

Fort Curtis, 106, 110, 119, 121

Fort Donelson, 193

Fort Monroe, 7–8, 22, 57, 58, 59, 76, 78, 92, 113, 137, 183, 210, 234; refugee flight to, 3–4, 24, 31, 47, 115, 251n6; labor at, 28–29, 31–34, 35–46, 53–54; impact of battle of Manassas, 30; impact of Peninsula campaign, 46–54; exemption from Emancipation Proclamation, 54–56, 57, 60; shelter at, 61, 63, 64–65, 67, 69, 71–72; violence against women at, 85–87;

removal efforts from, 87–91, 94–99; food rationing system at, 141–42, 144, 145, 146–50; census at, 151; and clothing relief, 158, 159; schools around, 193, 196–97; and attempts to preserve refugee lands, 213–14, 217, 219, 220–21. *See also* Hampton, Va.

Fort Pickens, 3

Fort Pickering, 66

Fort Pillow, massacre at, 132

Fort Sumter, 22

Forty-Sixth United States Colored Troops, 111–12, 119, 124–39 passim, 210, 230, 233, 234, 245–46

Fountain, Daniel L., 293n27, 293n28

Fourth United States Colored Troops, 147

Freedman's Village, 73, 78, 218

Freedmen's Bureau, 7, 212–13, 220, 237, 243, 251n4; and protection of refugee lands, 213, 215, 218; efforts of, to close refugee camps, 215–16, 221–29, 231, 236; and physical protection, 236, 237

free labor, 16, 21, 37, 195; Union's failure to implement, 38–40; claimed by refugees, 41–43; as new federal policy, 44–46; on leased plantations, 113–14, 123, 129–30; and role of stores, 164–65; postwar arrangements of, 223–29, 232–35; state laws inhibiting, 224; sharecropping as form of, 244–45. *See also* land; military labor, of refugees

Freetown, 74

Fremont, Maj. Gen. John C., 45

Friends Freedmen's Association of Philadelphia, 72, 153, 159, 164–66; Women's Aid Committee of, 160, 196, 288n23

Friends, Religious Society of. *See* Quakers

Fry, Gen. Speed Smith, 201–2, 205, 298n121

Fuentes, Marisa J., 16

Fugitive Slave Act, 3, 7

Fulton & Cairo Railroad, 274n12

gardens, 78, 153–56, 216

Garrard County, Ky., 174–78, 179, 181, 186, 189, 201, 230, 237

General Order No. 5 (Gen. John Wool), 43

General Order No. 34 (Gen. John Wool), 39–40

General Order No. 48 (Gen. Frederick Steele), 107–8

Gerteis, Louis, 277n38

Gettysburg, battle of, 121

Giles, Lucy, 37

Giles, William, 37

Glymph, Thavolia, 170, 280n90

"Go Down, Moses" (spiritual), 183

Goodrich's Landing, 123–24, 126–27, 135

government farms, 113, 209–10, 240

Grand Junction, Tenn., 109, 116

Grant, Gen. Ulysses S., 51, 113, 118–19, 132, 242

Great Britain, 160

Grey, William H., 235

guerrillas: terror of, 61, 88, 114, 136, 199; attacks of, on leased plantations, 129–33

guns, 47, 124, 206, 207; refugees armed with, 133–34, 233; Union regulation of, 134

Hahn, Steven, 276n24, 293n28

Haiti, 10, 11, 97–99, 174, 253n20

Hall, Theron E., 187, 192–93, 198, 202–5, 222

Hamlin, Hannibal, 73

Hampton, Va., 1, 3–4, 20, 79, 85, 147, 209, 217, 234, 235, 240; religious life in, 9, 34, 197, 217; occupation of, 25, 33, 37; evacuation of, 30–31; burning of, 32, 33; commerce in, 33–34, 48–53, 164–65; marriage in, 34–35; shelter in, 47; reaction to Emancipation Proclamation, 55–56; and violence, 85, 155, 220; removals from, 87, 89–91, 98–99; schools in, 146, 193, 198, 216, 220, 237; attempts to save refugee lands in, 213–15, 217, 237; closing of camps in, 216. *See also* Fort Monroe

Hampton Normal and Agricultural Institute (Hampton University), 237

Hampton Roads, 21, 22, 87

hard war, 141

Harpers Ferry, Va., 160, 189

Harrison's Landing, Va., 54, 264n133

Harrow, 225

88, 189, 299n141; persistence of slavery in, postwar, 221–22, 303n56; state laws protecting slavery, postwar, 224; Court of Appeals, 224. *See also* Camp Nelson, Ky.; Lincoln, Abraham: and Kentucky

Kentucky Bible Society, 207n100

Kentucky River, 182

Keokuk, Iowa, 94

kidnapping. *See* refugees: recapture of

Kock, Bernard, 98

labor. *See* free labor; military labor, of refugees; sharecropping; slavery

Lake Providence, La., 109–10, 119, 123–24

Lancashire, Great Britain, 160

land: claims of refugees to, 211–12, 216, 218–20; abandoned and confiscated land policies, 212, 214, 301n23; federal efforts to protect refugee lands, 212–13, 214, 217–18; private efforts to protect refugee lands, 213, 226, 228–29, 231, 236–38; freed peoples' efforts to rent or purchase, 213, 217–18, 228, 235–36, 239–40, 241–42; federal restoration of, to ex-Confederates, 214–16, 219–20, 232, 239, 240; freed peoples' resistance to restoration of, 216–17, 221, 222; white landowners' resistance to freed peoples' purchases of, 218, 220–21, 237; loss of value of, 306n120

Landau, Ohio, 225

landscapes, of refugee camps, 65–66, 70, 72–82; and high population density, 76–83, 211; and crowded spaces, white fears of, 77–78, 82, 122, 151, 163, 220, 226; and crowded spaces, black preference for, 78–82; urban spaces, 80–82, 133; and race and gender, 83–87, 94, 97, 229, 268–69n2. *See also* environment; islands; planned settlements; shelter

Lane Theological Seminary, 189

Langley, Dr., 211

laundresses, 109, 126–37 passim, 235; military oath of, 126–27; labor of, described, 127; Union army policy regarding, 127–29, 280n92; blamed for disorder, 128; and nursing duties, 135

laws of war. *See* Lieber Code

Lee, Mary Custis, 73, 218

Lee, Gen. Robert E., 73, 207, 214, 218

Lee plantation (Newport News, Va.), 25

Lexington, Ky., 208, 243

Lexington and Danville Turnpike, 181

Lieber, Francis, 62

Lieber Code, 13, 62, 86, 202

Lincoln, Abraham, 3, 10, 11, 14, 15, 45, 54, 55, 248; naming of park after, 73; and colonization, 97–99; and West Bogan case, 138–39; and Kentucky, 180–81, 186, 206, 294n33; abandoned and confiscated lands, policies of, 212, 214; death of, 214. *See also* Emancipation Proclamation

Lipsitz, George, 78

literacy, 42, 48–49, 195, 197, 241, 246. *See also* schools

Little Bethel, village of, 29

Lockwood, Lewis C., 34–35, 36, 37, 42–43, 44, 46, 47, 48, 54, 85, 98, 183, 197, 260n55, 261n83

Louisville, Ky., refugee settlement in, 221, 226

Lowell, Mass., 43

Lower Little Rock Road, 122

lumber, 49, 67–68, 71–72

lynching, 245

Madison County, Ky., 189

Magruder, Col. (and Gen.) John G., 30, 32, 258n35

Mallory, Charles King, 22, 24, 28, 213

Manassas, first battle of, 30, 258n32

Mann, Maria, 66, 109, 119, 122, 143, 152, 163, 168–72

Manning, Chandra, 253n23, 254n27

marriage: legal sanction of, 34–35, 78, 137, 245–46; weddings officiated by missionaries, 34–35, 137; interracial, 96; in slavery, 104–5, 275n29; wedding garments, 172; post-Emancipation, 245–46. *See also* families

martial law, 137, 225, 228

material culture, 12, 253n24. *See also* clothing; clothing relief; property ownership, of refugees; shelter

McClellan, Gen. George B., 46; army of, 47, 48, 49, 52, 53, 54

McDowell, Gen. Irvin, 258n32

McKeal, Frank, 106, 112, 233

McKeel, John, 112, 126, 233, 306n115

McKiel, Hester, 101, 116–17, 136

McKiel, Josiah, 101–5, 117–18, 136, 234, 273n2, 273 (nn7, 8), 274n12, 306n120

measles, 134–37, 210

medical care: inadequacy of army system of, 108, 301n29; refugees' informal practices of, 134–36; expansion of army system of, 135; medical director and inspector of freedmen, appointment of, 135. *See also* hospitals; illness and disease; nurses

Meigs, Montgomery, 203, 215

Memphis, Tenn., 66, 80, 87, 89, 109, 110, 114, 132, 133, 199, 210, 226, 234, 235

Meridian campaign, 93, 132, 134–35

Merrimac (ironclad), 46

Mexican War, 39

Mexico, 210

midwives, 246–47

migration patterns, of refugees: ; to areas of Union occupation, 4, 5–6, 25, 46–47, 57–61, 106–8, 112, 140–41, 187–88, 201, 206, 221; rural to urban, 80–82, 132–33, 152, 226; to Northern states, 94–96, 99–100, 122, 162, 225; to Haiti, 97–99; to Kansas, 241–44. *See also* colonization; islands; land; plantations, leased; removals, refugee; resettlement, postwar; Southern Homestead Act

military labor, of refugees, 26–29, 32, 35–36, 53–54, 106–39 passim; inspection of bodies for, 26–27; of women, 27, 32, 39–40, 112–16, 126–29, 259n38; and racial ideologies, 28; types of, 28–29; described, 35–36; and wage rates, 36, 39–41, 45–46, 80, 111, 113, 166, 227; and labor mobility, 36–37, 40–42, 264n133; and unpaid wages, 37–46, 55, 71–72, 108, 123, 146, 158, 234, 260n65, 275n6; certificates of employment for, 129; and wages received, 129; postwar claims to back pay, 234. *See also* laundresses; nurses; scouts and spies

military necessity: determinations of, 3, 27, 45–46, 50–55, 61, 66, 92, 97, 241, 247–48; and Emancipation Proclamation, 11, 54–55, 110; general principle of, 12–13, 44, 254n27; and humanitarianism, 13–14, 62, 95, 142, 187, 202–3, 222, 284n7; and shifts in Union strategy, 46–48, 132, 208, 210–211; and black recruitment, 110; and women, 115, 128, 185–86; of food rations, 142; of clothing, 158; of religious life, 182, 185, 204; of schools, 192–93, 199–200

military service, of refugees. *See* United States Colored Troops

Mill Creek, 69

Miller, Alfred, 246

Miller, Minos, 111

Milliken's Bend, battle of, 124–25

ministers. *See* religious life

miscegenation, 86

missionaries: as intermediaries between refugees and army, 13–14, 192, 295n60; and provision of physical relief, 162–67; teaching of, 192–200. *See also* American Missionary Association; Quakers; religious life; schools

Mississippi River, 66, 68, 69, 70, 102, 123, 230; islands in, 88–89, 91–92; Union control of, 114–15, 118–19, 129. *See also* islands

Mississippi Valley, 8, 16, 61, 62, 64, 76; refugee settlements in, 101–39 passim; migration of cotton planters to, 102–3, 136; reduction of Union troops in, 129–33. *See also* cotton production; Helena, Ark.; Mississippi River; Phillips County, Ark.; Vicksburg, Miss.

Missouri Hotel, 122

Mitchel, Gen. Ormsby, 74

Mitchelville, S.C., 7, 74, 199

Mobile, Ala., 210

Monitor (ironclad), 46

Monroe, La., 125–26

Moody, John, 33

Moss, Joseph, 228–29, 237, 305n92, 308n7

Mound Plantation, battle of, 124–26, 232

movement and mobility, of refugees: and decisions to flee slavery, 2–3, 24, 106, 112,

116–18, 137, 178, 187–99; and labor, 36–37, 39–41; regulated by military passes, 42, 91, 96, 225; forced by Union, 47–48, 54, 119, 122–24, 181, 201–2; Union limitations on, 89–91, 156; refugee attachments to place, 99–100, 227–28; discouraged by relief efforts, 162. *See also* migration patterns, of refugees; removals, refugee; resettlement, postwar; slavery: restricted movement in

Mt. Hebron Baptist Church, 177

Murfreesboro, Tenn., 151

Nancy, 206
Nansemond River, 73
Nashua, N.H., 43
Nashville, Tenn., 64, 67, 81, 93, 143, 235
Natchez, Miss., 235
National Freedmen's Relief Association, 13, 159
National Home for Disabled Volunteer Soldiers, 243
Neely, Mark, 272n73
negro cloth, 168–69
Nesbit, Scott, 253n23
neuralgia, 202
New Bern, N.C., 151, 158, 211
new materialism, 253n24
New Orleans, La., 6, 123, 193, 199, 210, 230
Newport News, Va., 21, 22, 24, 28, 29, 30, 31, 33, 35, 47, 51, 53, 87, 147
Newtown, 74
New York, N.Y., 42, 166, 196
Nicholasville, Ky., 201, 237
niter, 135
Norcum, James, 101
Norfolk, Va., 50, 78, 80, 81, 157, 162, 172, 211, 215, 219, 220
North Brookfield, Mass., 159
Northern states, 5, 8, 38; escape of enslaved people to, 5, 61, 96, 102; vagrancy policies of, 39–40; removals of refugees to, 94–96, 122; resistance of, to refugee resettlement in, 95–96, 162; refugee reluctance to move to, 99–100, 225. *See also* resettlement, postwar

Northwestern Freedmen's Aid Commission, 144, 158, 164
nurses, 109, 127

Oakes, James, 258n33
Obama, Barack, 8
occupation, Union army, 60; women and children, as occupiers, 109. *See also* land; plantations, leased
Ohio River, 189
Oliver, John, 53, 89–90
108th New York Regiment, 84
114th United States Colored Troops, 187, 207–10
124th United States Colored Troops, 201
Ord, Maj. Gen. Edward, 214
orphans: asylums for, 235–36; apprenticeship of, 236
overseers, 22, 24, 44, 76, 102, 123, 256n18
oystering, 20, 34, 155, 240

Paducah, Ky., refugee camp in, 221, 292n10
panics, economic, 102
Parrish, Ann, 21
Parrish, Edward, 22, 24, 33, 53
Parrish, John, 22, 24
Patterson, Dr., 103
Patterson, Isom, 103, 274n17
Patton, Stephen, 235
Paw Paw Island, 88, 133
Peake, Mary, 146
Peake, Thomas, 98, 146–47
Peninsula campaign, 46–54, 73; impact of, on federal policy, 54–55, 264n135
pensions, veterans', 233, 243, 246, 308n17, 309n26
Petersburg campaign, 147, 207, 214
petitioning, by refugees, 48, 262n104
Phelps, Col. John Wolcott, 25, 26, 27, 29, 31, 257n5, 258n31
Philadelphia, Pa., 42, 94, 160, 166, 171, 196, 197, 234. *See also* Friends Freedmen's Association of Philadelphia
Phillips County, Ark., 101–5, 119, 122, 123, 136–37, 230–36, 244–45. *See also* Helena, Ark.

285n33; defined, 10; sources about, 15–16; recapture of, by Confederates, 30, 80, 125–26, 130, 186, 201; organizing of, 41–43, 55, 172–73, 217–18; concern for personal security, 80, 81, 133–34; census of, attempted, 151. *See also* children; clothing; death; families; food; food rations; free labor; land; marriage; medical care; military labor, of refugees; plantations, leased; property ownership, of refugees; religious life; resettlement, postwar; schools; shelter; violence, racial; women; *and names of individual refugees*

Reidy, Joseph P., 73

relief efforts, private: organized by refugees, 172–73, 235–36. *See also* American Missionary Association; clothing relief; missionaries; Quakers

relief policies, federal, 284n22; and shelter, 61–62; antebellum, 62; and race, 62, 265n7; and food, 141–42, 145; and gender, 147–50, 285–86n37; and clothing, 158. *See also* humanitarianism; military necessity

religious life: black ministers, 9, 34, 42–43, 175–78, 183–85, 189–96, 197–98, 201, 204–6, 207, 212, 219, 229–30, 235, 241–43; antislavery Christianity, 25, 174, 189; worship services in camps, 34, 183; army chaplains, 108, 109, 113, 182; establishment of independent black churches, 176, 213, 229–30; and sacred spaces, 178, 183; pursuit of religious freedom, 181–82; Union army indifference to, 182–85; and music, 183; visibility of, 183; religiosity of refugees, 184–85, 244; Union army likened to God's army, 185, 188, 204; and gender, 185–86, 207; nonsectarianism, 189–92; black ministers' relationship to white missionaries, 190–92; churches threatened, 229. *See also* American Missionary Association; Exodus, analogy to; missionaries; slavery: religious life of enslaved; Quakers

removals, refugee, 83–100 passim, 122

Republican National Convention, 242

Republican Party, 242–43

resettlement, postwar, 223–28; resistance to return to home plantation, 223, 230; state laws inhibiting, 224; in Northern states, 225; in Mississippi, 225–26; and refugee preference for cities, 226

Restieaux, Capt. E. B. W., 202

Richmond, Va., 22, 46, 47; fall of, 207, 209

Rip Raps, 48

Roanoke Island, N.C., 99, 144

Roche's Plantation, 134

Rousseau, Gen. Lovell, 221

Royster, William, 201

Russell, LeBaron, 56, 90

Saint-Domingue. *See* Haiti

San Francisco, Calif., 159

Sanitary Commission, United States, 109. *See also* Mann, Maria

sanitation, problems of, 66

Savage, Immanuel, 35–36, 40, 46, 52, 53, 234, 240, 259n51

Savage, Susan, 35, 40, 46

Savannah, Ga., 212

Sawyer, Samuel, 109, 122

schools: destruction of, by Confederates, 122; establishment of, 146, 192–96, 210; for noncommissioned officers, 192–93; rates of attendance in, 193; and children, 193, 197, 235; progress of students in, 193–95; race and perceptions of learning, 194; visibility of, 195–96; books, 196–99; supplies, 196–200; night schools, 197; religious nature of, 197–98; physical spaces of, 198–200; on leased plantations, 199–200; vulnerability of, 199–200. *See also* American Missionary Association; industrial schools; literacy; Quakers

Schwalm, Leslie, 258n33, 277n43, 280n90

Scofield, Abisha, 162–63, 190–91, 200, 205, 228–29, 234, 237

Scott, Gen. Winfield, 3, 30, 32

scouts and spies, 29–30, 146

scurvy, 144, 210

Sea Islands of Georgia and South Carolina, 87, 113. *See also* Edisto Island, S.C.; Hilton Head Island, S.C.; Mitchelville, S.C.

Second Arkansas African Descent, 118

superintendents, 6–7, 14; of contrabands, 44, 46, 47, 52, 54, 55, 74, 85, 97, 109, 122, 146, 147, 151, 159; of freedmen, 87, 91, 113, 115, 116, 123, 130, 131, 133, 137, 199, 231; of Refugee Home, 203–5, 222; of Negro affairs, 210, 213, 214, 220

Sutherland, Daniel, 129

Susan, 22

Sweeney, Capt. Henry, 232

Syrett, John, 301n23

Tallmadge, Capt. Grier, 36, 41

Taylor, William E., 300n9

Taylor farm, 211, 300n9

Terrabonne Parish, La., 220

Thayer, Capt. A. L., 231

Third Virginia Cavalry, 22

Thirteenth Amendment, 230

Thirty-First Ohio Regiment, 143

Thirty-Fourth Arkansas Regiment, 122

Thirty-Sixth Iowa Regiment, 111

Thomas, Adj. Gen. Lorenzo, 91, 110–15, 187, 298n121; leased plantation policy of, 112–16, 130; marriage policy of, 137

Thomas, Col. Samuel, 88

Thornton, William, 184

Tiptonville, Tenn., 72

Trent River settlement, 211, 216, 217

Tucker, Catherine, 240

Tucker, Jane, 240

Tucker, Susan, 240

Tunnell Hill, 69, 93

Twelfth United States Colored Heavy Artillery, 206

Tyler, John, 198

Underground Railroad, 5, 61, 94, 96

Union army, 12–13; quartermaster's department, 3, 18, 28, 35, 36, 39, 40, 41, 44, 51, 61, 63, 67, 73, 91, 137, 149, 179, 192, 202, 203, 215, 233, 295n60; provost marshals, 15, 26, 48–49, 52, 116, 123, 134, 155; engineer's department, 28, 36, 233; subsistence, 28, 141–42; command, impact of changes in, 32, 39, 53, 106–8, 205, 214, 225; regulations of, 51, 63, 65, 127, 142–43, 278n45; department of Negro

affairs, 210, 300n4; demobilization of, 210–11, 233–34, 238, 243. See also names of individual armies and units; military labor, of refugees; military necessity; superintendents; United States Colored Troops

Unionist slave owners, 55, 117, 136, 264n138, 264n2

Union navy, 41

Uniontown, 73, 74, 78, 84–85, 93–94, 199

United States Colored Troops (USCT): recruitment of, 110–12, 186–88, 189, 299n141; white attitudes toward, 110–12, 214, 233; service in, 110–39 passim; as targets of Confederate violence, 125, 132, 186–88; and citizenship, 232–33, 276n24

United States Commission for the Relief of National Freedmen, 13

Urbana, Ohio, 225

vegetables, 34, 93, 131, 152–55, 210

Vicksburg, Miss., 8, 68, 69, 88, 89, 114, 127, 130, 132, 133, 134, 137, 148, 153, 225

Vicksburg campaign, 118–21, 129, 141, 214, 276n11; and USCT, 119

Vidalia, La., 84

violence, racial: incited by Union soldiers, 44, 54, 109, 110, 278n45; persistence of, from slavery, 108–9, 111–12, 133, 136–39, 189, 202, 273n7, 282n148; in reaction to slave flight, 117, 186, 206–7; in Mississippi Valley, by Confederates, 118, 123, 125, 129–33; against women, by Confederates, 188, 206–7; in postwar period, 224, 237–38, 241, 243. See also Elaine, Ark., massacre at; guerrillas; rape

Vlach, John Michael, 79

voting rights, 242, 247

Wade, Benjamin, 202

Ware, Thomas, 34, 48–49, 52

War of 1812, 21, 39, 174; flight of enslaved people during, 5

Washburn, Lt. Col. Peter, 29

washerwomen. See laundresses

Washington, D.C., 3, 11, 12, 13, 14, 17, 30, 33, 54, 60, 64, 65, 80, 98